Land/Scape/Theater

THEATER: Theory/Text/Performance

Enoch Brater, Series Editor

Recent Titles:

Land/Scape/Theater

Elinor Fuchs and Una Chaudhuri, Editors

Ann Arbor   THE UNIVERSITY OF MICHIGAN PRESS

Copyright © by the University of Michigan 2002
All rights reserved
Published in the United States of America by
The University of Michigan Press
Manufactured in the United States
of America
☺ Printed on acid-free paper

2005   2004   2003   2002   4   3   2   1

A CIP catalog record for this book is available from the British Library.

Library of Congress Cataloging-in-Publication Data

Land/scape/theater / edited by Elinor Fuchs and Una Chaudhuri.
p.   cm. — (Theater—theory/text/performance)
Includes index.
ISBN 0-472-09720--2 (alk. paper) — ISBN 0-472-06720-6 (pbk. : alk.
paper)
1. Theater.   2. Drama—History and criticism.   3. Landscape in
literature.   I. Fuchs, Elinor.   II. Chaudhuri, Una, 1951–
III. Series.
PN2020 .L32   2002
792—dc21   2002005412

In loving memory,
Lynda Hart and Linda Dorff.
And to new life,
Theresa Rachel Katz

Acknowledgments

We want to express our appreciation to Mark Dundas Wood and Amy Strahler Holzapfel for their research and editorial contributions to this project. In addition, we thank Prof. Edward S. Casey of SUNY Stony Brook, Martha Wilson of Franklin Furnace, Jeffrey Wexler of the Byrd Hoffman Foundation, Kari Hensley of La Pocha Nostra, Bil Schroeder of the Yale School of Drama, Mimi Johnson of Performing Arts Services, and Jackie Allen, Chris Jaehnig, and Gwendolyn Alker of New York University for their valuable assistance at different stages of our work. We are grateful to Per Hedström, Curator of the National Museum of Sweden, for his help in obtaining permission to use the Strindberg landscape painting that appears on our cover. We thank LeAnn Fields and Marcia LaBrenz of the University of Michigan Press for the interest and attention they have given this project since its inception. Most of all, we thank our contributors for taking up the challenge of elaborating a new paradigm for theater analysis. Their inspiring work expanded our own thinking on landscape, and led to what became an unusually collaborative and rewarding exploration.

Contents

Introduction: Land/Scape/Theater and the New Spatial Paradigm

Una Chaudhuri and Elinor Fuchs

> Suddenly landscape seems to be everywhere—an organizing force, an open sesame, an avant-garde emblem, alike in fiction and music, food and folklore, even for professors and politicians.
>
> —DAVID LOWENTHAL,
> *Landscape Meanings and Values*

> You and your landscapes! Tell me about the worms!
>
> —SAMUEL BECKETT,
> *Waiting for Godot*

The title of this book makes a connection that may strike some as improbable, if not perverse. In contrast to the open countryside and panoramic views that we associate with landscape, theater summons the very image of interiority: one imagines a stage "interior," inside a windowless performance space, inside an urban edifice, at the heart of a dense metropolis. Theater, whose great subject has been human action and feeling, has historically aligned itself on the side of culture and artifice in their long debate with "nature." Like Gogo, it has attended to the worms, not the landscape.

Yet it is in part because of this apparent dichotomy between theater and landscape that landscape can offer a framework for fresh thinking on modern theater. The distance between the two terms may mark an ideological blind spot, a traditional and naturalized refusal of certain considerations in favor of others. By suggesting a relation where one has not been recognized, this book aims to open a new conceptual space in theater studies.

The theater of the past century has challenged as never before the Aristotelian hierarchy. Demoted in theory and displaced in practice, the most privileged of Aristotle's six "elements," plot and character, have been undermined by a host of flexible dramatic structures and a gallery of fractured subjectivities. A pervasive new spatiality, of which scenography is only the most obvious site, has turned the Aristotelian hierarchy on its head: now spectacle may be the "soul" of the dramatic enterprise. As yet, however, no critical project has been devoted to rehabilitating this term so decisively slighted by Aristotle. The meanings that attach to landscape, we suggest, can elaborate the nature and implications of this "spatial turn" in modern drama and theater. Landscape names the modern theater's new spatial paradigm.

Yet while offering landscape as a positive countercategory, we cannot lose sight of the fact that our formulations arise within and share the antipositivisms of postmodern theory. Thus by the broken form of our title, *Land/Scape/Theater*, we want to acknowledge certain significant discontinuities and occlusions within the assumptions attached to the idea of landscape itself. The very word embodies an awkward conflict, straddling the gritty specificities of the material world and the idealizations of various aesthetic traditions. Una Chaudhuri's introductory essay, "Land/Scape/Theory," outlines the sources of some of these debates in the field of landscape studies.

Landscape is subject to as many meanings—and landscape studies to as many internal debates—as theater itself. As phenomenologist Edward S. Casey writes, landscape is "intrinsically *anexact*," for it escapes measurement; whatever escapes measurement must escape a quick and single definition as well.[1] The term itself arose in the visual arts in the seventeenth century, and not in discourse about actual natural formations on the ground. Thus landscape is classically a fine-arts term, and subdivisible by fine-arts categories, such as the beautiful, the sublime, and the picturesque. However, by the Romantic period, the term and all its subordinates began to flow back to the natural world itself. Landscapes came to be admired not only as works of art on canvas, but as signs of various relationships to nature itself, ranging from the economic to the spiritual.

In the twentieth century, landscape's third career began. A new interest in "vernacular landscape" opened the term to humble scenes as well as great, built as well as open, urban as well as rural. The term came to refer to the multifarious interplay between the land and human adaptations to and indeed *of* it. As a parallel movement, a new generation of art critics began to unmask the class biases of landscape art criticism. A new field of cultural landscape studies arose and was soon surrounded by a cluster of satellites exploring cultural and human geography, landscape architecture, urban studies, regional studies, ecology, art history, literary studies, and other fields. "It can hardly be doubted," the British geographer and theorist of landscape aesthetics Jay Appleton declared at a 1990 conference, "that the resurgence of interest in landscape since World War II has by now reached a dimension that warrants the use of the term, Landscape Movement."[2]

But for theater, why speak of this slippery, shape-shifting *landscape* at all, when *place* and *space,* whose meanings are easier to agree on, are available for use? While these terms play an important role in recent writings on theater—and indeed in many of the essays in this book—we believe *landscape* permits certain distinctions that are necessary to a theorization of the new spatial paradigm in modern theater. *Space* is too unfeatured for our purposes: every inch of space is just another inch of space. Or space may be qualified in ways unhelpful to our project, since we are not speaking of the performing space, the stage space, interior space, or even space in the sense of a "practiced place" in de Certeau's formulation.[3] If *space* is too unfeatured, *place* is overly particular. Landscape is more grounded and available to visual experience than space, but more environmental and constitutive of the imaginative order than place. It is *inside* space, one might say, but *contains* place. *Landscape* has particular value as a mediating term between space and place. It can therefore more fully represent the complex spatial mediations within modern theatrical form, and between modern theater and the world.

So what does it mean, to say that landscape, trailing all its diverse tributaries, offers a critical category for the understanding of modern and contemporary theater? And for that matter, why only modern theater? Weren't landscapes a feature of dramatic fiction and theatrical representation long before the modern period? Whether it is the wild mountainside where Pentheus was torn apart, Lear's storm-lashed heath, or Segismundo's desolate cave, landscape has always played a role in the creation of dramatic meaning, and a rethinking of classic plays from the perspective of landscape will yield fresh insights. But we believe that at the threshold of modernism, theater began to manifest a new spatial dimension, both visually and dramaturgically, in which landscape for the first time held itself apart from character and became a figure on its own. As the century moved on, landscape would encroach on the traditional dramaturgy of plot and character to become a perspective and a method, linking seemingly unrelated theatrical practices in staging, text, scenography, and spectatorship. In her introductory essay "Reading for Landscape: The Case of American Drama" Elinor Fuchs traces the convergence of these practices into a contemporary landscape dramaturgy.

Landscape was most famously linked to theater by Gertrude Stein. But her bold rubric, the *landscape play,* represents in fact a late moment in the development of a consciousness that reaches back to Ibsen's complex engagement with actual landscapes, and before him, to Wagner's idealization of landscape painting. The romantic/ironic ambivalence of Ibsen's landscapes transmutes into the more explicitly ecological concerns of Chekhov's dramaturgy, establishing one might say a "landed" landscape tradition in contrast to the more formalist "scapes" of the Stein lineage. By century's end, these lines of development have intertwined across a wide spectrum of space- and place-conscious performance. The range would include the pastoral-dispastoral imaginaries of Sam Shepard, Pina Bausch, and Heiner Müller, the national and border explorations of Robert Ashley and Guillermo Gómez-Peña, the cultural and linguistic excavations of Suzan-Lori Parks, Caryl Churchill, and Mac Wellman, the ecoperformances of Rachel Rosenthal, the fantasy mappings of Richard Nelson and David Hancock, and the extravagant landscapes of the Wilson-inspired Michael Counts. The range is suggested in the different directions taken by our recent work in the field, Una Chaudhuri's *Staging Place,* and Elinor Fuchs's "Another Version of Pastoral" in *The Death of Character.*

For the past two decades, new thinking in every area of theater has been concerned almost exclusively with the subjective—with contested representations of the human subject. This volume is intended as a step toward the restoration of the natural and built environment, and of the nonhuman order, to appropriate presence in considerations of dramatic form and meaning. Our general project of raising landscape-consciousness invites many different approaches and perspectives; thus this book is intentionally heterogenous, including the historiographic, cultural, linguistic, art-historical, formalist, theoretical, and just vividly descriptive. Yet we make no claims here to have produced a comprehensive survey: the field is excitingly wide open.

In the spirit of this volume's spatialized consciousness, we have mapped its diverse explorations into five perspectives. Section One presents our introductory "Overviews." Section Two, "Groundings," returns, as landscape itself invariably does, to the view of and from the ground. The goal of the essays in this section is to locate precisely the ways entire dramatic worlds and aesthetic forms can emerge from the landmarks, afflictions, and patterns of particular landscapes. Natalie Crohn Schmitt argues that it is the very specificity of certain sites underlying the plays of Yeats, rather than their symbolic or abstract quality, that produces his religious dramatic form. Similarly, Joseph Roach suggests that the traumatic memory of the Irish potato famine haunts the symbolic world of *Waiting for Godot.* Joining traditional rural landscapes here is the now equally familiar cityscape, which, as Stanton Garner Jr. shows in his discussion of two site-specific performances, transforms spectatorship along with dramatic structure, producing a thoroughly contemporary version of landscape theater.

"Steinscapes," Section Three, explores the dramatic territory opened up by Gertrude Stein's conceptualization of plays as landscape. Stein saw the stage itself as the ground on which landscapes of words could be arranged and put in motion. The first of the three essays, by Stein scholar Jane Palatini Bowers, inquires into the origins and logic of Stein's idea, particularly as it arose from the theory and practice of landscape *painting,* which Stein herself frequently cited and discussed. The aesthetics and formal principles that Stein imported from painting into theater are variously the subject of the following two essays. Marvin Carlson finds that Stein's idea of landscape as language has generated a flourishing American movement of linguistic dramaturgy revolving about real and fantastic landscapes. Finally, Marc Robinson explores the art-historical roots of landscape in the work of one of Stein's most notable successors, Robert Wilson.

Various ideologically and aesthetically driven departures from particular landscapes into wider geographic frames are the subject of Section Four, "Redirected Geographies." In the five essays included here, this larger view puts the spatializing impulse at the service of new accounts of experience, identity, and history. Edward Ziter charts the effects of new geographical and ethnographic information on the orientalist theater of late-nineteenth-century Britain. Charlotte Canning shows how circuit Chautauqua synecdochically fixed its version of civic values through its signature image of a brown tent set in the community landscape, redefining both the land and the community as functions of performance. Julie Stone Peters follows Artaud's journey into the Sierra Madre, tracing the flow from European aesthetics and spirituality to remotest Mexico and back into the expanded mystical landscape of later European theater. Matthew Smith explores surprising commonalities in the landscape idealizations and exclusions of two seemingly opposed theatrical figures, Richard Wagner and Walt Disney. The last essay in this section, by W. B. Worthen, reads contemporary Latino/a performance within the project of what one artist, Guillermo Gómez-Peña, calls "border aesthetics," pitched on (and against) the ambiguous geography of the "nation," and on the porous boundaries of identity itself.

Finally, the essays in Section Five, "Out of Space," suggest the extreme limit of the landscape idea, the point at which spatialization becomes an abstract principle, transmutable even into seemingly nonvisual realms. Daniel Gerould describes the "landscapes of the mind" in the symbolist drama that ushered in this century of landscape theater. Arthur Sabatini explores the "sonic landscapes" of Robert Ashley's operas, relating them to the composer's comprehensive geographical vision. Alice Rayner reflects on the disappearance of space in the cyberworld of interactive and digital performance, a disappearance ironically coupled with the persistence of the language of space and place that has arisen to describe it.

The reader may note that several of these essays center on dramatic text rather than stage performance. The emphasis is deliberate. In applying the landscape paradigm to the deep structure of written plays, and not merely to the scenographic practices and presentation styles they have inspired, we make a larger claim for the analytical value of our central term. It is not "news," after all, to informed students of theater, that field, or landscape, staging has been the dominant directorial approach of the postrealist theater, whether proscenium, environmental, or site specific. The important experimental directors of the past four decades, among them Jerzy Grotowski, Peter Brook, Joseph Chaikin, Richard Foreman, Robert Wilson, JoAnne Akalaitis, Andrei Serban, Anne Bogart, Elizabeth LeCompte, Robert LePage, and the late Reza Abdoh, have wrought countless variations on the dispersed visual field we associate with landscape and have contributed to the gradual retraining of the perspectival spectator. What is more difficult to discern, and therefore more important to theorize, is the landscape in the text. In a theoretical environment that has been habituated for a generation to the "linguistic turn," it is the spatial turn, not simply in the literal or naive space of the visible theater, but within and surrounding text itself, that needs to be brought to light.

In recent decades, a vigorous inquiry into the role of spatial experience in constructing cultural meaning has been under way in many fields, resulting in renewed interest in topography, geography, and mapping, as well as new attention to the specificity of place. These developments have had particular impact in the humanities with the accelerating recognition that the linguistic model does not offer a sufficient account of the real world in a time-collapsed global structure. Theater, with its long history of landscape representation and its more recent history of landscape practice, should now enter this burgeoning dialogue on landscape.

With one exception, every essay published here was written especially for this volume. In many cases, the essays were not part of an ongoing project for the contributors, although they may have resulted in one. As we, contributors and editors, have worked with our material, we have constantly attempted to widen our vision, striving to see what is before us, but obscured by earlier frames of analysis. We hope that landscape, in the many senses invoked here, will take its place among these frames, and that theater in turn will move into and inform the discussions of place, space, ground, geography, and mapping that are animating other fields.

NOTES

1. Edward S. Casey, "Landscape Revisited," address to the Society for Philosophy and Geography, New York, December 1998, 4.

2. Jay Appleton, "The Integrity of the Landscape Movement," in *Understanding Ordinary Landscapes,* ed. Paul Groth and Todd W. Bressi (New Haven: Yale University Press, 1997), 189. The volume documents a symposium at the University of California, Berkeley, in 1990 entitled "Vision, Culture, and Landscape," and contains a valuable bibliography.

3. Michel de Certeau, *The Practice of Everyday Life,* trans. Steven Rendall (Berkeley and Los Angeles: University of California Press, 1984), 117.

One

Overviews

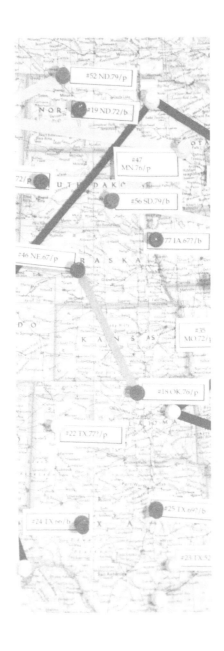

1

Land/Scape/Theory

Una Chaudhuri

On the theoretical scene of landscape, the theater makes a belated entrance. In spite of our widespread suspicion, first voiced by Gertrude Stein, that plays are landscapes, the theater has had no part whatsoever in the lively conversation—now a heated debate—about the history and meaning of landscape. The vast field of landscape aesthetics, founded on the genre of landscape painting but now extending to poetry, the novel, travel writing, architecture, and gardening, has completed a trajectory from innocent origin to current critique with hardly a mention of theater.[1] However, the stages of that process, and the terms of that critique, are enormously suggestive for an inquiry into the modern theater's relationship to landscape. In the critical eye, landscape painting went from an inspired and inspiring documentation of the wonders of the natural world, to "a way of seeing,"[2] an ideologically and psychologically revealing statement about our relation to the world around us, to a way of *not* seeing, of masking and occluding the unsavory truths about our relations to each other and to the land we supposedly share. That process must be acknowledged by any discipline now seeking to use the concept of landscape for its own investigations.

Before entering the complex field of landscape aesthetics, let us first pause to recognize that the term *landscape* is far from being contained within that or any other single field. The question "What is landscape?" has been asked in many different intellectual contexts and academic disciplines—art history, earth science, geography, history, architecture, urban planning, literature, to name only the most obvious—and answered in radically different ways. John Brinckerhoff Jackson, the founder of cultural landscape studies, admits that even after "twenty-five years [of] trying to understand and explain that aspect of the environment that I call the landscape . . . the concept continues to elude me."[3] Efforts to define the concept often proceed by distinguishing it from close relatives like nature,[4] wilderness,[5] environment,[6] scenery, and geography, but these distinctions seem to hold only as long as the writer remains present and vigilant: unsupervised, the distinctions blur and the terms mingle promiscuously.

Even the word *landscape* is notoriously difficult to define. Like the many other terms with which it shares the suffix *-scape,* from the familiar *cityscape, seascape,* and *dreamscape,* to the recently proposed *ethnoscape, financescape,* and *mediascape,*[7] the term *landscape* suggests a systematicity and a coherence that often prove elusive in applications. The fundamental fuzziness of the term makes it available for wide metaphorical use, as in vaguely poetic, evocative phrases like the *landscape of childhood,* the *landscape of desire,* the *landscape of ideas,* and so on. This lack of precise definition is not an index of cultural insignificance, however. On the contrary, the instability and ubiquity of the term reflect the cultural need for this concept, making it powerfully generative for many fields, including ours.

In common parlance, landscape is a familiar, even cozy, term, with general pleasant connotations masking its vagueness. The equation of landscape with idyllic notions of peaceful repose, even with enhanced health (organic food and "getting away from it all") persists in spite of the efforts of writers like Raymond Williams to thoroughly deconstruct the underlying oppositions that sustain it: city versus country, urban versus rural. The word *landscape* continues to conjure up images of the natural world that seem to be there either to be admired (the "prospect" landscape of fields and valleys), or peacefully enjoyed (the "refuge" landscape of shady glens and glassy streams), or revered (the sublime or monumental landscape of mountains, gorges, and canyons). As these very examples suggest, however, the "nature" that is landscape's subject[8] is never free of cultural coding, which usually reflects the history of certain genres of painting and certain practices of gardening and architecture. To follow this suggestion to its logical conclusion is to ask whether every landscape is not always in fact also a "culturescape."[9] And indeed, the principal definitional debate has occurred around the issue of whether landscape refers to an empirical reality, a piece of the world that is actually "out there," or is always a representation—an image, idea, rendering, conceptualization, or fantasy about what's out there. These two views—landscape as environment and landscape as discourse—initially correspond to the two major disciplines within which landscape has been studied systematically: the environmental sciences, particularly geography, and the humanities, particularly art history. Each of these discussions now has a substantial history behind it, yet only very recently have they begun to interact and integrate their projects (a development with great promise for fields, like ours, seeking to press the concept into service for our own analytical needs).

The word *landscape* itself is derived from the Dutch *landschap* (which in turn derives from Middle Dutch *landscap*, "land": *land + -scap* (collective suffix): "state, condition"). Closely related are Danish *landskab*, German *landschaft*, and Old English *landscipe*, with suffixes meaning "to shape" and also (as in the English *-ship*) "association" and "partnership."[10] Thus the word's etymology suggests a rich tapestry of meaning linking place to people, land to living—a tapestry that has only been fully appreciated and elucidated in the past half-century, in the discipline of cultural landscape studies.

Landscape and Society

> Landscape must be regarded first of all in terms of living rather than looking.
>
> —JOHN BRINCKERHOFF JACKSON

The study of landscape first entered geography when scholars at the turn of the twentieth century sought to record the elements of the built environment that were rapidly fading under the pressures of industrialization. An exemplary essay of this moment in landscape studies is "The Morphology of Landscape" (1926) by Carl Sauer, founder of the Berkeley school of cultural geography, which urged attention to human interaction with the biosphere over time, and to the role played by migration and regional cultures in shaping the landscape. The next decisive move occurred in 1951, when an unknown writer named John Brinckerhoff Jackson published the first issue of *Landscape* magazine, in which he claimed that "there is really no such thing as a dull landscape," and characterized every landscape as "a rich and beautiful book [that] we have but to learn to read."[11] The movement—neither a distinct discipline nor an academic department—spawned by Jackson's work is known as cultural landscape studies and has for the past fifty years been vastly extended through the work of loosely allied groups of writers and scholars from a large variety of backgrounds: geography, biology, anthropology, history, architecture, design, and literature.[12]

Jackson's paramount contribution to landscape studies was one that will resonate for students of modern theater, for it was a version of "no more masterpieces," as well as an understanding that the "kitchen sink" can be as dramatic as the drawing room. Jackson insisted that ordinary landscapes and everyday habitats could be as rich in information, as worthy of rigorous attention, and as valuable to our understanding of the human relation to the natural world, as the "masterpieces" of the built and the natural environment that had hitherto occupied the attentions of scholars and policymakers alike. Jackson's vigorous campaign for American "visual literacy" helped to constitute the field of landscape studies as a politically engaged discourse encompassing every conceivable form of human interaction with space: rural, urban, and suburban; domestic homes and corporate office towers, places of work and palaces of leisure, memorials to the past and transparent containers of the present. Contrary to the common usage (in which *to landscape* means "to prettify") landscape studies defines landscape as "including everything from city skylines to farmer's silos, from golf courses to garbage dumps, from ski slopes to manure piles, from millionaires' mansions to the tract houses of Levittown, from famous historical landmarks to flashing electric signs."[13] As such, landscape studies is a treasure house of information and interpretation for analyses of theatrical landscapes, which frequently use ordinary landscapes as their points of departure.

A discipline that bases itself on "reading the landscape" has significant points of contact with literary theory, especially with semiotics and deconstruction. Underlying the work of interpretation practiced by Jackson's heirs in cultural geography is the notion that landscapes are communicative devices that encode and transmit information, and that the skilled interpreter can learn to decode both their conventions and the specific messages they encode. Following hard upon this notion of the landscape as text, however, comes the recognition that landscapes, like texts, are not singular or stable signifying systems, and, further, that a single text is susceptible to many different readings. The assumed singularity of landscape, as implied, for instance, by the common notion of landscape as space that can be taken in at a single glance, has been strongly contested. D. W. Meinig famously laid out "ten versions of the same scene," to make the point that "even though we gather together and look in the same direction at the same instant, we will not—we cannot—see the same landscape."[14] The pluralism of landscape extends over time and place: it is not only that a variety of reading strategies can be brought to bear on a landscape but that cultures vary enormously in their relationship to landscape:

> In contemporary western societies [landscapes] involve only the surface of the land; in other parts of the world, or in premodern Europe, what lies above the surface, or below, may be as or more important. In the contemporary western world we

"perceive" landscapes, we are the point from which the "seeing" occurs. It is thus an ego-centered landscape, a perspective
landscape, a landscape of views and vistas. In other times and
places the visual may not be the most significant aspect, and
the conception of the land may not be ego-centered. . . . The
experience of landscape is too important and too interesting to
be confined to a particular time, place and class.[15]

To complete the logic of cultural relativism with regard to landscape, we should note, as many commentators on landscape do, that the
concept itself is inscribed with a peculiar cultural history. The word
landscape first entered the English language in 1598 as a painters' term,
meaning, as its Dutch counterpart did by then, "a picture depicting
scenery or land." It was not until almost half a century later that the
word was used in English to mean a view or vista of natural scenery.
This chronology suggests that landscapes in paintings led to the recognition of landscapes in real life.[16]

Perhaps this reversal of the usual life-art dialectic is not so surprising to our postmodern minds, accustomed as we are to the simulacra of
mass media, copies with no original, as Jean Baudrillard defined them.
Living after completion of the Disney dream of a totally constructed
environment, where everything in the landscape, including nature itself,
is manufactured, we are perhaps as distant as it is possible to be from the
experience that landscape theorists identify as originary, when the practice of landscape painting produced a new perception: the perception of
land as landscape. Crucially for us, John Brinckerhoff Jackson actually
characterizes that moment as a theatricalization of the world. In his classic essay "Landscape as Theater," Jackson argues that the Renaissance
metaphor of the *theatrum mundi,* the world stage, was the manifestation
of a synchronous development in the fields of art and geography: a new
conception of drama, matched by a new technology of stage representation, suddenly joined forces with a bold new geographical conception of
the world as a visual space. Landscape, then, was the framing, or staging,
of geography. The primary medium of this staging was in fact not theater
but painting.

Landscape Painting

The story that Kenneth Clark tells in his classic work on landscape
painting begins in the sixteenth century, when what he calls "the landscape of fact" succeeds the medieval "landscape of symbols." The latter

subordinates the sheer pleasure of perceiving nature to the moral and religious value of reading its otherworldly meanings. This impulse to allegorize the world, says Clark, persists even in the "most perfect form" of late
medieval landscape, as represented for him by the *Paradise Garden,* one of
many medieval renderings of the theme of the *hortus conclusus,* the
enclosed garden, paintings and tapestries that depict the Virgin in a walled
garden, with or without unicorns. Clark's discussion of the painting
installs a contrast, between the sensuous materiality of nature and its symbolic significance, that persists as one of the most contentious elements in
discourses on landscape (including discussions of the actual gardens,
enclosed or otherwise, that were one of landscape painting's first legacies
to the landscape itself). The *Paradise Garden,* writes Clark,

> distils a world of delicate, sensuous perception, where flowers
> are there to please the senses of sight and smell, fruit to satisfy
> the taste, and the sound of a zither, mingled with that of falling
> water, to delight the hearing. Yet all these sensations still have
> some immaterial quality, for they are conceived as testimonies
> of heavenly joy; and the picture is full of heavenly symbols, the
> fountain, the bird on the battlements, the Holy Child making
> music and the dragon of evil lying with his belly in the air. In
> Venice, a century later, these pleasures no longer reflected
> another world.[17]

The decisive development, from Clark's point of view, occurred a century later, in Venice and in the Netherlands, when a "resolute search for
truth"[18] brought artists to the actual topographies of the world around
them, and for the first time in the history of art, a sense of place entered
the picture. From this time forth, landscape painting was regularly celebrated for its alleged fidelity to nature, all the while continuing to satisfy
various spiritual and psychological desires, from the Virgilian to the
Wordsworthian, from reassurance about nature's friendliness to grim
warning of its otherness. But just as "the eighteenth century, that winter
of imagination," allowed the brave new landscape of fact to "degenerate
into topography,"[19] so also another stirring chapter in the history of
landscape, the fantasy landscapes of romanticism, devolved into the
stagey sentimentalities of the picturesque style. Clark follows his subject
beyond these impasses, passing through the "ideal landscapes" of
Claude Lorraine and Gaspard Poussin, the "natural vision" of the
impressionists and Constable (who represents, says Clark, the "final
stage in the development of man's relations with nature"), to the "north-

ern lights" of Turner and van Gogh, concluding with the "return to order" represented by Seurat and Cézanne. The story he tells through these stages presents landscape painting as "an act of faith," an ongoing expression, beyond orthodoxies and in defiance of materialism, of a "mystical sense of the unity of creation." Landscape painting is, in this view, the art of making paradise on earth:

> We are surrounded by things which we have not made and which have a life and structure different from our own: trees, flowers, grasses, rivers, hills, clouds. For centuries they have inspired us with curiosity and awe. They have been objects of delight. We have recreated them in our imaginations to reflect our moods. And we have come to think of them as contributing to an idea which we have called nature. Landscape painting marks the stages in our conception of nature. Its rise and development since the middle ages is part of a cycle in which the human spirit attempted once more to create a harmony with its environment.[20]

But Clark's *Landscape into Art* is no longer the reliable guide to the field that it once was. Along with Ernst Gombrich's classic essay "The Renaissance Theory of Art and the Rise of Landscape" (1953), Clark's text and its influential periodization of landscape painting are now the object of critique. In his recent collection *Landscape and Power*, W. J. T. Mitchell challenges the traditional view of landscape painting as a "revolutionary" genre that emerged in sixteenth-century Europe.[21] For Mitchell, this "postmedieval" and Eurocentric view of landscape (which ignores the counterevidence of the landscape arts of Hellenistic and Roman painters, but cannot finally stand up against the "overwhelming richness, complexity and antiquity of Chinese landscape painting")[22] is a "pseudohistorical myth" in the service of no less a political program than Western imperialism itself, with which it shares a history and a heyday.[23] Mitchell unpacks the ideological freight of the paragraph I just quoted, starting with the hefty baggage in Clark's liberally employed pronoun "we": "Who is this 'we' that defines itself by its difference from 'trees, flowers, grasses, rivers, hills, clouds' and then erases this difference by re-creating it as a reflection of its own moods and ideas? Whose history and whose nature is marked into 'stages' by landscape painting?" (6) Mitchell's next question is the crucial one, opening up the issue of history, of the role played by landscape in ensuring (by occluding) the triumph of a specific historical economic program, one that depends upon and therefore "naturalizes" an oppositional view of human beings and the world of nature. "What disruption" was it, asks Mitchell, that "required [the invention of] an art that would restore the 'human spirit' to harmony with its environment?" (6) Mitchell then introduces what he characterizes as the "skeptical" counterdiscourse on landscape, exemplified by a study like John Barrell's *The Dark Side of the Landscape*, which draws attention to the ideological and economic motives behind representations of landscape.[24] According to this now well established critical tradition, landscape painting is both a discourse and a cultural practice that silences discourse. Mitchell concludes with the following ironic reframing of Clark's "innocent" position:

> Clark's paragraph . . . may be read as still true if only its key terms are understood in an ironic sense: [if] the "different structure" of nature is read as alienation from the land; the "reflective" and imaginary projection of moods into landscape is read as the dreamwork of ideology; the rise and development of landscape is read as a symptom of the rise and development of capitalism; the "harmony" sought in landscape is read as a compensation for the screening off of the actual violence perpetrated there. (7)

Mitchell is not alone among commentators on traditional landscape theory who have shown that an enormous ideological investment lies behind the long-standing equation between the European Renaissance and landscape painting. This equation in turn rests on another one, that between landscape painting and perspective.

Landscape, Perspective, and "Visualism"

The emergence of the European landscape arts coincided with the discovery of the principles of perspective drawing, the quasi-mathematical system for representing three-dimensional space on a two-dimensional plane by organizing represented objects in relation to each other. As first used by Brunelleschi and thereafter formally presented by Alberti in *Della Pittura* (1435), the technique was widely received not as the artificial device that it actually was but as an almost magical means of revealing truth. Regarded as a fulfillment of the impossible dream of a medium that erased mediation, perspective completely transformed the field of representation. Beyond its transfiguration of painting, perspective soon furnished a model for the design of three-dimensional spaces in the real world—gardens,[25] buildings, streets, even rural estates and entire cities. The preeminence of perspective finally "came to condition the ordinary expectations of what the observing I/eye—that fixed point determining the lines along which forms were dispersed in perspective space—should perceive in the real environment outside the frame of the picture."[26]

The visual control provided by the technique was experienced by its first viewers as giving them a kind of supernatural access to the represented world. In fact it did just the opposite: far from bringing the viewer into the world shown in the painting, the success of the illusion depended on keeping him fixed in one position just outside the picture frame, firmly alienated from the landscape. The founding paradox of perspective as employed in landscape painting is that it appears to "give" us the world—especially the natural world, its favorite subject—just at the very moment that it removes it from us—or rather, us from it—most decisively. That we do not notice the loss is not surprising given what we gain: a mechanism for producing the imminently useful conviction that the world can be mastered by the eye. For behind the success of perspective and the glorification of landscape painting lies the privileging, the prioritization, of vision and visuality.

The extraordinary success of this reordering of sensory priorities in favor of vision was due in part to the support lent to it by European scientific revolutions from Copernicus to Newton. Galileo's formulation of science as an objective discourse on nature, susceptible to measurement and predictability and quite independent of the human observer, was later given philosophical support in Cartesian dualism, which construed the human mind as radically distinct from the world of matter, hence of space and place. The human being was, to Descartes, "a substance whose whole nature or essence consists in thinking, and whose existence depends neither on its location in space nor on any material thing."[27] The model of a distanced and disinterested observer produced by mechanistic science was effortlessly shared with landscape, which perspectivism had caused to be increasingly regarded as an object of contemplation.

The spectator of perspectival landscape art is formally an outsider, and the continued coherence of the picture depends on his remaining so. The thrilling effects achieved by perspective depended upon the distance and fixed position of the onlooker, and, further, upon denying both of these. The anxiety of that position—the outsider who is not permitted to know his exclusion—is considerably alleviated by the concomitant projection of passivity on the world represented. As Julian Thomas puts it, "Because landscape art presents the world from the point of view of the outsider, that which is inside the frame takes on the passive role of object, represented, manipulated and alienated, denied any agency of its own."[28] Unable to enter or alter the space of the world she or he is gazing upon, the spectator of landscape painting can take comfort in the conviction that it is a world over which she or he has conceptual dominion. The price of this alienation is a presumption of order, and a fantasy of social control as total spatialization ("A piazza for everything and everything in its piazza," as Marshall McLuhan joked).[29]

The connection between landscape painting and perspective intervenes dramatically in any effort to consider landscape as a medium of modern theater. In the theater, perspective is much more than the mere metaphor it is in everyday parlance. Perspective is one of theater's fundamental spatial techniques. Indeed, the history of the Western theater's relationship to space sustained a traumatic break when the principles of perspective drawing were introduced into the protocols of scene design by Sebastiano Serlio in the sixteenth century. The stage aesthetic that developed rapidly thereafter proved to be a costly bargain: with the illusion of depth now available to it, set design could supply astonishing degrees of realism, but only—and always—within the confines of the picture frame, the proscenium arch. Pushed outside this frame, banished from participating in the life-art dialectic that is theatrical process, the spectator became a viewer and had to relinquish the unique experiential mode of receiving art that is offered by this art alone. True, this new mode of spectatorship recast the ideal spectator as a sovereign, giving him a model of individuality, centrality, and authority to aspire to: the position in the auditorium from which the perspectival effects were seen to perfection. But the bargain was a Faustian one: the average spectator's chances of actually sitting in the "duke's seat" were nil, just as bleak as his or her chances of actually "mastering" the social world.

The actual position of the spectator of perspectival staging can perhaps best be understood in all its psychological implications with reference to a certain well-known theory of landscape. In *The Experience of Landscape,* Jay Appleton connects various subgenres of landscape to biological needs and urges identified in animal habitat theory. From this perspective, landscape appears as a series of strategic locations— "prospect," "refuge," "hazard"—available to the predator whose survival depends on successfully negotiating the various features of the land and its other inhabitants. He singles out the picturesque genre as especially pleasing because it places the viewer in the position of protected (safe) observer, viewing the scene from a partially hidden and pleasantly shaded spot, the "refuge."[30] Any framing of a natural scene that confers such a position of safety on the onlooker is an instance of the picturesque, a guarantee that it is "only a picture," and that the viewer is safely removed, "outside the frame, behind the binoculars, the camera, or the eyeball, in the dark refuge of the skull."[31] Thus proscenium staging can be thought of as an instance of constructing the "picturesque spectator," the ever-threatened and threatening predator, temporarily enjoying a moment of safety!

But (as the title of a well-known book on theater puts it) theater is not safe.[32] Certainly, the landscape theater that is the subject of this book comes into being on the far side of the shielded and sheltered theatrology inaugurated by perspective staging and perfected by naturalism. Landscape theater seeks to reanimate the life-art dialectic that realism had enclosed within its illusory four walls. In doing so, it seems to retrace the trajectory followed by the concept of landscape itself, from two-dimensional representation to three-dimensional environment, from a tract of land capable of being seen at a glance to an environment one can explore and inhabit.

The Politics of Landscape

> A landscape is built out of inclusions and exclusions; it is a
> structuring of knowledge and a valorizing of some things at
> the expense of others.
>
> —GARRETT A. SULLIVAN JR.

The connection between landscape painting and perspective makes it no accident, Denis Cosgrove[33] and others have argued, that the form should emerge in fifteenth-century northern Italy and Flanders, when new social relations needed legitimization in a new "politics of vision." The new way of looking at the land that was enshrined in landscape painting, or, to put it another way, what this form of painting did to land when it converted it into landscape, was to disengage it from hereditary patterns of tenure, habitation, and obligation. The landscape was the land as commodity, passive, inert, external to the observing self, able to be bought and sold at will. Extending this economic reading of landscape aesthetics, Charles Harrison contests the art-historical tradition that sees landscape painting as a genre that gradually grew out of the margins of other genres, notably portraiture. According to Harrison, landscape painting was rather a "form of alternative to portraiture or even of resistance to what portraiture tends to picture. . . . Landscape achieves autonomy as an artistic genre in England only when the countryside can be viewed as other than the property of the landed gentry."[34] Landscape marks the moment when "the countryside is viewable under some aspect other than its aspect as property." It becomes, at that moment, the "paradigmatic site of individual experience." In the writings on land-scape of which Clark's study represents a culmination, "response to landscape is taken as a measure of individuality."

An early stage of this use of landscape as evidence of a certain desir-able or even normative subjectivity has been explored in a brilliant arti-cle by John Barrell on the "politics of taste" in eighteenth-century En-gland. Barrell argues that a specific "correct taste" in landscape was one of several tests that determined nothing less than one's ability to think at a sufficiently abstract level, which in turn signified one's ability to grasp the public interest, and hence to participate in government. This way of legitimating political authority from within the discourse of civic humanism depended on an opposition between two kinds of landscapes, the ideal panoramic landscape of extensive prospects and encompassing views, and the enclosed, occluded, or limited landscape of nature's inter-esting but atypical (or "accidental") details. The crucial distinction was between the "universal" or permanent quality of the wide vista, which was said to show—and to be appreciated by those who understood and valued—the relations between things, versus the "accidental" and diverting specificity of the narrow view, appealing to ruder sensibilities. Thus the distinction between these two kinds of landscapes delineated (and authorized) a class distinction, dividing the world into those capa-ble or not capable of the abstraction needed to serve the "public inter-est." The underlying connection between landscapes and modes of intel-lection had very wide currency and regularly slipped from the literal to the metaphorical register, as in the following contemporaneous descrip-tion of the progress of knowledge:

> In all sciences, we rise from the individual to the species, from the species to the genus, and thence to the most extensive orders and classes [and] arrive . . . at the knowledge of general truths. . . . In this progress we are like people who, from a low and confined bottom, where the view is confined to a few acres, gradually ascend a lofty peak or promontory. The prospect is perpetually enlarging at every moment, and, when we reach the summit, the boundless horizon, comprehending all the variety of sea and land, hill and valley, town and county, arable and desert, lies under the eyes at once.[35]

Translating this passage out of the metaphorical register back into the discourse on literal landscapes, Barrell argues that this model of general knowledge as comprehensive vision implies a deficit of knowledge in certain quarters ("those who remain imprisoned within their few acres at the bottom of the eminence") that readily translates into a naturalized class distinction: "Those who can comprehend the order of society and nature are the observers of a prospect, of which others are merely the objects. Some comprehend, others are comprehended."[36] On this spatialization of class identity rested the civic notion that "it is particularly or exclusively the independent owner of a substantial freehold in land who is capable of exercising political authority."[37]

The cultural use of landscape to define subjectivity and confer identity can be seen even more clearly in the practice of landscape photography that flourished in England and elsewhere in the last three decades of the nineteenth century, when the cultural coding of landscape spread far beyond the elite circles of the landed gentry where it had originally taken root. The photographic representation of picturesque places (or "spots," as they were commonly called) invariably adopted an accompanying rhetoric of florid prose that drew heavily upon a fixed repertoire of images—the standard building blocks of the picturesque as cultural construct, paradoxically guaranteeing its authenticity as nature untouched by culture. John Taylor points out that "in 1884 it was said that suburbia might be growing but within five or six miles of each photographer's door there were abbeys, ancient places, birches, brooks, canals, cattle, churches, cottages, crags, crosses, dingles, farms, ferns, foxgloves, gables, ivy, lands, locks, oaks, ponds, rustic bridges, rustics at work, tombs, watermills, windmills, walls and woods."[38] The images produced by the growing army of landscape photographers gained in cultural and psychological importance to the same degree that the actual countryside itself became either more contaminated by culture (by progress or "development") or more difficult to gain access to (usually because of growing pressures on leisure time, and increased competition from urban entertainments). In a development that anticipates contemporary simulacral phenomena like Disney's aptly named World Showcase, the pictures "became talismans or touchstones, evidence that the landscape really did exist. The viewers could stay home, and still be incorporated in the array of feelings that would be evoked by landscape."[39]

Beyond evoking certain predetermined feelings, landscape was pressed into the service of nationalist ideology by giving a "face" to the nation, a face sufficiently distinguishable from those of other nations and sufficiently simplified so as to be easily recognizable and "quotable" as needed. In the case of England, the landscape was scoured (by photographers and others) for examples of its "ancient" and "natural" aspects, these being combined into a seamless image of a place not only worth belonging to but also worth fighting for. As one writer, presenting a collection of photographs entitled *The English Countryside,* put it:

> Prehistoric trackway, ancient village, sleepy town, the farmhouse in the hollow, the sheepfold on the hill—all have rendered their share in the making of England, and in the building up of that race whose sons are emulating on the battlefield the deeds of their forefathers set forth in the quaint inscriptions on the walls of many a village church or in the mouldering records of ancient boroughs.[40]

The ideological use of the landscape is perhaps nowhere more readily apparent than in America, where landscape painting played a decisive role in establishing a link (which persists to this day) between national identity and the land itself. The rhetoric of nineteenth-century romantic nationalism included the claim that the American landscape itself engendered nationalist sentiment. As E. L. Magoon put it in an essay forthrightly entitled "Scenery and Mind": "The diversified landscapes of our country exert no slight influence in creating our character as individuals, and in confirming our destiny as a nation."[41] Grand natural scenery, he goes on, "tends permanently to affect the character of those cradled in its bosom." In her study of landscape painting and cultural politics in nineteenth-century America, Angela Miller has argued persuasively against the "generally accepted view that the expression of national identity in landscape art was both natural and inevitable."[42] Departing from traditional discussions of American landscape art, which have tended to emphasize its relationship to concepts of nature and to Emersonian concepts of self (the "American mind" paradigm), Miller reads sentiments like Oliver Wendell Holmes's "Our Union is river, lake, ocean and sky,"[43] as part of "a cultural endeavor directed at consolidating a middle-class social identity utterly bound up with the civilizing mission."[44] The role played by landscape painting in this endeavor is, in Miller's account, complex and often contradictory, negotiating "the conceptual dilemma [of] how to build an integrated national self without sacrificing local identities."

The tension between landscape as locality and landscape as nation is, in fact, one of many instances of what Stephen Daniels terms "the duplicity of landscape,"[45] referring to the tension between thing and idea—matter and meaning, place and ideology—that seems to be the defining characteristic of landscape. An acute awareness of this difficult doubleness may lie behind the reluctance in the field of cultural landscape studies to engage the materials of art, including, of course, theater. This antiart tendency may be born of a need to valorize the "vernacular," but it is frequently stated as a choice of a complex sociality over a superficial visuality. As Paul Groth writes in the introduction to his recent collection of essays on landscape, "For writers in cultural landscape studies, the term landscape means more than a pleasing view of scenery. Landscape denotes the interaction of people and place: a social group and its spaces, particularly the spaces to which the group belongs and from which its members derive some part of their shared identity and meaning."[46] Another commentator on the two disciplines puts it as follows: "The landscape student is as interested in what has been built around such sublime sights as Niagara Falls, Yosemite National Park or Yellowstone's Old Faithful as in these spectacular landscapes themselves. Where the landscape artist might well have edited out the passing railroad, and the photographer might deliberately secure a pylon-free vista, . . . the landscape analyst is likely to question the logic behind such omissions, while asking why society would permit these mundane landscape elements to be erected around supposedly revered landscapes."[47]

This emphasis on the social as opposed to the aesthetic dimension of the landscape initially appears to divide this discourse on landscape from that of art history, but as recent controversies surrounding exhibitions of landscape paintings have shown, this particular version of the boundary between art and social life is getting weaker all the time. The now full-blown critical turn represented by "skeptical" studies like *The Dark Side of the Landscape* has begun to disrupt popular assumptions about the apoliticality of landscape art. An exhibition of American paintings held in 1991 at the National Museum of American Art was entitled "The West as America: Reinterpreting Images of the Frontier." Plaques on the walls near the paintings made the following (rather measured) point:

> Images from Christopher Columbus to Kit Carson show the discovery and settlement of the West as a heroic undertaking. A more recent approach argues that these images are carefully staged fiction, constructed from both supposition and fact. Their role was to justify the hardship and conflict of nation-building. Western scenes noted progress, but rarely noted

damaging social and environmental change. Looking beneath the surface of these images gives us a better understanding of why national problems created during the Westward expansion still affect us today.[48]

The exhibition went on to draw parallels between the settling of the West and American imperialism in Southeast Asia. The response to the exhibition was one of outrage, with senators threatening to cut off funds to the Smithsonian, and galleries out of town canceling the scheduled tour of the exhibition. A decade earlier, an exhibition of the paintings of Richard Nelson at the Tate Gallery in London had run into a similar controversy when its accompanying commentary implied, according to the outraged press, that "our greatest Augustan landscapist [was] a purveyor of 'elite culture,' who presents social inequalities in their most flattering light."[49]

Public controversies like these reveal that the shift in critical understanding of landscape painting—from objective representation, to way of seeing, to way of not seeing—is no longer contained within an academic discipline. It has entered the sphere of public culture, from whence it must invariably also inflect both the representation and the interpretation of theatrical landscapes. If, as Barbara Bender puts it, "the experience of landscape is too important and too interesting to be confined to a particular time, place and class,"[50] surely it is also too important and too interesting not to be *staged.*

NOTES

1. To my knowledge, the one and only recent book linking the two fields is Garrett A. Sullivan Jr.'s *The Drama of Landscape: Land, Property, and Social Relations on the Early Modern Stage* (Stanford: Stanford University Press, 1998). Denis Cosgrove's article "Spectacle and Society: Landscape as Theater in Premodern and Postmodern Cities," in *Understanding Ordinary Landscapes,* ed. Paul Groth and Todd W. Bressi, 99–110, does not deal with theater itself, only with the theatrical metaphor so ubiquitous in Renaissance thought and first explored by John Brinckerhoff Jackson, the founder of cultural landscape studies, in a brief but wide-ranging article: "Landscape as Theater," *Landscape* 23, no. 1 (1979): 3–7.

2. Denis Cosgrove, *Social Formation and Symbolic Landscape* (London: Croom Helm, 1984), 13.

3. John Brinckerhoff Jackson, "The Order of a Landscape: Reason and Religion in Newtonian America," in *The Interpretation of Ordinary Landscapes: Geographical Essays,* ed. D. W. Meinig (Oxford: Oxford University Press, 1979), 153–63.

4. Carl Sauer writes, "Culture is the agent, nature is the medium, the landscape is the result." "Landscape," in *Dictionary of Concepts in Human Geography,* ed. Robert P. Larkin and Gary L. Peters (Westport, Conn.: Greenwood, 1983), 141.

5. The title of a recent book by Paul Shepard makes the connection memorably: *The Cultivated Wilderness; or, What Is Landscape?* (Cambridge: MIT Press, 1997).

6. Ann Whiston Spirn suggests that at midcentury the word *environment* was preferred over the word *landscape* because of the Nazis' adoption of "blood and soil, a linking of native landscape and racial identity." *The Language of Landscape* (New Haven: Yale University Press, 1998), 17.

7. Arjun Appadurai, *Modernity at Large: Cultural Dimensions of Globalization* (Minneapolis: University of Minnesota Press, 1996), 33–35.

8. And which we continue to connect it with, as in Edward Casey's resolve to "attempt wherever possible to respect the elemental origin of *landscape* in the flora, soil, and other conceptions and configurations of the land [and use it to] refer primarily to the physiognomy of the land, the manner in which the land appears and is taken in." *Getting Back into Place* (Bloomington: Indiana University Press, 1993), 203.

9. Casey, *Getting Back into Place,* 232.

10. Spirn, *The Language of Landscape,* 17. See also "The Word Itself," in John Brinckerhoff Jackson, *Discovering the Vernacular Landscape* (New Haven: Yale University Press, 1984), 3–8.

11. John Brinckerhoff Jackson, "The Need of Being Versed in Country Things," *Landscape* 1, no. 1 (1951): 5.

12. The field is distinguished by a plurality of styles as well as of disciplines, ranging from the accessible "literary" style favored by Jackson's journal to the densely annotated and heavily researched scholarly style of such works as *The Making of the American Landscape,* ed. Michael P. Conzen (Boston: Unwin Hyman, 1990).

13. Peirce F. Lewis, "Axioms for Reading the Landscape: Some Guides to the American Scene," in Meinig, *Interpretation of Ordinary Landscape,* 11–12.

14. D. W. Meinig, "The Beholding Eye: Ten Versions of the Same Scene," in *Interpretation of Ordinary Landscapes,* 33. The ten views of landscape Meinig identifies are as *nature,* as *habitat,* as *artifact,* as *system,* as *problem,* as *wealth,* as *ideology,* as *history,* as *place,* and as *aesthetic.* A similarly pluralistic system for interpreting landscape is presented in the same volume by Peirce F. Lewis, who identifies four "Axioms for Reading the Landscape," each with numerous corollaries.

15. Barbara Bender, "Introduction: Landscape—Meaning and Action," in *Landscape: Politics and Perspectives,* ed. Barbara Bender (Oxford: Berg, 1993), 1.

16. *American Heritage Dictionary of the English Language,* 3d ed.

17. Kenneth Clark, *Landscape into Art,* rev. ed. (New York: Icon Editions, 1976), 17.

18. Clark, *Landscape into Art,* 39.

19. Clark, *Landscape into Art,* 105.

20. Clark, *Landscape into Art,* 1.

21. This is the view presented in the article "Landscape Painting" in *The Oxford Companion to Art,* in terms that make the problematics of the position quite apparent: "Until fairly recent times men [sic] looked at nature as an assemblage of isolated objects, without connecting them into a unified field. . . . It was in the European atmosphere of the early 16th century that the first 'pure' landscape was painted."

22. W. J. T. Mitchell, "Imperial Landscape," in *Landscape and Power,* ed. W. J. T. Mitchell (Chicago: University of Chicago Press, 1994), 9.

23. "If Kenneth Clark is right to say that 'landscape painting was the chief artistic creation of the nineteenth century,' we need at least to explore the relation of this cultural fact to the other 'chief creation' of the nineteenth century—the system of global domination known as European imperialism" (Mitchell, "Imperial Landscape," 10).

24. Other important considerations of landscape in this "skeptical" vein are Ann Bermingham, *Landscape and Ideology: The English Rustic Tradition 1740–1860* (Berkeley and Los Angeles: University of California Press, 1986); Simon Pugh, ed., *Reading Landscape: Country—City—Capital* (Manchester: Manchester University Press, 1990); and Alan R. H. Barker and Gideon Biger, *Ideology and Landscape in Historical Perspective: Essays on the Meanings of Some Places in the Past* (Cambridge: Cambridge University Press, 1992).

25. See, for example, John Dixon Hunt, *The Figure in the Landscape: Poetry, Painting, and Gardening during the Eighteenth Century* (Baltimore: Johns Hopkins University Press, 1976), 39–48.

26. Catherine M. Howett, "Where the One-Eyed Man Is King: The Tyranny of Visual and Formal Values in Evaluating Landscapes," in Groth and Bressi, *Understanding Ordinary Landscapes,* 87.

27. René Descartes, *Discourse on Method* (1637), quoted in David Pepper, *The Roots of Modern Environmentalism* (London: Croom Helm, 1984).

28. Julian Thomas, "The Politics of Vision and the Archaeologies of Landscape," in Bender, *Landscape: Politics and Perspectives,* 22.

29. Marshall McLuhan and Quentin Fiore, *The Medium Is the Massage* (New York: Bantam, 1967), 53.

30. Jay Appleton, *The Experience of Landscape* (London: Wiley, 1975).

31. Mitchell, 16.

32. Gordon Rogoff, *Theatre Is Not Safe: Theatre Criticism, 1962–1986* (Evanston, Ill.: Northwestern University Press, 1987).

33. Cosgrove, *Social Formation.*

34. Charles Harrison, "The Effects of Landscape," in Mitchell, *Landscape and Power,* 215.

35. Quoted by John Barrell, "The Public Prospect and the Private View: The Politics of Taste in Eighteenth Century Britain," in Pugh, *Reading Landscape,* 27.

36. Barrell, "Public Prospect," 28.

37. Barrell, "Public Prospect," 30.

38. John Taylor, "The Alphabetic Universe: Photography and the Picturesque Landscape," in Pugh, *Reading Landscape,* 181.

39. Taylor, "The Alphabetic Universe," 181–82.

40. Quoted by Taylor, "The Alphabetic Universe," 193.

41. E. L. Magoon, "Scenery and Mind," in *The Home Book of the Picturesque; or, American Scenery, Art, and Literature* (1852; rpt. Gainesville, Fla.: Scholars' Facsimiles and Reprints, 1967), 3.

42. Angela Miller, *The Empire of the Eye: Landscape Representation and Cultural Politics, 1825–1875* (Ithaca, N.Y.: Cornell University Press, 1993), 3.

43. "Brother Jonathan's Lament for Sister Caroline" (1861), in *The Works of Oliver Wendell Holmes,* 13 vols. (Boston: Houghton Mifflin, 1892), 12:284.

44. Miller, *Empire of the Eye,* 11.

45. Landscape "can neither be completely reified as an authentic object in the world nor thoroughly dissolved as an ideological mirage." Stephen Daniels, "Marxism, Culture, and the Duplicity of Landscape," in *New Models in Geography,* ed. N. Thrift and R. Peet (Boston: Allen and Unwin, 1990), 206.

46. Groth, "Frameworks for Cultural Landscape Study," in Groth and Bressi, *Understanding Ordinary Landscapes,* 1; emphasis added.

47. Stephen F. Mills, *The American Landscape* (Edinburgh: Keele University Press, 1997), 9–10.

48. Quoted in Stephen Daniels, *Fields of Vision: Landscape Imagery and National Identity in England and the United States* (Princeton, N.J.: Princeton University Press, 1993), 1.

49. Quoted in Daniels, *Fields of Vision,* 2.

50. Bender, "Introduction," 1.

2

Reading for Landscape:
The Case of American Drama

Elinor Fuchs

Every dramatic world is conditioned by a landscape imaginary, a "deep" surround suggested to the mind that extends far beyond the onstage environment reflected in the dramatic text and its scenographic representation.[1] This spatial surround both emerges from the text and shapes its interpretation, guiding the "visitor" to a reading in depth of the dramatic world's scale and tone. Until the end of the nineteenth century, this spatial ground served, like scenography itself, as a platform for human action. It provided, one might say, the "landscape preconscious" of the characterologically conscious text.

The signs of a shift from preconscious to conscious are everywhere to be found in the European dramatic texts of the end of the nineteenth century. In the symbolic avalanches of Ibsen, the threatened forests of Chekhov, the ecstatically open or pathologically closed worlds of Wedekind, the trembling atmospheres of Maeterlinck, and the *lehr*scapes of late Strindberg one can begin to see landscape itself as independent figure: not simply a support to human action, but entering it in a variety of roles, for instance, as mentor, obstacle, or ironist. The crossover of romantic landscape painting into scenography, the revitalization of allegory, and a growing awareness of landscape itself as endangered suggest the diversity of influences from which a fin de siècle landscape poetics of the theater was fashioned.

Modern American drama absorbed the heightened landscape dimension in these influential European models and brought it to bear even within a prevailing realism. This essay will interest itself in the deep landscapes of several American plays of the past half-century.

Within this interest, my special focus will be on the progressive exchange of position enacted in these plays between figure and ground—in other words, between character and landscape. As my discussion progresses from *Death of a Salesman* to *The America Play* to David Hancock's *The Convention of Cartography* it will also move through stages of human relationship to the land, from direct connection of foot, hand, and wheel, to more abstract and conceptual ties of geography and maps.

> Biff. *I stopped in the middle of that building*
> *and saw—the sky.*[2]

In "The American Ideology of Space," an article originating in a 1988 symposium at New York's Museum of Modern Art, the well-known theorist of American pastoral, Leo Marx, outlines three coexisting versions of America's myth of the land: primitivist, utilitarian, and pastoral. American primitivism equates civilization with corruption, he observes. It seeks to be as far away as possible in space and time from the great centers of European civilization, and to inhabit "the most distant, western edge of the mental map."[3] But wilderness ideology has always been a minority commitment, however passionately held. The predominant view of landscape in the United States is utilitarian: the wasteland must be civilized and put to work (65). In America, to master the land is to achieve Progress, an achievement happily found to coincide with the will of God. The third branch of American landscape ideology is the pastoral, Marx writes, a longing that seeks a balance between civilization and nature. The pastoralist belief in a "middle landscape" is not at odds with the instrumentalization of the land, but restrains and humanizes it (66–67). In postwar American society this pastoral strain found expression in the suburban backyard, the rainbow of promise, if not the pot of gold, at the end of urban flight.

Scratch the play of character in *Death of a Salesman* and one finds this spectrum of American landscape ideology precisely laid out in variations that stretch across three successive generations of fathers and sons. The play's deep landscape is linked at the outset with that strangest of pre-figures, Willy's elusive father. In realistic terms, nothing is less probable than that a midcentury salesman from Brooklyn would have sprung from a father who ventured across the United States in a covered wagon, selling homemade flutes all the way from Boston to the country's farthest western edge. The story is preposterous. Yet the flute-playing father is a kind of "big bang" in the landscape imaginary of *Death of a Salesman;* he occupies the pristine moment before the myth of the land splinters into conflicting ideologies. The presumably long-dead father is entrepreneur, pastoralist, and primitivist in one, a trinity of American relationships to the land.

In Willy's imagination, embodied in Miller's opening stage direction, the father and his flute bespeak a kind of Eden, a pastoral idyll of "grass and trees and the horizon" ("Overture," 5). Its primal scene is the family circle in Nebraska—no, South Dakota—no, *somewhere*—on the open road. "All I remember is a man with a big beard, and I was in Mama's lap, sitting around a fire, and some kind of high music," rambles Willy, sharing his final memory of a lost golden age with the spectral Ben (42). As brother Ben describes it in Willy's reverie, the covered wagon is no echo of the *illud tempus,* but a flute store on wheels, making money in every city "through Ohio, and Indiana, Michigan, Illinois, and all the Western states." In Ben's account, as improbable as Willy's, the covered wagon starts out in Boston and heads for the West, staking out a salesman's territory on a continental scale. "With one gadget [father] made more in a week than a man like you could make in a lifetime," he says dismissively (42–43).

As the legend continues, however, this forebear abandons both home and family for the Alaskan wilderness. The "wild-hearted" (42) father goes primitive (or entrepreneurial, we don't know for sure), abandons family, lapses into a conclusive silence, and produces in his son Willy a "temporary" sense of self (45). As the story unfolds, the landscape he leaves behind proves to be temporary as well.

Willy and his mythic brother are satellites put in motion by their perpetually moving father: the road dominates their landscapes. "I remember you walking away down some open road," Willy mistily recalls to Ben (41). Yet they are both on the road, Ben by train, Willy by automobile, for strictly instrumental ends. For Ben wealth lies in single-minded exploitation of the land, whereas for Willy the resources to exploit are human—smiles, slaps on the back, being "well liked." Miller ironically juxtaposes the expansive legend of Ben—for whom north equals south, and Alaska equals Africa (no difference: two place names beginning with *A,* and each a wilderness available to plunder)—against the shrunken horizon of Willy's outer borough compromise. Ben is after big game:

Willy. The Gold Coast!
Ben. Principally diamond mines. (42)

Not to be outdone as land-utilitarian, Willy, the timid pastoralist, lays a risible counterclaim to mastery of the land. "It's Brooklyn, I know, but we hunt too. . . . There's snakes and rabbits and—that's why we moved out here. Why Biff can fell any one of these trees in no time" (44).

Out of the mingled American land myths prefigured by Father, Ben has chosen a route of disciplined predation. To Ben, the woods could not be burning (Willy's strange apocalyptic cry), because they are in any case only timber. Marx recalls the early maps of the New World, their uncharted white zones floating between the coasts to depict the "boundless immensity and seeming emptiness, or ahistorical character" of the North American continent (63). Ben is as ahistorical as the foundational American narrative of "virgin" land. He is its figurative correlative. His landscape forms a vast, reproving backdrop to Willy's all-but-defeated pastoralism. Reproving yet supportive, for in the grip of real-life limitations, Willy still retains the illusion of an open frontier, even in a salesman's territory. For a salesman, he brags, "the sky's the limit" (79).

Willy's conflicted landscape (brilliantly suggested in Jo Mielziner's historic set, which later found its way into the stage directions of the printed text) is torn between the alienating density of the urban built environment, and the pastoral nostalgia stirred by the disappearing open space. His flashes of elegiac tenderness for the lost elms, the carrots in the garden, the "moon moving between the buildings" (63) give momentary respite from his striving for success and his shame at not achieving it. Yet even Willy's modest version of the pastoral ideal may not survive into the third generation.

For the younger figures, the utilitarian principle of wealth-extraction has been transferred to the dense "jungle" of the urban scene. Their battles are played out in the offices, elevators, and restaurants of the built landscape. Their pastoral pursuits are similarly less a relief from the success game than an extension of the instrumental principle to the sphere of recreation. Happy's dismal horizon is measured by his successful friend the merchandise manager, who builds a "terrific estate on Long Island," only to sell it after two months to build a new one (17). Bernard plays tennis on the weekends, a sign but also a variant of professional achievement. In mechanical parody of the ur-father's continental trek, Howard's son recites on the latest expensive gizmo, a tape recorder, the name of every state capital, but in alphabetical, not geographical or experiential, order.

Only Biff—but at the cost of terrible confusion—embraces in actual experience some mixture of drop-out primitivism and what Lawrence Buell describes as "new world pastoral," "the idea of vast territories of the actual globe subsisting under the sign of nature."[4] "We don't belong in this nuthouse of a city! We should be mixing cement on some open plain, or—or carpenters," Biff laments (55), even as he tries to fit himself to the shape of the marketplace. "What am I doing in an office, making a contemptuous begging fool of myself, when all I want is out there, waiting for me the minute I say I know who I am!" he cries, when the effort fails (125).

In the end the survivors of the Loman world are those who for better or worse do not dream of landscape and are comfortable within the opportunities and limitations of the urban world, Charley, Bernard, and Linda. The large background landscapes of the play resolve themselves finally into a gravesite, a landscape whose perpetual care, in the parlance of the cemetery industry, will be Linda's responsibility. The flute music, which suggested the freedom of the distant horizon at the beginning of act 1, reappears as ironic counterpoint to Linda's repeated cry to the dead Willy, so trapped by life, "We're free" (133).

A great cyclorama of the American landscape glints through the human drama in *Death of a Salesman*. Those who see *Salesman* as a Jewish play "in drag," so to speak, an Odets play inflated by pretensions to universality, might dismiss its landscape text as poetic decoration, masking a psychosocial narrative of urban (trans.: immigrant) culture. Yet a landscape reading frames the urban and generational issues in a longer, more impersonal, story of loss, greed, and illusion and may account in part for the play's felt mythic power.

When *Death of a Salesman* is discussed as a "tragedy of the common man," the measure of "common" is economic class. The play's landscape text, with its large background story of the disappearing frontier and the closing of the open road, offers another scale against which "common" may be measured. Even in his smallness, Willy is enlarged by a landscape imaginary of which he himself is only half-aware. Opening back in time and out in space from coast to coast and beyond to the colonized riches of Africa and Alaska, Miller's text is underlaid by a landscape pentimento that traces the career of American expansion as it consumes the continent. This underpainting shapes, yet never dissolves, the psychological and social lines of character. In Sam Shepard, this boundary begins to disappear.

Wesley. *I could feel this country close like it was part of my bones.*[5]

In many ways, Sam Shepard takes up where Miller leaves off, for instance replaying over and over the city/wilderness or city/pastoral divide between Biff and Happy. But in Shepard's landscapes, the dramaturgy itself shifts: at times, the story of the land is not just the underpainting on the canvas, but the painting itself. The Shepard landscape reverie, usually but insufficiently analogized to jazz, appeared early in his work. In his 1966 one-act *Red Cross,* set in a cabin that is something like a tree house, Shepard's three figures float off into fantasies in which they merge with landscapes of the imagination. Carol hurtles over a ski slope and turns into a gigantic murderous snowball, her head exploding and bleeding into the snow. Jim goes night swimming in the middle of a forest. In an extended riff, the Maid makes a first attempt to swim and drowns in agony only to revive as a tranquil sea creature with "water all around and dragonflies and water lilies floating by and little silver fish flashing around [me]."[6] The human disappears entirely as the maid becomes an invertebrate in a watery refuge.

Shepard's "family plays" of the 1970s, with their more continuous characters locked into fate-driven trajectories, are often seen as his return to realism. But on close inspection one finds some strangely porous figures who periodically act as transmitters or screens for landscapes. The land itself becomes a character in some of Shepard's plays, performing at times as agent, as in *Buried Child,* or as victim in *Curse of the Starving Class.*

Though *Buried Child* is the more conventional of the two plays, its ramshackle farmhouse is furnished with a magical landscape surround—"like a paradise out there."[7] Rain and sun play their symbolic roles accompanying the repression and then exposure of crime and guilt. The barren untilled fields yield miraculous crops of corn and carrots that disturbingly spill onto the stage. The ghost of the title, the murdered incestuous child, invades the stage as the final harvest. Shepard blurs the line between human and vegetable, between the crop that ripens on the land and the child who is given up by it: either way, the natural environment appears to be endowed with independent agency; it is the figure of fate in the fate tragedy.

By contrast, in *Curse of the Starving Class,* the sere southwestern land (and by extension all of rural America of the old subsistence economy) is more patient than agent. The land is Shepard's threatened tragic figure, presented, like an ancient suffering protagonist, a moment before the catastrophe. Its struggle to survive is for the most part visually unrepresented, but it is suggested in Weston's ironic cornucopia of indigestible artichokes, and most notably in the maggot-infested lamb whose zigzagging career of rescue and loss follows that of the land itself through the course of the play. After the final Hobbesian battle of all against all among Shepard's absurdly comic antagonists, the family farm will be bulldozed, subdivided, excavated, "developed"—as we are given to imagine—into strip mall or suburban condos.

In the "Note to the Actors" that prefaces *Angel City*, Shepard uses a landscape metaphor to describe the way characters should be performed in that play. They are not "whole character[s]" with built-in time lines of rational motivation, he says, but should take form as "painting[s] in space" created by the actors.[8] In *Curse of the Starving Class* one can extend this idea of characterization to actual landscape painting. In act 1, Wesley doesn't so much describe, as melt into, a night landscape. "I was lying on my back," he begins.

> I could smell the avocado blossoms. I could hear the coyotes, I could hear the stock cars squeeling [*sic*] down the street.

So far Wesley has only a heightened sensory awareness of the night landscape outside his windows. But then difference and distance collapse. Wesley's boundaries fall away. He does not so much sense the landscape as dissolve the "he" who senses.

> I could feel myself in my bed in my room in this house in this town in this state in this country. I could feel this country close like it was part of my bones. I could feel the presence of all the people outside, at night, in the dark. Even sleeping people I could feel. Even all the sleeping animals. Dogs. Peacocks. Bulls. . . . I could feel the space around me like a big, black world. (59)

In moments like these, Shepard's figures lose the separated status of dramatic character. "In its . . . endless recession in depth, landscape *draws us out*," writes Edward Casey in a piercing analysis. The response is not "in our mind, but . . . *in the body*."[9] Shepard's figures can lose boundaries, dissolving into a world that precedes a separated self.[10] At the same time, landscape itself loses apprehendable shape as scene. In Miller, landscape was omnipresent, yet stood back from character as picture. In this sense Miller's invocation of landscape was fundamentally mimetic. But in Shepard, landscape goes beyond picture. Landscape is "anexact," says Casey, always "more than a place" (4–5). Shepard shows us landscape *sans frontières*, foreground figure merging into background image, outward representation into inner state. This indistinguishability of foreground and background, inner world and outer reality, is literalized with comic horror in *Angel City*, where window and film screen merge, and the green slime that is advancing on Los Angeles oozes onto the stage and covers the faces of Rabbit and Wheeler.

> Before Columbus. *There is uh tiny land mass*
> *just above my reach.*
> Lots of Grease and Lots of Pork. *There is uh tiny land mass*
> *just outside my vocabulary.*[11]

The non-realist play texts of Suzan-Lori Parks do not so much invoke landscape as an image of a real scene in the real world, or as a deep sensing by and in the body (the separated and immersed versions of landscape as picture and as sensory experience), as conceive of dramaturgy itself as landscape construct. Stage as globe, as theme park, as museum, as geographic territory, as archaeological "dig," and as map are among the scenographic indications of a landscape dramaturgy. Repetition, choral structure, circular actions set in the real time of performance art, or set in pre- or post-*histoire,* all contribute to the spectator's sense of spatialization.

"We can no longer depend on a story-line unfolding sequentially, an ever-accumulating history marching straight forward in plot and denouement," wrote geographer Edward Soja, in his pathbreaking *Postmodern Geographies,* "for too much is happening against the grain of time. . . . Simultaneities intervene. . . . The new, the novel, must involve an explicitly geographical . . . configuration and projection."[12] The postmodern works of Parks, David Hancock, and others bear out this sense of reordered coordinates of time and space. Temporality is less an organizing principle of Parks's dramatic method than it is a memory (embodied by her figure Before Columbus) within her spatial world, one more element in a timeless present. "Yesterday today next summer tomorrow just uh moment uhgoh in 1317 dieded thuh last black man in thuh whole entire world," goes the circular refrain from *The Death of the Last Black Man in the Whole Entire World.*[13]

Yet despite the predominance of spatial forms and references in *Last Black Man,* the texture of actual landscape is almost wholly absent, as is the essential marker of landscape-as-picture, the horizon. Parks seems to have left behind the sensuous domain of landscape for the more abstract realm of geography. The neurophysiologist Erwin Straus wrote that "Sensory space stands to perceptual space as landscape to geography."[14] Indeed, many in *Last Black Man*'s chorus of figures are incarnated from the half-formed shapes of geographical legend: ancient Egypt makes an appearance with Queen-Then-Pharoah-Hatshepsut; the ancient Near East with Old Man River Jordan; biblical Israel with Ham, whose diasporic route ends on the slave coasts of Africa. An entire continent surges to imaginative view with Before Columbus. (Parks creates what could be thought of as a geo-orthography for this figure's historical epoch: in those days the "worl'" was "roun'; it hadn't yet acquired its deadly 'd.'") In the after-Columbus world, however, a very real landscape flickers across the mind whenever Black Man—hunted, hanged, electrocuted, pushed from heights—dies another death or finds his way back to the front porch he shares with Black Woman. She imagines the cultural landscape at one of his many executions: "Put thuh Chair in thuh middle of thuh City. Outdoors. In thuh square. Folks come tuh watch with picnic baskets" (107).

From Miller to Shepard to Parks one can follow a choreography of exchange between figure and ground, tracing a progressive spatialization of character. In Parks, characters such as Before Columbus and Old Man River Jordan not only begin to take on the function of setting, whether represented or unrepresented, but setting itself takes on a central attribute of character: it acquires memory. Black Man may be the hunted victim across the post-Columbian landscape, but his defiant other is the landscape of the memory rock summoned by Parks's writer-figure, Yes and Greens Black-Eyed Peas Cornbread, whose colorful name itself seems to have grown out of the land.

"You should write that down," scolds Yes, "You should write that down and you should hide it under a rock" (102). Yes has an urgent reason for converting the play's black geography into the linearity of a conventional historical narrative: "You should write it down because if you don't write it down they will come along and tell the future that we did not exist" (104). Yet even with the precaution of concealing an account of Black Man's life in the landscape, of hiding it under a rock, his memory is not assured. The white man can change the landscape. "You should write it down and you should . . . hide it all under a rock so that in the future when they come along they will say that the rock did not exist" (104).

Last Black Man is arranged in "panels," underscoring the figures as stationary icons of themselves rather than agents moving through time. Yet there is one great change at the end. Yes's final injunction to "write it down" no longer expresses fear of extinction; it becomes an assertion of survival. Writing is now for *us*, and even to teach *them*, not merely to save us from them. The writing is no longer hidden under the rock, but indelibly carved into the landscape.

You will write it down because if you don't write it down then
we will come along and tell the future that we did not exist.
You will write it down and you will carve it out of a rock. . . .
It will be of us but you will mention them from time to time so
that in the future . . . they'll know how they exist . . . so that in
the future . . . they'll know why they exist. You will carve it all
out of a rock so that in the future when we come along we will
know that the rock does yes exist. (130–31)

In the final moments of the play, Ham reveals that he was there on
the slave coast when they came to get his people. "I—was—so—po-lite,"
he confides, but "In thuh rock. I wrote: ha ha ha" (131). All the stage
figures riotously join the laughter. Black Man will be remembered by his
world kin, whose last laugh will resound from the very landscape. Black
Man is dug in "6 BY 6 BY 6" (130), the chorus announces at the end, but
the writing on the rock proclaims that what is interred beneath ground
will be inscribed above, written "in stone" on the visible landscape.

Parks sees her plays as contributions to the recovery of black memory and history. She describes her project as an excavation in the landscape of the dead: "Since history is a recorded or remembered event,"
and "because so much of African-American history has been
unrecorded, dismembered, washed out, one of my tasks as playwright is
to . . . locate the ancestral burial ground, dig for bones. . . , hear the
bones sing, write it down" (4). In the oddly literal way theater has of
making theory concrete and visible, Parks in effect aligns herself with
the cultural rather than the more traditionally visual analyst of landscape. She would agree, in Simon Schama's words, that the scenery of
landscape "is built up as much from strata of memory as from layers of
rock."[15] In creating a landscape dramaturgy that consciously recon-
ceives every element of the stage work spatially, Parks reflects the contemporary understanding that landscape is a primary lens through
which to comprehend human culture.

Gertrude Stein's famously gnomic utterances about her plays as
landscape can be reread through the lens of cultural landscape theory.
Acknowledging that streets and windows and even saints and convents
can all be part of a landscape, Stein said that "nothing really moves in a
landscape but things are there, and I put into the play the things that
were there."[16] But what if, as Stein might ask, there is no *there* there to
"put in?" In *The America Play*, history is no longer an excavation of
memory to form a record and recover truth, but a game of sorts, a fiction

created with historical materials. The insight leads Parks to an entirely different kind of landscape: not an enduring work of nature—a rock formed by the geologic solidity of the ages, but a cut-and-paste cultural construction: a theme park. Even worse (or perhaps even better) an *imitation* theme park. *The America Play,* as its title suggests, is a landscape play in the widest geographic sense, but the displays and buried treasures of the America it represents make no pretense of standing in for an historical record. Rather, these objects, and the theme park setting itself, question the very possibility of an authoritative history. The objects in the imitation Great Hole could be better seen as a playful version of what Pierre Nora has called *lieux de mémoire,* or sites of memory—cultural objects, places, and events on which to project stories that change with the needs of every generation.[17]

The landscape dramaturgy of *The America Play* is signaled both by its represented and unrepresented settings and the American cultural landscape they stand in for. The scene before the spectator—a kind of amusement park in act 1, then the site of an archeological dig in act 2—is a great hole, located somewhere out west "in the middle of nowhere."[18] The play is punctuated by a single temporal gesture: it takes place "after." Act 1, devoted to the performance by the black "Foundling Father" of the death of Abraham Lincoln, is set *after* Lincoln, in both senses of *after;* act 2 takes place at some point after the death of the Foundling Father.

As in *Last Black Man,* Parks spatializes her play through various strategies of repetition—doubles, circles, echoes, imitations, internal performances, even a return from the dead. Not only the language but the landscape setting itself echoes in multiple repeats: the great hole before us is actually an "exact replica" of the *real* Great Hole of History back East, where a jumble of historical look-alikes from different periods (Amerigo Vespucci, Marcus Garvey, Mary Queen of Scots, Millard Fillmore, and Tarzan) circle the grounds in peaceful coexistence, waving to the spectators. Yet the "real" theme park in turn stands in for the fakery of the "themed" built landscape of contemporary America, and at a deeper level, the fake reality of an American history that excludes black experience from its accounts. Even so, this layering and echoing of imitations and simulations and omissions stirs a nostalgia for a lost real: we detect its faint echo with no greater certainty than does Parks's Lucy, who in act 2 uses her hearing trumpet to scan the air, the subtle landscape, for vibrations from the past. A brilliant spatial conceit, the Great Hole is a precise metaphor for the peculiar atemporality created by the double erasure that is Parks's deep theme: the acute loss of African-American experience within a culture that erases its own history only to restore it as entertainment.

The America Play, by Suzan-Lori Parks, Yale Repertory Production, New Haven, 1994, designed by Ricardo Hernandez. (Photo by T. Charles Erickson.)

Parks's three central figures, the Foundling Father (or the Lesser Known) as Abraham Lincoln, his son Brazil, and his wife, Lucy, are attached to landscape by vocation. As he tirelessly informs us, Foundling Father was first of all a Digger. A figure possibly inspired by the first "Clown," or Gravedigger from *Hamlet,* he sees the world from the viewpoint of a hole in the ground. The fulfillment of his greatest dream would have been to dig the grave of Lincoln, to "put the Great Man in the ground" (160–61), though his skill led at length to an even greater tour de force of digging: the replica of the Great Hole of History. The venture itself was an epic tale written on the landscape. Half a century after *Death of a Salesman* with its haunting background of wilderness, Parks still acknowledges, if even as a joke, that in an "America" play you need a wilderness, for "wilderness is still the scale and measure of [the American] sense of landscape."[19] Brazil confides:

> [M]y Pa come out . . . West. . . . Come out here all uhlone.
> Cleared thuh path tamed thuh wilderness dug this whole Hole
> with his own 2 hands and et cetera (178–79).

In the next generation Brazil digs in the Great Hole to find traces of his dead father. Lucy (named perhaps after the hominid exhumed from another landscape) works not in soil but in air, which she scans for echoes of a vanished past. As echoes teach us, even sounds inhere in landscape.

"Nothing contains [landscape], while it contains everything," writes Casey.[20] Digging is the work of *The America Play*'s second act, though Brazil says he would "rather dust and polish," (185) an in-joke about the social ranking of field slaves and house slaves in the antebellum South. In between his archeological discoveries, Brazil puts down his shovel to enact the melodramatic gestures of mourning in which he has been trained, or to play the "State Capitals" geography game so fitting to the dramaturgy of landscape. Brazil's unearthed finds might be described as Nora's *lieux*, figurative sites of memory within the literal site of memory that is the Hole. Though physical site is not the only meaning of the French *lieu*, the idea of place hovers behind the many uses to which it lends itself. It is a term that can be justly claimed for landscape, as in a sense can Nora's entire project of spatial historiography.

"Lieux de mémoire exist because there are no longer any milieux de mémoire," writes Nora, observing that continuity of cultural memory is no longer part of everyday experience (1). The loss of memory, Nora observes, has led to a culture with a mania for "museums, archives, cemeteries, collections, festivals . . . relics of another era, illusions of eternity" (6). Parks's act 2 memorial Hole playfully represents this contemporary obsession as a landscape littered with collectibles, for instance George Washington's wooden false teeth (or their replica). As the "wonders" in her theme park are dug up, Parks traces both the loss of black historical memory and, with anarchic humor, celebrates the freedom to create it where none exists.

Crying "WONDER: HO!" (193), like a voyager to the New World sighting land, Brazil excavates a Tee-Vee that plays tapes of his "faux-father's" (184) Lincoln act. The blank television set, nothing in itself, yet capable of summoning every imaginable scene, symbolizes for Parks the desolation and opportunity of the contemporary historically deracinated moment. In much the same way, at the end of the play, the refurbished imitation Great Hole of historical memory, sparkling with fakes, stand-ins, copies, and simulacra, becomes a passing kind of Whole. In a comic reverse irony, Parks waves away the tragic implications of the black man's history as void, for at the end, son finds father, vocation, a usable history, and a nice chunk of real estate. The hole is not just negative space; it is a (w)hole, paradoxically both empty and complete like the theater itself. Which of us, Parks hints, does that much better in posthistorical America?[21]

> Ida's Demon. *Your experience and memories have hidden connections which can only be seen when you record your journey on a road map and view it from above.*[22]

In an important essay in Stephen Barker's *Signs of Change,* entitled "A Misreading of Maps," Bruno Bosteels traces some of the implications of the critical shift from historiography to geography.

> What thus currently seems to be taking place in some of the most fertile fields of literary, cultural, and philosophical studies is a gradual yet thorough displacement from text to territory. Abandoning the rhetoric of temporality, critical and theoretical inquiries today are increasingly moving towards the politics of spatiality. From a textual analysis of "writing" . . . the emphasis is shifting towards the cultural study of literary, artistic, and ideological forms of "mapping. . . ."[23]

Bosteels proposes a postmodern *poiesis* of cartography that would loosen the discipline of mapping from its historically representational, mimetic moorings. In David Hancock's *The Convention of Cartography* (itself something of a *lieux de mémoire* in New York theater history, given the unavailability of its text and the ratio of its fame to the numbers of spectators who actually saw it during a short run in a tiny playing space), the poetic function of maps suggests the validity—even for a discipline as seemingly removed from maps as theater—of Bosteels's observation.

The Convention of Cartography is festooned with maps and mapfragments. They variously appear in and as stage objects, and stand in for layers of deep and yet deeper landscapes. The maps refer to the destinationless journeys by bus and auto taken by Hancock's restless figures. Beyond the journeys, the maps point obliquely to the landscape itself, a melancholy American flatbed of all-night diners and crumbling motels seemingly arrested forever in the fifties. These landscapes emerge from a deceptively simple staging that takes place in two distinct parts, first a lecture-demonstration, then a self-guided tour through an adjacent "museum," with a brief coda in the lecture room. The spectators are drawn into and through multiple itineraries, traced against the background of the interstate highway system. But maps are just the exoteric sign of an almost mystical landscape nostalgia in the play. Hancock, like Parks, sometimes Wellman, and other contemporary playwrights creating new theatrical forms, exchanges normative plot and character for a geomythology of America. He is unusual, however, in locating his mythic America in the melancholy of cultural and industrial obsolescence, loss, and aging. The play is pervaded by the mood, if not limited to the locations, of the industrial rust belt.

In his lecture, Bill the "Curator," a role so far played only by Hancock himself, tells the audience about his years as a teenage runaway traveling the country by Greyhound with a drifter named Mike who once worked on the Alaska pipeline. Folk poet, philosopher of life, and "great artist," Mike made collage sculptures out of old, demeaned objects. He would collect postcards in Arabic from the 1936 World's Fair, old buttons that had lost their shirts, animal cards, pressed butterflies, tattered photos of complete strangers, odd matchbooks, back issues of *Mechanix Illustrated*, mildewed volumes in Greek, and frayed maps. When he had enough objects, he would glue a collage into any container that came to hand—an old cigar box or abandoned medicine cabinet would do—and scatter the art across the landscape at gas stations, pay toilets, diners, toll booths, highway overpasses, and rest areas. Mike's work expressed a great vision, an American landscape sown with art, and an art whose material is composed of memory and ruins, like the landscape itself.

Years later, college-educated, married, and himself an artist, the Curator's adult journey begins as he tracks the ailing, aging, Mike to Durham, North Carolina. Bill now devotes his time to retracing Mike's Greyhound bus journeys and retrieving his poems and sculptures. Mike himself appears only on video, but each discovery of his art marks his existence at a moment in time in a particular landscape, and each encapsulates memories of still other, remembered, scenes: "With this coffee in me," goes one of Mike's poems, written on a placemat in a Seattle diner,

> I can perceive a different reality from you. . . .
> I have the ability to go back in time just by staring at the
>   objects I find on the road.
> All those discarded relics have souls.
> In a spark plug I see evenings in motel rooms.
> In a wool hat I see meals in a diner in central
>   Pennsylvania.
> In a torn Esso road map, I see an empty Studebaker
>   along a back road. . . .

As we learn from the taped interviews with Mike that are shown at the lecture, Mike's spatial vision extends into esoteric landscapes of the soul:

> I'm beginning to think there's a subway tunnel deep inside this country. . . . It's a rumbling you feel only at night. . . . Secret underground trains. Like when they sent the Jews away. . . . Even in this day and age people are still being sent on the Journey. You realize you're on the Journey only after it is much too late. The only way out is through memory. (29)

For the spectator, uncertainty as to the ontological status of characters, stories, and objects in *The Convention of Cartography* becomes a substitute for dramatic conflict. The uncertainty is intensified by the concrete reality of the art objects and the seemingly authoritative maps. As a kind of joke for those who are convinced they are experiencing an elaborate fiction, and as a warrant of authenticity for those who accept the Curator's story as autobiography, a guide to the museum in the form of a military-style pin map is mounted on a wall. The map traces the Curator's journey of rediscovery. To each discovery is pinned the code from the Curator's "museology," which locates the artworks along the geographical circuit of Mike's travels and the Curator's retracings. For instance, Exhibit #43 TN.77?/p is the forty-third artifact of Mike's discovered by the Curator, was found in Tennessee (TN), was probably but not certainly (?) made in 1977 (77), and is a poem.

In contrast to this often hilarious cartological positivism are the geographical mysteries embedded in the maps left behind by the clairvoyant Ida, Mike's true love and sometime traveling companion, with whom he built stock cars in happier days. Ida, the third major figure in *Convention of Cartography*, who "appears" only by ghostly voice on tape, died half-mad in some state institution back in Michigan. One can distinguish among Hancock's three figures according to layers of landscape: the Curator with his attempt to organize the field is the chief cartographer; Mike was the great traveler, who spent a lifetime "always passing through" (21); but Ida was the deep geographer. Her maps, guided by the inner voice she called her Demon, were encoded with occult notations in the form of buttons and butterflies. Unfortunately, the code to these notations has been lost.

Maps play a teasing role in the performance: they seem to verify, indeed reify, the journeys within journeys within journeys described in the text, yet at the same time their opacity safeguards a mysterious inner spirit

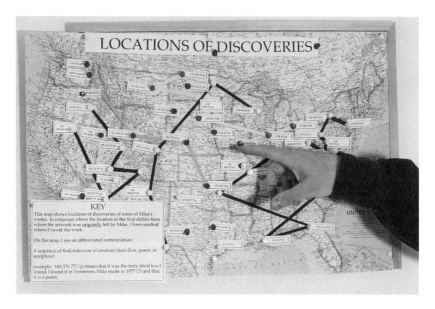

"Museological" map from *The Convention of Cartography,* with
hand of David Hancock as Curator, New York City, 1994.
(Photo by Nancy Hanway.)

alive with powerful, private relationships to the landscape. The intensity
these relationships can attain is suggested by Mike's final request:

> Whenever I pass through Indiana, there's this particular street
> that I look for off Route 80. It's got grass growing up out of it.
> . . . There are above ground swimming pools and barbecue sets
> in the back yards. . . . But it's all overgrown. The pieces to the
> swimming pools are all over the lawns. . . . That's the street
> where I want to be buried. You have to promise me that you'll
> bury me there. . . . I want my ashes spread in a stranger's back-
> yard. It's a certain peace there—you can only catch it out of the
> corner of your eye (33).

Like Parks in relation to the field of cultural landscape studies,
which helps in part to read her, Hancock, in his winking relationship to
the authority of maps, appears to be in playful consonance with contemporary thinking in geography. Just as a cultural landscape historian
might look at an urban horizon and see not an aesthetic skyline but a
spatial history of ethnic groups, trades, and technologies, so a cultural
cartographer would recognize, according to Denis Wood, that "[m]aps

are embedded in a history they help construct," that they serve particular interests, that those interests are expressed in signs and myths, and that histories are buried in the signs.[24] One might say that Wood describes the convention, or the conventions, of cartography. It is not an objective science, but a set of practices that can be unpacked with the skill that theater people normally reserve for character. Or turn the proposition around: human lives are constructed not only by the family romance or by the coordinates of cultural materialism, but by the complex codings of landscape and geography.

"Record all your memories while you're on the road," the Demon instructs Ida. "Your experience and memories have hidden connections which can only be seen when you record your journey on a road map and view it from above" (54). The perspective of the overview offered by maps is—whether maps appear or not—the perspective of a landscape dramaturgy toward which this discussion has been moving.

Gertrude Stein saw the view from above, looking down on the earth, as the formal viewpoint of the landscape play, On her first flight, taken across the United States during her 1935 lecture tour, she identified the overview as the essential perspective of artistic modernism. In the epilogue to *Picasso: The Complete Writings,* Stein described arriving at this insight:

> One must not forget that the earth seen from an airplane is more splendid than the earth seen from an automobile. The automobile is the end of progress on the earth, it goes quicker but essentially the landscapes seen from an automobile are the same as the landscapes seen from a carriage, a train, a wagon, or in walking. But the earth seen from an airplane is something else. So the twentieth century is not the same as the nineteenth century. . . . When I was in America I for the first time travelled pretty much all the time in an airplane and when I looked at the earth I saw all the lines of cubism made at a time when not any painter had ever gone up in an airplane. I saw there on the earth the mingling lines of Picasso, coming and going, developing and destroying themselves . . . and once more I knew that a creator is contemporary, he understands what is contemporary when the contemporaries do not yet know it.[25]

From a sufficient height, Stein perceived, even the greatest speed can be translated into the experience of space. Stein's insight into cubism as a view of the earth from the sky is, to Jean-François Lyotard, the essential perspective of landscape, which is embraced "whenever the mind is transported from one sensible matter to another, but retains the sensorial organization appropriate to the first. . . . The countryside for the townsman; the city for the farmer," and (I rearrange Lyotard's order of examples for emphasis) "the earth seen from the moon for a terrestrial."[26]

The late-century plays and theater pieces I have discussed find the view from the air more congenial than the view from the car. They survey entire regions, nations, and the planet itself. They express the principle of the territorial overview and of the map, in often playful ways, recognizing, as in Parks and Hancock, the untrustworthiness of official representations of history and memory. Their admixture of human and landscape, and their placement of memory in landscape, can be read as a postmodern version of the Renaissance memory theaters—the spatial memory systems that promised transcendent knowledge and recall of all earth and all heaven, "a vision of the world and of the nature of things viewed from a height, from the stars themselves"—revived in memory by Frances Yates.[27] The memory theaters of the Renaissance mages were on the pretemporal side of the modern, picturing a changeless and knowable universe. The new spatial theater marked by shifting and unstable *lieux*, in Nora's sense, may be arising on the posttemporal side of modernism. Time, with its historiographic determinism, has retreated, leaving behind such freshly interesting theatrical perspectives as landscape, territory, geography, and the map.

NOTES

1. Throughout my discussion I have used a variety of terms to refer to the landscape phenomena I explore, for instance *landscape imaginary, landscape consciousness, deep landscape, landscape surround.* All these terms should be understood as pointing to all the layers of landscape in a given work and their combined significance—the layer that is physically represented, the layer that is unrepresented but still part of the immediate action, and those that are merely suggested, adumbrated, or implied.

2. Arthur Miller, *Death of a Salesman,* in *The Portable Arthur Miller,* ed. Harold Clurman (New York: Penguin, 1977), 125.

3. Leo Marx, "The American Ideology of Space," in Stuart Wrede and William Howard Adams, eds. *Denatured Visions* (New York: Museum of Modern Art/Harry N. Abrams, 1991), 66. Marx prefers the term *space* to *landscape,* defining *landscape* reductively as "a pretty stretch of natural scenery" (62).

4. Lawrence Buell, *The Environmental Imagination: Thoreau, Nature Writing,*

and the Formation of American Culture (Cambridge: Harvard University Press, 1995), 54.

5. Sam Shepard, *Curse of the Starving Class,* in *Angel City, Curse of the Starving Class, and Other Plays* (New York: Urizen Books, 1978), 59.

6. Sam Shepard, "Red Cross," in *The Unseen Hand and Other Plays* (New York: Vintage, 1986), 154.

7. Sam Shepard, *Buried Child,* in *Seven Plays* (New York: Bantam, 1981), 132.

8. Shepard, *Angel City,* 6.

9. Edward S. Casey, "Landscape Revisited," paper presented to the Society for Philosophy and Geography, New York, December 1998, 9.

10. "To return to things themselves is to return to that world which precedes knowledge" (Merleau-Ponty, *Phenomenology of Perception,* ix, quoted by Casey, "Landscape Revisited," 1).

11. Suzan-Lori Parks, *The Death of the Last Black Man in the Whole Entire World,* in *The America Play and Other Works* (New York: Theatre Communications Group, 1995), 116.

12. Edward W. Soja, *Postmodern Geographies: The Reassertion of Space in Critical Social Theory* (London: Verso, 1989), 23. The force of arguments such as Soja's and Fredric Jameson's on mapping lead Jeanette Malkin to note that it has now "become a commonplace to speak of modernism as privileging time, while postmodernism privileges space." See Jeanette R. Malkin, *Memory-Theater and Postmodern Drama* (Ann Arbor: University of Michigan Press, 1999), 10. See also Edward S. Casey, *Getting Back into Place: Toward a Renewed Understanding of the Place-World* (Bloomington: Indiana University Press, 1993), 6–8.

13. Parks, *Death of the Last Black Man,* 101.

14. Erwin Straus, M.D., *The Primary World of Senses,* trans. J. Needleman (Glencoe, Ill.: Free Press, 1963), 318.

15. Simon Schama, *Landscape and Memory* (New York: Alfred A. Knopf, 1995), 6–7.

16. Gertrude Stein, "Plays," in *Lectures in America* (London: Virago, 1988), 129–30.

17. See Pierre Nora et al., *Realms of Memory: Rethinking the French Past,* trans. Arthur Goldhammer (New York: Columbia University Press, 1996). Many have questioned the translation of the French *lieux* into the English *realms.* I prefer *sites,* which includes, but is by no means limited to, spatial objects.

18. Suzan-Lori Parks, *The America Play,* in *The America Play and Other Works,* 159. All subsequent references are to this edition.

19. Don Gifford, "The Touch of Landscape," in *Landscape, Natural Beauty and the Arts,* ed. Salim Kemal and Ivan Gaskell (Cambridge: Cambridge University Press, 1993), 127–38, 129.

20. Casey, *Getting Back into Place,* 25.

21. A valuable discussion of the play exploring the hole/whole interplay may be found in Harry Elam and Alice Rayner, "Echoes from the Black (W)hole: An

Examination of *The America Play* by Suzan Lori-Parks," in *Performing America: Cultural Nationalism in American Theater,* ed. Jeffrey D. Mason and J. Ellen Gainor (Ann Arbor: University of Michigan Press, 1999), 178–92.

22. David Hancock, *The Convention of Cartography,* typescript, 54. One of the most admired of contemporary American theater texts, the occasion of an Obie Award for its 1994 New York production, and the source of many subsequent writing prizes and awards for its author, *The Convention of Cartography* has not yet been published. For further information on Hancock, see Fuchs, "False Memory Syndrome: The Memory Theater of David Hancock," *Theater* 29, no. 1 (1999), 83–88.

23. Bruno Bosteels, "A Misreading of Maps: The Politics of Cartography in Marxism and Poststructuralism," in *Signs of Change: Premodern, Modern, Postmodern* (Albany: State University of New York Press, 1996), 109–38, 113.

24. See Denis Wood with John Fels, *The Power of Maps* (New York: Guilford Press, 1992), table of contents.

25. Gertrude Stein, *Picasso: The Complete Writings,* ed. Edward Burns (Boston: Beacon Press, 1970), 88.

26. J.-F. Lyotard, "Scapeland," in *The Lyotard Reader,* ed. A. Benjamin (Oxford: Blackwell, 1989), 212.

27. Frances A. Yates, *The Art of Memory* (Chicago: University of Chicago Press, 1966), 144.

Two

Groundings

3

"Haunted by Places": Landscape in Three Plays of William Butler Yeats

Natalie Crohn Schmitt

> I am convinced that in two or three generations it will become generally known that the mechanical theory has no reality, that the natural and supernatural are knit together, that to escape a dangerous fanaticism we must study a new science; at that moment Europeans may find something attractive in a Christ posed against a background not of Judaism but of Druidism, not shut off in dead history, but flowing, concrete, phenomenal.
>
> —W. B. YEATS,
> *Essays and Introductions* (1937)

Three Yeats plays set out-of-doors, among his best, are precisely wedded to the landscapes—sacred wells and ruin—that he attributes to them: *At the Hawk's Well* (1916), *The Cat and the Moon* (1917),[1] and *The Dreaming of the Bones* (1919). In this essay, I examine the sites and their attendant myths in relation to the plays. I argue for the importance of landscape in Yeats's plays not merely as source but as substance. I show the relationship between the realistic settings in the plays, the supernatural they also represent, and Yeats's dramatic form.

The extent to which Yeats's description of the sites is precisely realistic, and, in two cases, the story told inspired by the mythology of the sites, has been given scant attention in the energetic search for literary sources and in the wealth of symbolic readings the plays have provoked. Consequently, the significance of these sites and myths in Yeats's drama has not been examined. Later critics who have sought to look at the plays as dramas—entailing dramatic actions—have, not surprisingly, overlooked the number of lines in Yeats's plays devoted in whole or in part to establishing the setting—in *The Dreaming of the Bones*, almost a third of them. The highly abstract staging that Yeats sought for his plays has also led critics to perceive the plays as esoteric and abstract.

Katharine Worth, for instance, tells us that the dance plays "take us into a kind of no-place." And Barton Friedman argues that the setting for the *At the Hawk's Well* is the mind of the playwright gestating the play.[2]

The plays' realistic descriptions of the landscapes and their attendant myths do not diminish the interest of the variety of related stories that critics have found—whether or not they all were, in fact, sources for the plays. When a variety of stories come together as one, Yeats regarded them as essentially truer. The search for literary sources does, however, reveal a kind of literary Darwinism at work: an assumption that it is literature that begets literature, an assumption fostered in this case by the fact that for most critics the literary sources are more accessible than the landscapes that also inspired them. For each play, I provide the descriptions of sites included in the literary sources that critics have cited—when indeed the literary source describes a site—to demonstrate that the actual site bears greater similarity to that described in the play than does any described in literary sources.

The realistic description of landscape in the plays does not necessarily invalidate the symbolic readings of the plays that critics have provided for them, although it does tend to make some of them seem far-fetched. The plays are unquestionably symbolic. Yeats sought, he said, a dramatic form "distinguished, indirect, and symbolic,"[3] and he himself provided symbolic readings of elements in his plays. But for Yeats the literal and symbolic (or, as he would see it, "natural and supernatural") are knit together; the symbolical is bound to the particular, and, in the plays under consideration here, that particular is primarily landscape.

The supernatural in the plays' sites is to be understood to a considerable extent as indwelling. For the Irish, as Yeats observed, the mythology of the landscape is "not symbols but realities."[4] In the western countryside dotted with ruins and the remembered sites of ancient rituals, including some that are still celebrated, the distinction between past and present, dream and reality, sacred and profane is unclear. Symbol and site are joined, as are the abstract minimal sets Yeats wanted for the stage and the realistic verbal description of the sites that he provides. Further, the form of the plays is essentially static, spatial, their stasis central to their religious meaning and intended effect. The plays are, I shall argue, inherently landscape plays, plays in which landscape is foregrounded and central to the experience that Yeats sought to provide.[5]

Sacred Well 1

In *The Cat and the Moon,* a lame beggar and a blind one, bound by their infirmities, have been together for forty years, the Lame Beggar traveling upon the Blind Beggar's back and guiding the way. The pair journeys to St. Colman's Well, known for its healing powers. As they walk, the Blind Beggar says that they had asked directions of a beggar at the crossroads, and he told them that the well was but a thousand paces and a few paces more under a big ash tree. Once at the well, St. Colman appears to the Lame Beggar "in the ash-tree . . . or up in the air."[6] He offers the beggars the chance to be either saved or cured. The Blind Beggar chooses to be cured and thereupon deduces that the Lame Beggar stole his sheep; he sees that he is wearing its black fleece. The Blind Beggar beats the lame one and departs. The Lame Beggar chooses to be saved. The saint, now upon the Lame Beggar's shoulder, instructs him to bless the road by dancing. As a blessed man, the Lame Beggar finds that he can dance. Three musicians, one of whom speaks the lines of the saint, invisible to all but the Lame Man, frame the piece with a verse about Minnaloushe, a black cat, creeping through the grass in moonlight.

F. A. C. Wilson, one of the earliest commentators on Yeats's plays and the person who began the critical tradition of focusing on the plays' literary sources and of providing primarily symbolic interpretations of them, found *The Cat and the Moon* to be "one of the most concentrated pieces of symbolism in all Yeats's work."[7] Yeats himself first described the play as slight, but nonetheless encouraged symbolic readings by providing a few of his own. In the preface to the first edition of the play, he said that "perhaps" when, in the play, "the Saint mounts upon the back of the Lame Beggar, he personifies a certain great spiritual event which may take place when Primary Tincture . . . supersedes Antithetical" (*VPl*, 805). The implied reference is to Yeats's wholly symbolic *A Vision*. Further esoteric readings, following this invitation to provide them, have so obscured the play's humble beginnings in realistic description of the site and its attendant myth that Richard Taylor, among others, tells us that "the effort Yeats made in notes and prefaces to associate the figures in *The Cat and the Moon* with Irish legend and St. Colman's Well in particular, is strangely inconclusive."[8] But in prefaces to both his editions of the play, Yeats did identify the site and its attendant myth, and his adherence to precise description of that site is remarkable.

"The Well itself," Yeats wrote in the 1924 edition of the play, "is within a couple of miles of my Galway house, Thoor Ballylee, and is sacred to St. Colman, and began a few years ago to work miracles again, rejuvenated by a Gaelic League procession in its honour. There is some story, which I have half forgotten, of a lame man and a blind man's arrival at it, though not their quarrel there" (*VPl*, 805). The second preface, 1935, is even more explicit:

A couple of miles as the crow flies from my Galway house is a blessed well. Some thirty years ago the Gaelic League organised some kind of procession or "pattern" there, somebody else put a roof over it, somebody else was cured of a lame leg or a blind eye or the falling sickness. There are many offerings at the well-side left by sufferers; I seem to remember bits of cloth torn perhaps from a dress, hairpins, and little pious pictures. The tradition is that centuries ago a blind man and a lame man dreamed that somewhere in Ireland a well would cure them and set out to find it, the lame man on the blind man's back. I wanted to give the Gaelic League, or some like body, a model for little plays, commemorations of known places and events, and wanted some light entertainment to join a couple of dance plays. (*VPl*, 806–7)

St. Colman Mac Duagh founded a church in A.D. 610, the extensive remains of which lie just west of Gort, the town nearest to Thoor Ballylee. There are a number of St. Colman's wells in the area, all thought to be restorative of health.[9] The St. Colman's Well in the play, one and one-half miles as the crow flies from Yeats's house, is a well-recognized feature of the Gort landscape. It is shown on the local map of Kilmacduagh, as are ruins and other sacred wells, which continue to be significant features of the Irish landscape. The map also features a drawing of the well, children's copies of which I saw on the wall in the Kiltartan grammar school not far from the well.[10] The well lies in a grassy field off the road between Gort and Labane, two miles south of Labane and approximately a thousand paces from the road leading to Thoor Ballylee. Since 1901, it has been covered by a dome put up by the Gaelic League; a stone near the well, carved in Gaelic, commemorates the event. Despite its dome rising above the field, the well cannot be seen where it lies, three hundred yards to the west of the road, and it was necessary for me to ask directions to it. In Yeats's play, the Blind Beggar asks the lame one, "Look well now, can you see the big ash-tree that's above it?" The Lame Beggar replies, "No, not yet" (*VPl*, 793). I asked directions, not of a beggar at the crossroads, as did the characters in Yeats's play, but of an old woman in a nearby farmhouse. I was struck by the precision of the directions given me both to the well and to other locations in Ireland, although the directions were given in yards, not in Yeats's more timeless paces. In town, I had been told that the well was three hundred yards past the level crossing, on the left, in the middle of Fahey's field. When I got there, I found the tall stump of an old tree next to the well, posi-

St. Colman's Well: "I see it all now, the blue sky and the big ash-tree and the well." (Photo by the author.)

tively identified from photos by forest botanist Richard Dodd as a European ash of approximately three hundred years of age.[11]

That the saint in Yeats's play is in the tree is what Irish beliefs would suggest. Janet Bord and Colin Bord, scholars of holy wells in Ireland and their mythology, observe that the wells are commonly located next to trees and not merely because the wells are in rural areas but also because the trees or bushes themselves have special significance. Many holy wells appear to have a particularly important tree or bush growing beside them: "Their principal significance seems to be as a relic of ancient tree worship, which once may have been as important as water worship"[12]—and, like the wells, they were involved in healing.

Bord and Bord speculate that the association has to do with "the receptive, inward-looking nature of the well and the vital, outward-growing nature of the tree";[13] that is, tree and well belong together like saint and sinner and black cat and white moon in the play: they are opposites. They report that ash trees were so venerated that it was thought to be extremely unlucky or even dangerous to break a bough of one. Lady Gregory, when she was collecting folklore at the turn of the century, was told the following: "There were ash trees growing around the blessed well at Corker, and one night Deeley, the Uncle of Pat Deeley that lives beyond, and two other men went to cut them down, to get the makings of a car-body. And the next day Deeley's lip was drawn down—like this—and water running from it for the rest of his life. I often see him; and as to the two other men, they died soon after."[14]

When Yeats wrote *The Cat and the Moon,* its well, presided over by St. Colman, was regarded, as it had been for centuries, as a healing well. It continues to be so regarded, albeit by a dwindling percentage of the population: Mondays and Thursdays in October, before St. Colman's feast day on October 29, are thought to be most propitious, and rounds of it are still made on those days. In 1993, I was told, the well was "all decked out" that year for the feast day.[15] Various offerings—candles, plastic flowers, and religious figures—continue to be left there. In the play, Yeats describes "the things praying people put on the stone, the beads and the candles and the leaves torn out of prayer-books, and the hairpins and the buttons" (*VPl*, 800).

The Lame Beggar instructed by the saint to dance to bless the road is again a realistic detail. Yeats recounts having seen such dancing at Kiltartan.[16] Dancing at the crossroads was a traditional magical means to reinaugurate the province and the four quarters of the universe.[17] The earth itself, in Irish mythology and in Yeats's later work, is sacred.

A story of the blind man and the lame man, the lame man upon the blind man's back, both healed at St. Colman's Well, was told to me in Gort by someone who did not know Yeats's play on the subject. In the grammar school near the well, the schoolteacher showed me a framed legend of the well documented by a G. Quinn PP (parish priest) in 1840:

> According to tradition Rina Rynagh when about to give birth to her child became the object of the king's wrath. Prophecy told him that her child would be the greatest of their lineage. He ordered that she be thrown into the river at Kiltartan with a stone around her neck. She was preserved by Providence. Two clarics found her, one partly blind, the other partly lame. They took her some distance where the child was born. There they wished to baptise the child but there was no water. They scooped the earth and a fountain gushed forth beside a large tree. The lame claric put water to his limbs and was healed, the blind put it to his eyes and he saw, crying out La Ban. Hence the name of the district Labane. This well has been visited and rounds made down through the years to the present day.

The legend is accompanied by an unsigned and undated picture of a young girl sitting on a flat stone by the well. Whether there was a flat stone and a wall at the site previously, as described in Yeats's play, I was unable to determine. Sacred wells were regularly protected by circular stone enclosures,[18] and this one may have been so protected before the more ambitious dome was built. Yeats represented his story absent the dome not only because the myth is older than the dome but also because it is too Christian and too recent for his age-old tale and leaves the well in a confining darkness that is neither uplifting nor magical, as are the events in Yeats's play.

Yeats first stayed at Lady Gregory's Coole Park, just south of the well, in 1897 and returned there each summer. He loved the countryside and, as he states, had seen the well prior to its covering. In 1917, he purchased Thoor Ballylee and spent his summers there until 1922. The old farmwoman told me that she often saw Yeats walk by that way from Thoor Ballylee to Coole Park.

Some aspects of realistic description, not landscape, serve to support the idea of the play's realistic details. In the 1935 preface to the play, Yeats positively identifies "the holy man in the big house at Laban," to whom the beggars refer, as Edward Martyn of nearby Tulira Castle, and his cousin and inseparable friend—"the old lecher from the county of Mayo"—as George Moore of Moore Hall in Mayo, both of whom were living when the play was written.[19] Yeats thought that his audience would understand the reference and suggests cutting it before an audience that would not (VPl, 808). Minnaloushe, the cat in the musicians' verse, was the black cat of the Gonnes with whom Yeats was staying when he wrote the play.[20]

Various other sources for the play have been provided. Taylor gives as a possible source the legend of Cruachan recorded in Lady Gregory's Cuchulain of Murithemne: "According to the legend of 'Cruachan,' Nera, who had entered the hill of the sidhe, saw a blind man with a lame man upon his back making his way each day to a well to see if the king's crown were still safely hidden there."[21] The most frequently suggested source is Synge's Well of the Saints. George Brandon Saul, for instance, points to a similarity between the Blind Beggar's first speech, "I see it all now," and the words of Martin Doul's in Synge's play after his (temporary) cure from blindness.[22] Taylor sees a closer relationship to Synge's source for the Well of the Saints, André de La Vigne's Moralité de l'aveugle et du boiteau, in which the afflicted pair are cured by sacred relics carried in a passing procession, whereupon the blind man is delighted but the crippled one curses the saint for destroying an easy life. In Yeats's version, Taylor says, "the whole is enacted before the symbol [sic] of Tree and Well."[23]

Some of these stories, all of them, or others, and even the expression "the lame leading the blind," may have been additional sources for Yeats and confirmed for him the truth of the experience it represented: "When I had finished," he said, "I found them [lame and blind man] in some medieval Irish sermon as a simile of soul and body, and then that they had some like meaning in a Buddhist Sutra" (VPl, 807). There is no reason to doubt, however, that the landscape and its attendant myth are, as Yeats said, his primary inspiration. The point of Yeats's vague reference to the story as "some story . . . half forgotten, of a lame man and a blind man's arrival at it," is, as he makes clear in the next few lines of the preface, that "the spectator should come away thinking the meaning as much his own manufacture as that of the blind man and the lame man had seemed" Yeats's (VPl, 807). The plays were to induce a state where thought becomes reality and reality becomes his and the spectator's thought. The landscape's story is to occur as if it were both real and a vision. Yeats was interested in the idea of the interrelationship of perception and creation[24]—so evident in Irish mythology.

Nonetheless, the very realistic source of the play makes some readings that have been provided seem strained. Some of the most elaborate symbolic readings have to do with the distance to the well specified by the beggar at the crossroads: "one thousand paces and a few paces more" (VPl, 793). Wilson interprets the distance as the pilgrimage of history between two points of highest civilization. "Each step the Blind Beggar (the masses) takes represents a year's progress toward the millennium, and he has already taken over a thousand."[25] Thus Wilson reads the play primarily in terms of Yeats's cyclical theory of history, but also in terms of the human life-cycle as expressed in the relation of soul and body, and reincarnation. Taylor believes that the beggars represent not peasant and aristocrat, as Wilson believes, but objective and subjective principles in search of wholeness and that the thousand paces parody Yeats's A Vision: "Up to this point there has not been much comedy, except for the anti-heroic conception of deformed beggars as heroes and the parody of Yeats's theory of historical cycles in the thousand-odd steps they count out to find the well."[26] A. S. Knowland, observing that there is no corroboration from elsewhere in the play for either Wilson's or Taylor's interpretation of the number of paces, concludes that "the beggar at the crossroads, considered within the prevailing tone of the play, seems to suggest not so much Wilson's solemn 'conjunctio oppositorum' or Unity of Being, as a comic reduction of the

Daemon figure who directs the hero to the place and moment of his decision."[27]

At the very least we should bear in mind, as Yeats reminds us, that we are "among dreams" (VPl, 807) and should come away thinking the meaning as much our own manufacture as that of the blind and lame man had seemed his.

Sacred Well 2

In *At the Hawk's Well,* an old man has waited fifty years beside a well on a windswept, treeless hill for the waters of immortality to rise in it. The well is guarded by an ominous hawk/woman/witch. From across the sea, the Irish mythical hero Cuchulain has come boldly in search of this well in which the waters rise only occasionally. The water rises. The old man, who claims to have been repeatedly kept from the waters by its hawk guardian, sleeps. Cuchulain is enchanted away from the well by the hawk. The three framing choral musicians cannot understand why anyone would be lured from comfort to such a desolate place.

The several books on Yeats country, though their authors never elaborate the relationship between landscape and Yeats's work, provide elemental testimony to such relationship.[28] Critics, offering innumerable symbolic interpretations of *At the Hawk's Well,* have labored in a seemingly unrelated tradition. Thus Helen Vendler states that in analysis of the play "the first question that arises concerns the well: where did Yeats find his symbol, and what does he mean by it?"[29] But the well is more than a symbol: the play includes Yeats's vivid description of an actual well, his climb to it, and its attendant myth.

In county Sligo, at the northeast end of the Ox Mountains one mile northeast of Coolaney,[30] is Hawk's Rock (Carraig-an-Seabhach), about fifteen miles southwest of the town of Sligo, Yeats's childhood summer home. In 1889, T. O'Rorke, a local priest, privately published a history of the area, familiar to Yeats, in which the rock is described as an aerie on the face of a precipice, from which the hawks come whirling and screaming on the approach of an intruder.[31]

The rise of land nearest Hawk's Rock is Tullagan Hill, 430 feet above sea level, "a steep hill," as in the play (VPl, 405), and rising abruptly in the midst of an untilled field. Strangely, approximately ten feet from the top of this hill on the east side and marked by a cairn and a cross is a well, Tullagan Well, one of the marvels of early medieval Ireland. It is described in the fourteenth-century *Book of Ballymote* as the eleventh wonder of Ireland. "The property of that well is, it fills and ebbs

Tullagan Hill. The miraculous well is very near the top left. "The old thorn trees are doubled so / Among the rocks where he is climbing." (Photo by the author.)

like the sea" a mile and a half distant.[32] Estyn Evans, writing in 1966, observed that until recently rounds were made at the well in the month of August as they had been, he believes, since prehistoric times.[33] My local innkeeper told me, as fact, that the water rose and fell in the well according to the tides.

Bord and Bord claim that the ebbing and flowing of wells in Ireland is well documented.[34] Further, for reasons of changes in topography, rainfall, or other natural changes, or for reasons of human interference, wells cease to flow temporarily or permanently, and such changes in water supply in a well are often thought to result from some insult to the well.[35] I seem neither to have insulted the well nor to have stayed long enough to see any change in water height. I saw the well, approximately two and one-half feet across, with only a little water in it, this covered with algae and a rotted fern leaf. "I but see / A hollow among stones half-full of leaves," says Cuchulain (*VPl*, 405). Reg Skene suggests that the words "that hollow place" seem "to open up the well *symbol* sugges-tively" (emphasis added). "Is there," Skene asks, "a hollow place sur-rounded by stones in every man's life capable of mysteriously filling itself with the divine presence?"[36] More simply, what would one call a virtually dry well?

Tullagan Well is marked by gray boulders on three sides and a wooden cross. "And are there not before your eyes at the instant / Grey boulders. . . ?" asks the Old Man (*VPl*, 404). Yeats did not include the cross, which is likely to have been there in his day. In its place he imagines three hazel trees that "drop their nuts and withered leaves" into the well to mark the site as one of more primitive magic (*VPl*, 404). I doubt that hazel trees were ever near the rather barren rocky top of Tullagan Hill. The Old Man, more accurately, describes the well-site as a place "where nothing thrives" (*VPl*, 403). In Ireland, the hazel tree has been long venerated, and its traditional association with the sacred well is known to go back to the Celts.[37] "The Hazel tree," according to Yeats, "was the Irish tree of life or of Knowledge, and in Ireland it was doubtless, as elsewhere, the tree of the heavens."[38] The waters of sacred wells were very commonly thought to grant longevity or eternal youth.

Next to the well is a large flat stone, the only such stone anywhere in sight:

> The guardian of the well is sitting
> Upon the old grey stone at its side,
> Worn out from raking its dry bed,
> Worn out from gathering up the leaves.
> (*VPl*, 400–401)

I saw no hawks. Whether Yeats did or not, it would have taken no great stretch of the imagination to envision the well-guardian at this site—with the Hawk's Rock in view—as a hawk. Well-guardians were common both in fact and in mythology. Most common among the supernatural guardians were ghostly women in white and, after that, fairies. Such fairies, who had been described to Yeats and Lady Gregory, were in control of the well's powers and could cure illness and grant wishes.[39] The water divinity did not generally take the form of a witch, but there are occasional references to witches as keepers of sacred wells. More often the well custodian was simply referred to as an old woman, one who had the knowledge and power necessary to keep the well functioning. Philip Dixon Hardy, writing in 1840, makes reference to actual contemporary well-guardians.[40] Some of them, Bord and Bord tell us, were priestesses with lineages going back to pagan times; others were merely old women living in cottages near the wells who would help visitors in the ritual involved in return for small payments.[41] But a well's guardian spirit need

not have been human; the hedgehog, frog, fish, eel, and even the fly have
been reported as well-guardians. In some instances, the guardian was of
a malicious or evil nature. Those making pilgrimages to wells are said to
have maintained a healthy respect for well-guardians since they knew
that the guardians would react favorably only if approached deferen-
tially.[42] In the context of such mythology and the site, the
hawk/woman/witch well-guardian at Tullagan Well seems quite logical.

The day I was on Tullagan Hill, a stiff wind blew from the north, the
direction of Ballysadare Bay. In the play the chorus observes "a man
climbing up to a place / The salt sea wind has swept bare. / . . . The wind
that blows out of the sea." (VPl, 399, 401) True to observations made by
the Old Man, there are no houses in the vicinity and certainly no great
house—"no house to sack among these hills" (VPl, 404). The site is isolated and at sunset could be eerie. "The sun goes down in the west. / . . .
/ Night falls; / . . . / I am afraid of this place," report the musicians (VPl,
400, 401).

I believe that Yeats's ascent of the hill was, like mine, the seemingly
easiest one—proceeding from the north through a field and up the east
side, around the hill's northern rock face—for in the play Cuchulain
approaches on this side, the side with the well. The ascent is marked by
small hawthorn trees: "broken rocks, / And ragged thorns," the "old
thorn-trees are doubled" (VPl, 401, 403). Evidence of cattle remains on
the way. Thus, the well in the play logically has "a guardian to clean out
the well / And drive the cattle off" (VPl, 402–3).

Taylor argues that the reference to Aoife in the play sets it in Scotland.[43] Perhaps. The play also seems set nearer the sea and in a harsher
landscape than is Tullagan Well. Certainly, Yeats greatly extended the
times between the well's reputed ebbings and flowings: the Old Man in
the play claims that, in his fifty years of waiting, the well has flowed only
three times. But the evidence suggests that Tullagan Well was the site
with which Yeats began his play.

An often noted, apparently autobiographical (i.e., realistic) reference in the play is relevant here. Yeats was fifty when he wrote the play.
The Old Man in the play had been patiently waiting at the well for fifty
years. In the two years following the writing of the play, Yeats proposed
again to Maud Gonne (her husband, from whom she had separated, had
just died), and then to Maud Gonne's illegitimate daughter. When she
too refused, he suddenly married Georgie Hyde-Lees. It is as if Yeats, like
Cuchulain in At the Hawk's Well, had decided that life was for the taking,
not the waiting.

Scholars have provided a large number of literary sources for the play, the stories of which are myths neither directly related to Cuchulain nor to the well near Hawk's Rock. Some of these sources do include descriptions of landscape that, if nothing else, attest to the fact that stories about sacred wells and their powers, sacred wells with special trees beside them, and sacred wells with guardians are numerous. Chief among literary sources suggested is the magic well of Connla in various versions presented by the writer A.E., by a seer, Dorothy Hunter, by the historian Standish O'Grady, and, most suggestively, by Yeats himself. In O'Grady's *History of Ireland,* Connla's Well, the source of the Shannon, has beside it a hazel tree with bright crimson nuts that provide knowledge to all who eat them.[44] In some versions of the story, a rowan (ash) tree replaces the hazel.

The description of Connla's Well closest to that in *At the Hawk's Well* (and to Tullagan Well) is found in two visions invoked by Yeats, one in December 1897, the other in January 1898, for members of the Order of the Golden Dawn, the order of Christian Cabalists to which Yeats belonged. In the first of these visions, Yeats transported the members "to a mountainous district where in the midst of the hills we found ourselves before an ancient well. Leaning over the well on our left grew a mountain-ash laden with red berries." In the January vision, they arrived at the well, like Cuchulain in the play, after a sea journey: "At length we came to a further shore bare of trees save only a few hazel bushes (seen only by . . . [Yeats]). Broken rocks and boulders . . . were strewn around."[45]

The second most frequently cited source is the myth of Slieve Gullian: On this mountain grew "the hazels, whose magic clusters might assuage that hunger of the spirit which know no other assuagement. . . . Here beneath those nine hazels, their immortal green and their scarlet clusters, sprang the well of the waters of all wisdom. Three dreadful queens guarded it. Sometimes they smile, seeing afar some youth wandering unconsoled."[46]

A source for the play provided by Taylor is the No play *Yoro:* "Living in this mountain, under the shade of a pine tree, and using the water of the fountain as medicine, and prolonging our age, how hopeful are we, how happy our prospects."[47] Birgit Bjersby also suggests "Tubber Derg, or The Red Well," which is said to be in a rocky place, near a hazel glen.[48]

Numerous, often elaborate, symbolic interpretations of the play have been provided. Yeats tells us in his notes to his play *Calvary* that he regards certain birds, including hawks, as symbols of subjectivity (*VPl*, 789). Oliver St. John Gogarty said Yeats referred to the hawk-woman as

intellect.[49] In the program for the play's initial performance, the play was
subtitled *The Well of Immortality*. The wind, Yeats said, he generally
used as a symbol of vague desires and hopes: "wind and spirit and vague
desire have been associated everywhere. . . . I follow much Irish and
other mythology, and the magical tradition, in associating . . . the West,
the place of sunset, with fading and dreaming things."[50] For Yeats, however, symbolic and real, were indissolubly intertwined.

Ruin

In *The Dreaming of the Bones,* a participant in the 1916 Easter post office
uprising, from which he is now fleeing, climbs in the dark to the top of
a desolate hill in the Burren, the eerie unearthly gray limestone outcrop-
pings unique to the region that make up the hill above the ruins of Corcomroe Abbey, from whence, at dawn, he is to spot a boat in the bay to
take him to an Aran island. The Young Man is guided by two figures who
turn out to be the ghosts of the historical Diarmuid and Dervorgilla,
lovers who betrayed Ireland in the twelfth century by inviting the Normans to enter the country. Souls in purgatory, they seek forgiveness
from the Young Man. However momentarily tempted, he will not provide it.

Because *The Dreaming of the Bones* is the only one of Yeats's plays to
make explicit use of contemporary history, few literary sources for it
have been provided. It is the only play for which some critics have
acknowledged the realistic locale described. Others are less sensitive to
the specific Irish landscape invoked. Maeve Good tells us that for *The
Dreaming of the Bones* "there are three levels of vision before us, or three
overlapping landscapes: first the landscape created by the staging of the
play; next the political landscape of Ireland as seen by the Young Man;
and finally the spiritual or daimonic landscape of the dead."[51]

In the language of the play, another altogether realistic landscape is
described and is central to the play. Of the critics who have seen the relationship of the play to landscape, Liam Miller is best: *The Dreaming of the
Bones* is set "in the neighbourhood of the ruined Cistercian Abbey of
Corcomroe in County Clare, a barren rock-strewn peninsula, near the
Atlantic coastline. This enormous monastic ruin, sacked during the
'Protestant' Reformation, with the hills rising behind it out of the stony
landscape and the tombs of the ruined Abbey, . . . surely suggests the
sense of 'dreaming back' into the historic past with which the play is
concerned."[52] A. Norman Jeffares and Knowland note that the use of the

Corcomroe Abbey from "the grey stone to the northeast." "All about the hills / Are like a circle of agate or of jade." "We're almost at the summit and can rest, / The road is a faint shadow there; and there the Abbey lies amid its broken tombs." "The white road to the Abbey of Corcomroe." (Photo by the author.)

names of towns near Corcomroe Abbey in the play—Muckanish, Aughanish, Finvara, and Bailevelehan—gives the scene an objective reality.[53]

What is more interesting in the play is the precise landscape description: of the graveyard beside the ruined church down "the narrow lane / Where mourners for five centuries have carried / Noble or peasant to his burial" (*VPl*, 767) and of the isolated unroofed church with its interior ancient tombs, the church itself lying amid broken tombs, and all surrounded by the strange desolate Burren, so haunting that it is easy to think of it as haunted. I was completely alone there. The only other very noticeably living presences were the circling noisy birds, as in the play: "birds cry in their loneliness, / But now they wheel about our heads" (*VPl*, 763–64). Behind the stone wall in the pasture beyond the apse of the church lies "the shallow well and flat stone / Fouled by the drinking cattle" (*VPl*, 767).[54] I have seen it twice, once befouled, and, unfortunately, when I returned with a friend and my camera, once not.

Abbey Hill. "Even the sunlight can be lonely here, / Even hot noon is lonely." "They have drifted in the dance from rock to rock." (Photo by the author.)

Abbey Hill, the hill that the lonely traveler in the play climbs in the dark, is not far from Lady Gregory's seaside house, Vernon Lodge. The 795-foot hill lies, as Yeats describes it, to the northeast of the abbey.[55] The isolation of the place, the shrill birds that one can hear even at some height away from the church, and what geology books unfailingly describe as the desolate nature of the Burren,[56] made me, like Yeats's traveler, afraid on my ascent. "Why does my heart beat so? . . . Birds cry, they cry their loneliness. / Even the sunlight can be lonely here" (*VPl*, 762–63). Like Yeats's traveler, I tried to reassure myself that "I should not be afraid in County Clare." Ascent through Abbey Hill's rocky creviced surface in the dark would be treacherous, as the play makes clear: I "would break my neck / If I went stumbling there alone in the dark" (*VPl*, 765). At the same time, the wide stretches of bare limestone with their strange "*pseudo*-artificial"[57] flatness would allow for the dance "from rock to rock" of the play's ghostly couple. The top of the hill is round, as Yeats describes it in the play. The Young Man in the play is to look for an Aran coracle to put in either "at Muchanish and the rocky shore / under Finvara," both of which can be clearly seen from the top of Abbey Hill.

In the distance the limestone hills appear to be gray-green. It has often been remarked that the description of the hills in the play as "a grey-green cup of jade, / Or maybe an agate cup" (*VPl*, 763) is a reference to the bridal cup in the No play *Nishikigi*, which Yeats acknowledged as a source for *The Dreaming of the Bones*, although it was not a source for the play's landscape. It should also be noted that the limestone hills of the Burren encircling the abbey look, if not like a cup, like a more expansive gray-green bowl. "And I cannot but believe," remarked Yeats, "that if our painters of Highland cattle and moss-covered barns were to care enough for their country to care for what makes it different from other countries, they would discover, when struggling, it may be, to paint the exact grey of the bare Burren Hills . . . those grey mountains that still are lacking their celebration."[58] Yeats painted them in words.

In the play, the Young Man fears that the sound he hears is that of a policeman on horseback. The Stranger (Diarmuid) explains that it is rather "an old horse gone astray / . . . wandering on the road all night" (*VPl*, 765). His further lines suggest something supernatural. *The Burren Region* tourist brochure provides the following: "Many stories are told of the [mythical] Maire Ruadh's life, and death. One story of her death, still told in the Burren . . . [concludes] 'So the living woman never rode back that way. . . . But of a stormy night you'll hear the heavy feet of the stallion, and him galloping the road.'"[59]

The Cistercian Abbey itself was founded by the O'Briens around 1200. Donough O'Brien, whom Yeats describes in the play as being buried near the church altar, was one of a group of Irish nobles who invited the Scots to invade Thomond and take it from the king.[60] Thus, the Young Man asserts that "it was men like Donough who made Ireland weak" (*VPl*, 769). When they were defeated, Donough escaped from the battlefield at Athenry but was killed in 1317 near the abbey.

Diarmuid was slain in 1172; Dervorgilla died in 1193. Diarmuid MacMurrough, king of Leinster, ran off with Dervorgilla, daughter of the king of Meath and the wife of Diarmuid's host, Tegernan O'Rourke of Breffni, and was consequently banished. He sought to regain Leinster with help from England, where Henry II gave him an army under Strongbow. Thus Diarmuid initiated the Norman invasion of Ireland and the seven centuries of foreign domination that followed. Diarmuid and Dervorgilla logically ask absolution from the Young Man seeking to rid Ireland of English domination: their action eventuated in the Easter Uprising of which the Young Man was a part.

Vendler convincingly provides a literary source for the play that is other than *Nishikigi*: "The Vision of Hanrahan the Red," a version of the

story of Diarmuid and Dervorgilla (there called Dermond and Der-
vadilla) that Yeats recounted in *The Secret Rose*.[61] On the basis of this
source, Vendler reads the play as a love story and believes that "later topical analogies with Irish affairs which suggested themselves naturally to
Yeats in 1917 are, if not irrelevant to the unraveling of the meaning of
the play, at least not its central concern. . . . [Therefore] the main
difficulty with *The Dreaming of the Bones* is that there is no necessary
connection between the lovers and the Young Man."[62] The strong sense
of landscape present in the play, provided by the many lines entailing its
description, argues against Vendler's criticism. Although the church was
destroyed during the Protestant Reformation in the sixteenth century, it
is easy to associate its ruins with these ghostly figures who brought in
the Normans. The avaricious Normans, among other barbarities that
they committed, desecrated altars and plundered and destroyed
churches.[63] Diarmuid and Dervorgilla, like Donough O'Brien, are part of
Ireland's violent history, of which this harsh landscape and ruin and
tombs are so evocative. As Wilson observes, during the 1916 rebellion
fighting was heavy in this part of the west, and the play contains a reference to the British troops' vandalism there.[64] Yeats himself feared that
the contemporary political reference in the play might be "too powerful."[65] And indeed the play was not performed in Ireland until 1931
because of its political import.

Wilson points out that No legends are always traditionally associated with some particular genius loci and cannot conceivably be transplanted at a dramatist's whim, whereas Yeats originally thought to set
The Dreaming of the Bones in the Wicklow mountains just south of
Dublin and then changed the site.[66] He went to considerable lengths to
wed the play to the new location. Wilson himself observes that the Burren is "clearly an apt environment for a ghost-play" and that it is logical
that the ghosts might come to Corcomroe and to the tomb of Donough
O'Brien, who shares with them the stigma of having called in a foreign
army against the Irish people.[67] The play, as Anthony Bradley comments, helps to create the sense of a place both untouched by the English from whom the Young Man is fleeing and of an idealized rural community of peasants and nobility, far from the unheroic life of the urban
middle class.[68] How the Young Man may have gotten to Corcomroe
Abbey, some hundred miles as the crow flies from Dublin, is not clear.

"One method of distinguishing Yeats's more successful plays from
the others," Peter Ure usefully suggests, "is to observe that in them the
story is *about* the place, . . . that the characters have come to just this
place, and no other anywhere in the world, so that this story may hap-

pen."[69] I would argue that this is as much true of *The Dreaming of the Bones* as of *The Cat and the Moon* and *At the Hawk's Well*: the characters must come to the place they do and to no other. Moreover, the place is an actual place literally described, and it is critical to Yeats's intentions, as I will show, that it is so.

Eighteen years after *The Dreaming of the Bones,* Yeats wrote:

John Synge, I and Augusta Gregory, thought
All that we did, all that we said or sang
Must come from contact with the soil, from that
Contact everything Antaeus-like grew strong.[70]

Natural/Supernatural

A number of critics have examined the question of the relationship between Yeats's poetry and nature, and they are not in agreement. Observing that Yeats was leading a fight against naturalism with its emphasis on the workaday, democratic, and scientific modern world, Edmund Wilson, like many critics, overlooks his precise representation of nature.[71] Patrick Rafroidi states that while Yeats wrote to Katharine Tynan in 1888 that "we should make poems on the familiar landscapes we love," he finally considered art superior to nature. Nature merely embodied "'the inspired intuitions of the mind.'"[72] To the contrary, Sister Bernetta Quinn argues that, although Yeats did not observe the Catholic faith, his poetry proved him to be an Irishman by its evident sharing in the Irish love of their landscape.[73] And Donald Davie comments that "the wonder of Yeats's career is his having made poetry of world significance out of a landscape so much at the edge of things, so unrepresentative in the twentieth century, as the landscape of Ireland. . . . So far as poetry in English is concerned, the landscape of Ireland is positively Yeats's single-handed creation."[74]

Yeats did not merely love the Irish landscape. His view of nature was profoundly religious; he was interested in concrete phenomenal Druidism, not the institutionalized Judeo-Christian tradition. "All about us," he explained, "there seems to start up a precise inexplicable teeming life, and the earth becomes once more, not in rhetorical metaphor, but in reality, sacred."[75] Yeats sought not only to make the landscape vivid but also to make it come alive with the past and the supernatural. To this end, he asserted, artists should retell or even create legends "haunted by places."[76] František Déak usefully observes that the French symbolists—whose ideas were both akin to and very influential on

Yeats's own—and the avant-garde in general can be characterized by their transfer of issues traditionally associated with religious life into the aesthetic domain.[77]

Yeats was pleased to acknowledge that he knew and borrowed stories from literary sources. The landscape and its legend—or the legend that Yeats provided for it—and the literary sources were to come together as one. If "Japanese poets, too, feel for tomb and wood the emotion, the sense of awe that our Gaelic speaking country people will sometimes show when you speak to them of Castle Hackett or of some Holy Well" and if "the ghost lovers in *Nishigiki* remind me of the Aran boy and girl who in Lady Gregory's story come to the priest after death to be married," then so much the better for Yeats's theory of reality.[78]

Yeats also claimed painting as an important source. In explaining his use of analogies from painting in a series of lectures on poetry, Yeats said: "I began my own life as an art student and I am a painter's son, so it is natural to me to see . . . analogies"[79] between painting and poetry.

The concept of landscape art influenced Yeats's very subject matter. The word *landscape,* a product of the seventeenth century, suggests a scene more or less natural, not exclusive of humans and their works, but away from cities and their busyness. Ruskin's writings on landscape painting had helped make it a much-discussed subject; his ideas on truth to nature in landscape painting, of which Yeats had evidently read little, were nevertheless part of the intellectual climate in which Yeats lived.[80] Landscape art was the most prominent form of painting in England in the eighteenth and nineteenth centuries. In the English landscape painting of the Romantics, representations of ruins served to intensify solitude and as reminders of a fleeting world. Mountain scenery, pregnant with religion and poetry, was evocative of loneliness, spirits, and death. "It is," Yeats said, "a natural conviction for a painter's son to believe that there may be a landscape that is symbolical of some spiritual condition and awakens a hunger such as cats feel for valerian."[81] Yeats found such landscapes in Blake's painting and in that of his followers Samuel Palmer and Edward Calvert.[82] The plays were to provide such landscapes in words.

The analogy of plays to pictures was a logical one for Yeats. Yeats conceived of poetry as "region," an idea he first formulated in 1889.[83] In so doing, Yeats followed the Pre-Raphaelites and the Romantics before them in violating the classic distinction Gotthold Lessing had drawn in *Laocoon* (1766) between the visual arts as conveying their ideas and emotions in a single moment, and literature as conveying them over time.[84] Of all the literary forms, drama (including Lessing's own) was, of course, the one most especially dedicated to the representation of action developing over time. It was the literary form least like landscape. Many of Yeats's plays, the later ones in particular, are very brief because Yeats wished for them to be in effect an extended moment, the moment of tragic ecstasy, the spiritual condition he wished to evoke. Insofar as possible, the plays are reduced to that "moment of exaltation, of excitement, of dreaming."[85] The form of the plays is essentially spatial.

Of literary genres, the age-old Irish poetry called *dinnseanchas* may have been a source of inspiration for Yeats, as both Caroline MacDonogh and R. F. Foster have recently implied.[86] These poems and tales relate the original meanings of place-names and thus constitute a form of mythological etymology that melds the legendary and the local. But if *dinnseanchas* served as a source of inspiration, Yeats did not know how to accommodate it to his drama. He remarks: "When I first began to write poetical plays for an Irish theatre I had to put away an ambition of helping to bring again to certain places their old sanctity or their romance. I could lay the scene of a play on Baile's Strand, but found no pause in the hurried action for descriptions of strand or sea or the great yew-tree that once stood there; and I could not in *The King's Threshold* find room, before I began the ancient story, to call up the shallow river and the few trees and rocky field of modern Gort."[87]

French symbolist drama constituted an important and acknowledged literary model. Symbolist drama, as Déak observes, is static because it attempts to dramatize the liminal situation, the moment of the hero's self-conscious transformation or initiation, or its failure. Edgar Allan Poe's essay, "Philosophy of Composition," read by the symbolists as a theory of theater, asserts that since all intense excitements are through physical necessity brief, the length of the poem must be determined by the degree of excitement intended.[88]

Even more than symbolist drama, Japanese No drama guided Yeats in writing landscape plays. Prior to 1913, when Yeats first became familiar with No, he had been unable to establish a sense of place in his plays because of what he had perceived to be dramatic action's essential urgency. But he saw that in the less than urgent *Nishikigi,* for instance, "the tale of the lovers would lose its pathos if we did not see that forgotten tomb where the hiding fox lives among 'the orchids and the chrysanthemum flowers.'"[89] Many No plays, Yeats observed, "began with a traveller asking the way with many questions."[90] His use of this convention is clearly evident in *The Cat and the Moon, At the Hawk's Well,* and *The Dreaming of the Bones.* In each of the plays, the characters travel, with guidance, to a holy place in the landscape where past and present, natural and supernatural meet. As in No, the action then consists of the "meeting with ghost, god, or goddess at some holy place or much-legended tomb."[91] As in French symbolist drama, the central character travels to a liminal state, to transformation or the failure to achieve that transformation. In *The Dreaming of the Bones,* the tragedy of the central character's failure to achieve that transformation is to evoke, as Yeats believed great tragedy did, the experience of ecstasy in us.[92]

Yeats commented that while he first chose faraway places and Arcadia for the scenery of his art, he convinced himself that he "should never go for the scenery of a poem to any country but . . . [his] own" and then to places long familiar to him.[93] His comments, above, on *On Baile's Strand* and on *The King's Threshold* make clear that, even in these early plays, he wished to call up the specific characteristics of the sites in which he envisioned them to be set, but he did not know how to do so. Ecstasy is here on earth in "the minute life of long familiar things and symbols and places,"[94] in "landscapes we love." All but five of the twenty-four plays in *The Collected Plays of W. B. Yeats* are clearly set in Ireland. Of the exceptions—*Calvary, The Resurrection, The Shadowy Waters, The Player Queen,* and *A Full Moon in March*—two are about Christ, one with Irish characters is set at sea, and the location of only two is indeterminate. It became increasingly central to Yeats's view of reality that the plays are both set in a real landscape he knew well and representative of the supernatural. Naturalism and symbolism are to come together as one, "overflowing, concrete, phenomenal." His art, built of particulars he knew well, represented the union of opposites.

The staging Yeats sought for his landscape plays was in marked contrast to the realistic scene he called "to the eye of the mind." The setting for *The Dreaming of the Bones,* for instance, is "any bare place in a room close to a wall. A screen, with a pattern of a mountain and sky, can stand against the wall, or a curtain with a like pattern hang upon it, but the pattern must only symbolise or suggest" (*VPl,* 762). As in symbolist theater, Yeats sought to create stage decor with his language. In the words of the symbolists, "the speech creates the set."[95] The dance plays were written to be performed in a drawing room with actors and audience not separated by lighting or by a stage. In *At the Hawk's Well,* the Old Man is to enter through the audience.[96] Prior to the performance, one of the costumed musicians can, if necessary, tend to the lights. At the opening of *The Dreaming of the Bones,* one musician is to enter and then two others; the first is to stand singing while the others take their places; then all three are to sit down against the wall by their preset instruments—a drum, a zither, and a flute—or they are to unfold a cloth as at the opening of *At the Hawk's Well.* The singing and the narration of the musicians are thus to be clearly presentational. To indicate the climbing of Abbey Hill, the actors are to circle the stage at four different times. The play's three central figures are only referred to as Young Man, Young Girl, and Stranger. The Stranger and the Young Girl (Diarmuid and Dervorgilla) are to be masked. The musicians are to be made up so that their faces resemble masks. Far from any realism in acting style, Yeats wrote at one time that he wished for his actors to rehearse in barrels so that their movements would not detract from their words. The plays are written in verse. Yeats made some experiments with actors speaking to the psaltery, a stringed instrument used in early music, to remove their speaking further from the patterns of normal speech. In *The Cat and the Moon,* the Lame Beggar's dance to drum taps is to be like that of a puppet (*VPl,* 805). The movements of the figures in *At the Hawk's Well* are to suggest marionettes (*VPl,* 401).[97]

Just as naturalism and symbolism are to come together as one in Yeats's plays, so do the realistic setting described and the abstract setting represented here. The representation is to be at once intimate and remote. Literal words and abstract stage are to be joined together as are natural and supernatural. We are to hear one and to see the other. Sight and sound are to be combined, not redundant as in naturalistic theater, where one merely mimics the other.

Even those who have argued for the importance of landscape to Yeats's work have misunderstood its role. John Unterecker wrote to Sister Bernetta Quinn that he could not "think of any writer who more successfully transforms the real world in which he is rooted into the unreal but related world of inter-connected literary symbols."[98] But it is critical to Yeats's view of reality that both the real world and the unreal are present at once, not that one is transformed into the other. It is for this reason that, as Elizabeth Louizeaux states, "in Yeats's finest poems landscape as symbol never takes precedence over the landscape as experienced." But she adds that vision is the predominant sense to which his poetry appeals.[99] Not so: Yeats was a poet who wrote ever-so-carefully arranged sounds and rhythms.[100] Certainly his theater art was always one of synthesis.[101] It is the union of one and many, sight and sound, movement and stillness, here now on the stage and there then in Gort—art and landscape—that is central to his work and to his view of reality.

Yeats was not a naturalist if by that is meant a view of nature not haunted. For him natural and supernatural are wed. In the west of Ireland, with its landscape dotted with ruins and cairns of every age, art and life, past and present, Celtic beliefs and Christianity, dead and living, reality and dream, natural and supernatural freely intermingle. Pointing to the significance of his book *Mythic Ireland,* Michael Dames writes as follows: "Irish myths offer an insight into the original nature of human dwelling on earth, and now that the estrangement of our own civilization from a previously deified natural order is recognized as a self-destructive aberration, it may be Ireland's archaic legacy begins to assume new relevance."[102] This thought echoes Yeats's exactly. Yeats sought to make the landscape's myths, or the myths of it that he created, as much a part of our perception of the landscape as that of any country person's. His effort, in contrast to that of the people from whom he and Lady Gregory collected stories, was self-conscious and deliberate. The plays I have discussed in this essay originated in or were profoundly influenced by Yeats's response to landscape—a religious response, if you will, that he would have us share.

NOTES

1. The present essay is reprinted, with few changes, from *Comparative Drama* 31, no. 3 (1997): 337–66, by kind permission of the editors. In *Comparative Drama* the essay is accompanied by fourteen photos. *The Cat and the Moon* was not actually published until 1926. In "The Landscape Play: W. B. Yeats's *Purgatory,*" *Irish University Review* 27, no. 4 (1997): 262–75, I propose an actual site for *Purgatory* as well.

2. Katharine Worth, *The Irish Drama of Europe from Yeats to Beckett* (Atlantic Highlands, N.J.: Humanities Press, 1978), 4; Barton Friedman, *Adventures in the Deeps of the Mind* (Princeton: Princeton University Press, 1977), 12.

3. W. B. Yeats, *Essays and Introductions* (New York: Collier, 1968), 221.

4. W. B. Yeats, *Autobiographies* (London: Macmillan, 1955), 416.

5. For an excellent account of landscape plays see Elinor Fuchs, "Another Version of Pastoral," in *The Death of Character: Perspective on Theater after Modernism* (Bloomington: Indiana University Press, 1996), 92–107.

6. *The Variorum Edition of the Plays of W. B. Yeats,* ed. Russell K. Alspach (New York: Macmillan, 1966), 798. Subsequent references to this edition are identified by the abbreviation *VPl* and appear in my text in parentheses.

7. F. A. C. Wilson, *Yeats's Iconography* (New York: Macmillan, 1960), 129; William Empson, "Mr. Wilson on the Byzantium Poems," *Review of English Literature* 1 (1960): 56. Empson refers to Wilson as a symbolist critic.

8. Richard Taylor, *A Reader's Guide to the Plays of W. B. Yeats* (New York: St. Martin's Press, 1984), 119.

9. J. Fahey, *The History and Antiquities of the Diocese of Kilmacdaugh* (Dublin: M. H. Gill and Son, 1893), 111–12. The well is misidentified as one

near St. Colman's birthplace in Corker in *Place Names in the Writings of William Butler Yeats,* ed. James P. McGarry with additional material by Edward Malins (Gerrards Cross: Colin Smythe, 1976), 78.

10. The pictures were all drawn from the same perspective as the picture on the map and thus they are likely to have been copies of that picture rather than drawings from life.

11. *Fraxinus excelsior* (personal communication with Richard Dodd, University of California, Berkeley).

12. Janet Bord and Colin Bord, *Sacred Waters: Holy Wells and Water Lore in Britain and Ireland* (London: Granada, 1985), 77.

13. Janet Bord and Colin Bord, *Earth Rites: Fertility Rites in Pre-industrial Britain* (London: Granada, 1982), 103.

14. Bord and Bord, *Sacred Waters,* 78. The same story appears in Fahey, *History and Antiquities,* 112, but the trees are hawthorns, and the well in Corker is specified as that of the birthplace of St. Colman.

15. Correspondence with Gerald Keane, local historian, Gort. Keane, to whom locals had referred me when I asked the whereabouts of the well, was, when I went to seek him in October, doing rounds at the well. When I found him, he was taking up a collection to restore the well. He showed me a picture of his parents at the dedication of the well and had become, in effect, the well's guardian.

16. W. B. Yeats, *The Celtic Twilight* (Gerrards Cross: Colin Smythe, 1981), 11.

17. Michael Dames, *Mythic Ireland* (London: Thames and Hudson, 1992), 133–35.

18. See illustrations in Philip Dixon Hardy, *The Holy Wells of Ireland* (Dublin: Hardy and Walker, 1840), passim.

19. Yeats describes them as "bound one to the other by mutual contempt" (*Autobiographies,* 401).

20. A. Norman Jeffares, *A Commentary on the Collected Poems of W. B. Yeats* (Stanford: Stanford University Press, 1968), 211.

21. Taylor, *A Reader's Guide,* 120. Taylor (119) also suggests the kyogen *Kikazu Zato,* which Yeats had read and in which a blind man and a deaf man play tricks on one another based on their infirmities. The setting in this play is unrelated to that in *The Cat and the Moon.*

22. George Brandon Saul, *Prolegomena to the Study of Yeats's Plays* (Philadelphia: University of Pennsylvania Press, 1958), 76–77.

23. Richard Taylor, *The Drama of W. B. Yeats: Irish Myth and the Japanese No* (New Haven: Yale University Press, 1976), 146–47.

24. Natalie Crohn Schmitt, "Ecstasy and Insight in Yeats," *British Journal of Aesthetics* 11 (1971): 260.

25. Wilson, *Yeats's Iconography,* 153.

26. Taylor, *A Reader's Guide,* 120.

27. A. S. Knowland, *W. B. Yeats, Dramatist of Vision* (Totowa, N.J.: Barnes and Noble, 1983), 147.

28. The site of *At the Hawk's Well* has been identified in at least four such books: Sheelah Kirby, *The Yeats Country* (Dublin: Dolmen Press, 1962), 24; Susan Cahill and Thomas Cahill, *A Literary Guide to Ireland* (New York: Charles Scribner's Sons, 1973), 168; McGarry, *Place Names,* 52; and Alain Le Garsmeur and Bernard McCabe, *W. B. Yeats: Images of Ireland* (New York: Macmillan, 1991), 51.

29. Helen Hennessy Vendler, *Yeats's "Vision" and the Later Plays* (Cambridge: Harvard University Press, 1963), 204.

30. Not to be mistaken with nearby Collooney.

31. Terence O'Rorke, *The History of Sligo Town and County* (1889), 1:18, as quoted in Kirby, *The Yeats Country,* 23–24. Cahill and Cahill, writing in 1973, describe small hawks whirling from their nest there (*Literary Guide to Ireland,* 168). They may be merely reiterating O'Rorke.

32. *The Irish Version of Historia Britonum of Nennius,* ed. and trans. James Henthorn Todd (Dublin: Irish Archaeological Society, 1848), 197–99. According to Arthur Gribben, accounts of this miraculous well actually go back to a thousand-year-old *dinnseanchas,* a compilation of place-name lore (*Holy Wells and Sacred Water Sources in Britain and Ireland* [New York: Garland, 1992], 13). Cahill and Cahill write, "Hill of Tullaghan, at the top of which a brackish holy well sometimes rises" (*Literary Guide to Ireland,* 168). Nennius describes the water as sweet. It looked too brackish to try.

33. Estyn Evans, *Prehistoric and Early Christian Ireland: A Guide* (New York: Barnes and Noble, 1966), 192.

34. "A number of wells whose water ebbed and flowed have been recorded, this variation in water level said to be caused by a nearby river or by the sea, according to whichever is the closest." Bord and Bord further tell of the well Ffynnon Leinw in Cilcain parish (Flint), much written about by antiquarians because of its ebbing and flowing that took place twice daily. The well water would mysteriously diminish when the tide, from the sea seven miles distant, was in, and increase when it was out. "Its water source," they explain, has "been tapped by the Hendre Mine," so that "Ffynnon Leinw is now fed by surface water and no longer ebbs and flows, so this well-documented phenomenon cannot be scientifically investigated" (*Sacred Waters,* 81–82).

35. Ibid., 78.

36. Reg Skene, *The Cuchulain Plays of W. B. Yeats* (New York: Columbia University Press, 1974), 135.

37. Bord and Bord, *Earth Rites,* 101–2.

38. *The Variorum Edition of the Poems of W. B. Yeats,* ed. Peter Allt and Russell K. Alspach (New York: Macmillan, 1987), 177.

39. Bord and Bord, *Sacred Waters,* 112–13.

40. Hardy, *Holy Wells of Ireland,* 98.

41. Bord and Bord, *Sacred Waters,* 116–18.

42. Ibid., 119–22, and see also 123 for notice of a prominent evil guardian spirit in Scotland, Cailleach (Old Wife), who was believed to dwell at the side of a loch in the form of a heron.

43. Taylor, *Drama of W. B. Yeats*, 134.

44. Standish O'Grady, *History of Ireland*, 2 vols. (London: Sampson Low, 1881), 1:127.

45. From a record of meetings of the Order quoted by Birgit Bjersby, *The Interpretation of the Cuchulain Legend in the Works of W. B. Yeats* (Uppsala: Lundequist, 1950), 43.

46. Standish O'Grady, *Selected Essays and Passages* (Dublin: Talbot Press, 1918), 339; cited in Wilson, *Yeats's Iconography*, 38. According to W. G. Wood-Martin, *History of Sligo*, 3 vols. (1892; rpt. Sligo: Antiquarian Books, 1990), 3:360, who quotes an O'Curry to the effect that there were several springs in ancient Ireland "each surrounded (it is said) by nine imperishable hazel trees, from which showers of ruddy nuts were dropped periodically into the spring." Those who ate the salmon that ate the nuts became wise.

47. Motokiyo Zeami, *Yoro*, as quoted in Taylor, *Drama of W. B. Yeats*, 122.

48. Bjersby, *Interpretation of Cuchulain Legend*, 42, citing *Stories from Carleton*, intro. W. B. Yeats (1889; rpt. New York: Lemma, 1973), 117–82. Other sources mentioned that are in various ways suggestive but the landscapes of which bear little resemblance to that in *At the Hawk's Well* are the pool of Bethesda in John 5:2–9; William Morris's medieval romances *The Well at the World's End* and *The Water of the Wondrous Isles;* John Millington Synge's *The Well of the Saints;* A.E.'s "The Fountains of Youth," *Irish Theosophist* 5, no. 12 (1897): 221; these are cited by Bjersby, 41–44.

Further sources cited are the Irish legend of Cuchulain and the two yoked white birds recounted by Yeats in *Visions and Beliefs in the West of Ireland,* comp. Lady Gregory with two essays and notes by W. B. Yeats (Gerrards Cross: Colin Smythe, 1970), 362; Standish Hayes O'Grady, "Niall and the Loathly Hag," *Silva Gadelica* (London: Williams and Norgate, 1892), 370–72; Jeremiah Curtin, "The Prince of the Lonesome Isle," in *Myths and Folklore of Ireland* (1890; rpt. Irvine, Calif.: Reprint Services, 1990), 101–6; an early Yeats poem, "The Old Age of Queen Maeve," in *Variorum Poems,* 180–87, and an early Yeats story "Dhoya," in Ganconagh [pseud. W. B. Yeats], *John Sherman and Dhoya* (New York: Cassel, 1891), cited by Wilson, *Yeats's Iconography,* 34–38; "The Well of D'Yerre-in-Dowan," in Douglas Hyde, *Beside the Fire: A Collection of Irish Gaelic Folk Stories* (London: David Nutt, 1890), 129–41, cited by Saul, *Prolegomena,* 49; and "The Heart of the Spring," in W. B. Yeats, *Mythologies* (New York: Collier, 1969), 171–76, cited by Natalie Crohn Schmitt, "Intimations of Immortality: W. B. Yeats *At the Hawk's Well*," *Educational Theatre Journal* 31 (1979): 506.

49. Oliver St. John Gogarty, *It Isn't This Time of Year at All!* (Garden City, N.Y.: Doubleday, 1954), 245.

50. Yeats, *Variorum Poems,* 806, 808.

51. Maeve Good, *W. B. Yeats and the Creation of a Tragic Universe* (Totowa, N.J.: Barnes and Noble, 1987), 57.

52. Liam Miller, *The Noble Drama of W. B. Yeats* (Dublin: Dolmen Press, 1977), 237.

53. A. Norman Jeffares and A. S. Knowland, *A Commentary on the Collected*

Plays of W. B. Yeats (Stanford: Stanford University Press, 1975), 159. Book 3 of W. B. Yeats's novel *The Speckled Bird* is also set in the vicinity of Corcomroe Abbey.

54. This well is probably on the spring that is located at the abbey, the Latin name of which is *Sancta Maria in Petra Fertilis,* Our Lady of the Fertile Rock.

55. "But now they [the birds] wheel about our heads; and now / They have dropped on the grey stone [of the hill] to the northeast" (*VPl,* 764).

56. Burren, from *boireann,* is Irish for "rocky place"; for example: "The desolate, rocky upland of the Burren" (*Irish Geographical Studies in Honour of Estyn Evans,* ed. Nicholas Stephens and Robin E. Glasscock [Belfast: Queens' University of Belfast, 1970], 116). "The burren district of Clare is notable for scenery of a peculiar character, unique to Ireland. Wide stretches of bare limestone there prevail, trenched with gaping crevices, deep gorges, and valleys separating terraced hills, the *pseudo*-artificial appearance of which, combined with an unusual sterility of the region, impresses the beholder with a sense of weird desolateness" (J. R. Kilroe, *A Description of the Soil-Geology of Ireland* [Dublin: Alex Thom, 1907], 12).

57. Kilroe, *Description of Soil-Geology,* 101.

58. Yeats, *Essays and Introductions,* 208–9.

59. *The Burren Region* tourist brochure (Limerick: Mid Western Regional Tourism Organisation, n.d.).

60. The notable tomb in the church, in the north wall and with an effigy, is that of Prince Conor na Siudaine O'Brien (d. 1267), grandson of the founder of the church. The effigy is one of only two early Irish royal monumental effigies extant. Whether Donough is also buried there or whether Yeats mistook or substituted one for the other, I have not been able to determine. Important people tended to be buried close to their church's high altar.

61. *The Secret Rose, Stories by W. B. Yeats: A Variorum Edition,* ed. Philip L. Marcus, Warwick Gould, and Michael J. Sidnell (Ithaca, N.Y.: Cornell University Press, 1981), 215–20.

62. Vendler, *Yeats's "Vision,"* 187, 194.

63. In 1202, Corcomroe Abbey was damaged by fire and then occupied by Irish and English soldiers. "No structure in the monastery was left without breaking and burning, except the roofs of the houses alone, and even of these a great portion was broken and burned" (*Annals of Loch Cé: A Chronicle of Irish Affairs from A.D. 1014 to A.D. 1590,* ed. and trans. William Mounsell Hennessy, 2 vols., Chronicles and Memorials of Great Britain and Ireland, no. 54 [London: Her Majesty's Stationery Office, 1871], 1:225, as quoted in Arthur Champneys, *Irish Ecclesiastical Architecture* [London: G. Bell and Sons, 1910], 234).

64. Wilson, *Yeats's Iconography,* 205.

65. *The Letters of W. B. Yeats,* ed. Allen Wade (New York: Macmillan, 1955), 26.

66. Wilson, *Yeats's Iconography,* 204. Wilson provides no source for this information, but David R. Clark has kindly provided me with information about an early manuscript of the play (National Library of Ireland, MS. 8775) to this

effect. The manuscript, moreover, specifies a mountain and nearby villages (personal correspondence). So Yeats had set out to make this site very specific.

67. Wilson, *Yeats's Iconography,* 204–5.

68. Anthony Bradley, *William Butler Yeats* (New York: Frederick Ungar, 1979), 160–61.

69. Peter Ure, "The Plays," in *An Honoured Guest,* ed. Denis Donoghue and J. R. Mulryne (London: Edward Arnold, 1965), 153.

70. W. B. Yeats, "The Municipal Gallery Revisited," in *Variorum Poems,* 603.

71. Untitled essay by Edmund Wilson in *The Permanence of Yeats,* ed. James Hall and Martin Steinmann (New York: Macmillan, 1950), 26–27.

72. Patrick Rafroidi, "Yeats, Nature, and the Self," in *Yeats, Sligo, and Ireland,* ed. Norman Jeffares (Gerrards Cross: Colin Smyth, 1980), 189, 193. Rafroidi (193) quotes from Robert O'Driscoll, *Yeats and the Theatre,* ed. Robert O'Driscoll and Lorna Reynolds (Toronto: Macmillan; Niagara Falls: MacLean-Hunter, 1975), 9. Rafroidi's chief evidence is Yeats's "Sailing to Byzantium." He argues against William Empson's reading (in "Mr. Wilson") of the poem's line "Once out of nature I shall never take / My bodily form from any natural thing" as tongue-in-cheek. For Yeats's letter to Katharine Tynan, see *Letters of Yeats,* 99.

Evidently in high dudgeon because she believed that Yeats had just dismissed a nature poem of hers as but "a flawless lyric," Dorothy Wellesley, a minor poet and an intimate friend who was however not the most perceptive judge of his work, asserted that Yeats is like "most of the Celtic poets" in that he is "not concerned with nature at all." She added that "his lack of observation concerning natural beauty was almost an active obsession," then went on to suggest, "it is possible that to this racial characteristic must be added his extremely poor sight. His small dark eyes turned outwards, appear like those of a lizard and as though at times they were hidden by a film" (*Letters on Poetry from W. B. Yeats to Dorothy Wellesley,* intro. Kathleen Raine [London: Oxford University Press, 1964], 173). There is no doubt that Yeats's eyesight was poor; see Joseph Hone, *W. B. Yeats, 1865–1939* (New York: Macmillan, 1943), 142. I hope the evidence here makes clear that Yeats could see trees, rocks, mountains, birds, wells, and ruins and be moved by them.

73. M. Bernetta Quinn, O.S.F., "Symbolic Landscape in Yeats: County Galway," in *The Hidden Harmony: Essays in Honor of Philip Wheelwright* (New York: Odyssey Press, 1966), 15.

74. Donald Davie, "Landscape and Poetic Focus," *Southern Review* 4 (1968): 687. For readings pertaining to Yeats's views on nature, see also Liam Miller, "Yeats's West," *Ireland of the Welcomes* 28, no. 3 (1979): 17–32; Barbara Hardy, "Verge or Limit: Responses to Simple Nature," *Yeats Annual* 7 (1990): 68–80; Paul Scott Stanfield, "Yeats and Balzac," in *Yeats and Politics in the 1930s* (Basingstoke: Macmillan, 1988), 112–44; Paul de Man, "Symbolic Landscape in Wordsworth and Yeats," in *The Rhetoric of Romanticism* (New York: Columbia University Press, 1984), 125–43; John Crowe Ransom, "The Irish, the Gaelic, the Byzantine," *Southern Review* 7 (1941–42): 517–46; Elizabeth Bergmann

Loizeaux, "Yeats's Early Landscapes," *Yeats* 2 (1984): 144–64; Heather Martin, "W. B. Yeats: More Realist Than Idealist," *Canadian Journal of Irish Studies* 9, no. 2 (1983): 77–80; and R. N. Snukal, *High Talk: The Philosophical Poetry of W. B. Yeats* (Cambridge: Cambridge University Press, 1973).

75. "Notes" to *The Words upon the Window Pane* (1934), in *VPl*, 970. "In our land . . . there is no river or mountain that is not associated in the memory with some event or legend. . . . I would have our writers and craftsmen of many kinds master this history and these legends, and fix upon their memory the appearance of mountains and rivers and make it all visible again in their arts, so that Irishmen, even though they had gone thousands of miles away, would still be in their own country. Whether they chose for the subject the carrying off of the Brown Bull or the coming of Patrick, or the political struggle of later times, the other world comes so much into it all that their love of it would move in their hands also" (Yeats, *Essays and Introductions,* 205–6). "Perhaps some day a play in the form I am adapting . . . [for performance in London] may excite once more, whether in Gaelic or in English, under the slope of Slieve-na-mon or Croagh Patrick, ancient memories" (ibid., 236).

76. W. B. Yeats, "A Note on National Drama," in *Literary Ideals in Ireland,* by John Eglington, W. B. Yeats, A.E., and W. Larminie (1899; rpt. New York: Lemma, 1973), 19: "Our legends are always associated with places, and not merely every mountain and valley, but every strange stone and little coppice has its legend, preserved in written or unwritten tradition. Our Irish romantic movement has arisen out of this tradition, and should always, even when it makes new legends about traditional people and things, be haunted by places. It should make Ireland, as Ireland and all other lands were in ancient times, a holy land to her own people."

77. František Déak, *Symbolist Theater: The Formation of an Avant-Garde* (Baltimore: Johns Hopkins University Press, 1993), 131. Yeats wrote, "I am very religious and deprived by Huxley and Tyndall, whom I detested, of the simple-minded religion of my childhood, I had made a new religion, almost an infallible Church of poetic tradition, of a fardel of stories, and of personages, and of emotions, inseparable from their first expression, passed on from generation to generation by poets and painters with some help from philosophers and theologians" (*Autobiographies,* 115–16).

78. Yeats, *Essays and Introductions,* 232.

79. Opening to the second lecture, as quoted by Robert O'Driscoll, "Yeats on Personality: Three Unpublished Lectures," in O'Driscoll and Reynolds, *Yeats and the Theater,* 27.

80. Elizabeth Bergmann Loizeaux, *Yeats and the Visual Arts* (New Brunswick, N.J.: Rutgers University Press, 1986), 50.

81. Yeats, *Autobiographies,* 74.

82. Loizeaux, *Yeats and Visual Arts,* 50.

83. See ibid., 48–49.

84. *Laocoon: An Essay upon the Limits of Painting and Poetry* was translated into English in 1836 and was well known in the latter half of the nineteenth cen-

tury. Loizeaux makes clear that the Pre-Raphaelites often took subjects for painting from literature (*Yeats and Visual Arts,* 13).

85. Yeats, *Essays and Introductions,* 242–43. The plays represented "overflowing turbulent energy, and marmorean stillness," "a moment of intense life" (*Essays and Introductions,* 255; *Explorations* [New York: Macmillan, 1962], 153). W. J. McCormack notes the synchronic rather than diachronic axis in *Purgatory* (*Ascendancy and Tradition in Anglo-Irish Literary History from 1789 to 1939* [New York: Oxford University Press, 1985], 378). The synchronic axis is, in fact, the more prominent one in many of Yeats's later plays.

86. Caroline MacDonogh, "August Gregory: A Portrait of a Lady," in *Rural Ireland, Real Ireland?* ed. Jacqueline Genet (Gerrards Cross: Colin Smythe, 1996), 116; and R. F. Foster, *W. B. Yeats: A Life,* vol. 1: *The Apprentice Mage* (Oxford: Oxford University Press, 1997), 186. See also Seamus Heaney, "A Sense of Place," in *Preoccupations: Selected Prose, 1968–1978* (New York: Farrar, Straus and Giroux, 1980), 131–32.

87. Yeats, *Essays and Introductions,* 233.

88. Déak, *Symbolist Theater,* 128, 66.

89. Yeats, *Essays and Introductions,* 233.

90. Ibid., 233.

91. Ibid., 232.

92. See Schmitt, "Ecstasy and Insight," 261–62.

93. Yeats, *Variorum Poems,* 843–44.

94. Yeats, *Essays and Introductions,* 296. In the early plays the central characters go to heaven. In later ones they are earthbound: "We are in the midst of life and there is nothing but life" (*Letters of Yeats,* ed. Wade, 728).

95. Déak, *Symbolist Theater,* 125, 222.

96. Mallarmé's *The Book* (1885) was to take place in his apartment; as its performer, Mallarmé was to enter through the space between the audience's chairs (Déak, *Symbolist Theater,* 89).

97. Déak points out that puppetlike movement was also common in symbolist theater. It was consistent with other aspects of symbolist acting: hieratic gesture, stylized posing, and monotone declamation, all of which were part of a broader attempt to introduce hieraticism and ritual into art as well as everyday life (*Symbolist Theatre,* 237 and passim).

98. Quoted by Quinn, "Symbolic Landscape in Yeats," 157.

99. Loizeaux, "Yeats's Early Landscapes," 163, 144.

100. For an analysis of the sounds and their significance in *Purgatory,* see Schmitt, "Curing Oneself of the Work of Time: W. B. Yeats's *Purgatory,*" *Comparative Drama* 7 (1973–74): 310–33.

101. "I would have all the arts draw together," Yeats wrote in 1937, "recover their ancient association, the painter painting what the poet has written, the musician setting the poet's words to simple airs, that the horse-man and the engine-driver may sing them at their work" (*Essays and Introductions,* ix).

102. Dames, *Mythic Ireland,* 9.

"All the Dead Voices": The Landscape of Famine in *Waiting for Godot*

Joseph Roach

> You and your landscapes!
>
> —GOGO TO DIDI,
> *Waiting for Godot*

Theodor Adorno situates *Endgame* at history's end. He raises but does not exhaust the question of whether the end of history remains within history—whether it produced the consciousness that implicates Beckett's work in its own time or moves outside of it, providing a position from which to contemplate with maximum disinterestedness the terminal crisis that brought it forth. Prying partially loose the intellectual grip of the universalizing, existentialist "Theatre of the Absurd," Adorno releases *Endgame* into the topical company of "every aspiring drama of the atomic age." He amends this generality with the important distinction that as a dramatic parody—one that ironically recycles superannuated forms "in the epoch of their impossibility"—*Endgame* stages in its vertiginous silences and demonic shtick the most appalling insight of the postapocalyptic world: "The violence of the unutterable is mimed by the dread of mentioning it."[1] This is a failure of language quite different from the one plumped up by the metaphysicians of absurdity.

To insert *Waiting for Godot* into such a critical framework requires a redirected but not wholly revised historical perspective. One bridge between the two works appears in the two landscapes, a different scene of desolation in each play, evoked by Beckett's actual and implied stage directions. They verge on a modernist-minimalist revival of the pathetic fallacy. Both *Endgame* and *Godot* personify their settings as malign by means of theatrical self-referentiality. This malignity is reciprocated by a notable peculiarity of Clov and Estragon: scenery makes them angry. Exasperated, standing on his ladder at the porthole in *Endgame*, the usually docile Clov lowers his telescope and turns to answer Hamm's annoyingly urgent query with one of his own: "What in God's name could there be on the horizon?"[2] Already framed by an exterior scene—"A country road. A tree. Evening"—Estragon's petulant outburst in act 2 of *Godot* covers even more explicitly agrophobic ground: "Recognize! What is there to recognize? All my lousy life I've crawled about in the mud! And you talk of scenery! (*Looking wildly about him.*) Look at this muckheap! I've never stirred from it!"[3] The historical provocation for such alienation is clearly suggested in *Endgame* by the violent end attributed to every living creature in "Nature": "All is . . . . Corpsed" (30). The historical motives for topographical alienation in *Godot* are at once more elusive and more ironic: "Charming spot," says Estragon, facing upstage; "Inspiring prospects," he adds, facing the auditorium; "Let's go," he concludes, cuing in Vladimir's crucial exposition about their given circumstances: "We can't. . . . We're waiting for Godot" (10).

Blurbed as "a modern morality play, on permanent themes," *Waiting for Godot* (written in 1948 and first performed in 1953) has challenged critics of every generation and intellectual camp to elucidate its tenebrous allegory. This strenuous endeavor was not made any easier by Samuel Beckett's notorious disinclination to clarify his intentions. He insisted that his words meant what they said—no more, no less. This is undoubtedly true, but the yawning gulf of the unsaid, which opens up like a gallows beneath the clever patter of the dialogue (not to mention under the ponderous weight of academic critics), threatens to leave dangling any strong reading of this play. Famously, had Beckett known the true identity of Godot, he would have said so. With the Scylla of vulgar reduction on one side and the Charybdis of mystified humanistic universality on the other, Adorno's essay navigates the tricky waters of historical context. The catastrophes of which "Towards an Understanding of *Endgame*" speaks are of sufficient scope and specificity to reconcile Beckett's resistance to meaning and his engagement with the crisis of the late twentieth century, "a culture reconstructed in the shadow of Auschwitz."[4] That is as clear and as devastating as the annihilated world that Clov sees on the gray horizon. But what about the "muckheap"— the road, the tree, the low mound, the ditch, the bog—with which Estragon reproaches Vladimir? "You and your landscapes!" he fumes. "Tell me about the worms!" (39).

The natural-historical landscape of *Godot* is desolate but not empty. In addition to a tree with five leaves and handful of the living (Vladimir, Estragon, Lucky, Pozzo, and the boy), it is thickly populated by disembodied voices. In other words, it is haunted. From Ibsen on, modern drama has been troubled by ghosts.[5] Their ubiquity stems in part from the fact that they conveniently represent the past that is dead but that refuses final interment. The preternatural sounding of "All the dead voices" in act 2 of *Godot*, a lyrical passage as unsettling as it is dramatically inevitable, captures the intensity of this convention as poignantly as any in the canon of modern drama. It can easily be imagined as a musical number, like an operatic duet, which can be performed on its own in a concert (and separately anthologized among Beckett's greatest hits) but which acquires its fullest power only in its proper context:

> *Estragon.* All the dead voices.
> *Vladimir.* They make a noise like wings.
> *Estragon.* Like leaves.
> *Vladimir.* Like sand.
> *Estragon.* Like leaves.
>   (*Silence*)
> *Vladimir.* They all speak at once.
> *Estragon.* Each one to itself.
>   (*Silence*)
> *Vladimir.* Rather they whisper.
> *Estragon.* They rustle.
> *Vladimir.* They murmur.
> *Estragon.* They rustle.
>   (*Silence*)
> *Vladimir.* What do they say?
> *Estragon.* They talk about their lives.
> *Vladimir.* To have lived is not enough for them.
> *Estragon.* They have to talk about it.
> *Vladimir.* To be dead is not enough for them.
> *Estragon.* It is not sufficient.
>   (*Silence*)
> *Vladimir.* They make a noise like feathers.
> *Estragon.* Like leaves.
> *Vladimir.* Like ashes.
> *Estragon.* Like leaves.
>   (*Long silence*) (*Godot*, 40)

As is typical among the moderns, the dead are seen as something of an imposition. Like intrusive visitors, they speak only of themselves. They certainly accumulate in significant numbers: "Where are all these corpses from?" Vladimir wonders. "These skeletons," Estragon corrects him (41), insisting on a distinction that typifies Beckett's way of marking the passage of time by noting the progress of decay: "It's never the same pus from one second to the next" (39). Time (one might say history) narrows the relationship between the people and the land: "A charnel-house! A charnel-house!" Vladimir exclaims (41), summing up the sonorous detritus by locating the macabre source of its abundance.

Clever stage directors have found that the references to corpses and skeletons in *Godot* play well when the actors insinuate that they refer insultingly to the audience. This is hilarious indeed. But it can also draw in the audience as a kind of surrogate chorus, representing the dead as restless witnesses to the ineffectual efforts of the living actors to summon them into fullness of being. Like the dead, they are present in the consciousness of the quick, but they are also invisible on the horizon. Pozzo reports that after nearly a full day on the road with Lucky, he hasn't seen anyone else: "yes, six hours, that's right, six hours on end, and never a soul in sight" (16).

The poetic and dramatic tension of "All the dead voices," then, arises from the onomatopoetic reproduction of echoes that only the characters can hear in a landscape hollowed by loss. The acoustical gravity of this absence deepens cumulatively in the five excruciatingly placed silences. In an opera (or melodrama), the chorus and orchestra would enter there. But in Beckett's theater, silence mocks the speakers, threatening the finality of an evacuation that they have experienced as only partially complete: "The air is full of our cries" (58). The phantom sound plot (the rustling, the murmuring) thus supports the mise-en-scène of the skeletonized landscape. As the vibrations that make up sound diminish, they are commonly said to "die out" or "decay" (*OED*). As they do, the sensations of the listeners reorganize themselves into memories. Wings, leaves, and feathers may reasonably be supposed to have rustled. But these are not the only whispers in Vladimir and Estragon's evocation of "All the dead voices." It must have been the ashes that murmured.

Scholars who have written about the poet they call "the Irish Beckett" have noted the Irishness of the landscape in *Waiting for Godot*. They have done so in the contexts of literary influence and biographical affinity or disaffection, coming down even to the details of Beckett's sore feet on his walking tour through the countryside of Connemara in 1931.[6] What they have not pursued, except by implication, is what seems most obvious in light of Adorno's "violence of the unutterable": that the landscape of the Irish countryside, particularly in the west country, was created by the actions or inactions of historical persons as well as by the workings of God or nature.

Like the "abode of stones" of which Lucky speaks in his thrice-repeated naming of Connemara (*Godot*, 28–29), rural Ireland is haunted by dead voices. To anyone who is prepared to listen, they speak of the consequences of the potato famine, or the Great Hunger, the effects of which endured long after its deadliest years, 1845–51. Successive seasons of potato blight and the failure of the British authorities to respond effectively doomed those unlucky enough to depend for a living on what they could dig from the ground. As the roots turned black in their hands and they were forced from the land by eviction or hunger, millions emigrated and at least a million more starved. Entire villages disappeared, and with them memories and traditions, the prolific cultural life of premodern Ireland. Exiles in their own land, the homeless wandered the highways deprived of everything, even a destination. Resonant in the memories of witnesses to the tattered columns of walking skeletons shuffling along the dreaded "Famine Road" to nowhere was the low wailing they sent up, a wordless prayer for mercy in face of the terrible quiescence of God. They died in the ditches where they lay down, the children first, their mouths stained green from eating grass. When the road finally emptied, the silence descended: "A country road. A tree. Evening."

This silence hangs over the Irish landscape like a shroud. After the Great Hunger it was especially evident in the notable disappearance of music from the land. George Petrie's salvage ethnomusicology, *The Ancient Music of Ireland* (1855), describes the unsettling effect of such an evacuation on the nerves of famine and immediate postfamine visitors:

> The "land of song" was no longer tuneful; or, if a human sound met the traveller's ear, it was only that of the feeble and despairing wail for the dead. This awful, unwonted silence, which, during the famine and subsequent years, almost everywhere prevailed, struck more fearfully upon their imaginations, as many Irish gentlemen informed me, and gave them a deeper feeling of desolation with which the country had been visited, than any other circumstance which had forced itself upon their attention.[7]

Petrie's scene of desolation makes it clear that the topography itself, the "pastoral plains" as well as the "dreary bogs," stood as a mute memorial to "the calamities which, in the year 1846–7, had struck down and well nigh annihilated the Irish remnant of the great Celtic family."[8]

The 150th anniversary of the famine has drawn attention to the profundity and duration of that silence. There can be no question about the Great Hunger's impact as history, but its traumatic hold on cultural memory has been deferred, displaced, even disavowed. With some notable exceptions, literature has approached the subject of the Great Hunger with a tact bordering on amnesia.[9] The closets are so full of bones, to borrow the Beckettian image of Tracy Chapman, that the doors won't close.[10] Of course the specter of mass starvation does tend to make people avert their gaze and turn their minds to other subjects: "The violence of the unutterable is mimed by the dread of mentioning it." But the landscape of the Irish famine, as Lucky's so-called nonsense speech intimates, remains in plain sight and within earshot—the sparsely peopled countryside, the wind in the ruins, the rocks scattered like bones under an indifferent sky: "the tears the stones so blue so calm alas alas on on the skull the skull the skull the skull in Connemara" (*Godot,* 29).

Beckett's own staging of *Waiting for Godot* gives some suggestive hints about the appearance of the landscape as he envisioned it. In all of his productions, he ignored his own stage directions and substituted a stone for the "low mound." This stone was big enough for one actor to sit on, but not two.[11] In his production notes, he explicitly associated the environment of the play with the landscape evoked in Lucky's monologue: "It is all about stones, about the world of stones."[12]

One indisputable connection between *Waiting for Godot* and Ireland stands out: the food is terrible. This is even more noticeable when it is abundant: "Funny," says Estragon, "the more you eat the worse it gets" (14). Abundance, however, is not the typical experience here. The desperation associated with food by the characters is performed through the extraordinary elaboration of the vaudeville business with which they acquire, exchange, share, and consume it. Estragon brings up the subject of food by "violently" announcing his deprivation: "I'm hungry!" (13). He spent the previous night in a ditch and was beaten by unidentified assailants (7). Now food preoccupies him. Vladimir, turning his pockets inside out, can offer only some turnips, which Estragon rejects, and one carrot: "Make it last," Vladimir cautions, "that's the end of them" (14). Beckett's personal selection of the properties for his own stagings of *Godot* is very suggestive in this context: "the carrot was usually pitifully small, another example of diminishing resources."[13]

The final, miserable carrot does important work of dramatic exposition. In the longer arc of the action of the play, it prepares for the moment of the last of the radishes in act 2. This second pathetic offering Estragon, despite his bone hunger, has to reject, and the reason he gives evokes some of the most painful accounts of the onset of potato blight:

"It's black" (44). In the more immediate liaison of the scenes in act 1, the carrot routine sets up the cruel humor of Pozzo's picnic. After Lucky unpacks the supper of a bottle of wine and chicken, Pozzo begins to eat "voraciously, throwing away the bones after having sucked them" (17), while Vladimir and Estragon distract themselves from the painful sight of watching him feast by examining Lucky's running sores. Then Estragon begs for the discarded bones after Lucky, who has first refusal as Pozzo's lackey, turns them down, which disconcerts his master: "I don't like it. I've never known him to refuse a bone before" (18). Estragon "begins to gnaw" the refuse, scandalizing Vladimir, who won't be thrown a sop, even though he too has hungrily watched while the banquet proceeded.

Beckett's actively performative imagery of animality, death, scarcity, and his repeated use of words like *violent* in connection with hunger and food converge in the little song that opens act 2. Another bleak lyrical interlude, Vladimir's ditty heightens the perception that deprivation, violence, and punishment are the normal expectation for those whose physical needs transgress against the prevailing maldistribution:

> A dog came into the kitchen
> And stole a crust of bread.
> Then cook up with a ladle
> And beat him till he was dead.
>
> Then all the dogs came running
> And dug the dog a tomb
> And wrote upon the tombstone
> For the eyes of dogs to come:
>
> A dog came in the kitchen
> And stole a crust of bread.
>
> (37)

And so forth, as if fighting over the last scrap were a daily ritual as efficacious as waiting for Godot. The similarly canine (and circular) impression made by Lucky's mute obedience does not end when his master throws him a bone. Of Lucky's weeping at the threat of abandonment, Pozzo says, "Old dogs have more dignity" (21), a line that occasions the master's callous rumination on the constant quantity of the world's tears: no sooner does one person begin to cry, than another stops (22). The prevailing action of the play is one of circularity and stasis, as has often been pointed out, but it is also one of subtraction, as if the diminishing number of organs (Pozzo eyes, Lucky's tongue) and the growing number of skeletons have some connection with the dwindling supply of carrots, radishes, and bread crusts. And why wouldn't they? As Pozzo philosophizes in his self-satisfied way, blaming indifferent nature, "That's how it is on this bitch of an earth" (25). But *Waiting for Godot,* in its characteristically Beckettian corporeality, proffers more tangible agents of catastrophe than the abstractly malign operations of an absurd universe, while at the same time it does not (because it need not) abandon the general proposition of nihilism.

In *Texts for Nothing,* Beckett, second-guessing himself like a well-made playwright clearing up weak motivations, asks a suggestive question about Pozzo: "Why did Pozzo leave home, he had a castle and retainers [?]"[14] In the play, Pozzo thinks that he might have left his half-hunter back at "the manor" (31). The image of the absentee landlord, living off the sweat of his starving bondmen, preening himself over the way he indulges them, suits Pozzo, especially in the harrowing metonym of the rope that joins him to Lucky, first as a chain, then as a lead. His attitude toward his slave is specific. Harmonizing with the category of mid-nineteenth-century political economy that wrote off surplus populations of putatively inferior people as expendable, Pozzo's ideology prompts him to think of selling Lucky at the fair as leniency: "The truth is you can't drive such creatures away. The best thing would be to kill them" (21).

That Vladimir and Estragon initially misrecognize Pozzo as Godot himself connects him with the elusive landlord of the larger estate. Consistent with the imagery of feudal obligations to vassals, inquiries about Godot's nature turn to his provision of food. When Vladimir interrogates the boy, he asks: "Does he give you enough to eat?" (34). The boy's reluctant and evasive answer is not reassuring. Set against the starved landscape, it is one of those many expositional plantings in the play that culminate in the final nonappearance of the greatest absentee of them all.

This is not Brecht. Beckett the poet successfully evades abduction by worthy causes as a condition of his austere, ironic compassion. But *Waiting for Godot* does not evade history. As soon as the refugees that Peter Hall was the first to call "tramps" begin to take stock of their rotten tubers along "a country road" in an "abode of stones," history and memory come into play. They proliferate in the dramatic silences that sensitized listeners cannot but hear as choric.

The evocation of geographical and historical specificity in dramatic images, however, does not foreclose more general implications. The

necrology of the play explicitly includes *all* the dead voices. That the setting of *Waiting for Godot* could be "at once Ireland and anywhere"[15]
makes Adorno's contention about the historical situation of *Endgame*
even more readily applicable to the earlier work: the landscape of famine
is an all-too familiar one at the beginning of the twenty-first century, and
there exists plenty of evidence to suggest that instead of a belated
episode of premodern catastrophe, the cold-blooded modernity of the
Great Hunger in Ireland foreshadows an apocalyptic global landscape
yet to come. "Sweet mother earth!" is how Estragon generalizes the
prospect, voicing the apostrophe of nurture withheld as a bitter oath
(53). History in Beckett's play, like so much else in the work of this most
physical of playwrights, is made palpable, present to the senses even as
absences—a silence, a stillness, an unbroken horizon. His art mimes the
"violence of the unutterable" in a place—at once remembered and
prophesied—where the bounty of the earth is bestowed on the profusion
of its graves.

NOTES

1. Theodor Adorno, "Towards an Understanding of *Endgame,*" in *Twentieth
Century Interpretations of Endgame,* ed. Bell Gale Chevigny (Englewood Cliffs,
N.J.: Prentice-Hall, 1969), 86.

2. Samuel Beckett, *Endgame* (New York: Grove Press, 1958), 31. Further
citations to this edition will be given in the text.

3. Samuel Beckett, *Waiting for Godot* (New York: Grove Press, 1954), 39.
Further citations to this edition will be given in the text.

4. Adorno, "Understanding of *Endgame,*" 106.

5. For an authoritative account, see Marvin Carlson, *The Haunted Stage: The
Theatre as Memory Machine* (Ann Arbor: University of Michigan Press, 2001).

6. Eoin O'Brien, *The Beckett Country* (Dublin: Black Cat Press; London:
Faber and Faber, 1986), 305–7; John P. Harrington, *The Irish Beckett* (Syracuse:
Syracuse University Press, 1991), 177; Mary Junker, *Beckett: The Irish Dimension*
(Dublin: Wolfhound Press, 1995), 47–50; see also J. C. C. Mays, "Irish Beckett,
a Borderline Instance," in *Beckett in Dublin,* ed. S. E. Wilmer (Dublin: Lilliput
Press, 1992), 133–46; Rodney Sharkey, "Irish? Au Contraire! The Search for
Identity in the Fictions of Samuel Beckett," *Journal of Beckett Studies* 3, no. 2
(1994): 1–18; and Vivian Mercier, *Beckett/Beckett* (Oxford: Oxford University
Press, 1977).

7. George Petrie, *The Petrie Collection of the Ancient Music of Ireland*
(Dublin: Society for the Preservation and Publication of the Melodies of Ireland,
1855), xii.

8. Petrie, *Petrie Collection,* xii.

9. Terry Eagleton, *Heathcliff and the Great Hunger: Studies in Irish Culture* (London: Verso, 1995), 11–26.

10. Cited in Peter Quinn, "Closets Full of Bones," in *Irish Hunger: Personal Reflections on the Legacy of the Famine,* ed. Tom Hayden (Boulder, Colo.: Roberts Rinehart, 1997), 234–40.

11. *The Theatrical Notebooks of Samuel Beckett,* vol. 1: *Waiting for Godot,* ed. Dougald McMillan and James Knowlson (New York: Grove Press, 1994), 89.

12. *Theatrical Notebooks,* xiv.

13. *Theatrical Notebooks,* 109.

14. Samuel Beckett, *Texts for Nothing* (London: Calder and Boyars, 1974), 27.

15. Eagleton, *Heathcliff,* 282.

5

Urban Landscapes, Theatrical Encounters: Staging the City

Stanton B. Garner Jr.

Critical analysis dissipates the privilege of the lived in urban society. It is only a "plane," or a level. Yet analysis does not make this plane disappear. It exists—as a book. Who reads this open book? Who crosses over its writing? It is not a well-defined subject and yet a succession of acts and encounters constitute on this plane itself urban life, the *urban*.

—HENRI LEFEBVRE,
Writings on Cities

Taking to the Streets

In March 1991, the Living Theatre presented *Rules of Civility and Decent Behavior in Company and Conversation* at their theater on East Third Street in New York City. The play was an adaptation by Hanon Reznikov of a list of 110 rules of conduct that George Washington transcribed as a teenager. "An extraordinary amalgam of good intentions and social myopia" (in Reznikov's words), these rules address issues of practical etiquette (seating arrangements, table manners, when to tip one's hat) and moral behavior (the importance of conscience, reverence toward God).[1] The company presented Washington's injunctions through a series of exercises, rituals, and audience interactions. Dressed in military combat garb, they explored counterpoints and connections: between behavioral and ethical prescription and the complexity of actual human relationships, between social regimentation and the militarism of the United States' recently completed operations against Iraq.

Eleven years after attending this production, what persists in my memory is the play's concluding sequence, in which the actors led the audience outside for a candlelight peace vigil. As we stood on the four corners of Avenue C and Third Street, Alphabet City stretched to our north, south, east, and west in a quartet of darkened vanishing points.

Traffic passed by, as did the occasional pedestrians and neighborhood residents, glancing at us with curiosity or bemusement, ignoring us. Like much of the rest of the play, this closing gesture was marked by a certain earnestness, but it was not without its power (the war was still very much alive as a collective trauma) or its visual beauty. As a nexus of meanings, the moment was resonant, and this resonance was caught up in landscape, environment, location. Superimposed on Valley Forge was the road to Basra; echoed in our candlelight vigil was the rhetoric of a thousand "points of light" and the televisual images of rocket flares over Baghdad. Looming over everything was the city itself, and the act of crossing from the theater to the streets outside became the most overt of the many border and boundary issues that the play as a whole sought to explore. The question of (in)civility was taken to the streets, and New York as a whole disclosed itself as the play's mise-en-scène.[2]

Such moments have their lineage, stretching back through earlier Living Theatre productions (like *Paradise Now*) and other performance events of the 1960s avant-garde to plays like *Waiting for Lefty* that violated the boundaries between theater and city, auditorium and street. In the West, of course, theater has always been intricately tied to the city and its forms of culture. From the Athenian civic and religious festivals, through the public and private theaters of the early modern period, its history parallels the progression(s) of Western urbanism. In North America, theater construction followed the westward migration of settlements in a kind of cultural Manifest Destiny. Marvin Carlson reminds us that "the stability of theatre as an element does not mean that its urban role is stable but, on the contrary, that it has been able to accommodate itself to a variety of urban functions as the city around it has changed."[3] Whether it inhabits the center or the margins of the city, theater has always been deeply implicated in the structure and interplay of civic meanings. At times, theater has constituted an overt reading of the urban text: one thinks of the fifteenth-century pageant theater, which literally traversed the medieval city in a meaning-charged cognitive mapping. But even when the theater has been characterized by a more familiar architectural immobility, it has often devoted itself to the city, its relationships, and its forms of life and culture, both exploring and constructing these meanings within a cultural imaginary. Here, one thinks of the city comedies of Middleton and Dekker, or the plays of Restoration London, with their urbane settings (St. James Park, the Strand). As the genre of location, social network, and detail, comedy, of course, finds a natural home in the densely particularized urban fabric.[4]

In *The Place of the Stage* (1988), Steven Mullaney explores the cultural and ideological place of the late-sixteenth-century public theater within the symbolic topography of Elizabethan London.[5] And in *Places of Performance* (1989), Carlson considers the importance of urban location to the spatial semiotics of theater and theatrical performance. But given the obvious centrality of the city to theatrical culture (and vice versa), it is remarkable how little attention has been paid to the functioning of theater within the urban landscape and how little consideration is given to the parameters of theater as a specifically urban institution and practice. In part, this is a function of the theater itself and the operations by which theatrical performance tends to suspend, render invisible, the fields (spatial, temporal) of actual location. As in earlier periods, playwatching today forms part of a wide network of social practices, and these practices—purchasing tickets, traveling through the city, approaching the theater facade and marquee, milling about the sidewalks and streets during intermission, eating out—negotiate the urban landscape in a number of ways. At the same time, even in most avant-garde theater dramatic performance is constituted, to varying degrees, through the suspension of this contextualizing. Those signals that do manage to penetrate the boundaries of theatrical performance— the rumbling of the subway beneath the New York Public Theater, ambulance sirens—act as uncanny reminders of what is bracketed out, returns of the urban repressed.

It is important to resist this bracketing, to read against the perceptual occlusion of the cityscape, in order to understand the place(s) of theater within the city's material and cultural environment. For while its dramatic locales may reflect a nostalgia for the rural and the undeveloped (the forest of Arden, the fjords of Norway), theater is the most urban of cultural forms. This became particularly true in the twentieth century, when the city itself underwent radical transformation, metamorphosing from the massed population centers of the nineteenth century, through the city center with suburban ring, into what William Sharpe and Leonard Wallock call the "decentered urban field" of the contemporary/postmodern city.[6] Returning twentieth-century theater to its urban contexts allows us to consider its function within a modern and contemporary urban practice. In representational terms, the theater of the past one hundred years has served as a medium for exploring the idea of the city, reading its meanings, exploring the terms of its cultural legibility. In terms of actual performance, more recent theatrical experiments—in particular, Fiona Templeton's 1988 *You—the City* and *Mugger Music,* a 1996–97 performance piece by a group of Manchester-based artists—have explored the relationships between theater and the city, tested and extended the boundaries of theater as a mode of urban experience, and foregrounded the intersecting ecologies of performance and spectatorship.

Theater and Urban Legibility

At the center of the many disciplines (and interdisciplines) that concern themselves with the city—urban studies, architecture, urban planning, cultural geography, environmental psychology, landscape studies, urban sociology, and cultural studies—are questions of spatial *legibility*. In his 1960 study *The Image of the City*, Kevin Lynch used the term to describe the ease with which the parts of a cityscape can be recognized and organized into a coherent pattern.[7] Influenced by the semiotic notion of the city as "urban text," subsequent urban analysis has extended the notion of legibility to include the intricate structures of historical, spatial, socioeconomic, and cultural meanings that constitute the modern urban landscape. In this sense, contemporary urban analysis constitutes the academic edge of a broader set of concerns that link municipal planners, architects, and urban dwellers alike: the nature of the meanings inscribed in districts, neighborhoods, structures, sites of encounter; the city as place and idea; and the terms and limits of its readability. As the city expands its boundaries and its definition, and as the culture of the twenty-first century becomes increasingly urbanized, the pursuit of urban intelligibility stands as a dominant cultural activity.

Given that the contemporary city is both a geographical locale and "a category of thought and experience," it is not surprising that the literary and performative arts should have played such an important role in the cognitive/interpretive activity by which the modern city is mapped and, in a sense, constructed.[8] As James Donald writes, "In order to imagine the unrepresentable space, life, and languages of the city, to make them liveable, we translate them into narratives."[9] It is hard to imagine Dublin apart from its fictional representation in James Joyce's fiction, and the development of the "idea" of the European and North American city over the past 150 years is, in large part, a product of the literary cities of such writers as Charles Dickens, Upton Sinclair, Virginia Woolf, and contemporary urban novelists. Literary preoccupation with the urban is particularly pronounced, of course, among modernist writers. Modernism as a literary movement was deeply involved in the cosmopolitanism, technological and stylistic innovation, multiplicity, and dislocations of urban experience. Malcolm Bradbury notes, "Modernist art has had special relations with the modern city . . . in its role both as cultural museum and novel environment."[10] But literary naturalism was also grounded in the modern metropolis, and postmodernist writers have likewise shown an interest in the modern city, its archaeologies and geographies, and its possibilities of meaning and encounter. Across the spectrum of literary movements and styles—realist, modernist, and postmodernist—the modern city has often been taken as a prototype of literary form.

Despite the centrality of theaters—traditional and avant-garde—to the modern city's cultural and social landscape, drama has tended not to be considered in the company of fiction, poetry, or film as a mode of imagining the city.[11] This omission is surprising, for dramatic representation in the twentieth century was deeply concerned with the modern and postmodern cityscapes and the changing meanings with which they have been invested. In its avant-garde forms, theatrical modernism demonstrated a recurrent fascination with the metropolis as a repository of cultural meanings and as a field of social and exteriorized psychological conflict. Jean Cocteau's *Wedding on the Eiffel Tower* is set against the background of "a bird's-eye view of Paris"; in keeping with the play's conflation of the photographic and the pictorial, Irène Lagut's setting for the original production depicted this panorama as a patterned cubist landscape.[12] Bertolt Brecht's *Drums in the Night* sets its narrative of postwar Germany against an expressionistic city terrain, while the Chicago of *In the Jungle of Cities* (subtitled *The Fight between Two Men in the Gigantic City of Chicago*) is a place of mythic size and lawlessness, labyrinthine and predatory, a phantasmagoria of American capitalist urbanization. The second half of Eugene O'Neill's *Hairy Ape* moves through a differently stylized urban field: from Fifth Avenue to Blackwell's Island to the waterfront, its New York is both an arena of social demarcations and something more nightmarish—the projection of inner alienation, a theatrical echo of T. S. Eliot's "Unreal City."

Because of its representational limitations, realist and naturalist drama has tended to rely on more explicitly metonymic strategies for staging urban landscapes. Tennessee Williams's *The Glass Menagerie,* for instance, represents St. Louis as a whole through the Wingfield apartment, its adjoining alley, and other immediate surroundings; Williams comments in his stage directions: "The Wingfield apartment is in the rear of the building, one of those vast hive-like conglomerations of cellular living-units that flower as warty growths in overcrowded urban centers of lower middle-class population."[13] As these remarks suggest, the materiality of the realist stage—the density of its object-world— itself functions metonymically to suggest the perceptual and material density of urban experience. Materially invested in this way, the realist mise-en-scène works in often striking efforts to map the city and its social and subjective meanings. George Bernard Shaw's plays, for example, offer a dramatic cartography of late-nineteenth- and early-twentieth-century London. Chancery Lane in *Mrs. Warren's Profession,* northeast London in *Candida,* the symbolic contrast of Wilton Crescent and West Ham in *Major Barbara*—Shaw maps this London in terms of its demographic boundaries, its zones of socioeconomic belonging and exclusion. The London that emerges in Shaw's drama is one of legibility and intellectual transparency, offering itself to totalizing classification. In the character of Henry Higgins—who boasts, "*I* can place [any man] within two miles in London. Sometimes within two streets"—Shaw offers an analogue of the playwright as urban ethnographer.[14]

Exploring the more fluid parameters of an "expressive" or "poetic" realism, the canonical plays of postwar American theater extended the pursuit of urban intelligibility to the psychological and sociological landscapes of midcentury urbanization. *A Streetcar Named Desire* appropriates the city of New Orleans both poetically and allegorically, gesturing toward its history of cultural encounter and mapping its psychic attractions and terrors (the streetcar, of course, is the principal spatializing metaphor here). Arthur Miller's *Death of a Salesman* draws upon a more explicitly expressionist stagecraft—"towering, angular shapes" surround the Loman house—in its portrayal of a New York that counterpoints (and menaces) the memories of more pastoral times.[15] In Edward Albee's *Zoo Story,* the same city is mapped with the detailing of an itinerary: as the play's characters sit in Central Park, they recount their movements through the city with cartographic precision, and the urban text disclosed by their conversation is invested with meanings both public and covert (the west side of the park as a gay meeting place, for instance). At the same time, as Jerry's monologue indicates, the New York presented in Albee's play is a city of widespread alienation, with eccentric individuals living in isolated apartments. As in the subway car of Amiri Baraka's *Dutchman,* hurtling through "the flying underbelly of the city," the unexplained violence of the play's conclusion suggests the fundamental unreadability of contemporary urban experience.[16]

With *A Zoo Story,* one can observe the emergence of a different, more contemporary image of the city, increasingly opaque, characterized by a deepening dissociation between individual experience and the wider urban text. Subsequent drama tends to reject the globalizing glance that pretends to contain the city as material/cognitive terrain. In the postmodern world of Sam Shepard's *Angel City,* the paradigmatically postmodern Los Angeles has been reduced to its mediatized image, knowable only in cinematic and televisual terms. A place of images, it demonstrates, as Edward W. Soja writes, the "growing power of an urban hyperreality, of simulations and simulacra."[17] To the extent that the city exists in these plays as material environment, it has disintegrated into atomized locales. The characters of David Mamet's *American Buffalo,* for example, inhabit a backstreet urban world. The Chicago that surrounds them is evident largely in the urban detritus of Don's Resale Shop, which mirrors the larger city in a kind of broken archaeology. Unlike the city of Lorraine Hansberry's *Raisin in the Sun,* whose neighborhoods are transparently overwritten with the history of successive migrations, the Chicago of *American Buffalo* is ultimately unknowable (what hospital is Fletch in?) and (for the play's two-bit characters, at least) uninhabitable in other than marginal, dissociated spaces. This cognitive impasse is echoed in Stephen Poliakoff's British city plays of the 1970s. One of the central characters in *Hitting Town* refers to the unnamed Midlands city in which he grew up: "Whole center has changed—me and my sister used to know a different place. Imagine being locked in here, the rest of your life unable to get out."[18] With the memory of the Birmingham bombing still fresh, the city is now menacing, defamiliarized, its only form of legibility the graffiti that marks its wall.

The Theatricality of Urban Space: Performing the City

As this brief survey suggests, representations of the urban landscape in twentieth-century drama are remarkably varied in their symbolic and cognitive appropriations of the modern and contemporary city. At the same time, both avant-garde and more traditional drama tend to share a certain conservatism in addressing actual urban terrains. The very transportability of urban representations in this drama—*Angel City* opened at the Magic Theater in San Francisco, *A Streetcar Named Desire* opened at the Barrymore Theater in New York, and many of the plays mentioned above have played in nonurban theaters—underscores (as we have seen) the extent to which traditional theater depends on the suspension, or deactivation, of the specific urban environment.

More radical practitioners of twentieth-century theater challenged this experiential deactivation and sought to reinterrogate the relationship between the theater and its urban landscapes. With its strategies for breaking down the boundaries separating audience and stage, twentieth-century environmental theater and scenographic practice sought to incorporate the material context of performance within the theatrical event itself. From the Soviet restaging of the storming of the Winter Palace in Petrograd and Max Reinhardt's outdoor production of *The Merchant of Venice* in Venice to Peter Brook's use of the Théâtre des Bouffes du Nord and its proletarian north-Paris location for the work of his International Centre of Theatre Research, the city has regularly formed part of an avant-garde redefinition of performance space. In 1991, the London International Festival of Theatre (LIFT) devised a program entitled "Lifting London," which featured site-specific theater and performance works mounted throughout metropolitan London.[19] More specifically political theater groups—the Living Theatre, the Performance Group, Bread and Puppet Theater—have likewise claimed the urban milieu as performance landscape, thereby linking theater with other modes of civic and urban performance: parades, pageants, other public events, street entertainment. The flourishing of political street theater during the 1960s and 1970s reflected a broader radical understanding of the city as political field. In this sense, Bread and Puppet's New York street processions and the performances of the San Francisco Mime Troupe in city parks worked to occupy and revoice the urban text with strategies similar to those of the civil rights marches, antiwar demonstrations, sit-ins, and other forms of urban protest. Such performances—theatrical and nontheatrical alike—evoked Brecht's *Street Scene* and its suggestion that the roots of political theater can be discovered at the intersections (pun intended) of urban encounter, performance, and spectatorship.[20]

This tradition of activist urban theater remains: one thinks of John Malpede's Los Angeles Poverty Department (LAPD), which elicits theater from the margins of urban culture, and the "invisible theater" of Augusto Boal, which foregrounds and performs the structures of power that constitute the city's relational infrastructure. Jan Cohen-Cruz's anthology *Radical Street Performance* documents recent appropriations of urban space for performative interventions by artists as varied as Belgrade's Dah Teatar, Calcutta's Suman Chatterjee, and New York's Circus Amok.[21] But the political and performance culture that sustained activist street theater during its heyday have clearly undergone profound changes. While individual artists and groups continued to claim the streets for political performance, other urban theater artists of the late 1980s and 1990s pursued more broadly environmental strategies of framing and defamiliarization, exploiting theater's modes of seeing and presentation in order both to engage the city's material and social landscapes and to disclose the wider theatricality of urban space. Rejecting the immobility of conventional spectatorship, these works explore the intersections of theatrical and urban practice. As such, they extend the impulse evident in theatrical urban representation—to locate the terms of the city's legibility and the parameters of its inhabitability—into the field of actual encounter. If, as Henri Lefebvre suggests, the city is "not only a language, but also a practice," then *You—the City* and *Mugger Music* extend the quest for urban intelligibility into the very practices— walking, seeing, interacting—that constitute the city as a *lived* field of spatial meanings.[22]

The works of urban environmental theater I am concerned with here have their genealogy, one with strong roots in the visual and sculptural arts. Among the practitioners of what Allan Kaprow calls "assemblage, environments and happenings" in the late 1950s and 1960s, the urban landscape emerged as a particularly complex performative and interactive field. The work of German artist Wolf Vostell is striking in this regard. In *Cityrama I,* held in September 1961, spectators were sent on a route through a Cologne still scarred by war and instructed to perform specific activities at twenty-six designated sites. In *Ligne Petite Ceinture,* mounted the following year, participants were sent on a bus around Paris and instructed to notice the cityscape revealed along this route: "Keep a look out for the acoustic and at the same time optical impressions. Noises—cries—voices—walls with placards torn or hanging down—(décollages) debris—ruins etc."[23] In both events, the city was transformed into the theatricalized space of performance, and its landscape became the material for shaping acts of artistic and spectatorial consciousness. Cited and defamiliarized in this way, the city's routes and locales became scenes where the historical, the everyday, and the artistic displayed their overlapping claims. The boundaries between the urban and the aesthetic became radically unsettled; no longer backdrop, the city was refigured within "the total art of décollage."[24]

In his May 1976 theater piece *Light Touch,* environmental artist Robert Whitman offered a similar framing of the city's urban fields. *Light Touch* was mounted in a warehouse on Washington Street near the docks in New York's Greenwich Village. In the work's central sequence, the lights were extinguished and a sliding warehouse loading door was opened across from the seated spectators. Through the floor-to-ceiling opening—a makeshift proscenium, bounded by flowing curtains on either side—the city, subtly theatricalized, became its own performance. Like the background sounds in a John Cage composition, the city's sensory texture—lights, sounds, movements, the passing of cars—emerged as a kind of found art, now stripped of the familiarity that normally rendered it unnoticed. When a truck eventually pulled up at the loading dock and its contents were unloaded—an apple, a cement block, and a kitchen sink—these objects stood in the spotlight as precipitates, representatives of a sort, from the newly luminous urban field.[25]

In sketching out the genealogy of contemporary urban environmental theater, one might also point to the work of Squat Theatre, the expatriate Hungarian group that settled in New York in the late 1970s. Performing in a building on West Twenty-third Street, the company incorporated the city as found environment into their theatrical productions. In *Andy Warhol's Last Days* (1978), the audience sat facing a stage beyond which was a ground-floor storefront window. At various points throughout the play, film projections directed the audience's attention to scenes throughout the city: a performer with an Andy Warhol mask, for instance, rode a horse through the streets of the financial district. A video camera and microphones brought the scenes and sounds of the street to a monitor inside. When curtains were drawn from the window in the work's final act, the city became an even more radical presence in the performance. As outside spectators gathered and looked in, the inside audience found itself doubled and unsettled by the spectatorial cross-gaze. Like Whitman's door frame, the storefront window rendered the urban field itself a performance. As Theodore Shank writes, "Members of Squat Theatre have said that they came to realize while still in their Budapest apartment that when they looked into the windows of other apartments, natural everyday actions took on a theatrical quality."[26] Framed by the window and by the act of theatrical watching, the streets, figures, and actions of the West Side Chelsea neighborhood— and, by extension, the city as a whole—became a multiply theatricalized space, constituted through overlapping acts of performance and spectatorship. The demarcations between theater and city were destabilized, and the latter asserted itself as the work's ultimate performance field.

Landscapes of Urban Encounter: You—the City

Ten years after *Andy Warhol's Last Love, You—the City*—a play by British-born poet, playwright, and director Fiona Templeton—was mounted in New York (*You—the City* was performed from May 18–June 5, 1988; subsequent productions have been held in Ljubljana, London, The Hague, Zurich, and Munich). Described in the introduction to the published text as "an intimate Manhattanwide play for an audience of one," the performance was structured to provide individual spectators with a sequence of encounters at twelve locations in Times Square and the Hell's Kitchen area to its west.[27] Spectators (or "clients," as they were referred to) arrived by appointment at ten-minute intervals at an office building at One Times Square, where they were greeted, asked to fill out a questionnaire (with questions like "Why You?"), and passed on to a fictional "executive." Like those of the play's other performers, the executive's speech was a monologue with occasionally cryptic sentences addressed to "you." When this particular encounter was completed, the client was led by a second performer to the street and a continuing sequence of encounters with (among others) a "consumed consumer," a street person, and a woman who addressed the client through a two-way mirror in a room within a Forty-sixth Street club called the Harlequin. The client was eventually driven to a playground between Ninth and Tenth Avenues, where a series of further encounters began: in this second "act," the client actually encountered other clients at later and earlier stages of their movement through the play's itinerary. Clients passed each other in an elaborately choreographed crossover on a basketball court; in a nearby apartment, encounters were staged with different clients and performers in the same room. At a specified time in the apartment scene, each client received a phone call. After crossing the playground a second time, the client was brought to a cafe, where she or he received a program and had a chance to share the experience of You—the City with performers and other clients. Twenty-two clients could be accommodated during each day's performance (which ran from 3:00 to 8:20 P.M.), and fake clients were deployed at the beginning and end of each cycle to ensure the required circulation and crossovers. The timing of each encounter was worked through to the minute, and contingency arrangements were developed in case anything failed to go according to schedule. During any day's run, You—the City required fourteen performers and a sizable support crew.

In his essay "Walking in the City" (one of the chapters of his 1974 book The Practice of Everyday Life), Michel de Certeau contrasts two mutually contesting modes of apprehending the city. Reflected in the view from the 110th floor of the now-vanished World Trade Center, the "panoramic city" is an essentially theoretical entity, an administrative construction that erases the complexity and density of actual urban practice within a fiction of pure readability. In contrast to this totalizing image is the city from below and within, the city as it is traversed, mapped, and obscured by everyday practices like that of walking. "Beneath the discourses that ideologize the city, the ruses and combinations of powers that have no readable identity proliferate."[28] As a mode and practice of urban habitation, walking the city becomes a way of redrawing the city's landscape, appropriating its routes and landmarks, creating shadows and ambiguities within the urban text. "Walking affirms, suspects, tries out, transgresses, respects, etc., the trajectories it 'speaks.'"[29] Like the graffiti on New York subway cars, walking constitutes a subversive rhetoric whose opacity and subjective contours mock the panoptic fantasies of modernist/utopian urbanism.

By theorizing walking as a mode of urban practice and clarifying the issues of legibility that such practices negotiate, de Certeau's essay offers a useful reference point for considering the experience of urban habitation performed in Templeton's play. "The long poem of walking," for de Certeau, forms part of the wider tactical repertoire of everyday practices by which individuals trace their own paths through the landscape of functionalist rationality.[30] A sense of this subjective creativity is clearly evoked in *You—the City*. Templeton writes: "In theater that uses more than one site . . . the movement of the mind, in the body, through the order of their successive resonances, and the resonances of the four-dimensional topography thus traced, reflects the city itself" (144). But walking in *You—the City* (and its companion modes of locomotion, including riding in a taxi) occupy a different, more complicated, field of assertion and encounter than de Certeau's transgressive *flânerie*. Whereas de Certeau's urban pedestrian exercises a transgressive agency, the participants in *You—the City* undertake a spatial journey that is both choreographed and (in large measure) scripted. Subject to the performance constraints of Templeton's script, the act of walking engages a challenging, often ambiguous interaction of the internal and the external, of self and other. Templeton notes: "Like an analogue of the mind in the world and vice versa, the city is an experience of simultaneous interiority and exteriority" (144). It is also, one might add, an experience of the simultaneously private and public. Denied the theater's insulated space, the solo spectator/participant in Templeton's play undergoes a series of encounters that explore the line between the personal and the anonymous in urban interactions: addressing a security guard, riding in a cab, encountering a street person. As one of the reviewers of the London production observed, "The experience is immediately reminiscent of other occasions where intimacy is artificially induced: therapy, prostitution, fortune-telling, being button-holed by a looney."[31]

The title *You—the City,* therefore, addresses less the transgressive presence of the "you" within "the city" than the relationship between the two and the terms by which each comes to inhabit (at times, invade) the other. What marks Templeton's play is the extent to which language mediates the individual's encounter with the city. Clients are taken through a Manhattan of storefronts, churches, streets, and playgrounds, and they are exposed to the sounds, smells, and gritty surfaces of this urban environment. But the New York disclosed by *You—the City* is also a wordscape, and its interpersonal fields are encountered discursively. The play's script is an often surreal pastiche that alternates between stock phrases (one of the performers is encouraged to improvise using "well-known public songs, ads, bywords, fictional clichés, idioms, billboards visible as you walk along" [12]) and more subjective meditations. Oscillating in and out of sense with the associative logic of surrealist automatic writing, Templeton's text approximates a kind of transurban speech, a running stream of language—overheard, received, thought, spoken—that constitutes the city as interrelational space. That this text is passed on (like the clients) between the play's performers underscores the jointly monologic and collective nature of urban discourse.

The pronoun *you,* of course, is at the center of this discursive stream. As the performers question, address, and harangue the client over the course of the play's two and a half hours, *you* is established as one of the play's principal scenic terrains. What is the relationship of this *you* to the spectator and to the performer's equally intimate/depersonalized *I?* Templeton's text plays freely with the shift between the individualized and the collective; like the strip-show club's dividing screen, which superimposed the client's own reflection on a ghostly image of the performer, the deployments of *you* as a performance variable foregrounded the unclear boundaries of identity and encounter. Toward the end of the play, the client is invited to "make YOU yours" (123) and to assume the power of speaking *you* within the play and the city that serves as its setting. By this point, the pronoun has been disclosed as a field of subjective and collective experience as interwoven as that of the city itself. Given that the power of *you* is now deployed by the former target of the play's linguistic interrogation, the *I* from which it will hereby be spoken is similarly decentered. Like the clients who cross each other on the basketball court, the categories *I* and *you* are interchangeable; in the play's linguistic circularity, the pursuit of each entails the discovery of the other: "You don't recognize your wall-eyed self till you see a stranger" (9).[32]

In a survey of contemporary environmental performance, Steve Nelson raises questions about the transgressiveness of Templeton's piece. Noting that the play's verbal text makes no explicit references to the actual locales surrounding it and that the spectator/client has few opportunities to intervene in its scripted textuality, Nelson suggests that

Basketball court scene from Fiona Templeton's *You—the City*, New York City, 1988. (Film by Jeff Preiss, photo courtesy of Fiona Templeton and Franklin Furnace.)

You—the City hinges, finally, on voyeurism and simulated experience. The play's words "serve to insulate performer and client from the real world at the same time they play against the grain of the piece's environment—the edgy, threatening world of New York City's streets."[33] Certainly, *You—the City* does operate within a suspension of consequence (this is, after all, only theater), and its mysterious chain of encounters does require a certain trust on the part of each spectator radically different from the usual mode of being-in-the-city (as one participant expressed it, "You knew you weren't going to die" [2]). But Nelson's judgment overweighs the insularity of the play's governing strategies. The surrounding city was an active component in the performance of *You—the City,* and this presence was felt in the neighborhood-specific meanings that the play's encounters evoked (street person, strip joint exchange) and in the environmental signals that formed an explicit part of the play's scenic field: "Use the geography and its inhabitants to the full," one of the performer instructions reads: "Give your silences time to let the surroundings provide the text" (102).

The urban field and its unpredictabilities impinged upon the performance in more radically interactive ways, as well. Tourists sought to intervene in one exchange between a client and the fictional street person, and nearby street vendors became concerned during one encounter between a client and the histrionically gesturing "concerned consumer" (in the streets, of course, such histrionics are read as derangement). On the last day of the London production, a street demonstration was held in a mainly Bengali section of Spitalfields, where the second half of the play was being conducted. For the performers of *You—the City,* the line between performance and urban reality was even more precarious, the potential for accident and interruption even greater. Performers playing the cab driver had to contend with actual Manhattan traffic, while those stationed in Hell's Kitchen themselves became features of the urban environment and its narratives: one female performer was known as the "Cat Lady" by neighborhood Puerto Ricans, another was thought to be a cop on the lookout for crack fiends, and several were approached by a local pimp. In playful subversion of the play's performative boundaries, children at the playground memorized the performers' lines and often chimed along in unison.

As these anecdotes suggest, *You—the City* problematizes the notion of the urban real essential to Nelson's critique. By appropriating the city itself as theatrical milieu, Templeton's play sought to defamiliarize the cityscape and interrogate the terms of its disclosure. A blurring of boundaries was central to this dynamic. Moving through the play's itinerary, spectator/clients found themselves caught in an ambiguity of framing. Were individuals performers or "real" people? Reading for clues, some clients imagined performers where none were present (one woman started to go off with a real panhandler who approached her). Unsettling the boundaries between the real and the theatrical in this way, the city itself was disclosed within an ambiguously performative mode. One client described going home after participating in the play: "When I saw these kids threatening each other, when I saw guys in a huddle in the subway, when someone addressed me, it all seemed like it was part of the show or the scenery" (133). As Templeton herself observed, "Clients go off afterwards wondering what line they draw between spectacle and the real just to get themselves home" (139).[34] Such confusions result, in part, from the discontinuities between the protected space of Templeton's play and the urban milieu in which it took place. But they also result from a more radical revelation. For the city performed by *You—the City* is itself deeply theatricalized, constituted through rituals, scripted utterance, performance acts, spectatorship, scenes of encounter. Seen in this way, the urban real is less an ontological given than an intersubjective construct, "performed" at multiple sites, continually renegotiated. By exploring the ways in which the urban landscape frames itself, Templeton's disclosure of the city—of being-in-the-city—raises questions crucial to the theater and its urban fields: How does performance (re)frame the environment in which it takes place? How does the city (re)frame the performances that take place within it? And how does theater as a specifically urban form intersect with the broader theatricality of urban life?

From Urban Warren to Cybercity: Mugger Music

Mugger Music, a more recent experiment in urban environmental theater, also explores the intersections between theatrical disclosure and the city's own modes of habitation, encounter, and spectatorship; at the same time, through a series of different performative strategies, it offers an even more intensified focus on the cityscape as a repository of urban meanings. The piece was first mounted in Manchester, England, on May 11, 1996, by Nick Crowe, Jane Gant, Graham Parker, and Ian Rawlinson. All four artists were associated with the Loading Deck, a studio theater in central Manchester. Since its establishment in May 1993 (and in connection with the Index Theatre Co-operative, 1989–95), the Loading Deck has developed and sponsored a series of site-specific performance and installation works designed to explore the "variety of contexts that

make up the end of century urban warren."[35] Its September 1994 production *The Alphabet of Dogs* was set in the Oliver Machine Works, a
large abandoned Manchester factory that was appropriated as a representative of other urban industrial sites abandoned by an increasingly
postindustrial world. Manchester, of course, is a resonant city for such
an installation: as the first industrial urban center (Friedrich Engels used
it to demonstrate the squalor of capitalist urbanization in *The Condition
of the Working Class in England*), the city has struggled to find its place
within the economic transformations of capitalist postmodernity.

   Mugger Music extended this exploration of the city's urban terrain
and industrial legacy. Staged over a period of twenty-four hours, the
piece involved single performers leading individual audience members
on a route along the River Medlock, which runs through Manchester;
they left every half hour, and each itinerary took roughly ninety minutes
to complete. Participants were led to and past a number of sites and into
particular buildings: a hotel lobby, a snooker hall, the Loading Deck
itself. The choice of the Medlock as performance site was strategic. In
the words of the works' authors/designers,

> The Medlock is a largely hidden river since a lot of old ware-
> houses and railway arches back onto it and it is thus rarely vis-
> ible to passers by. So although Manchester was founded on the
> river, years of cultural, industrial and physical sedimentation
> have accumulated to rewrite and disguise it. *Mugger Music*
> takes this sedimentation as its starting point and considers
> how the processes of cultural and ideological sedimentation
> also construct the cities we live in.[36]

Alternatingly visible and invisible, the Medlock became both register
and metaphor of urban overwriting, transformation, and neglect.

   In June 1997, Crowe, Parker, and Rawlinson remounted *Mugger
Music* in New York under the auspices of the Lower Manhattan Cultural
Council.[37] The piece was performed in a series of routes and locations
throughout New York's financial district, and though its sequence of
activities followed the Manchester production in many ways, its itinerary was adapted to the very different material, historical, and economic
landscape of lower Manhattan. As in Manchester, participants departed
at thirty-minute intervals over a twenty-four-hour period (midnight to
midnight).

   After being met by a guide at a prearranged time and place, each
participant was given a tape player with headphones, as in an organized
walking tour, and told to listen. This tape featured a series of recorded

Nick Crowe and Graham Parker on the set of *Mugger Music,*
New York City, 1997. (Photo by Ian Rawlinson.)

questions ("In which city do you live? How long have you lived there?
Were you born in that city?") and the anonymous voices of people
responding. Throughout the walk, each participant listened to an additional tape featuring urban sounds and conversations. Over the course of
the seventy-five- to ninety-minute performance, each was brought to a
number of sites where she or he engaged in prearranged rituals. Participants were taken to the Millennium Hotel, past the Vietnam Memorial
and the New York Stock Exchange, into a suite in the New York Technology Center. Outside the Chase Manhattan Bank headquarters, the
guide read the bank's mission statement. At a deli, each participant was
asked to purchase something with her or his own money. Earlier, each
was instructed to engrave her or his name with a pin on a card-shaped
piece of wax. These objects played their part in a dynamic of exchange:
the signed wax was taken from the participant and replaced with a similar card from another participant, and the purchased item was taken
from the participant (a ritualized mugging?) and left on a table at an
abandoned historic restaurant. In this semidarkened restaurant, the participant was invited to drink a glass of milk from a refrigerator in the
middle of the room, and the empty glass was left on the table with oth-

ers that had been left before in an expanding "found" installation. Performed in this way, the city was disclosed as a field of traces, marked by the steady accumulation of objects at once personal and anonymous. As Ginger Strand noted in her review of the piece, *Mugger Music* "provided a means for reimagining urban space, and contemplating one's role in the creation of the palimpsest that is the late twentieth-century city."[38]

In a meditation on the nature of onstage and offstage in both city and theatrical performance, one of the most interesting sequences in *Mugger Music* took place in a loft. Having brought the participant into a room containing documentation and organizational materials for the performance piece (maps, schedules, equipment), the guide went to another room. There, he (the guides in both productions were male) took advantage of one of the few opportunities to rest during the piece (and during a day spent walking the city): he would sit, eat or drink, change clothes. All of this was visible on a closed-circuit monitor to the participant in the main room. The experience of watching this performance of offstage life suggested the shifting boundaries between the public and the private; as a stage in the participant-guide encounter, it established unexpected intimacy in a relationship that had maintained a certain distance and reserve up to this point. At the same time, of course, this disclosure took place during a moment of absence and disembodiment. That its intimacy was experienced, voyeuristically, through video technology underscored the increasingly mediatized, displaced nature of contemporary encounters.

Mugger Music was organized in terms of "one performer leading one audience member through the immense complexity of a city occurring before them."[39] Like *You—the City,* it sought to defamiliarize the city for those who had learned to screen out its material and human landscapes. The choice of the financial district for the New York production was motivated, in part, by the desire to challenge this screening and to offer a more phenomenologically and cognitively direct encounter with the urban built environment:

> In New York, possibly more than any other place on earth, people tend to walk with a real sense of purpose and a fixed destination. Partly because of the layout of the streets and partly as an act of survival. There's very little drift. One of the interesting things about the financial district is obviously the break up of the grid at that point, which gives us a kind of starting point for physically altering people's usual criteria for movement.[40]

One of the work's participants describes both the experience of defamiliarization and the blurring of perceptual frames brought about by the work's strategies of disclosure:

> I begin to see things. Chunks of crud, elderly men wearing eye-liner, braless young woman on Rollerblades (today it will hit ninety), pathetic looking young junior execs with badly sprayed cowlicks emerging from the 4–5 express. I wonder how many have been placed by the artist.[41]

In its engagement of urban environment, the piece was structured to exploit the city's rhythms and cycles. While each participant was given an experience with its own beginning, middle, and end, the performance as a whole, taking place over twenty-four hours, was grounded in the city's diurnal transformations: night, dawn, rush hour, midday, rush hour, what evening life the financial district affords, night again. But while *Mugger Music* constructed time with an almost classical unity, it refused a totalizing view of the city: no Joycean Bloomsday here. Just as the walking route represented only one set of trajectories through the city's urban landscape—different mappings of the performance event would yield different itineraries of encounter—individual performances constituted only a segment of this temporal whole. Even as guide and participant engaged with a material and human totality, the moment was shadowed by other moments, other urban incarnations and possibilities: evening by the memory of the city's daytime throngs, midday by the silence of the streets at night. Like the Manhattan skyline, evident here only in partial and receding views, the city existed both inside and outside the field of vision.

Theatricalizing urban space through acts of scripted walking, *Mugger Music* was clearly influenced by *You—the City*. At the same time, the cities disclosed by the two pieces are radically different. The city explored by Templeton's play remains the metropolis we have known for most of the century—singular, mappable, voiceable through the shared space of interpersonal encounter. Deploying a dramaturgy of tracings, excavations, and electronic transmissions, *Mugger Music*, by contrast, rejects the notion of the singular city with its continuous time and space in favor of the postmodern city, multiple, decentered, increasingly mediatized. Superimposed on the New York of skyscrapers—the mappable landscape of buildings and streets, the city of aerial postcards and "I Love New York" campaigns—were other New Yorks. As in Manchester, there was the city sedimented with history, the archaeological city, the city as palimpsest. Counterpointing the imposing monuments of real estate speculation were structures like the eighteenth-century Fraunces Tavern, ghostly reminders of earlier moments in the city's physical and demographic history. To walk the streets of lower Manhattan and enter its structures was to negotiate the boundaries between the owned and the disowned and to encounter the spaces of a residual urban fabric. There was also the invisible city (to borrow Italo Calvino's title) embodied in the buildings and people of the financial district. Standing behind the material and human congestion of Wall Street and its surroundings at midday was the city as a nodal point within late-century capitalism, the New York of financial markets and futures trading, a city defined less by its physical boundaries and urban infrastructures than by its place within the flow of multinational capitalism. In this network of urban elsewheres, Tokyo and London are closer than Jersey City or White Plains.

Though subject to its own competing structures of legibility and illegibility, in short, the physical New York of *Mugger Music* was also invaded by other spaces, palimpsestic traces, postmodern modes of spatial relationship that subvert the geographical integrity of the traditional and modern cities. In this city, dominant, residual, and emergent exist within a field that is temporally and spatially discontinuous, multiply determined. The performance strategies of *Mugger Music* gestured toward this reconceptualization of the urban in one final, striking way. After rejoining the guide in the loft, the participant was photographed by another performer. These "mug shots" were collected and uploaded on the Internet as an artistic installation in its own right. As Crowe and his collaborators explained,

> One of the recurrent strands of the work is this accumulation of trace material from people, whether that's their name being etched or their trace on a video camera. We see the Internet . . . as a site just like any of the others we use. It's a place to leave a trace.[42]

Mugger Music and the projects out of which it emerged formed the subject of a number of interlocking websites, including the Total New York website, which (until it was discontinued in fall 1999) featured information, interviews, and photographs related to the performance event. This cyber-installation was intriguing in the ways it explored and extended the notion of performance documentation, complicating *Mugger Music*'s phenomenology of traces and proliferating its channels and modes of access. For one thing, the theater event itself further surrendered its spatial and temporal coordinates and its demarcations between the live and the mediated. This extension of the art/performance moment into the different spatiotemporality of the Internet recalled Crowe's geographical extravaganza *One Day and All of the Night,* a live/interactive web project held on the 1996 World AIDS Day in which video cameras filmed the change between day and night over a twenty-four-hour period at four sites around the globe.[43]

The cyber-record of *Mugger Music* as a performance event expanded the piece's exploration of postmodern urbanness. If *Mugger Music* engaged the city's sensory and cognitive fields, its localized strands of meanings and allusion, it also evoked the virtual city, deterritorialized, dematerialized, digitally global. As a 1994 British Channel 4 program on the virtual city claimed, "The chaos of American urban sprawl belongs not just to the city of steel and glass, but also to the other city—the phantom city of media and information. With most resources devoted to it, it is the cyber-city which is accelerating faster than the real urban space."[44] Cities like Lagos, Jakarta, and Mexico City, their infrastructures buckling under uncontainable population and material growth, may temper such a claim. But the nature of the urban is clearly changing, and emerging from the explosion of telecommunications is a rival metropolis, with its disembodied geography of televillages, cyber cafes, and information superhighways.

"Any city is too complex to reduce to a single meaning," the play's designers note. "We just establish. . . an intimate contact and ritual structure that allows people to block out or receive as much information as they choose to."[45] Such contact, *Mugger Music* suggests, can be complicated and elusive; the city's sounds are both live and recorded on tape, and its channels of encounter are increasingly technologized. The implications of this multiple-channeled urban disclosure are profound—both for our understanding of the contemporary city and for the field of postmodern theater and performance. In both spheres, we find ourselves faced anew with questions of boundaries, materiality, representation. If the contemporary city is a site of displacement, traces, and mediatization, then its staging involves a similar negotiation between two kinds of landscapes, the physical and the dematerialized, the archaeological and the virtual, the inhabited and the empty.

NOTES

1. Hanon Reznikov, "Director's Note," program for the Living Theatre, *Rules of Civility and Decent Behavior in Company and in Conversation,* n.p.

2. When the company performed the play in Rome, they held the candle-light vigil outside the American Embassy on the Via Veneto; the Embassy called the police and the company was forced to disperse (John Tytell, *The Living Theatre: Art, Exile, and Outrage* [New York: Grove, 1995], 347).

3. Marvin Carlson, *Places of Performance: The Semiotics of Theatre Architecture* (Ithaca, N.Y.: Cornell University Press, 1989), 7.

4. See, for instance, Gregory W. Dobrov, ed., *The City as Comedy: Society as Representation in Athenian Comedy* (Chapel Hill: University of North Carolina Press, 1997).

5. Steven Mullaney, *The Place of the Stage: License, Play, and Power in Renaissance England* (Chicago: University of Chicago Press, 1988).

6. William Sharpe and Leonard Wallock, "From 'Great Town' to 'Nonplace Urban Realm': Reading the Modern City," in *Visions of the Modern City: Essays in History, Art, and Literature,* ed. William Sharpe and Leonard Wallock (Baltimore: Johns Hopkins University Press, 1987), 11.

7. Kevin Lynch, *The Image of the City* (Cambridge: MIT Press, 1960), 2–3.

8. James Donald, "This, Here, Now: Imagining the Modern City," in *Imagining Cities: Scripts, Signs, Memory,* ed. Sallie Westwood and John Williams (London: Routledge, 1997), 181.

9. Ibid., 186.

10. Malcolm Bradbury, "The Cities of Modernism," in *Modernism, 1890–1930,* ed. Malcolm Bradbury and James McFarlane (Harmondsworth: Penguin, 1976), 97.

11. See, for example, *Literature and the Urban Experience: Essays on the City and Literature,* ed. Michael C. Jaye and Ann Chalmers Watts (New Brunswick, N.J.: Rutgers University Press, 1981), which features a range of essays on poetry and fiction but only one article on theater.

12. Jean Cocteau, *The Wedding on the Eiffel Tower,* in *Modern French Theatre,* ed. Michael Benedikt and George E. Wellwarth (New York: Dutton, 1964), 101.

13. Tennessee Williams, *The Glass Menagerie* (New York: New Directions, 1945), 21.

14. George Bernard Shaw, *Pygmalion* (Harmondsworth: Penguin, 1941), 26.

15. Arthur Miller, *Death of a Salesman* (Harmondsworth: Penguin, 1949), 11.

16. Amiri Baraka, *Dutchman,* in *Selected Plays and Prose of Amiri Baraka/LeRoi Jones* (New York: William Morrow, 1979), 71.

17. Edward W. Soja, "Postmodern Urbanization: The Six Restructurings of Los Angeles," in *Postmodern Cities and Spaces,* ed. Sophie Watson and Katherine Gibson (Oxford: Blackwell, 1995), 135.

18. Stephen Poliakoff, *Hitting Town, Plays: One* (London: Methuen, 1989), 96.

19. Claire Armistead, "LIFTing the Theatre: The London International Festival of Theatre," in *Contemporary British Theatre,* ed. Theodore Shank (Houndmills: Macmillan, 1994), 160. Commercial theater has likewise shown an interest in site-specific interactive productions, as evidenced in the highly successful *Tony and Tina's Wedding* (1988)—currently playing in over thirty cities—and its

New York offshoots: *Bernie's Bar Mitzvah* (1992), *Grandma Sylvia's Funeral* (1994), and *Aunt Chooch's Birthday* (1998).

20. Bertolt Brecht, "The Street Scene" (1938), *Brecht on Theatre,* ed. and trans. John Willett (New York: Hill and Wang, 1964), 121–29. I am indebted for this suggestion to Elinor Fuchs, who (with Una Chaudhuri) offered valuable comments on a draft of this essay.

21. Jan Cohen-Cruz, ed., *Radical Street Performance: An International Anthology* (London: Routledge, 1998).

22. Henri Lefebvre, *Writings on Cities,* trans. and ed. Eleonore Kofman and Elizabeth Lebas (Oxford: Blackwell, 1996), 143.

23. Allan Kaprow, *Assemblage, Environments, and Happenings* (New York: Harry N. Abrams, 1966), 246. Vostell's 1973 performance piece *Berlin Fever* began with nearly one hundred participants driving from various parts of West Berlin to an empty area near the Berlin Wall (see Allan Kaprow, "Non-theatrical Performance," *Artforum* 14 [May 1976]: 45–46).

24. Kaprow, *Assemblage, Environments, and Happenings,* 243.

25. For a discussion of *Light Touch,* see Bruce Wilshire, *Role Playing and Identity: The Limits of Theatre as Metaphor* (Bloomington: Indiana University Press, 1982), ix–xiv. See also David Bourdon, "It's Happening Again," *Village Voice,* April 19, 1976; and Don McDonagh, "Artists' Theater Is Happening Again," *New York Times,* May 16, 1976.

26. Theodore Shank, "Squat Theatre," *Performing Arts Journal* 3 (fall 1978): 62.

27. Fiona Templeton, *You—the City* (New York: Roof Books, 1990), ix. Subsequent references to this edition of *You—the City,* which includes descriptions, instructions, and excerpts from the responses of performers and participants, are indicated parenthetically.

28. Michel de Certeau, *The Practice of Everyday Life,* trans. Steven Rendall (Berkeley and Los Angeles: University of California Press, 1984), 95.

29. Ibid., 99.

30. Ibid., 101.

31. Tom Lubbock, review of *You—the City* (London production), *Independent,* July 5, 1989. See also John Howell, review of *You—the City, Artforum* 27 (October 1988): 151; and C. Carr, "Is That You?" in *On Edge: Performance at the End of the Twentieth Century* (Hanover, N.H.: Wesleyan University Press/University Press of New England, 1993), 159–61.

32. For a discussion of language as a mode of spatial negotiation, see Stanton B. Garner Jr., "The Performing 'I': Language and the Histrionics of Place," in *Bodied Spaces: Phenomenology and Performance in Contemporary Drama* (Ithaca: Cornell University Press, 1994), 120–58.

33. Steve Nelson, "Redecorating the Fourth Wall: Environmental Theatre Today," *TDR* 123 (fall 1989): 88.

34. In an e-mail note to me (March 10, 2000), Elinor Fuchs described her experience as a participant in *You—the City:*

The event in its entirety suggested a vast secret spectacle—invisible to uninitiated passersby, who occupied the same street space but not the same spatial consciousness, only partly manifest to the "client," but suddenly revealing its intricate geometry in the basketball court. *You—The City* was an experiment in "consciousness-raising," as if to say—if all our movements could be incised into the urban landscape and the incisions seen *as* incised, what beautiful shapes and patterns we would trace.

35. "Stalk[4]: *Mugger Music* by Manchester's LOADING DECK," *Nettime Web Page,* n.d., <http://mediafilter.org/ZK/Conf/Conf_Email/January.21.1997 .03.01.02> (June 26, 1999).

36. "Current Projects: *Mugger Music,*" *Index Arts Co-operative Web Page,* n.d., <http://www.u-net.com/set/index/mugger.html> (June 26, 1999).

37. *Mugger Music* was performed in New York over twenty-four hours on June 10 and 14, 1997, and over five hours on June 12. I would like to thank Nick Crowe for clarifying points about both productions.

38. Ginger Strand, review of *Mugger Music, Theatre Journal* 50 (May 1998): 268. At one point, the guide dropped the participant's "ticket stub"—a cigarette stub—down a subway grating into a pile of other cigarette butts. Strand asks: "But this particular butt was a symbol, not detritus—it was different. Or was it?" (270). For an additional discussion of the New York production see Heidi Reitmaier, review of *Mugger Music, Sculpture* 17 (January 1998): 70–71.

39. "The Loading Deck Presents *Mugger Music,*" *Stalk Web Page,* n.d., <http://www.backspace.org/stalk/mugger.html> (June 26, 1999).

40. Nick Crowe, Graham Parker, and Ian Rawlinson, "Concrete Metropolis: *Mugger Music* Takes Manhattan, Part One of Three," interview by Tyler Thoreson, *Total New York Web Page,* June 6, 1997, <http://www.totalny.com/city /metropolis /part 1/> (May 19, 1999).

41. Tyler Thoreson, "Concrete Metropolis: I've Been Mugged, Part Three of Three," *Total New York Web Page,* n.d., <http://www.totalny.com/city/metropolis/part3/> (May 19, 1999).

42. Crowe, Parker, and Rawlinson, "Concrete Metropolis." The Internet performance site for *Mugger Music,* including photographs, was located at the *Total New York Web Page,* n.d., <http://www.totalny.com/city/metropolis/part2 /wall3.html> (May 19, 1999).

43. An internet record of *One Day and All of the Night* can be found on the *ArtAIDS Web Page,* n.d., <http://filament.illumin.co.uk/artaids/oneday /docu.htm> (June 26, 1999). Video cameras were placed in Australia, Hungary, the eastern United States, and western Canada.

44. Channel 4, *Once upon a Time in Cyberville,* 1994, program transcript, quoted in Stephen Graham, "Imagining the Real-Time City: Telecommunications, Urban Paradigms and the Future of Cities," in Westwood and Williams, *Imagining Cities,* 31.

45. Crowe, Parker, and Rawlinson, "Concrete Metropolis."

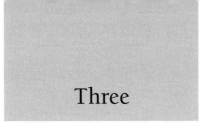

Three

Steinscapes

6

The Composition That All the World Can See: Gertrude Stein's Theater Landscapes

Jane Palatini Bowers

In a lecture in 1935 entitled "Plays," Gertrude Stein explained that the theater works collected in her volume *Operas and Plays* are landscapes and that they were inspired by the landscape around her summer house in Bilignin, France. If one were to approach Stein's so-called landscape plays expecting to find them set in Bilignin or to represent the French countryside (or any countryside for that matter), one would be disappointed, for the plays do not evoke a sense of place. When Stein calls her plays landscapes, she is drawing an analogy to a genre of art—the landscape painting. In imagining her plays as landscape paintings, Stein was able to free herself from dramatic conventions and to experiment with new forms that had their source in contemporary painting, not in dramatic literature.

The analogizing of the verbal to the visual had frequently served to liberate Stein from the restrictions of literary convention. Her very self-identification as a twentieth-century avant-garde writer was connected to parallels between her own career and those of her painter friends. She describes her 1905 novella *Melanctha,* for example, as "the first definite step away from the nineteenth century and into the twentieth century in literature," and she links this giant step for literature to a corresponding one for painting taken by Picasso and Matisse during the same winter in which she was writing *Melanctha:*

> It had been a fruitful winter. In the long struggle with the portrait of Gertrude Stein, Picasso passed from the Harlequin, the charming early italian period to the intensive struggle which

was to end in cubism. Gertrude Stein had written the story of
Melanctha the negress, the second story of Three Lives. . . .
Matisse had painted the Bonheur de Vivre and had created the
new school of colour which was soon to leave its mark on
everything.[1]

Out of her identification with painters, she conceived of the poems
in *Tender Buttons,* written between 1911 and 1912, as still lifes and of
many of the prose pieces written in the twenties and thirties as portraits.
Her aim in both instances was to create analogs to visual forms by verbal
means but not through conventional mimesis. Stein rejected narration,
description, and dialogue—the writer's usual arsenal for the depiction of
the experiential world outside the text. Like any writer, she would look;
she would listen; she would meditate. Then in a daring departure from
the usual writerly behavior, she would arrange her words like so many
brushstrokes, often defying grammar and therefore meaning, and working out patterns that to her mind corresponded to the object or person
that had instigated the still life or portrait. She claimed not to be concerned that the resulting piece did not immediately call its subject to a
reader's mind. Her goal was to pull readers after her into the twentieth
century by imposing a different form of imaginative activity on them
than they were used to. Rather than focusing on the writing's reference
to nontextual reality, readers were to appreciate Stein's twentieth-century compositions in and for themselves, for the harmonies and patterns, relations and rhythms resulting from the arrangement of their
components.

In conceiving of a play as a landscape, then, Stein was following a
pattern she had established early in her career, looking to the visual arts
for a model of creative activity. Of course, the connection between landscape and theater did not originate with Stein but has a long tradition
embodied linguistically in the word *scene* with its application to both
worlds. In his essay "Thought and Landscape" Yi-Fu Tuan defines landscape as a "space in which people *act*," or "*scenery* for people to contemplate" (emphasis added).[2] In the same spirit, but centuries earlier,
theater was "a word much used in the titles of books of travel and [geo-
graphic] description," according to John Brinckerhoff Jackson.[3] On the
other side of the metaphoric field, dramatists of the sixteenth and seventeenth centuries made frequent use of the *theatrum mundi* topos, and
during the same period, the Italians developed the proscenium stage that
borrowed its vanishing point perspective and disposition of loci in space

from landscape painting. In linking theater to landscape, Stein alluded to a centuries-old practice.

In Stein's case, the correspondence between landscape and the play text provided a solution to what she perceived to be troubling aspects of the theater experience from the point of view of the spectator. When Stein tells the story of her "life in the theater," which she does in her lecture, "Plays," she presents herself very much as a member of the audience for most of that life. In fact, she had had no experience of theater other than that of a spectator when she sat down to write her first play, *What Happened,* in 1913. As a spectator to the performance of a play, Stein found that the visual elements and the spoken language interfered with each other.

> I became fairly consciously troubled by the things over which one stumbles over which one stumbled to such an extent that the time of one's emotion in relation to the scene was always interrupted. The things over which one stumbled and there it was a matter both of seeing and of hearing were clothes, voices, what they the actors said, how they were dressed and how that related itself to their moving around. . . . Then I began to vaguely wonder whether I could see and hear at the same time and which helped or interfered with the thing on the stage.[4]

Costumes, sets, and even action and gesture—the spatial or visual elements of performance—are available to our understanding all at once, in the moment that we perceive them. The language of the play, by contrast, proceeds linearly. (At least, this was the case in the sorts of plays that Stein would have seen during her years of regular attendance at the theater in the late-nineteenth-century United States.) A spectator understands what she hears by following the line of words from one moment to the next, total comprehension occurring only at the end point of the line. Stein felt that what she saw at the theater distracted her from what she heard. To be distracted from the words was to lose their sense. On the other hand, to concentrate on the words was to dilute the intensity of the visual effect. Further complicating the theater experience for Stein was her own state of mind, her "emotion" as she puts it, which is "either behind or ahead of the play at which you are looking and to which you are listening." "So," she concludes, "your emotion as a member of the audience is never going on at the same time as the action of the play."[5] According to Stein, the conflict among the succession of visual stimuli, the rhythms of the spectator's consciousness and emotions, and the progression of language in the service of plot and characterization produces a "nervousness" in the spectator.

Stein reports having had an experience at the age of sixteen that suggested a possible solution to her difficulties with theater. She saw Sarah Bernhardt perform in San Francisco:

> I knew a little french of course but really it did not matter, it was all so foreign and her voice being so varied and it all being so french I could rest in it untroubled. And I did. . . . It was better than the theatre because you did not have to get acquainted. The manners and customs of the french theatre created a thing in itself and it existed in and for itself . . . there were so many characters . . . and you did not have to know them they were so foreign, and the foreign scenery and actuality replaced the poetry and the voices replaced the portraits. It was for me a very simple direct and moving pleasure.[6]

In short, Stein discovered that the most satisfactory theater experience for her was one in which language was no more nor less expressive than gesture and in which experiencing the performance provided more pleasure than understanding the play.

When Stein turned to the writing of plays herself, almost twenty-five years after seeing Sarah Bernhardt in San Francisco, she apparently sought, by creating landscape plays, to duplicate that "simple direct and moving pleasure" she had earlier experienced. She explains her intention retrospectively in her 1935 lecture:

> I felt that if a play was exactly like a landscape then there would be no difficulty about the emotion of the person looking on at the play being behind or ahead of the play because the landscape does not have to make acquaintance.[7]

"Making acquaintance" requires what Stein calls "progressive familiarity," a gradual process occurring over time. In theater terms such a process is accomplished through narrative and discursive means, in other words, through language used to advance plot, create character, and provide exposition. However, if the play is in a foreign language that one does not understand, then one cannot follow plot and dialogue, and thus one is "relieved," to use Stein's word, of the necessity of "making acquaintance." Similarly, if one were to eliminate from a play all narrative and discursive elements and to conceive of the play not as telling a story but as forming a landscape, one could create a theater experience that did not require its audience to "make acquaintance." Such an experience would allow audiences to "rest untroubled" in space, rather than compelling them forward in time. As Stein tells it, she therefore decided to write plays that were like landscapes.

Stein saw the natural landscape itself as a composition, simply waiting to be transposed into a play.

> The landscape has its formation . . . not moving but being always in relation, the trees to the hills the hills to the fields the trees to each other any piece of it to any sky and then any detail to any other detail. . . . And of that relation I wanted to make a play and I did, a great number of plays.[8]

This formation or composition of the landscape to which Stein refers is as much a cultural artifact as literature, art, or architecture; that is, landscape is not the same as nature or geography. In a landscape, as Mark Roskill observes in his excellent book on the history of landscape, "Nature in its ongoing organic life and richness of display is suborned to the needs of culture, from which it then takes its meaning."[9]

Landscape is a way of seeing, the imposition of a point of view upon nature. The principles of composition that cause us to contemplate a landscape in a particular way are learned and culturally determined. Originally an Anglo-Saxon word that meant simply a tract of land, *landscape* fell out of use until it was revived by Dutch painters in 1600 to refer to their representations of a scene. *Landscape* in its modern usage, then, signified first a kind of painting and only later the view or prospect itself.[10] The word as a designation of something in the environment, the view we see, suggests artfulness. As Jackson writes, landscape "is *always* artificial."[11] It is always a composition, whether created as such by a landscape architect or organized that way by the eye of the perceiver, trained by art to compose the view. As Stein points out in "Composition as Explanation," moreover, it is not the natural world that changes from generation to generation but our way of viewing it and our way of using it: "The only thing that is different from one time to another is what is seen and what is seen depends upon how everybody is doing everything. . . . Everything is the same except composition."[12]

It follows that landscape as a genre of painting "symbolizes an already represented world which is inescapably the world of human concepts and values."[13] To Stein's way of thinking, the first people to see and to express the composition of a generation are, in fact, its artists. Thus, for Stein, landscape represents the artist's imaginative power. She is not alone in her view of landscape as an expression of the potency and primacy of the artist's imagination. Salim Kemal and Ivan Gaskell remark that "the apocryphal story of the 'invention' of landscape painting is that an artist in his studio set down on canvas his friend's recollections of his travels: his landscape owed little to the painter's eye and much to the imagination."[14] Indeed, in his important essay "The Renaissance Theory of Art and the Rise of Landscape," Ernest Gombrich argues that the theory of landscape painting, denoting the artist's creative genius, among other things, preceded the practice of representing actual instances of natural beauty. According to Gombrich, it was Leonardo da Vinci who developed "the first complete aesthetic theory of landscape painting—even before the first landscape had come into existence."[15] Gombrich quotes a passage about landscape in the *Paragone* in which Leonardo "probes deep into the motive powers of the creative process itself."[16]

> If the painter . . . wishes to bring forth sites or deserts, cool and shady places in times of heat or warm spots when it is cold, he fashions them. So if he desires valleys or wishes to discover vast tracts of land from mountain peaks and look at the sea on the distant horizon beyond them, it is in his power; and so if he wants to look up to the high mountains from low valleys or from high mountains towards the deep valleys and the coastline. In fact, *whatever exists in the universe either potentially or actually or in the imagination, he has it first in his mind and then in his hands.* (Emphasis added)[17]

In the twentieth century, the artist who had the potential universe in his mind and then in his hands was, according to Stein, Pablo Picasso. In an uncanny echo of Leonardo's words, she writes about Picasso's power to create the composition of the contemporary landscape:

> One must not forget that the earth seen from an airplane is more splendid than the earth seen from an automobile. The automobile goes quicker but essentially the landscapes seen from an automobile are the same as the landscapes seen from a carriage, a train, a waggon, or in walking. But the earth seen from an airplane is something else. So the twentieth century is not the same as the nineteenth century and it is very interest-

ing knowing that Picasso has never seen the earth from an airplane [in 1938], that being of the twentieth century he
inevitably knew that the earth is not the same as in the nineteenth century, *he knew it, he made it,* inevitably he made it different and what he made is a thing that now all the world can
see. (Emphasis added)[18]

The difference between nineteenth- and twentieth-century landscape is
a result of a change in the way of seeing, anticipated by the artist and, to
a certain extent, created by him. Twentieth-century landscape painting,
in fact, drew upon the kinds of expanded perception that mechanical
flight made possible. But Stein presents Picasso as a kind of mythic
figure, an Icarus, who can see the landscape from the air without benefit
of an airplane. This mythic foresight (and "oversight"), this ability to
penetrate to the very heart of nature to reveal what has not previously
been seen is, according to Stein, the essence of Picasso's genius—and his
genius, like Leonardo's, is expressed in the landscapes he imagines and
creates.

Our changing way of seeing the landscape, which Stein finds characteristic of the twentieth century, actually began somewhat earlier, in
the last decades of the eighteenth century. Previously, artists had used the
one-point perspective to structure landscape. As Mark Roskill explains,
such a perspective "entails recognition on the viewer's part, and
identification with, the position of the single 'seeing eye,' placed at the
same height as the vanishing point toward which the lines of recession
set up within the pictorial representation converge." Roskill continues:

> It is a way of seeing in which an effectively disembodied indi-
> vidual has sovereign power of command over a section of the
> world that is physically separated from him and made subject
> to its own autonomous principles of structuring. . . . But in the
> last decades of the eighteenth century a fundamental change in
> the authority of that kind of view is set on foot, and this
> change can be associated specifically with the development of
> the panorama.[19]

The panorama was a landscape painted on the inside walls of a circular
building or rotunda, lit from the top. Spectators stood on a platform at
the center of the building, and by moving about on this platform, they
had a 360-degree view of the painted landscape.

In her lecture "Pictures," written, like the lecture on plays, for her

1935 tour of the United States, Stein herself tells of the remarkable experience of viewing a panorama and of its effect on her way of responding
to landscape paintings (and indeed to all paintings):

> The first thing I ever saw painted and that I remember . . . see-
> ing and feeling as painted . . . was the panorama of the battle of
> Waterloo. I must have been about eight years old and it was
> very exciting. . . . It was . . . a continuous oil painting, one was
> surrounded by an oil painting and I who lived continuously out
> of doors and felt air and sunshine . . . felt that this was all dif-
> ferent and very exciting. . . . I remember standing on the little
> platform in the center and almost consciously knowing that
> . . . there was no feeling of air, it just was an oil painting and it
> had a life of its own and it was a scene as an oil painting sees it
> and it was a real thing which looked like something I had seen
> but it had nothing to do with that something that I knew
> because the feeling was not at all that not at all the feeling which
> I had when I saw anything that was really what the oil painting
> showed. It the oil painting showed it as an oil painting.[20]

Though Stein here affects a childlike naïveté and wonder, she very
astutely identifies just what it was about panoramas that changed the
nature of landscape painting. In the first place, the source of perception
in a panorama is not the single-eyed, fixed gaze but the entire body that
can project the perceiver into the landscape. From that position, the
imagination is free to construct the image from multiple perspectives.
The panorama thus encouraged a new way of looking at landscape and a
new relationship of self to environment.

As a viewer of a panorama, moreover, one becomes aware of the
processes of illusion themselves, and they become part of the attraction
or thrill of the experience. Stein sees the painting of the battle of Waterloo *as* a painting. This excites her. As she remarks elsewhere in her lecture on pictures, her acceptance of an oil painting as a painting rather
than as a representation of something else is the key to her enjoyment of
this art form. "Resemblance," she declares, is a "pleasurable sensation,"
but it is also a "human weakness," and it is most definitely not the "business" of the oil painting:

> [W]hether it [the oil painting] is intended to look like some-
> thing and looks like it or whether it is intended to look like
> something and does not look like it it really makes no differ-

ence, the fact remains that for me it has achieved an existence in and for itself . . . as being an oil painting on a flat surface and it has its own life.[21]

We will remember that Stein claimed that the French theater of Sarah Bernhardt also "existed in and for itself." Indeed, in that it revealed and reveled in its own paintedness, the panorama turned painting into a kind of theater or performance. The panorama was only one of many such spectacles, including the diorama, from the late eighteenth through the early twentieth centuries, in which landscape was the key subject and that foregrounded the mechanics by which the illusion was created.

Stein remarks that the panorama has a life of its own, quite apart from its relationship to a life outside itself. This is exactly the quality she claims for all oil painting that interests her and for the Sarah Bernhardt play as well. It is a quality she prizes above all others. This self-contained liveliness, or existence in and for itself, is a mark of twentieth-century landscape painting. The space of the twentieth century, as Mark Roskill points out,

> is a space in which the artist's acts situate themselves in relation to one another, so as to take on purpose and direction without any reference to an experiential unity that can be taken as serving as ground for those relations, other than that of the unfolding logic of creation that warrants the works appearing as they do. . . . [W]hat counts as a genuine image of nature or record of experience—as against what is "found" within the act of making—becomes confused or obscured. Such is the case with the landscapes of Cubism from 1908–9 on, and in Pablo Picasso's and Georges Braque's case more endemically so.[22]

If the appearance of a twentieth-century landscape painting is determined more by "the unfolding logic of creation" than by its fidelity to the scene it purportedly represents, and if "what is found in the act of making" a landscape painting counts more than what is found in nature itself or in the artist's experience of it, then the twentieth century witnessed an extreme elaboration of the idea that landscape painting is a sign of the transformative power of the artist's imagination and the creative agency of his or her hand.

Though Stein approved of these tendencies of twentieth-century landscape, and particularly of Picasso's cubist landscapes, away from mimesis and toward self-reflexivity, she clung, rather nostalgically, to the notion that the landscape was an expression of national character. In Picasso's case this meant that his 1909 cubist paintings of the country-side around Horta de Ebro in Spain expressed the Spanish character not only because Picasso was Spanish but, more to the point, because the landscape he painted was. Writing in 1938 about Picasso's 1909 cubist paintings of the Spanish landscape, Stein declares:

> These three landscapes [of Horta de Ebro] express exactly what I wish to make clear, that is to say the opposition between nature and man in Spain. . . . [A] small number of houses gives the impression of a great quantity of houses in order to dominate the landscape, the landscape and the houses do not agree, the round is opposed to the cube, the movement of the earth is against the movement of the houses. . . . I have here before me a picture of a young French painter, he too with few houses creates his village, but here the houses move with the landscape, with the river, here they all agree together, it is not at all Spanish. Spaniards know that there is no agree-ment. . . . [I]t was natural that a Spaniard should express this in the painting of the twentieth century, the century where nothing is in agreement.[23]

Here, human creation and nature so interpenetrate in Stein's under-standing that she barely distinguishes between them. Nature has formed the imagination of the artist and is at the same time a figment of that very imagination. More importantly, Picasso's ability to anticipate and create the contemporary composition is a function of his nationality. The twentieth-century way of seeing and the Spanish way of seeing are confluent. In Stein's personal mythology, the only other country fit to produce an artist capable of realizing the composition of the twentieth-century landscape is the United States: "While other Europeans were still in the nineteenth century, Spain . . . and America . . . were the nat-ural founders of the twentieth century."[24] Not surprisingly, the Ameri-can who would join the Spaniard, Picasso, in founding the twentieth century and expressing its composition in landscapes was Gertrude Stein, whose medium was not paint but language and whose venue was not the art museum but the theater.

I have elsewhere called Stein's compositions for the theater "lang-scapes."[25] I adopted this coinage to suggest the centrality of language in the theater landscapes Stein creates and to bring to light her crucial insight that the landscape is itself a kind of language that the greatest artists can read and that they use as the ground of compositions in their own languages of paint or, in Stein's case, words.[26] These compositions, if they are in the language of paint, need not look like the experiential landscape; if made of words, as Stein's lang-scapes are, they need not be "about" the landscape; they need only be compositions according to the principles of relationality articulated by the landscape or discovered by the artist in the process of composing.

One might reasonably expect that a play imagined as a landscape would use language sparingly and would instead specify a series of pictures that theater practitioners would be expected to bring into existence. Thinking rather of Stein's plays as lang-scapes, we can understand why they are never silent and why the air of the theaters in which they are produced is dense with their words, filling the ear as, in print, they fill the eye. These are landscapes made entirely of language, word compositions in the same sense that the experiential landscape is a tree-hill-stream composition. As for the physical realization of her plays, though Stein intended that they be performed (she was not writing closet dramas),[27] she took only a vague interest in their staging, happily deferring to the collective judgment of producers, set designers, composers, choreographers, and directors, for she had few fixed ideas about how her plays should be realized, and she did not provide detailed stage directions. It follows that Stein's plays are not landscapes in the sense that they dictate particular ways of using theater space to those who would stage them or to those whose theater praxis they were to influence. Rather, Stein's plays are lang-scapes in the sense that they showed her contemporaries a new kind of composition for the theater of the twentieth century and suggested that language might play a central role in that composition. Few of her contemporaries seemed to get the message, however, and it was not until after her death that American theater showed any sign of her influence.[28]

With landscape painting rather than dramatic literature as her model, Stein could release language from the requirement that it tell a story, create psychologically believable characters, or convey sequential thinking. Narration, psychology, and intellection work to dismantle the simultaneity of spatial structure. Seeking simultaneity through language, Stein used words in her lang-scapes as a painter might place objects in the field of a painting, as though they were related to each other spatially, that is, visually on the page and sonorously in the air. Her language assumes a materiality equal in presence to the materiality of the other elements of the performance event. Stein's verbal compositions for the theater resist the temporal thrust of speech and the linear sequence of thought and narration. Each utterance in a Stein play is meant to be responded to as we respond to space—as a totality, present in each instant but not connected to subsequent instances except by juxtaposition or echoing. A Stein play comes into being as a series of perspectives. Its whole is not experienced as a unit but as an accumulation of multiple engagements of the listening self with the spoken and sung words. For the American Stein as for the Spaniard Picasso, juxtaposition, simultaneity, and multiple perspective are the relational principles expressed by the land/lang-scape.

Like Picasso's cubist landscapes, in which nothing is in agreement and where art and artifacts oppose themselves to nature, Stein's plays oppose the normal, the natural—or what we think of as natural—course of the theater event. Instead of moving with the actor and the action, her plays oppose them and create a kind of verbal stasis within theater time, much as a landscape painting extracts a moment from time's flow and freezes it in a visual space or as a "natural" landscape interferes with the processes of nature.[29] Within this stasis, Stein scripts an event not normally represented in the theater of her time: the writing of the play.

The work that most clearly exemplifies the concept of play as langscape is *Four Saints in Three Acts* (1927),[30] which had its original staging in 1934 and has been produced recently (in 1996) by Robert Wilson.[31] The text of *Four Saints* initiates a performance; it provides the songs for singing, the words for speaking.[32] At the same time, however, it counteracts the very performance it initiates in a kind of countertext, a written text that asserts itself at every moment and that slows the pace of the performance. The supertitles at Lincoln Center, the New York venue of the Robert Wilson production, were a serendipitous but entirely appropriate manifestation of a theater piece in which what was written imposes itself on and alters our experience of what is heard.

In the normal course of a theater event, as we know, speech and action, the essentials of drama, are dynamic and move along a continuum. Performance also takes place in space and is a visual as well as a temporal phenomenon. The flow of speech and action is checked, as it were, by the way the eye perceives the performance in space—instant by instant. Really then, the dynamism of performance, while it is continuous, is more like a succession of present instants than a seamless flow. It is at once continuous and discontinuous. The actor, the set, and the text can either increase continuity or decrease it. Actors are arguably the source of greatest continuity in a performance because they are *in propriae personae* always present and always the same. They occupy space *and* they continue. They are present to the eye in each separate moment of performance, but they are also the conduit of speech and action on their journey forward through time.

The text of *Four Saints* emphasizes the discontinuity of performance rather that its continuity. In this respect, Wilson's production complemented the play, whereas John Houseman's 1934 staging attempted inappropriately but understandably to impose narrative continuity on it, just as Virgil Thomson's musical scoring dresses what is essentially a static and syntactically fractured text in the borrowed robes of fluid melodies. The structure of *Four Saints* seems to militate against its actors in their function as conduit of the current of performance. It opposes their dynamism and, in a sense, prevents them from acting. Stein tried to minimize the intervention of the actors between herself and the audience and to attain direct contact with us. In other words, she attempted to write the actor out of the play and to write the writer into it. In her occupation as author of the text, Stein is actually a presence in *Four Saints,* and the play is, like all landscape art, a testament to and a celebration of the imaginative power and creative agency of its maker.

Almost two-thirds of the text is composed of authorial statement. In setting the words to music, Thomson obscured this fact in production by parceling out the authorial commentary to two figures (called "commere" and "compere"), both of whom seem in performance to be stage directors, a strategy that Wilson retained. Even at that, however, these "characters" discuss not so much the performance of the play—the stage business—as they do the composition—the business of writing. At the beginning of the play Stein maintains a running commentary on the writing process (and progress): self-criticism, self-encouragement, progress reports, plans and preparations for writing, and discussions of the difficulty or ease of writing. Once the play gets well under way, once Saint Ignatius and Saint Therese begin to speak, then Stein does not so much discuss the text that is being written or urge herself to write more of it, as deal with the written text as a plan for performance. However, it is a plan that is never settled because we are meant to perceive the writing and the performance as simultaneous acts. Like the panorama of the Battle of Waterloo that so enthralled Stein as a child, *Four Saints* calls attention to its own constructedness.

There are a Saint Plan and a Saint Settlement among the cast of characters, and the necessity of planning and settling is brought up at intervals throughout the play, most often when Stein or her saints are having difficulty deciding how the plan is to be settled. The refrain—"How many

John Houseman's production of *Four Saints in Three Acts* at the
Wadsworth Athenaeum, Hartford, Connecticut, 1934.
(Photo courtesy of the Beinecke Library, Yale University;
White Studios.)

saints are there in it?" is one of many similar and often repeated questions:
"How many acts are there in it?"; "How many nails are there in it?"; "How
many floors are there in it?"; "How many doors?"; "How many windows?"; and "How much of it is finished?" The lang-scape *Four Saints,*
these questions suggest, is like a house under construction: it will eventually be completed, but in the meantime it is a work in process, and questions about its nature as a whole cannot be answered.

The question of how many saints are in the play has several
answers, all of which beg the question:

Saint Therese. How many saints are there in it.
Saint Therese. There are very many many saints in it.
Saint Therese. There are as many saints as there are in it.
Saint Therese. How many saints are there in it.
Saint Therese. There are there are there are saints saints in it.
[Stein then names seven saints, hardly a complete list.]
Saint Therese. How many saints are there in it.

Saint Cecilia. How many saints are there in it.
Saint Therese. There are as many saints as there are in it.
Saint Cecilia. There are as many saints as there are saints in it.
   (28)

In the penultimate scene (in which Saint Settlement and Saint Anne say that "there can be two Saint Annes if you like"), Stein writes:

> They have to be.
> They have to be.
> They have to be to see.
> To see to say.
> Laterally they may.
>   (47)

If we see saints, they exist. Accordingly, in the last scene, Stein specifies that the saints ("All Saints") be lined laterally to the left and right of Saint Ignatius for our perusal. As the play ends, we can count the saints and answer one of the questions posed in the text but never answered by it.

As for the number of acts, the title promises us three, but the title, written first, cannot possibly measure the play, which has not yet been written. In fact, the play has four named acts, but there are three first acts, two second acts, two third acts, and a fourth act, making a total of eight acts. The only certainty regarding the number of acts in the play is that which is obvious at the end: "Last Act. / Which is a fact." No matter how many acts there are in it, the play is certain to finish. It is only when the play is finished that we will know how many acts there were in it, just as the number of doors, windows, floors, and nails in a house cannot be determined until the building is complete, for even the most carefully laid plans can be changed.

Any performance of *Four Saints* is certainly preplanned. The written text and the score exist, and they provide the "plan" that the performance will follow. However, we are made to feel that the plan is being created in our presence, as the performance proceeds. For example, Stein writes the play so that during performance she will seem to be feeding the actors their lines. That is, an unattributed statement, for instance, "Who settles a private life," is followed by the same statement ascribed to a saint:

Saint Therese. Who settles a private life.

Often the saints behave like a ventriloquist's dummy, who, when instructed, "Say hello, Charley," says, "Hello Charley." By echoing their own names in their lines, the saints bring Stein's instructions, the side text, into performance. The inclusion of the side text in performance occurs also with act and scene divisions, as when the announcement of a new scene rhymes with the first line of text in that scene: "Scene X / When"; or when the scene announcement has a syntactical connection to the first line: "Scene VI / With Seven"; or when there is a homophonic connection between scene announcement and first line: "Scene One" in the side text echoed by "And seen one" in the main text. Of course, a production could ignore the connection Stein makes between written notation and spoken text, but the connection is there nonetheless. Stein tried to make the written text an element of performance, and Thomson assisted her by scoring the act and scene divisions and character ascriptions so that every word written must be sung.

Four Saints also abounds in the use of conditionals, adding to the sense of tentativeness in the play. As might be expected, this effect is most intense in the first half. As it takes shape, the play leaves fewer questions unanswered. But in the beginning, almost nothing has been determined. After a five-page deliberation about how Saint Therese and Saint Ignatius are to appear when they first enter (whether sitting or standing, moving or still, on stage or off), Stein writes:

> Saint Ignatius could be in porcelain actually.
> Saint Ignatius could be in porcelain actually while he was
>   young and standing.
> Saint Therese could not be young and standing she could be
>   sitting.
> Saint Ignatius could be in porcelain actually actually in porce-
>   lain standing.
> Saint Therese could be admittedly could be in moving seat-
>   ing. Saint Therese could be in moving sitting.
> Saint Therese could be.
> Saint Ignatius could be.
> Saint Ignatius could be in porcelain actually in porcelain
>   standing.

(20)

Because the verb *to be* is in its conditional form, the text never does answer the question of how the actors are to be disposed on the stage. Of course, this dilemma must be resolved in performance, but the text fights against the resolution that the performance must achieve.

Stein is also fond of stage directions that, if followed, would immobilize the actors. (This is another comfortable fit between Wilson and Stein in that he too slows down his performers.) When Saint Therese finally appears on stage, she is described as being "very nearly half inside and half outside the house." Neither in nor out, but somewhere in between, poised on a threshold, Saint Therese is, as Stein writes, "[a]bout to be." As for Saint Ignatius, Stein commits herself momentarily to having him stand and then immediately launches into a passage that epitomizes the text in process:

> Saint Therese seated and not standing half and half of it and not half and half of it seated and not standing surrounded and not seated and not seated and not standing and not surrounded and not surrounded and not not not seated not seated not seated not surrounded not seated and Saint Ignatius standing standing not seated Saint Therese not standing not standing and Saint Ignatius not standing standing surrounded as if in once yesterday. In place of situations. Saint Therese could be very much interested not only in settlement Saint Settlement and this not with with this wither wither they must be additional. Saint Therese having not commenced. (17)

The passage tells us that Saint Ignatius is simultaneously standing and not standing and that, Saint Therese, who was about to be, has not yet commenced. In the meantime, the question of whether she is to sit or stand has not yet been decided.

Paradoxically, the contradictory directions and conditional suggestions that immobilize the performance, turn the writing of the play, the process of composition, into a performance event. The representation of the process of composition in the performance violates the most basic convention of realistic drama: that the play be a fictive but lifelike utterance detached from the circumstances and conditions of its creation. Rather than calling attention to its artfulness, realistic theater hides its constructedness and the imaginative power and control of its creators, be they playwrights, directors, or actors; in realistic theater their efforts are meant to be invisible. In violating this convention, Stein exposes the mimetic fallacy of realistic theater and shows us that all theater, like all landscape, is an illusion, the creative product of its artists.

Robert Wilson's production of *Four Saints in Three Acts* at the
New York State Theater at Lincoln Center, New York, 1996.
(Photo by Stephanie Berger.)

The Thomson/Grosser arrangement of the text somewhat obscured
its purpose and meaning by ignoring the improvisational illusion that
Stein creates and by disguising the authorial voice, assigning Stein's
speeches to the saints or to the commere and compere. But in the origi-
nal text, Stein never relinquishes her hold, never withdraws as the play-
wright usually does. "When this you see," she writes, "Remember me."
Even when the written text becomes a song, Stein, the poet, is its singer.
The "arias" as originally written are passages of unassigned text. Even
"Pigeons on the Grass" is a Stein song, although Thomson had Saint
Ignatius sing it. In an interview, Stein explained the genesis of this aria:

> I was walking in the gardens of the Luxembourg in Paris. It
> was the end of summer the grass was yellow. I was sorry that it
> was the end of summer and I saw the big fat pigeons in the yel-
> low grass and I said to myself, pigeons on the yellow grass,
> alas, and I kept on writing pigeons on the grass, alas . . . until
> I had emptied myself of the emotion.[33]

By incorporating the moment of creation and the improvised product of that moment into the work to be performed, Stein violates the temporal boundaries between the creation of the written text and its performance.

The improvised quality of the written text, its very eventfulness, immobilizes the performance. Like Saint Therese, who is half in and half out, the performance itself is suspended in a kind of limbo. It consists entirely of preparation. It begins with a narrative that prepares for a play ("Four saints prepare for saints . . . In narrative prepare for saints" [11]),[34] followed by a play that prepares for a performance and ends with the only fact, which is the last act. Even Stein's inspiration for Saint Therese and Saint Ignatius suggests immobility. Stein explained that she had imagined Saint Therese as being like the photographs she saw in a store window, of a girl becoming a nun—still shots, one following another, a process divided into the static moments of its unfolding. Stein refers to this image of Saint Therese within the play as she refers also to Saint Ignatius as a porcelain statue, which she later explained was an actual figurine, again in a Parisian store window, which she imagined to be Saint Ignatius.

Saint Therese, the photograph, and Saint Ignatius, the statue, are represented in a play in which even the syntax of the sentences tends toward a kind of suspended animation. Though commissioned as an opera libretto, most of the text is composed of choppy, flat prose, its vocabulary pared to the most ordinary and unmelodic monosyllables. Stein's characteristic repetition is very much in evidence in *Four Saints* with, for an extreme example, the phrase "Once in a while," repeated twenty-six times in succession. Many of the sentences in *Four Saints* remind us of a record that has caught the phonograph needle in one groove; some seem like a kind of mirror writing where the words that come into the text are immediately reflected in reverse order. Many passages come to us in stages, like revised compositions where the variations are never erased. Within her stalled sentences and passages, Stein minimizes or manipulates grammatical indicators of activity. Verbs are often eliminated and sentences replaced by noun phrases, such as "pigeons on the grass." The preferred verb form is, in any case, the participle, most often used as a verbal as in "Saint Therese seated" or "Saint Ignatius standing." The effect of the verbal is to picture the subject in a steady state. By favoring such verbs, Stein suggests that the performance be a series of still moments, in which action is transformed into a quality.

For the theater audience, Stein's lang-scape, *Four Saints,* creates an experience very much like that Stein herself had on the platform within the panorama of Waterloo or that any one of us might have before a twentieth-century landscape such as the cubist paintings of Stein's friend Picasso or the abstract expressionist landscapes of Willem de Kooning. Because the text does not impel us forward in time, we can suspend our normal anticipatory response to theater and engage the event in a meditative way, suspended in the experience of the thing in and of itself. Though this lang-scape purports to be about saints, it does not take its meaning from history or biography or from any temporal form of experience outside of the lang-scape itself—the sound of its words, the accidental juxtapositions, the odd relations of one set of words to another. The play's emphasis on process rather than on progress toward resolution empowers us as spectators to enter and to leave the lang-scape wherever we will, free to choose our vantage points and to create meaning, a meaning that shifts as our attention shifts.

Because Stein uses language to immobilize action, we in the balcony are like the passengers in a plane. We know that we are moving and that the earth moves with us, but the landscape down below appears to be still, a space without apparent reference to time. To the doubting, those who would insist that time cannot stand still in a play and does not in *Four Saints,* Stein offers the following parable about the magpies in the sky to which she refers in the course of the play:

> Magpies are in the landscape that is they are in the sky of a land-scape, they are black and white. . . . When they are in the sky they do something that I have never seen any other bird do they hold themselves up and down and look flat against the sky.
>
> A very famous French inventor of things that have to do with stabilisation in aviation told me that what I told him magpies did could not be done by any bird but anyway whether the magpies at Avila do do it or do not at least they look as if they do do it. They look exactly like the birds in the Annunciation pictures the bird which is the Holy Ghost and rests flat against the side sky very high.[35]

Despite the doubts of the expert, the hapless French inventor who serves as her foil, Stein maintains that moving birds stand still against the sky. Impossible? Perhaps, but then Stein insists only that the birds seem stationary. Stein perceives them so because she has learned from the painters of Annunciation pictures to see the landscape in this way. Here again, Stein attests to the power of the artist to alter our perception of nature. It is not too fanciful to see Stein's feat in *Four Saints* as comparable to the immobilization of the magpie in the paintings of the Annunciation. Through her "black and white" birds, the words of her text, she conveys an impression of stasis convincing enough to affect our perception of the play in performance. When the written words exist as perceptible and energetic language (live birds), they still appear motionless, as do the stage activities they instigate. In this twentieth-century landscape, where words make time stand still, we can see Gertrude Stein, the playwright, at work.

NOTES

Portions of this essay have been adapted from my book *"They Watch Me as They Watch This": Gertrude Stein's Metadrama.* Copyright © University of Pennsylvania Press. Reprinted with permission of the publisher.

1. Gertrude Stein, *The Autobiography of Alice B. Toklas* (1933; rpt. New York: Vintage, 1990), 54.

2. Yi-Fu Tuan, "Thought and Landscape: The Eye and the Mind's Eye," in *The Interpretation of Ordinary Landscapes,* ed. D. W. Meinig (Oxford: Oxford University Press, 1979), 90.

3. John Brinckerhoff Jackson, *The Necessity for Ruins and Other Topics* (Amherst: University of Massachusetts Press, 1980), 8.

4. Gertrude Stein, *Lectures in America* (1935; rpt. Boston: Beacon Press, 1985), 114–15.

5. Ibid., 93.

6. Ibid., 115–16.

7. Ibid., 122.

8. Ibid., 125.

9. Mark Roskill, *The Languages of Landscape* (University Park: Pennsylvania State University Press, 1997), 2.

10. Edward Relph, *Rational Landscapes and Humanistic Geography* (London: Croom Helm, 1981), 22.

11. John Brinckerhoff Jackson, *Discovering the Vernacular Landscape* (New Haven: Yale University Press, 1984), 156.

12. Gertrude Stein, "Composition as Explanation," in *Writings, 1903–1932* (New York: Library of America, 1998), 526–27.

13. Charles Harrison, "The Effects of Landscape," in *Landscape and Power,* ed. W. J. T. Mitchell (Chicago: University of Chicago Press, 1994), 216.

14. Salim Kemal and Ivan Gaskell, introduction to *Landscape, Natural Beauty, and the Arts* (Cambridge: Cambridge University Press, 1993), 3.

15. Ernest Gombrich, "The Renaissance Theory of Art and the Rise of Landscape," in *Norm and Form: Studies in the Art of the Renaissance* (New York: Phaidon, 1966), 111.

16. Ibid., 112.

17. Quoted in ibid., 111–12.

18. Gertrude Stein, *Picasso: The Complete Writings* (Boston: Beacon Press, 1985), 88.

19. Roskill, *The Languages of Landscape,* 80–82.

20. Stein, *Lectures in America,* 63.

21. Ibid., 79 and 61.

22. Roskill, *The Languages of Landscape,* 196.

23. Stein, *Picasso,* 54.

24. Ibid., 39.

25. See Jane Palatini Bowers, *"They Watch Me as They Watch This": Gertrude Stein's Metadramas* (Philadelphia: University of Pennsylvania Press, 1991), especially pages 25–71.

26. In landscape studies, the parallel between landscape and language has been drawn by John A. Jakle in *The Visual Elements of Landscape* (Amherst: University of Massachusetts Press, 1987); and most recently by Anne Whiston Spirn in *The Language of Landscape* (New Haven: Yale University Press, 1998).

27. When Stein began writing plays in 1913, she sent several of them to Mabel Dodge in the hopes that she would be able to get them produced in New York. Dodge suggested that the plays be published instead. Stein firmly declined: "No decidedly not. I do *not* want the plays published. They are to be kept to be *played*" (Gertrude Stein to Mabel Dodge, [?] 1913, Yale Collection of American Literature, Beinecke Library). Stein objected not only to the idea of her plays as closet dramas, available only in print, but also to the idea that they were suitable only for minimal staging or for staged readings in the context of a literary salon or art society. In 1944 and 1945 Stein made various efforts to have *Yes Is for a Very Young Man* produced, even translating it into French for a proposed production at the American Army University at Biarritz under her supervision. However, she abruptly withdrew her play from this production because, as Alice Toklas explained in a letter to Carl Van Vechten, she objected to a "workshop performance," that is, a production without scenery, and to a "hand-picked audience" (November 19, 1946, *Staying on Alone: Letters of Alice B. Toklas,* ed. Edward Burns [New York: Vintage, 1975], 32). Stein's interest in having her plays performed notwithstanding, only four of her nearly one hundred plays were produced in her lifetime—one, *Four Saints in Three Acts,* as an opera, and another, *They Must. Be Wedded. To Their Wife.,* as a ballet called *A Wedding Bouquet.*

28. It can be argued that Thornton Wilder, who met Stein in 1935 and remained a good friend until her death in 1946, was influenced by Stein, especially in *The Long Christmas Dinner* and his other one-act plays. As for Stein's more recent influence, see Bevya Rosten, "The Fractured Stage: Four Avant-Garde Productions of Gertrude Stein's *Doctor Faustus Lights the Lights,*" Ph.D. diss., City University of New York, 1998.

29. For a discussion of landscape painting as "the transient captured," see Kenneth Clark, *Landscape into Art* (New York: Harper and Row, 1976). John

Brinckerhoff Jackson explores the idea of the natural landscape as a place "where we speed up or retard or divert the cosmic program and impose our own" (*Discovering the Vernacular Landscape,* 156).

30. Though it is subtitled *An Opera to Be Sung,* and though it is an opera by virtue of the music created for it by Virgil Thomson, I consider the text of *Four Saints* a play, not an opera libretto. As is the case with *A Lyrical Opera Made by Two to Be Sung* (1928) and *Madame Recamier. An Opera* (1930), there are no textual characteristics that distinguish *Four Saints* from Stein's plays of the same period. Moreover, Stein herself seems to have had trouble maintaining the generic distinction. The manuscript of *Madame Recamier* bears the subtitle *An Opera,* but when Stein mentions *Madame Recamier* in a letter to Henry McBride, she writes, "I have written a real play a poetic meditative conversational drama about Mme. Recamier, I think even the small or big theaters might act it it is so like a real play . . . a really truly play" (October 25, 1930, Yale Collection of American Literature, Beinecke Library). Similarly, she refers to *Four Saints* variously as an opera, a play, and a drama in *Everybody's Autobiography* (1937; rpt. New York: Vintage, 1973), 48, 98, 111, 114, 193, and 194, and in *Lectures in America,* 125, 129, and 131. The nature of Stein's collaboration with Thomson is emblematic of her attitude toward opera as a formal imposition on her characteristic style. According to Thomson, after he had set some of her pieces to music, he suggested that they write an opera together. Thomson claims that they agreed as to their opera's theme ("the working artist's working life") and its form ("classical Italian opera," *opera seria,* which "required a serious mythological subject with a tragic ending") (Virgil Thomson, *Virgil Thomson* [New York: Alfred A. Knopf, 1966], 90–91). Despite this "agreement," Stein went off on her own to write *Four Saints* , and, without further consultation with the composer, she presented him with the finished "libretto," which—he must have noticed— bore little resemblance to classical Italian opera.

31. *Four Saints in Three Acts* premiered at the Wadsworth Athenaeum in Hartford, Connecticut, on February 8, 1934, directed and produced by John Houseman (making his debut), with choreography by Frederick Ashton and sets and costumes by Florine Stettheimer. For a full account of this production as a significant cultural event see Steven Watson, *Prepare for Saints: Gertrude Stein, Virgil Thomson, and the Mainstreaming of American Modernism* (New York: Random House, 1999). The 1996 staging of the opera was a production of the Lincoln Center Festival and the Houston Grand Opera, conceived, designed, and directed by Robert Wilson with costumes by Francesco Clemente and lighting by Jennifer Tipton.

32. The text of *Four Saints* referenced here is that published in *Operas and Plays* (1932; rpt. Barrytown, N.Y.: Station Hill Press, 1987), 11–47. All citations are to this edition and will appear parenthetically.

33. Gertrude Stein, typescript of a tape-recorded interview with William Lundell for the National Broadcasting Company, New York, October 12, 1934, Yale Collection of American Literature, Beinecke Library.

34. Stein actually begins *Four Saints* with a narrative seemingly unrelated to the play itself, a story of "what happened today." Using the past tense, Stein tells of a trip to the country on a beautiful day and of a visit (presumably later in the day) from a "he," who "said he was hurrying" (12). The visitor's conversation is reported using the narrative convention of indirect discourse. In the manuscript of *Four Saints* (Yale Collection of American Literature, Beinecke Library), the visitor's speech ends at the bottom of one notebook page, and Stein begins the next notebook page with a cautionary note: "This is how they do not like it." Since "they" do not like it, the format of the text changes from lengthy paragraphs, suitable to narrative, to a succession of single lines, and from a narrative of what happened today to an invitation to "imagine four benches separately." To "imagine four benches" is to move outside the text, but not back in time to a world of which the text is a report or a representation, but forward, to a world that the text is going to create—a movement from narrative to playwriting, from story to lang-scape.

35. Stein, *Lectures in America,* 129.

7

After Stein: Traveling the American Theatrical "Langscape"

Marvin Carlson

It is a critical commonplace among art historians that the coming of romanticism brought to prominence an essentially new subject in painting—the landscape. The new attention given by the Romantics to landscape has been somewhat less remarked in theater studies, though surely every student of British theater history or of the history of scenic design is aware of the key role in the shifting of design orientation played by Garrick's hiring of Philip Jacques de Loutherbourg as his designer, the first major stage designer whose training was in landscape painting rather than in architectural design. The new orientation not only shifted emphasis from interior to exterior scenes but, much more significantly, from stock (usually architectural) settings to settings created to suit the needs of the individual production, from the all-purpose bourgeois salon of comedy or *palais à volonté* of tragedy to scenery that, as nineteenth-century playbills used to boast, was "painted on purpose."

This new attention to enveloping the physical action of the drama in a specific physical setting uniquely appropriate to this action became a goal not only of natural landscapes like those de Loutherbourg designed for Garrick but also for a new sort of architectural interior. The physical setting became, as Victor Hugo characterized it, another actor in the play:

> Exact locality is one of the first elements of reality. The speaking or acting characters alone do not engrave on the soul of the spectator the faithful impression of facts. The place where such a catastrophe occurred becomes a terrible and insepara-

ble witness of it, and the absence of this sort of silent character makes the greatest scenes of history in the drama incomplete. Would the poet dare to assassinate Rizzo elsewhere than in Mary Stuart's chamber? stage Henri IV elsewhere than in the rue de la Ferronier, obstructed with drays and carriages? burn Joan of Arc elsewhere than in the old marketplace?[1]

Romantic dramatists, as often interested in internal as in external settings, created not only historical dramas featuring figures like Mary Stuart or Henri IV, where the kind of specific locale Hugo mentions was now normally sought, but also dramas taking place in a landscape of the imagination, like Byron's *Manfred* or Mickiewicz's *Forefather's Eve*. With the coming of realism, these landscapes of the imagination disappeared almost entirely from European stages, to reappear with the symbolist theater and other reactions to realism at the end of the century.

Despite the power of the innovative dramaturgy at the end of the nineteenth century, realism remained, and still remains, the dominant dramatic mode in the Western world, and particularly in the English-speaking nations. The visual environments of staged productions in these nations are still far more likely to echo the detailed domestic interiors of Ibsen's middle period than, for example, the dream landscapes of Strindberg.

Alongside this familiar, mainstream tradition, however, there continued all through the twentieth century, a significant, if much less attended, alternative theater, some of the leading practitioners of which formed the focus of Marc Robinson's 1994 study with the provocative title *The Other American Drama*.[2] In his book, Robinson considers a series of innovative, nonrealistic dramatists not as members of a specific antirealistic tradition, but as important contributors to the texture of the modern American theater, often neglected because they fall outside the hegemonic concept of American drama as basically a drama of realism.

Four of the six dramatists considered by Robinson are important members of the contemporary scene: Sam Shepard, Maria Irene Fornes, Adrienne Kennedy, and Richard Foreman, and around them could be grouped many other important current playwrights, such as Eric Overmyer, Suzan-Lori Parks, Len Jenkin, and John Jesurun, who are contributing in varied and significant ways to the nonrealistic "other American drama." Although these dramatists naturally offer a wide range of approaches to their art, all reject, in one way or another, the highly predictable machinery of the "well-made" drama of realism. Like all other features of conventional dramaturgy, the imaginary world that surrounds their dramatic action and its landscape undergoes striking changes.

As interest in nonrealistic drama has grown in the United States, new attention has been directed toward Gertrude Stein, now widely considered (as she is in Robinson's book) the pioneer of this alternative dramaturgy. Jane Bowers has called attention to the fact that Stein herself referred to her major plays and operas, written between 1920 and 1933, as landscapes. Recognizing that Stein's plays rarely if ever are involved, as landscape would seem to be, with the verbal depiction or evocation of a scene, but that they nevertheless are involved with spatial configurations of language itself that, like landscapes, frame and freeze visual moments and alter perception, Bowers suggests a more accurate neologism for such plays, *lang-scapes*.[3]

Although of the various contemporary experimental dramatists I have mentioned, only Richard Foreman has specifically called attention to his relationship to Stein, all of them share her indifference to traditional plots and character development, and most of them have, like Stein, replaced these concerns with exploration of the structures, sounds, and evocative possibilities of language itself. Thus in their work, as in hers, language itself becomes a landscape, but in a variety of ways that much extend the possibilities of langscape as an aspect of the contemporary theater beyond that employed by Stein or discussed by Bowers.

As Bowers perceptively observes, language itself takes on a kind of spatial configuration in Stein, but this configuration continues in Stein to operate largely on the linguistic level, in the spatial arrangements of words and phonemes, stressing, as Elinor Fuchs has suggested, a pattern wholly present to itself in the moment of perception.[4] The term *langscape* takes on a much richer range of evocation when we move from Stein to those more recent experimental American dramatists I have cited, almost all of whom move outward from Stein's spatial arrangements of language in general to verbal explorations of the language of space itself, of geography, of mapmaking, of travel, even of astronomy. These plays often contain detailed evocations of presumed surroundings, but unlike the detailed physical landscapes of naturalism, created for the eye, these langscapes are often not actually seen, but are created rather for the ear and the imagination.

Of the American experimental dramatists being considered here, Richard Foreman, who has acknowledged his indebtedness to Stein, indeed often seems closest to her if one considers only his written texts. The highly distinctive realization of these texts on stage (since Foreman is also his own director and designer) takes one in quite another direction. Although the fascinating, cluttered interiors Foreman creates are very much his own, they have a certain relationship to some of the early visual stage reactions against realism in the symbolist and expressionist theater, which often presented psychic projections of the play's central figure in the form of strange visual terrains—landscapes of the soul. So overwhelming is the visual physical detail of a typical Foreman production that a spectator may not at first notice that Foreman commonly mixes actual physical landscapes with verbal langscapes, often in a consciously disjunctive and disruptive fashion. "As the texts of my plays became increasingly fragmented in order to echo the truth of psychic life," he has stated, "I wanted the scenery to do the same."[5]

Anyone who has seen a Foreman production will have been struck by the complexity and multiple suggested meanings of its visual surroundings, but amid the barrage of visual and aural material, one may not notice that there is also a verbal langscape only partly congruent with the landscape actually seen. Since Foreman consciously layers his visual worlds so that they simultaneously represent many interpretive possibilities, the constant shifts of his language often pick up one layer after another, encouraging in the audience a floating or multiple perception of the setting. Sometimes, indeed, language claims a landscape frankly different from what our eyes perceive. To give only a single striking example, Jack, in *The Cure,* observes of his surroundings at one point, "Look, it is indeed a rock-strewn landscape," but he is in fact then on a chair midstage holding a single large rock that he has just brought there (127). The "rock-strewn landscape" exists only in its verbal evocation and in the synecdochic rock.

Such a verbally sustained metaphorical and psychic landscape, found here and there in Foreman's work, can be discerned in much of contemporary American experimental theater in circumstances as varied as the languages and imaginations of its creators, but surprisingly often playing a central role in the imaginative world of the drama. Langscapes of the psychic imagination, recalling the earlier experiments of symbolism and expressionism, often characterize not only the work of Foreman, but perhaps even more strikingly that of Adrienne Kennedy, who also powerfully mixes actual physical landscapes of psychic projection with verbal langscapes. The imaginary worlds evoked in her innovative early plays—the jungle, the hotel room, the Victorian castle imagined by Sarah in *Funnyhouse of a Negro* or the imagined Tower of London and related sites in *The Owl Answers*—clearly take the audience into the psychic world of the central character. Something of this approach operates even in Kennedy's much more abstract *Sun,* where Man, the only speaker, repeats as a continuing refrain, variations of the line, "I keep on thinking landscapes / flowers and water views / of the coast of Italy / cloudbursts lilies," landscapes that exist only in the language and the audience's imagination.[6]

The works of Sam Shepard, probably the best known of this group of contemporary American experimental dramatists, provide clear examples of both a more traditional and a more innovative use of language-created landscape. Shepard's four major "realistic" dramas of the late 1970s and early 1980s, *Curse of the Starving Class, Buried Child, True West,* and *Fool for Love,* relate language and landscape (probably not at all coincidentally) in a manner already quite familiar to audiences used to the tradition of Ibsen and Chekhov. The parched farmland outdoors in *Starving Class,* the cornfield in *Buried Child,* the prairie in *True West,* the desert in *Fool for Love,* like the attic in Ibsen's *Wild Duck* or Chekhov's cherry orchard, serve as complex repositories of symbolic and psychic reference, but all of these locations remain solidly anchored within the objective world of realism and naturalism. The conventions of this dramatic tradition assume an objective reality for them, even when they are offered to the audience's imagination only by language. Indeed the tradition of what semiotic theorists have called diegetic space was not original with realism; it dates from classic theater, and I have considered its various forms and interpretive implications elsewhere.[7]

Shepard's earlier, less traditional, and less well known plays are much closer in spirit and practice to those of the other dramatists I am considering. Here psychic and symbolic landscapes are essentially linguistic creations, existing only in the dialogues or, more commonly, in what Jack Gelber has called the "volcanic monologue . . . Shepard's favorite form of address."[8] Indeed, the "volcanic monologue," with its pyrotechnic linguistic display, is a favorite form of address for most of these experimental American dramatists, and a particularly favored location for the presentation of a geography generated by language.

Almost all of Shepard's plays, from the very beginning, have single settings, but while these in the midseventies became more detailed and realistic in the tradition of drama descended from Ibsen's middle period, Shepard's earlier works are essentially and often specifically bare stages, on which the characters create and travel through imaginary settings entirely by the use of language. This is precisely the case in Shepard's first extant play, *Cowboys #2,* in which the two characters play out scenarios in an imaginary vaguely western landscape created entirely by their words. In *Mad Dog Blues,* the setting is described as "an open, bare stage. All the places the characters move through are imagined and mimed"—places that include various parts of the United States, tropical jungles, oceans, and desert islands, some based on actual locations, others derived from legend or folklore. Stu, sitting in his (realistic) bathtub in Chicago, creates a series of imaginary worlds in elaborate monologues, but his companion Joy also directly participates in this process, converting, by language, his tub into an oceangoing vessel, a game in which Stu enthusiastically joins:

> *Joy.* Look at the fish. (*Stu leans over and looks*)
> *Stu.* Them's barracuda, lady.[9]

Elinor Fuchs has perceptively suggested that in both Stein and Maeterlinck, the spatial principle represented by landscape has virtually replaced the temporal principle, quoting Gurnemanz's haunting line to Parsifal, "Here time turns to space."[10] For Stein and Maeterlinck, however, this implied a landscape of stasis, while some of the most interesting contemporary American experiments return langscape from stasis to movement by literally "turning time into space" through language, and thus allowing characters to wander in time as if it were space.

The best-known example of this is surely Eric Overmyer's fascinating *On the Verge, or the Geography of Yearning,* both titles suggesting something of its highly unconventional physical setting. In this play, three Victorian lady explorers, already having explored such exotic domains as the Amazon, the Himalayas, and the jungles of Africa and Southeast Asia, embark together through a strange langscape into terra incognita. As they penetrate it, they gradually become aware of two related effects. The first is that this new world is created from language. As Mary notes in her journal, "I have begun to dream in a new language. My imagination seems to sculpt the landscape."[11] The second is that, as Mary proposes soon after, "the strange words in our mouths" in fact come from the future: "with each step, each chop of the machete, we are advancing through the wilderness of time as well as space. Chronology as well as geography" (133).

On the road, the women encounter denizens of the brave new world of the future and mysterious artifacts such as eggbeaters and laser video discs, but language remains the grounding of this world, as a striking sequence near the end of the play reminds us again. Begged by her companions to give them "the lowdown on the future" before her final departure, Mary goes into a kind of trance and throws out a catalog of miscellaneous yet oddly linked items such as "Non-dairy creamer. Non-profit foundations No-fault insurance." And "Pulsars. Fiber optics.

Remote control. Double Think. Think tanks." The revelatory stage direction that introduces this strange catalog stresses its geographical subtext: "She osmoses, uttering each new word as if it were being spoken for the very first time. Coining place names for a map of the New World" (163–64). The metaphor of the map, the nexus of language, location, and landscape, is a particular favorite of most of the playwrights I am considering, and I will return to it again later.

Another important modern American dramatist for whom language is a central concern is Suzan-Lori Parks. "Language is a physical art," Parks suggests. "Words are spells which an actor consumes and digests—and through digesting creates a performance on stage."[12] In all of her plays Parks builds complex worlds of words, but *The America Play,* probably her best-known work, provides an interesting contrast to Overmyer's *On the Verge,* since it also depicts a dramatic world in which time has become landscape, although in this case the landscape is the past rather than the future. The setting, according to the stage directions, is "A great hole. In the middle of nowhere. The hole is an exact replica of the Great Hole of History."[13] In the Great Hole, Lucy explains, "you could see thuh whole world without goin too far. You could look intuh that Hole and see your entire life pass before you. Not your own life but someones life from history, you know" (197). Instead of Overmyer's detritus from the future—eggbeaters and laser disks— Parks's Great Hole is littered with debris of the past, "one of Mr. Washington's bones, a glass tradin bead, lick-ed boots, circulars, freein papers." The objects again are evoked by language, but language itself intrudes among the artifacts: "Uh house divided" "4score and 7 years uhgoh," "thuh last words.—And thuh last breaths" (189, 192).

Yet another play with a "geographical" title, the unpublished "Land of Fog and Whistles," by a leading experimental American dramatist, Mac Wellman, provides yet another variation on the langscape of cultural detritus. If the perspective was on the verbal and physical clutter of the future in *On the Verge* and of the past in *The America Play,* in "The Land of Fog and Whistles" it is on the future viewed as past. In this dramatic monologue, which Wellman calls a "language-piece," a "ghostly Scheherazade" recalls features of a series of nine previous "worlds"— these features made present to her audience only through her words—a first world of "thick cloth and cinnamon," a second world of "pork pie hats, furbelows, cheez whiz, elastic straps, and a certain sense of purely personal entitlement," and so on, with the doom of nuclear destruction hovering over all.[14] This piece, with its dead narrator evoking a ghostly past, suggests a kind of Western No play, but without the promise at the end of peace and release, rather of a "mad and meaningless" movement from place to place creating empty episodes endlessly repeated.

The cultural clutter that fills these three plays is a common feature of the world evoked by much contemporary nonrealistic American drama, clutter not only of physical objects, as in any work by Foreman, but, more strikingly in view of the theme of this essay, of language itself. Mac Wellman and Len Jenkin in particular, and often Sam Shepard and John Jesurun as well, almost obsessively evoke langscapes of a folkloric or semimythic America, one of the most striking features of which is the detritus—physical, verbal, and psychic—that constantly threatens to overwhelm its anguished inhabitants.

The other striking feature of these langscapes, as I have already mentioned, is that, unlike the landscape of painting (and of Stein's imagination), they are not statically displayed before the eyes of character or spectator, but are unstable, constantly metamorphosing terrains forcing their inhabitants into incessant if often confused motion. Here another insight of Stein's seems particularly appropriate. Speaking not of drama, but of the American psyche, she suggested that "it is something strictly American to conceive a space that is filled with moving, a space of time that is filled always with moving."[15]

Certainly this sense of movement, or more accurately lack of a stable grounding point for the dramatic world being presented, is a strikingly common theme in most of the dramatists I am discussing. The stable, indeed claustrophobic Ibsenian living rooms of the realist tradition are here often replaced by open, shifting landscapes as the characters travel through realms of the imagination, by foot in Overmyer's *On the Verge,* by subway car in Kennedy's *The Owl Answers,* by carnival funhouse ride in Jenkin's *Dark Ride* or automobile in his *Limbo Tales,* first by airplane and later by automobile in Jesurun's *Faust: Imperial Motel,* by "Greyways" bus in Wellman's *Whirligig* and interplanetary spaceship in his *Albanian Softshoe,* by foot, limousine, bus, and ship in Shepard's *Mad Dog Blues.* The Mayor's opening line in Jenkin's *American Notes* indeed strikes deep into the American psyche and into the psyche of these American dramatists: "Bound for somewhere, Buddy?"[16]

Mac Wellman's *Three Americanisms* is essentially a fugue (or as Wellman calls it an elegy) on the theme of movement through a langscape filled with cultural clutter. It begins with the provocative line, "I am running on empty in a region infinitely sparse, infinitely many" and goes on to develop both the motif of movement ("I am walking," "I am trudging," "I am riding," "We are en route"), the motif of the desolate but cluttered surroundings ("flying bricks, stoves, car doors, bins, tray tables, coat hangers, typewriters and screen writers, waste paper baskets, all whistle about in the red clangor of the hot wind . . ."), and often the two motifs articulated together ("I am galloping through a region of rusted jumbos, atomic glimmerglass, archaic rosebuds, mystic armadillos and borderline hayrakes").[17]

Even when the characters of these plays are not physically moving, like the speaker in Wellman's *Three Americanisms,* through an unstable, shifting, and culturally cluttered terrain, their minds and their language are constantly preoccupied with an attempt, inevitably unsatisfactory, to locate themselves within it. This quest generates a language obsessed with landscape, location, and geography, with the creation and description of langscape, as in the already cited opening speech of the Mayor in *American Notes.* "You moving on to somewhere cause you think this ain't it," the Mayor observes, and indeed America offers an overwhelming amount of "somewhere" for its restless souls to wander in. As the Mayor remarks, this is not a "tiddlywink country like Alboonia you step outta your shack to take a piss and if the wind's right you are watering foreign soil."[18] By contrast, America, the Major warns the traveler, is a complex, challenging, and disturbing terrain:

> I got a good idea where you're headed. Why you know there's nine rivers between here and there, and you moving like you gonna get there Tuesday. There's the Muskinggum, an' the Chatahoochie, the Raritanic, the Monongahoola, the Gahoola-monga, the Belly-Up, the Snake, and the Skunk. Whooooooo! You counting? There's one so fearsome it either doesn't have a name or I'm scared to tell it. (6)

This sort of catalog survey of a selection of America's bizarre and multifarious place-names, a langscape device employed in a number of plays by both Jenkin and Wellman, echoes a popular poem by an earlier writer fascinated by the exuberance, variety, and often highly unconventional nature of such names, the ballad "American Names" by Stephen Vincent Benét. Benét announced himself in love with the varied and vigorous names on the American landscape, the "sharp names that never get flat . . . Tucson and Deadwood and Lost Mule Flat." These he contrasted with the "thin and worn" place-names of Europe, elegant and smooth, but also familiar and unexciting.[19]

The contrast that Benét records is echoed in more general and more theoretical terms in a 1991 article by Susan Stanford Friedman that extends this characteristic of American place-names out into the American language in general. Friedman suggests that "in relation to British

English and its partial parent French, American English is heteroglossic, polyglot, multivoiced, and many-tongued—a language of the rebellious, postcolonial subject that refuses the orthodoxy of its precursor."[20]

Wellman and Jenkin, like Benét, clearly delight, as weavers of linguistic structures, in this rebelliousness and unorthodoxy, but their emphasis is distinctly different. While Benét emphasizes his personal pleasure as a balladeer in the linguistic exuberance of the American langscape, Jenkin and Wellman strike a distinctly more desperate note, and one that reflects an America far less secure and self-congratulatory than that of Benét and his era. The vast American landscape now threatens a vertiginous rootlessness, and its polyglot geographical nomenclature seems less a mark of imaginative exuberance than of the filling of this vast landscape with uprooted fragments of borrowed history and culture, at best overwhelming the characters with abundance and complexity and at worst poisoning their surroundings with alien and unassimilated debris.

The contrast between the linguistic landscape of Benét and that of these contemporary dramatists is beautifully illustrated by a key speech in Mac Wellman's *Whirligig,* a bravura linguistic monologue that is one of the hallmarks of Wellman, as it is of Sam Shepard. Wellman's Bus Driver announces that, as the bus has "spontaneously combusted out by the dump near Milwacky," there is no transportation available to a dizzying variety of locations that read like a manic parody of Benét:

> Crow, Port Tobacco, Loyalsock, Baraboo, Washington, Salem, Cheegago, Webster, Troy, Utica, Carthage, Beanbag, Thorpe, Hog Eye, Noodle Oblong, Santa Claus, Rabbit Hash, Bumble Bee, Wink, Zigzag, Jackass Gulch, Gouge, Hang Town, Bug, Humbug Flat, Defeated, Raccoon, Okay, Custard, Brindle, Dead Man, Horsetail, not to Puppytown, by ways of Centipede, Paint Pot, One-Eye, Puke, and Rat-trap, nor through Chuckle head, Shinbone, Dead Mule, Ground Hog's Glory and Poverty Hill, where nothing don't grow no more owning to a radioactive constitution of stroobontium seepage.[21]

The linguistic exuberance of this onomastic riff by no means hides the recurring notes of defeat, disaster, and disequilibrium that so many of the names evoke, but perhaps even more significant is the framing of this catalog by images of toxic dumps, leaching into and destroying a once pure and healthy countryside. The leaking nuclear reactor and contaminated dump are central images in Wellman's imaginative landscape, the end product and central symbol of the poisoning of the American landscape by the detritus of modern Western civilization. These images are particularly clear in the four interrelated plays that make up Wellman's "Crowtette"—A *Murder of Crows, The Hyacinth Macaw, Second-Hand Smoke,* and *The Lesser Magoo.* The epicenter of the "Crowtette" is the midwestern town of Gradual, located downwind of the never seen but often mentioned "big reactor" and the "county dump." The smoking radioactive reactor and leaking storage dumps suggest a whole network of social and cultural poisons from Wellman's contemporary America, where an ominous vision of both present and future rests on the unstable and poisoned ground of a wasteful and destructive past, repressed but never obliterated.

More disturbing still, the combined American passions for continual movement and the covering of the landscape with litter is not confined to this country, nor, it now appears, even to this planet. Not content with reciting the terrestrial names of his bus's possible trajectory, Wellman's driver continues on with an equally bizarre collection of planetoids and asteroids, among which the play imaginatively travels, Thule and Teucer, Khufu, 1931 PH, Tyche, and so on. *Whirligig* offers no description of these apparently colonized astral worlds, but another Wellman terrestrial/celestial drama, *The Albanian Softshoe,* includes a more detailed interplanetary cruise that is a nightmare version of the naive celestial voyages of Saint-Exupéry's Little Prince. The junk and litter that covers the planetoids shows all too clearly their connection with Wellman's American landscape, confirmed by one of the few living inhabitants, an American farmer who has come here to escape the encroaching blacks. The psychic and linguistic debris of an oneiric middle America has here leached out into an equally cluttered, confused, and endangered cosmos.

It is easy to see why language, rather than wood, paint, or canvas, has become the preferred medium for presenting the shifting and cluttered landscapes of such dramatic worlds, since it shares with them multiple and constantly shifting referentiality. The langscapes of these American dramatists would fit very uneasily into the stable locales of the traditional illusionistic stage, and an attempt to fix them is doomed to frustration. It is striking how often the metaphor of the useless map occurs in these dramas, a warning that the stable configurations of cartography, like those of the illusionistic stage, are ill-suited to the shifting and unstable landscapes that these dramatists represent in the fluid and protean material of language. The *Whirligig* Bus Driver's warning that a search for the locations he mentions on the map may well be in vain finds parallels in many other works I have mentioned. The lady explorers in Overmyer's *On the Verge* are frankly moving through "Terra Incognita," by definition outside the fixed world of maps.

In the shifting geographies of Wellman and Jenkin maps do exist and indeed are frequently consulted, but their inadequacy in representing the imaginary langscapes of these plays is a recurring motif. The protagonist in Jenkin's *My Uncle Sam* visits a travel agency attempting to get to a mysterious Port Desire. Consulting a world map held by his assistant, the agent remarks, "We can't send you there if we can't find the place. Be sensible. How about Australia?" Sam perseveres: "Look again, will ya. That's the world. It's gotta be there somewhere," only to be informed, "Ah! There's the little bugger. Port Desire. Sorry. You can't get there from here."[22] In Shepard's *Mad Dog Blues* a similar problem plagues Yahoodi, who possesses the pirate captain's map to his buried treasure but admits, "This is a hard map to follow," and is ultimately forced to go wherever the captain leads him.[23]

Even more unstable is the setting in the book being translated that serves as the framework of Jenkin's *Dark Ride*. As the Translator figure himself explains in the play:

> The Chinese setting itself is also subject to debate. I've come to believe it may well be a fiction. I'm almost certain that the book relies on geographical information about China plagiarized from a certain Children's Picture Atlas of the World . . . though at times the author seems to have either misread this source, or is deliberately inventing locations that never existed.[24]

The towns of Gradual and Bug River, central locations in Wellman's "Crowtette" plays, are seemingly solidly located on the Bug River and Route Six, but when characters consult maps in an attempt to fix their precise location, as they do a number of times in these plays, their search is always troubled. Nella opens the cycle explaining in the first speech in *A Murder of Crows* that her surroundings "don't fit on the map right," while the strange Mr. William Hard subsequently argues that the inhabitants of Bug River really should not even put up a sign marking the community. "I'd never post that," he observes. 'It' be too much an abject certainty. . . . Where I come from's on no map."[25] In *The Hyacinth Macaw,* Susannah insists that she has "seen the map with the town of Gradual written all over, and Bug River too. A sharp red snake of a wriggle." But Dore, who knows her snakes, responds that "the devil put it there, to delude the mapmaker." "I love all maps," Dora confesses, "but not for what they tell me of the world. The world is a useless thing without the soul's commission."

It is really this "soul's commission" that determines the geography, and the cartography, of Wellman's Middle American community, its unstable geography reflecting an unstable and clearly threatened national psyche. Not all of the contemporary American langscape dramatists share the apocalyptic vision so common in Wellman, though a similar specter haunts a number of them, most strikingly Shepard and Jenkin. All, however, share a very twentieth-century, and particularly American, concern—that we are moving rapidly and often meaninglessly through a world that is simultaneously desolate and cluttered by the debris of the past, much of it unhealthy.

Further, in depicting this vision, they share a concern with the impact of the "soul's commission" upon the physical settings of their plays. More in the tradition of Strindberg than of Ibsen, they all recognize the close relationship between psyche and landscape, even to the extent of viewing the latter as a creation or projection of the former. At least two major characteristics set them apart from a dramatist of psychic projection like Strindberg, however, and for all their differences in tonality and technique, allow them to be considered as dramatists sharing a similar vision. First is the particularly American kind of psychic world they create. Second is the filtering of this world not through a personality, as in Strindberg, but through language, the medium that we have come to realize shapes not only the psyche's cognition of the world but perhaps the psyche itself. It seems altogether appropriate that some of our most perceptive and thoughtful contemporary dramatists have abandoned the concrete stage of detailed physical settings that suited so well the age of positivism and the celebration of the empirical methodology of the physical sciences, and in its place have developed forms of stage geography that reflect the widely held view that everything about us, even our physical universe, is in fact a product of language. Further, because they are also writers for the theater, which is traditionally concerned with both language and space, they have taken this preoccupation with language in a particularly theatrical direction, developing it as a spatial as well as a linear construct.

NOTES

1. Victor Hugo, *Oeuvres complètes,* 18 vols. (Paris: Club français du livre, 1967), 3:63.

2. Marc Robinson, *The Other American Drama* (Cambridge: Cambridge University Press, 1994).

3. Jane Palatini Bowers, *"They Watch Me as They Watch This"*: *Gertrude Stein's Metadramas* (Philadelphia: University of Pennsylvania Press, 1991), 26.

4. Elinor Fuchs, *The Death of Character: Perspective on Theater after Modernism* (Bloomington: Indiana University Press, 1996), 95.

5. Richard Foreman, *Unbalancing Acts* (New York: Pantheon, 1992), 64.

6. Adrienne Kennedy, *Sun,* in *Adrienne Kennedy in One Act* (Minneapolis: University of Minnesota Press, 1988), 71. *Funnyhouse of a Negro* and *The Owl Answers* are also in this volume.

7. Marvin Carlson, "Indexical Space in the Theatre," *Assaph* 10 (1994): 1–4.

8. Jack Gelber, "Sam Shepard: The Playwright as Shaman," introduction to *Angel City and Other Plays,* by Sam Shepard (New York: Applause, n.d.), 3.

9. Sam Shepard, *Five Plays* (New York: Bobbs-Merrill, 1967), 10.

10. Fuchs, *Death of Character,* 96; Richard Wagner, *Parsifal,* English libretto version Stewart Robb (New York: Schirmer, 1962), 7.

11. Eric Overmyer, *On the Verge,* in *Anti-Naturalism* (New York: Broadway Play Publishing, 1989), 131.

12. Suzan-Lori Parks, "Elements of Style," in *The America Play and Other Works* (New York: Theatre Communications Group, 1995), 11.

13. Parks, *The America Play,* 159.

14. Mac Wellman, "The Land of Fog and Whistles," typescript, 53.

15. Gertrude Stein, "The Gradual Making of the Making of Americans," in *Lectures in America* (Boston: Beacon Press, 1985), 161.

16. Len Jenkin, *American Notes* (New York: Dramatists Play Service, 1988), 6.

17. Mac Wellman, "Three Americanisms," fourth draft typescript, 1, 2, 3, 6, 10.

18. Interestingly, Mac Wellman also often cites Albania as the generic "other" to his imagined America.

19. Stephen Vincent Benét, *Selected Works* (New York: Holt, Rinehart and Winston, 1966), 367.

20. Susan Stanford Friedman, "Weavings: Intertextuality and the (Re)Birth of the Author," in *Influence and Intertextuality in Literary History,* ed. Jay Clayton and Eric Rothstein (Madison: University of Wisconsin Press, 1991), 161.

21. Wellman, *Whirligig* (New York: Theatre Communications Group Plays in Process, 1989), 11.

22. Len Jenkin, *My Uncle Sam* (New York: Dramatists Play Service, 1984), 19.

23. Shepard, *Angel City,* 163.

24. Len Jenkin, *Dark Ride* (New York: Dramatists Play Service, 1982), 12–13.

25. Mac Wellman, *A Murder of Crows* (Los Angeles: Sun and Moon Press, 1994), 7, 61.

8

Robert Wilson, Nicolas Poussin, and *Lohengrin*

Marc Robinson

"It moves," wrote Gertrude Stein, trying to sum up what she meant by a "landscape" play, "but it also stays."[1] She had already identified the same contradiction in landscapes themselves: A flock of magpies flying overhead seems fixed against the blue background of the sky, she said. Likewise, an apparently stable setting is in fact always changing. Clouds dissolve or rearrange themselves; the light shifts to reveal new contours and colors in familiar things; trees blur with every breeze. The landscapes we inhabit, like those Stein creates in her drama, seem permanently precarious—humming, as if they owe their composure to a miraculously coordinated effort by all its elements, including the observer, who affirms the arrangement by studying it closely.

This kind of vision also "moves but stays." For Stein it is a vigorous, stubborn act—attentiveness more than mere looking—as spectators address and readdress the same beguiling scene in the hope of understanding it fully. As they do so, they mimic Stein's own yearning for an intimate connection with her subjects—to "feel the melody of any one," as she writes in "Portraits and Repetition," and "get back to the essence of the thing contained within itself"[2]—a goal she further shares with those of her protagonists who compulsively review the institutions and mechanisms binding them to one another. (The speakers of *They Must. Be Wedded. To Their Wife.* are typical.) Her theater's famously repetitive language is the instrument (and evidence) of such engagement: Each cycle of description marks the continuation of attention; eventually such "insistence" (Stein's preferred term for repetition) forms the only solid ground in a world where figures won't thicken into characters and incidents won't collaborate on a narrative.

Both sides of this equation—Stein's persistence in the face of her subject's elusiveness—are integral to her theater. She resists both randomness and, at the other extreme, schematism. While her style is essentially austere—she almost never changes the subject—that subject deepens over the course of the play, revealing ever more intricate relationships among her speakers: "The more familiar a thing is," as she writes in "Pictures," "the more there is to be familiar with."[3] Elsewhere, she expands on these principles of familiarity and relationship in explaining why she wants to link theater and landscape:

> I felt that if a play were exactly like a landscape then there would be no difficulty about the emotion of the person looking on at the play being behind or ahead of the play because the landscape does not have to make acquaintance. . . . The landscape has its formation . . . as after all a play has to have formation and be in relation one thing to the other thing. . . . [T]he story is only of importance if you like to tell or like to hear a story but the relation is there anyway. And of that relation I wanted to make a play.[4]

This desire also sustains the theater of Stein's most loyal disciple, Robert Wilson. His own landscape aesthetics were first discussed by Richard Foreman in an influential review of Wilson's *The Life and Times of Sigmund Freud* (1969). Wilson's theater, he writes, "is not a straining after more and more intense 'expression' of predetermined material, but is a sweet and powerful 'placing' of various found and invented stage objects and actions."[5] This "compositional" approach results in a "'field' situation" (as Foreman calls it) designed to stimulate the spectators' capacity for comparative seeing: We learn to sense the magnetic tension linking figures placed far apart from one another, for instance, or the fraught relationship between a figure and a nearby object—a kind of visual counterpoint that also structures the larger relationship between the actors and the stage itself. When the light brightens and a small space suddenly seems boundless and uncharted—or when the horizon disappears behind a wall of buildings—it is the actors' new orientation in the landscape, rather than anything they say or do, that determines the nature of our involvement. As Foreman writes, "the specific 'aesthetic' emotion of lucidity replace[s] the more melodramatic emotions of both daily life and most theatre."[6]

Foreman's review of *Freud* established a vocabulary for discussing several other works Wilson staged in the 1970s, among them *Deafman Glance* (1970–71), *KA MOUNTAIN AND GUARDenia TERRACE* (1972), and *The $ Value of Man* (1975). Many of these pieces were stocked with disparate figures and objects, each participating in multiple dramas unfolding simultaneously, as still more images scrolled across the stage, replenishing the tableau. The most detailed record of these performances inevitably distorts their structure: Stefan Brecht's exhaustive chronicle of *Deafman Glance* (in *The Theatre of Visions*) is arranged in 113 numbered paragraphs—"#19. The waiter has been shaking a cocktail mixer and now serves the drink dexterously to the big frog." "#95. The ox stands, its belly lights up"[7]—that impose a single order and pace of perception where many are equally valid (notwithstanding the inevitable linearity of any performance). Accounts of *KA MOUNTAIN* are even more deceptive: Few spectators (if any) saw everything that happened over the seven-day continuous performance, staged at many different locations on Shiraz's Haft Tan Mountain.

Edwin Denby caught the right mix of delight and exasperation shared by many of Wilson's earliest spectators when he described his experience at *Freud:* "I felt like leaving, because I was so irritated at not being able to follow anything, but then . . . I started looking at the whole stage at once. . . . That was the way to look, not at anything in particular, but . . . to keep looking, and if you do get interested in one thing in particular . . . remember after a minute or two to let your eyes travel."[8] As he did so, learning to relinquish what he saw as forcefully as he seized it, he preserved the "lucidity" Foreman admired: It's as if Wilson feared the stage would muddy, and his imagery would lose its sparkle, if its surfaces were disturbed by scrutiny. Leo Bersani, in a brief discussion of Wilson's early work in *A Future for Astyanax,* calls this same approach "visual mobility," and then sharpens the definition: Wilson's spectator is "self-scattering" alongside the fragmented figures onstage, who by their own gracefulness teach us to jump as easily from situation to situation, unsentimental about what we see (or don't see).[9] The pleasures of such intentionally distracted vision—and of visionary states—overwhelm any pull from the opposite direction: the more focused work of introspection, the more painful experience of self-consciousness.

Such a relaxed (but engaged) mode of staging and seeing fosters equally organic analysis. Just as Wilson implies that he submits to natural laws when structuring a work—"I use the kind of natural time in which it takes the sun to set, a cloud to change, a day to dawn," he once said, correcting an interviewer who had said his theater runs in slow motion—spectators learn to allow patterns to emerge easily from the elements and events on view.[10] Watching one of Wilson's landscape dramas, we don't feel obligated to relate everything we see to a central situation, much less a figure—even when, as in *Einstein, Freud, Stalin,* even *Curious George,* the titles imply that someone does in fact enjoy preeminence. Nor do we rank images according to their capacity to further a thematic premise, something that we do instinctively in our memory of most productions. Wilson's dramatic structure is egalitarian, organized according to Stein's definition of sequence: "The natural way to count," she said, "is not that one and one make two but . . . one and one and one and one and one."[11] Each image invites contemplation and triggers associations all its own, even as it helps sustain the larger imaginative world deepening around it. Such a mise-en-scène is fluid and decentralized— it recalls Appia's vision of "rhythmic spaces"—or rather it is organized around many centers: Each object or figure seems, for the duration of our fascination with it, to have occasioned the entire landscape. For this reason, Wilson insists on preserving the affective and perceptual distance between stage and audience—even as his colleagues in the vanguard theater of the 1960s and 1970s were crossing that boundary. It's not merely a matter of taste: He fears that the immediacy prized by other theater artists leads to a kind of imaginative, even moral myopia. Wilson's theater, by contrast, urges us to register both a thing and the empty, umarked space around it. His performers—breathing monuments and bas-reliefs—compel attention less for their humanity than for their service as landmarks in an intricately mapped image-world. We discover the consequences of presence (not just its beauty) as they ripple through the environment and subtly alter our approach to every other element in the mise-en-scène. Another paradox: Because many elements on Wilson's stage seem self-contained, we work harder to connect them to others and perceive their context, something we take for granted in more seamless theater.

Paul Schmidt, Wilson's frequent collaborator in the 1980s and 1990s, once described the change from personal experience:

> I once had a house in Texas. A small house with a garden, and I had filled it with beautiful things—furniture, carpets, drawings, silver, glass, flowers. . . . Then I went to New York for a few years to work and left it to Bob Wilson, with all the beautiful things it contained. A few months later I came back, [and] I didn't recognize it. Everything was still there, but everything had been changed. . . . Objects had been placed next to one another in what to me was a senseless arrangement. . . . It all made me anxious. . . . But after a few days, little by little, slowly, I started to feel a pleasure that charmed me more and more. For

I began looking at the things that surrounded me. Bob knew, by some art, how to arrange them in a way that made me look at them, and to look at them as themselves. I realized that I had previously arranged everything in the house as a frame for myself; I had confined the things in it to the background.[12]

Fundamental as this principle is to Wilson's aesthetic, it would nonetheless be wrong to conclude that it results in impersonal art, or (despite his protestations to the contrary) that his productions resist interpretative approaches that consider anything other than structures and sequences. (The latter was Craig Owens's view; at the opposite and equally reductive extreme is Jill Johnston, who has turned many of Wilson's productions into autobiographical dramas about fathers and sons.)[13] Schmidt himself avoids the temptation to see Wilson's work in purely formal terms: Later in his description of the Texas house, he writes that "Bob had brought things out into the world—or rather he knew how to create a world of mutual affinities between us and objects." Schmidt's amended observation reminds us that the objects and their compositions aren't only interesting in themselves; just as important is the way they make us rethink the figures in their midst, integrating them more completely with their setting.

While Wilson may obey the "deindividualizing impulse" to create work in which "the audience is not so much following relationships between characters as relationships among places or channels" (as Elinor Fuchs writes persuasively in *The Death of Character*),[14] it doesn't necessarily follow that the patterns render the figures irrelevant. In fact, in many pieces he seems to argue for an expanded definition of conduct, one that recognizes objective correlatives for human endeavor and feeling in many elements of a given production, as he works variations on archetypal experiences in visual, aural, and gestural languages. In other words, far from being indifferent to psychological concerns, Wilson implies that most theater doesn't do them justice. It has oversimplified them in obedience to the rule of causality, or trimmed them to fit the biography of discrete characters—figures unable to suggest all the implications of their experience.

KA MOUNTAIN may go the furthest in subordinating performers to their landscape, yet even here Wilson's investigation of space is occasioned and controlled by a human figure—if not a character exactly, then someone emblematic of our shared nature. Wilson's synopsis, a series of apparent station-names reproduced in the program, begins by referring to "the old man," "the journey," and "the body"; only then does it move out to the "ocean," a "horizontal zone" and "people as trees," before finally returning to the old man.[15] The subtitle confirms the intimate source of its epic structure: *A Story of a Family and Some People Changing.* Just as Wilson's landscape theater won't let you consider individuals apart from their surroundings (as the Texas house teaches), neither can you know a space without taking into account those populating it. Figure and ground derive their value from one another.

It's a mark of Wilson's critical rigor that in practice such an alliance never looks as effortless as it sounds. The figure-ground relationship is negotiated throughout a production—this process often forms the only plot—as his performers emerge from the tableaux to offer themselves as standards of measure for the surroundings, then recede again, while the ground seems to shift, the climate to change, and all elements, including the figures, must stake new claims to their territory. In a number of works, these cycles are complicated by a steady dilation of the landscape; even the representations of actual places are enveloped by a cosmic idea of space. For the spectator accustomed to filtering his or her own perception of the stage through the eyes of a surrogate onstage, the change is especially disorienting. After working to establish a web of associations among people and settings, Wilson now unmoors his figures, denying them reference points for their identities. It's as if Wilson were reaching toward a Platonic ideal of space, impossible to master with our primitive imaginative compass—a zone of which the visible stage is only a tiny fraction. Wilson's production of Marguerite Duras's *The Malady of Death* (1991) condenses this process to its essential sequence: As a man and a woman measure the limits of their ambiguous relationship, the back wall of their room—a dark, shallow chamber—seems to slide open, wider after each scene, revealing bright white light. By the end, the characters are completely exposed, and geography itself, with its apparatus of borders, perimeters, interiors and exteriors, has been overwhelmed by abstract space. The stage no longer reflects the couple back to themselves, shoring up each person's embattled ego; neither does it frame their intimacy, nor cushion their difficult encounters, nor even give shape to their ultimate estrangement. Landscape sheds all previous emotional connotations to speak only of itself, casting in relief the helplessness of its onetime inhabitants.

When Wilson has himself described related sequences in his theater, he elaborates Stein's landscape poetics with additional terms borrowed from painting. Individual scenes, he says, also fulfill rules of perspective analogous to those in still lifes and portraits. (Wilson's version of the latter form is more direct and less cubist than Stein's.) The portraitist's close attention to a figure is matched by the most constrained episodes in a production (often staged in a corner of the stage or in front of the curtain), while the still life artist's interest in relationships among phenomena guides the scenes unfolding at a middle distance. As they alternate with landscape scenes, which provide a panoramic view of the stage and synchronize individual actions with the movement of the whole, the action expands and contracts, which in turn makes us aware of our own changing relationship to the stage. This, rather than narrative or emotional development, establishes the dramatic structure.

Wilson records this action on textual, gestural, and temporal levels as well; in doing so he awakens us to the contingency of our own language, bodies, and way of telling time. At moments in *A Letter for Queen Victoria,* for instance, the performers seem to be sounding the space whenever they speak, opening it up for viewing, rather than talking to one another or to us. They also lose themselves in their own speech, as Wilson severs language from speakers, distributing words around the stage in columns, forests, and ziggurats projected or painted on the backdrops. (*A Letter for Queen Victoria* announces the objectlike nature of words in the title, and the published script further encourages us to think of the page as we already think of the stage—a space to be designed, on which language has a presence as significant as that of any actor.) *Einstein on the Beach* (1976) demonstrates a similar approach in terms of gesture. The actors' fastidious finger movements in the prologue and later knee-plays eventually open onto a group of dancers spinning freely across a vast empty stage, arms stretched out like weathervanes. For all their weightlessness, they cleave to the ground, as if by obeying its topography they are rebuking the pair in the knee-plays, who chart space from a distance, hoping for knowledge from their coded, calculating gestures. Finally, in many productions time itself surrenders to the same centrifugal force. Scenes that seem to correspond to specific contexts—the antebellum South, Japan in the 1850s, postwar Germany—are reabsorbed into biological time. *Deafman Glance,* for instance, ends with a small house sinking into the ground, the top of a pyramid flying up to the sky, and all the performers going down a hole in the floor, from which, a moment later, a group of apes emerges—a kind of reverse evolution.

The most ambitious demonstration of this centrifugal motion, and the most suggestive of its largest implications, is *the CIVIL warS* (1983–86), Wilson's five-part work originally planned for production in Germany, Italy, Holland, Japan, and the United States—a project in which the dilating action within individual parts mirrors Wilson's own

Deafman Glance, by Robert Wilson, New York City, 1971.
(Photo by Martin Bough.)

Part 4 of *CIVIL WarS,* by Robert Wilson, Cologne, 1984. (Photo
by Clarchen Baus-Mattar.)

global conception of the entire production and his globe-circling efforts to complete it. Throughout *the CIVIL warS,* Wilson treats the stage as a blank, erasable slate, on which can be read the efforts of disparate figures to mark it with their image. *The CIVIL warS* includes figures recognizable as Frederick the Great, Garibaldi, Commodore Perry, Abraham Lincoln, and Robert E. Lee, who nonetheless shed their personal attributes as they become monuments to the social and emotional energies of their ages. Such an allegiance is expressed literally in the German section, when Frederick looms paternally over a miniature model of Berlin. A similar relationship is consummated in the Rome section, when Lincoln appears as a proscenium-high puppet walking godlike over his setting, then falls slowly backward until he's prone, hovering several feet off the ground, almost the width of the stage. Lincoln's body, emblem of his time, now becomes a second horizon line, border of his space.

Yet from the very start of *the CIVIL warS,* Wilson trains us to look critically at these mergers of individuals and landscapes. The first scene of the German section (intended also as the opening of the completed work) depicts two astronauts surveying a silhouette of a continent—it vaguely resembles Africa—hanging upright from the flies, a form so large it becomes a kind of upstage wall. It seems summoned by and subject to the astronauts, who move up and down ladders that themselves slide left and right, as if together they can organize the territory under their supervision. But moments later this ambition collapses, as the continent breaks in two. The rupture is a startling synopsis of every civil-war narrative. It also reorients those who recognize history solely by the deeds of its leading actors: Lincoln's and Lee's omnipresence notwithstanding, *the CIVIL warS* gives pride of place to cultural and geographic bodies. Later in the production, Wilson cites American imperialist designs on Japan, the war between France and England, the multiple divisions of Germany, as well as more elemental episodes of national upheaval, such as the Lisbon earthquake, described here by Voltaire. Human participation in (or responsibility for) all these events is subordinated to primeval forces. The ambitions and maneuverings of a Frederick (for instance) seem nothing more than reflections of a larger and less intelligible design, arranged on a cosmic level, predating his own emergence. In one sequence, Wilson shows a film of swimming polar bears; in another, a film of buildings exploding. Still other scenes, distributed throughout *the CIVIL warS,* subordinate human protagonists to various gods and goddesses, larger-than-life animals (a snow owl, a pair of giraffes), and other, hybrid figures—all of whom (he implies) are attuned to the universe's rhythms with an intensity unknown to their human charges.

Wilson once described his blending of different national histories in *the CIVIL warS*—and, within those histories, of the wild and the domesticated, the fantastic and the familiar—as "showing the shared nature of human experience among all peoples . . . a great affirmation of the oneness of humanity and the possibility of universal accord."[16] Yet if *the CIVIL warS* had actually succeeded in fulfilling this aim, how much less interesting it would be. Wilson is saved from false optimism (and thus from sentimentality) by his own dramatic structure, in which each element retains its independence even while sharing the same space and time. The implications of such fragmentation are manifold. Wilson's staging suggests an approach to history on guard against the generalities and reductions of history-writing itself. His world-sized epic remains more interested in molecules than in systems; follows detours as assiduously as the main stream of events; and values the unassimilated incident even as Wilson ponders the possible existence of a hidden grand scheme. The many images of cohesion in *the CIVIL warS*—families, generations, nations, cultures, eras—exist as unattainable ideals, their chronic dissolution only increasing their attractiveness.

Such a fragmented conclusion should seem inevitable from the start. After the silhouette of the continent splits in two, white light pours through the gap. The rupture prepares us to see all subsequent landscapes in *the CIVIL warS* as temporary and contingent, despite Wilson's ease at establishing new ones throughout the work and despite each section's allegiance with a particular city. Indeed, into the void disappear political notions of geography—a social order maintained by our system of nations and the history of our efforts to contain and characterize them. Meanwhile, a turtle continues its slow progress across the floor, seeming to press the stage into place. As at the end of *Deafman Glance,* there remains only this humble, elemental mode of occupying the ground—one unavailable to the humans who would seize it instead. It may be fitting, then, that *the CIVIL warS* was never staged in its entirety. After trying to encompass the globe with his art, Wilson unintentionally enables us to see his work in the form most suited to both its content and implicit ethics: The five parts survive as separate points in space, undiminished by linear connection and resisting the mapmaking of even the most expansive imagination.

Such Stein-influenced dispersal is the style by which Wilson is most easily identified, but there are a number of works in which he closes down the stage, delimiting its boundaries and turning his attention inward. We follow suit: Instead of seizing the opportunity Wilson has afforded us in his earliest pieces for undirected viewing (in the manner Bersani described), we submit to a plan—training our eye in principles of decorum and economy. The *Medea* prelude to *Deafman Glance* (presented, when I saw it in 1987, as a self-sufficient piece), and his stagings of *Alceste* (1986), *Hamletmachine* (1986), *Madama Butterfly* (1993), *Pelléas and Mélisande* (1997), and especially *Lohengrin* (1998) share an almost monastic temperament, despite their obvious differences in text and music. These Wilson productions are distrustful of ornament, modest in their deportment, saluting self-control and economy as they complete a tightly reasoned argument about perception. The "sweet and powerful placing" Foreman identified now obeys an even more apparent logic, as if Wilson were working out all the possible solutions to a visual problem or all the applications of a single gestural principle. In this regard, these productions seem to participate in an extraordinary rite of self-criticism, or at least self-questioning, requiring us to redefine Wilson's relationship to his Stein inheritance. If, in his early works, the "moving" seemed to overwhelm the "staying," now the balance shifts, and staying reasserts itself. Wilson seizes and maps space that he elsewhere might have surrendered to, demonstrating the procedures by which landscape (or nature generally) becomes geography—landscape organized, if not fully understood. These are the same procedures that he seemed determined to overthrow in other pieces. Here, the landscape toys with, and sometimes even rebukes, its inhabitants, nowhere more so than at its horizon—a favorite location on Wilson's stage, where his figures are silhouetted against a luminous, color-saturated sky.

In the director's most Steinian works, these upstage tableaux seem emblematic of his own desire to transcend the limits of his form: The stage seems to swell outward, its inhabitants on the verge of departure. But in other, more austere pieces, the horizon becomes an impassable border. Instead of proposing escape, it enforces self-discipline; to wait there for the stage to dilate, or a journey to begin, seems (to this Wilson) romantic and naive. In his production of *Hamletmachine*, Wilson argues the principles behind all these works. His stage is a kind of revolving box (appropriate to the black box at New York University where the production was first presented) in which furniture and other scenery shifts ninety degrees after each segment. The multiple points of view should open up the landscape; instead, they reaffirm its claustrophobia. Those spectators easily seduced by the horizons in Wilson's proscenium stagings experience particular disillusionment: A black curtain is drawn across a cyclorama with each rotation; on an adjacent wall a new horizon is revealed—but its promise of expansiveness is now no longer to be trusted. It doesn't stay visible for long, and indeed, after the final rotation, all screens are curtained and no escape seems possible. While this has been going on, the actors have been shrinking the landscape further: As they repeat the same movement pattern after each scenic shift, they advance no action, reveal no character, change nothing. Their performance is the gestural equivalent of the exitless space.

In this and other pieces, among Wilson's most emotionally open, such a severe style counters the subject matter. Reason is brought to bear on conditions which usually forgive unreason—Hamlet's disgust, Butterfly's longing and humiliation, Alceste's grief, Medea's rage, even Svetlovidov's nostalgia (in Chekhov's *Swan Song,* staged in 1989). The self-consciousness of Wilson's performers reorients spectators in other ways as well: In other productions, the figures often beckoned us to marvel at magnificent, if not always visible, landscapes. The famous crowd of black "mammies" pointing at the sky in *Deafman Glance* introduced attitudes of wonder that would be adapted by the couple in the caboose in *Einstein on the Beach* and the deep-sea-diving Robert E. Lee in the Rome section of *the CIVIL warS*. Not here: Now Wilson's performers gaze on far more circumscribed territory—their own bodies, and the small circle in which they are able to act. As they complete delicate gestures, or walk as if still learning the sequence of steps, or simply stand still and listen, their characters seem to abstract their emotions from themselves, thereby mastering them.

In all these works, passion spends itself on such procedures, which are affirmed, in turn, by the landscape's own contraction. The machine-like design of *Hamletmachine* is only one of many closed systems Wilson devises to prevent his performers from forgetting where they are. In each production, they are forced to acknowledge an ever more insistent space, adjusting themselves according to its demands, even as their characters surrender to feeling, or take refuge in their intimacy with one another. The set of *Swan Song*—the three sides of a provincial theater's stage, its tall gray walls broken only by windows placed too high to see through—is a cell out of *Endgame*. The protagonist of Brecht's *Oceanflight* (which Wilson staged in 1997) is surrounded by five identically dressed doubles, trapping him in a hall of mirrors. In *Alceste,* the landscape is vast, deep, and inviting only at the start. As an airborne cube seems to spin closer to the audience, the space grows more oppressive, culminating in Alceste's descent to an even more confining underworld.

By resisting the outside world, or banishing it altogether, Wilson is able to study in greater detail the spaces between his characters, testing their alliances or measuring their estrangement. Only a few steps separate Medea from her children—it's a route she travels four times in the prelude to *Deafman Glance,* twice with a glass of milk, twice with a knife. The length of a boardwalk and of a winding path in *Madama Butterfly* seems to predict, and then become permanent and taunting emblems of, Butterfly's inevitable separation from Pinkerton. Pelléas, Golaud, and Mélisande negotiate their own relationships across the space of numerous triangles and circles—the well where Golaud finds Mélisande, the ring he gives her, the vault where he threatens Pelléas, the sloping distance between Mélisande's tower and the forest floor—shapes that Wilson returns to obsessively in his otherwise restrained production. Sometimes Wilson will narrow the focus even further in order to analyze the self's relationship to the self. At the end of *Oceanflight,* after depicting Lindbergh's flight across the Atlantic, Wilson adds as a kind of coda an excerpt from *Notes from Underground,* which confines his hero within a spotlight, allowing him only the tiniest of movements. By isolating the flier's simplest gestures—fingers tapping at the air—in a space where the actor can see no further than his hands, Wilson seems to have found the innermost impulses prompting all the other, more spectacular ways Lindbergh had confronted empty space. The scene recalls Wilson's well-known comment about Einstein: Working on *Einstein on the Beach,* the director grew fascinated with a series of photographs in which the physicist's left finger and thumb always touch to form an oval of empty space. "In that, he knew what he knew," Wilson said, as if certain that the body's lacunae themselves would reveal the structure of the cosmos, inner space providing the key to outer space.[17]

Wilson has credited his sensitivity to the relationships between bodies and space to Cézanne—"my favorite painter," he told Arthur Holmberg. "My work is closer to him than to any other artist." The NYU production of *Hamletmachine,* he added, is "like a Cézanne painting in its architecture. Cézanne simplified and purified forms to reveal classical structure and composition."[18] Yet an even richer source for Wilson's formalism may be Cézanne's chosen master, Nicolas Poussin. ("I plan to do Poussin over again," Cézanne famously said, "but from nature.") To a disciple of Gertrude Stein, Poussin may seem an alien figure—how does one reconcile his centripetal classicism with her centrifugal modernism?—yet for Wilson they are natural kin. Under the sign of each artist, he teaches his spectators to look beyond the figures onstage toward the structures controlling their behavior and relationship to one

another. Indeed, the best description of Stein's frozen-fluid quality—
"staying" while "moving"—comes from a neoclassical source: Winckelmann, writing about the *Laocoon,* praises the sculptor's ability to render
a scene that is "sedate, but active; calm, but not indifferent or drowsy."
In a separate discussion of the *Niobe and Her Daughters,* he writes that
the figures "seem to have been formed, not for the expression of the passions, but simply for the lodgement of them."[19] Emotion arrested by
craft, then offered up for analysis: the core principle of classicism
expresses the same desire for clarity that motivates Stein's—and Wilson's—own art.

In the presence of a Poussin painting, a student of Wilson will
immediately recognize the rules of deportment. Like Wilson's actors,
Poussin's own figures appear to be radiating and conducting energy
simultaneously—both radio tower and lightning rod. The two artists
often arrange their protagonists in attitudes of benediction—palms held
up like signs—or of instruction, an index finger pointing to an important thing. (Bonnie Marranca has drawn attention to the significance of
similar gestures in Wilson's most overtly religious production, *Four
Saints in Three Acts.*)[20] Other figures in their compositions address more
territory. They unfold their arms to reveal the splendor at their feet, as if
they hoped to settle the space merely by acknowledging it, or they gesture upwards: From the sky might come guidance needed to thrive on
land. These figures look caught between animate and inanimate states,
the earthly and the otherworldly. They appear to have just touched
down, like disguised gods, and are still trying to ingratiate themselves
with their unsuspecting hosts. On the verge of action even when at rest,
they seem to believe that one need only set the tempo of one's own
movements in order to control the tempo of history itself.

The charged equilibrium in Poussin's compositions responds to his
subjects. He favors moments when the balance of power among his
figures is about to shift, or the focus is about to swerve. Solomon judges
between rival women claiming to be a baby's mother; Eliezer pauses
before selecting a wife from a group of thirteen candidates; Hercules
decides which woman—Vice or Virtue—will guide him across the landscape, and through the life, stretching out behind him. Each exemplifies
heightened awareness (including self-awareness) freed of self-consciousness. As Anthony Blunt and others have pointed out, the faces
confirm the bodies' self-control. Their features are rarely unguarded—
no Romantic ecstasy even for those whose condition would justify it.
Like Wilson's faces, these are held in place by the force of expectation,

inquiry, or sober understanding—as if what they were looking at were already part of the past.

Both Poussin and Wilson seek the essential structure of individuals (as well as of artifacts and landscapes)—the form beneath personality and other facades, what Hazlitt in his own essay on Poussin calls "the first integrity of things."[21] On discovering it, what had seemed a world of endlessly proliferating species now adheres to a single scheme, geometry—a truth Poussin made explicit in his famous drawing of a group of young artists at work in their shared studio, one of whom studies a little stage displaying a sphere, a cone, and a cylinder.[22] These become the shared language in a dialogue among all the elements of a given composition: The "statement" of a reclining body (for instance) is answered in the curve of a river; a cluster of figures emulates the disposition of a cluster of buildings. The body is capable of revealing psychological structure as well. In language that anticipates Wilson's own ideas, Poussin wrote: "Just as the letters of the alphabet are used to form our words, so the forms of the human body are used to express the various passions of the soul and to make visible what is in the mind."[23] (A theatrically minded viewer of Poussin will inevitably recall similar attempts at codification by Goethe; and it is to his famous "Rules for Actors" that one turns to begin tracing the development of the comparable performance style.)

Despite these satisfying correspondences, it would be misleading to imagine Poussin treating his figures as mere signposts to the features of his landscapes. There is a moral vision motivating his exercise. The painter abstracts the natural world so as to understand the terms of his residence in it: When he traces the lines of a family group against the lines of a horizon, for instance, or itemizes the spheres and cubes used to build both a city square and the crowd filling it, Poussin proposes an unsentimental, because rigorously empirical, understanding of companionship and social membership. His figures enjoy their place in the world because the entire landscape joins in affirming it; their presence is never accidental but obeys the same rules by which the surrounding city or countryside has itself been settled. This interest in context motivates Poussin to bind each of his figures to one another as well. As Blunt has shown, individuals reach across the canvas to forge alliances; one torso rhymes with another; legs fall into parallel lines, like cables holding the scene together, extending beyond themselves toward the edges of the painting. All these formal procedures demolish the Romantic fantasy of the solitary individual, responsible to no one but himself, by his actions affecting nothing but his own destiny.

In such a landscape, where Poussin anatomizes both individuals and their communities, the work of seeing assumes heightened importance; and it is on this subject that the relationship between Wilson and Poussin seems most profound. In a well-known letter, Poussin wrote:

> There are two ways of looking at objects, one is simply to see them, the other is to consider them carefully. Simply seeing means nothing more than naturally taking in with the eye the form and appearance of the thing seen. Looking at an object and considering it carefully, however, . . . involves making a special effort to understand a particular object fully: thus one can say that the simple seeing of an object is merely a natural process, while what I call *prospect* is a function of reason.[24]

Poussin argues this distinction repeatedly, in paintings that take vision as their implicit subject, regardless of their other, more apparent themes. In *The Triumph of David* (1632), for instance, a crowd of onlookers commands more attention than the returning hero: A group positioned on a stagelike elevation in the center of the painting even seems to be performing the act of looking. One of the objects of its attention, a marching figure, carries a large curved horn that encircles his head, framing it, giving his profile the formality of a coin face—a picture within a picture. A mysterious small item at the edge of the scene, an upside-down piece of the facade, confirms Poussin's self-reflexive intentions. It looks like an abstract version of a scene-designer's model—and its placement in the lower-left corner makes it a caption, preparing us to think about structure rather than sentiment before we move into the painting itself.

A later painting, *Landscape with a Man Killed by a Snake* (1648), uses a different strategy to achieve similar ends. Here (as the speaker named "Poussin" explained in the famous 1730 dialogue scripted by François Fénelon)[25] the passions incited by the title accident, depicted in the foreground, are controlled by the different kinds of visual access of three different witnesses, positioned along a winding road and in the surrounding countryside. As we mark the cause-and-effect of the observers' responses, we too travel up the road, and through the painting. Sight—the figures' and our own—becomes as precise a procedure for marking the space as physical action—and as it does so, that space seems to grow in significance, until it edges aside Poussin's ostensible subject. While Poussin implies that his landscape occasions an investigation of character, it would be equally true to say that the characters support an investigation of the landscape. (This shift in emphasis occurs throughout

Landscape with a Man Killed by a Snake, by Nicolas Poussin.
(Photo courtesy of the National Gallery, London.)

Poussin's oeuvre. The psychological richness of such works as *Landscape with the Body of Phocion Carried out of Athens* and *Landscape with the Ashes of Phocion Collected by His Widow* emerges less from the circumstances recounted in the titles than from the pathos in the relationship between the tiny, resolute figures and the grand, indifferent landscape. Wilson of course takes the same spatial approach to emotion.)

The purest of Poussin's classical constructions, *The Holy Family on the Steps* (1648), suggests the beneficial consequences of all these forms of disciplined seeing. Poussin has equipped Joseph with a T-square and a compass—as if assuring the viewer that even this, the most exalted and mysterious of narratives, is as intelligible as nature itself to all those educated in measure and proportion. But elsewhere he hints at the uncertainty motivating his style. Blunt reports that he regularly spoke of wanting people to "read" rather than merely look at his paintings—as if he felt vexed by the fact that viewers could seize his imagery all at once, and envied the way prose harnessed readers to the sequence of sentences. Only thus can the artist hope to control when and how his audience reaches conclusions about what it sees. Poussin's need to discipline his viewers originates in a desire to contain his subject, voiced in a series of maxims that together serve as his definition of art. "Nothing is visible without boundaries," it reads in part. "Nothing is visible without light. . . . Nothing is visible without distance. Nothing is visible without instrument."[26] This much may seem self-evident, but to Poussin the "visible" can never be taken for granted: He paints as if he had just fought and won a battle against invisibility, and feared that at any moment his subjects might disappear again. The tranquility of his paintings seems zealously guarded, each formal mechanism keeping at bay, just beyond the frame, numerous threats to his subject's clarity.

This anxiety is literalized in his many landscapes and interiors consisting of frames nested in frames—squares etched into the pavement or floor, the grooves of a field under harvest, the canopy of a bed, a crowd arranging itself around a central figure, the arch of a nave, a larger arch of trees, buildings surrounding a piazza. As soon as we let our eye wander, we're banked by a frame, our attention frozen momentarily before we're sent looking in a new direction, only to encounter another border. Yet in a painting that speaks directly about this technique, Poussin comes to an unexpected conclusion. His final self-portrait (1650) surrounds the artist with seven frames—three belong to paintings leaning against a wall in the background, four more make up the complicated design of a doorway. Yet none of them contains more than a portion of Poussin's body. He floats in front of them, resisting their appeals. Each of the frames expresses both the painter's desire to hoist into art something as mercurial as identity and, at the same time, the fear that he might just succeed. Stein's language again seems apt: The painter, "moving" as his innermost character tries to remain elusive, is at war with his craft, designed to make things "stay."

Poussin's notion of "prospect"—and, more specifically, his use of the frame to cultivate reasoned seeing and his ultimate ambivalence over its effects—anticipates Wilson's own interest in the degrees of attention, an interest that finds its most sustained expression in his staging of *Lohengrin*. The saga of Elsa's mysterious betrothal—Lohengrin agrees to marry her only if she vows, in turn, never to ask his name or origin— unfolds in a symbolic landscape as expressive of the characters' fate as is anything they do. The king's rigid alliance with the Judgment Oak, Lohengrin's arrival and departure on the river, Elsa's hesitant procession across the castle courtyard to her wedding, and her anxiety erupting in the claustrophobic bridal chamber—Wilson fulfills Wagner's scenic specifications by obeying principles of emotional geometry familiar from Poussin, reducing Wagner's landscape to its minimalist essence, and

Robert Wilson's production of *Lohengrin,* Zurich, 1991. (Photo by Schlegel und Egle Pressfotografen.)

thereby making explicit how the landscape exposes or traps, supports or abandons, the characters trying to feel at home in it.[27]

Over the course of the opera's three acts, the director maneuvers a set of large illuminated boxes—squares, *L* shapes, vertical posts, and horizontal bars—in order to build and dismantle what comes to resemble a huge frame, scheduling its transformations according to the temperaments of the characters it contains. As with Poussin, the relationship between the frame and its image resembles the tension between reason and passion—the artist's technique subduing his subject's volatility. Indeed, in its glacial, inevitable progress the decor seems to reproach the characters for their instability, Wilson seeking the tectonic causes of their psychological shifts. He also uses his setting to dramatize a war between trust and doubt. Elsa's rapturous love for Lohengrin freezes, contracts, and finally shatters as she submits it to ever more insistent questioning within Wilson's frame. What began as pure feeling, guided by instinct, changes into analytic thought. Such an attitude is the opposite of the faith that Lohengrin, in declaring himself knight of the Grail, has himself pledged to uphold.

The musical equivalent of Lohengrin's faith is heard in the opera's prelude, and Wilson's version of it introduces the terms of the debate filling the next three acts. In a program note, Wagner described the story motivating the music: "Out of the clear blue ether of the sky there seems to condense a wonderful yet at first hardly perceptible vision"—the Holy Grail—which "grows and grows until it seems as if the rapture must be dispersed by the very vehemence of its own expansion."[28] Baudelaire reworked this theme in his own landscape fantasia on the music: "I found myself imagining the delicious state of a man in the grip of a profound reverie," he writes in "Richard Wagner and *Tannhäuser* in Paris," "in an absolute solitude, a solitude with an immense horizon and a wide diffusion of light; an immensity with no other decor but itself."[29]

Wilson closely follows both descriptions in his own production. When the curtain rises, a long band of hazy white light, spanning the width of the proscenium, glows at the foot of a blue cyclorama. The stage is otherwise empty, sunk in shadow. It looks frosted, as if by an Arctic dawn. The stage awakens into unease as the light band shines brighter, trembles, and then detaches from the horizon and inches upward. As it continues its ascent, the stage seems to undergo a series of climate changes. One half of the screen blushes a pale rose, then blanches, then hardens to blue once again; the other half meanwhile shifts from white to pale green to gray. (As many have observed, Wilson's design in this scene seems indebted to the watery surfaces and eroded edges of Mark Rothko's mature paintings—many of which are commonly referred to by critics and by Rothko himself as landscapes.)[30]

Having done justice to Wagner's vision, Wilson now marks its limits. Toward the end of the prelude, another bar of light appears: This one is an illuminated box rather than a projected glow. It is vertical, almost as high as the stage itself, its white light unclouded. As the box descends from the flies, it restores gravity to the hitherto weightless stage; it also crops the ever expanding screen of light and color, changing an open field into a measured plot. It's as if Wilson were planting the flag with his pole of light, staking his claim to the stage. (In fact, the box represents Wagner's Judgment Oak.) We're forced to look back down at the ground for the first time since the opera began, and thus to register deliberately what we take for granted in all theater. But Wilson emphasizes more than the floor in this sequence: With the lightbox's descent, the air itself suddenly seems thick, resistant, a substance to be tested, the way one takes the temperature of water or measures the acidity of soil. When the box lands, Wilson has sounded his space.

He next defines his time. By appearing on the near side of the screen, the vertical bar seems to announce the present tense: We're jolted out of our Baudelairean reverie, recalled from the Grail's mystical past. We're also asked to confront time in its purest form, undiluted by any reference to a specific era or incident. Among the many gnomic statements Wilson has offered over the years to explain his work, the most recurrent directs our attention to the intersection of vertical and horizontal lines on his stage. "First there is a line that rises from the center of the earth and extends through the universe"—a line, he has said, that signifies time. Wilson's image seems to adapt Stein's idea of the "continuous present": Unlike conventional visualizations of time—one date or event following another—Wilson's line stretches upward even as it stays rooted in one place. He continues: "This temporal line is crossed by a second line, which forms space. The tension between these two lines interests me."[31]

His *Lohengrin* expresses this interest directly, of course, but Wilson has said that all his productions enact the encounter of the two lines throughout the duration of a performance. One envisions a series of such intersections spanning his stage, forming a web capable of catching even the subtlest moments of behavior and most fleeting sensations, fixing them in place. Concrete applications of this basic structure are everywhere on his stage. Horizontal and vertical units of scenery, the right angles of furniture, and especially the deportment of the actors themselves, arms darting out like so many branches from the trunks of rigid bodies: All reiterate Wilson's crosshatched image of time and space, by their sheer presence referring us back to the structure of the entire landscape. The director's practice resembles the way a painter squares an empty canvas before transferring his or her preparatory drawings. Yet the painter expects the grid to disappear eventually, obscured by invention, while in Wilson's theater each figure or piece of scenery draws the grid again, until by the end we are looking at it before, or at least along with, the spectacle behind it. Such a device only enhances the force of Wilson's imagery—the way a landscape seen through a many-paned window can be more beautiful than one seen outdoors.

As the work of measuring and cropping continues, and the other pieces of the frame glide into place (representing the Scheldt River, another tree, and the sky), the director carries out several projects at once. On an expository level, he underlines Wagner's own dramatic structure. The opera's plot consists of the single action of moving indoors, from the banks of the Scheldt to the castle courtyard to, deeper inside still, the bridal chamber, where the asking of the forbidden question serves to catapult the opera back to the river landscape. Wilson's frame both establishes the border between inside and outside and assigns distinct values to each space: Outside is for belief; inside is for analysis, however fateful. Within this gross structure are numerous smaller spatial transactions. Here, too, the assumption of power, emotional as well as political, is expressed in terms of entrances; narrative development becomes a matter of footsteps. In act 2, Ortrud knows she has scored an advantage when Elsa invites her into the women's quarters. In act 3, Elsa asks her husband's name right after Friedrich breaks down the door of the bridal chamber—his act a literal version of Elsa's own violation of the couple's security.

Wilson's attention to the act of moving indoors also directs attention to the political background of Elsa and Lohengrin's romance. The Swan Knight hasn't arrived in Brabant only to rescue Elsa; he pledges also to defend the nation against an invasion by its Hungarian enemies. Wilson's illuminated posts and lintels signify fortified national borders as much as they do the features of a river and castle landscape, just as the space within those boundaries is contested on more than romantic or spiritual grounds. The Hungarians aren't the only threats to Brabant's sovereignty: The unresolved question of succession—Is Elsa the king's rightful heir, now that her brother Gottfried is missing, or is Friedrich, urged on by Ortrud?—by itself teaches us to see any appearance onstage as a seizure of territory.

Finally, the decor focuses on our own space. Like one of Wilson's actors anatomizing a gesture, we are made aware of the separate stages by which we seek an object for our curiosity, then secure it with our scrutiny: We see ourselves seeing. Moreover, as soon as the first piece of the emerging frame takes its place, Wilson disputes the romantic expectations of an audience trained to surrender to Wagner's music—what the composer approvingly called the "emotionalizing of the intellect," resulting in our "self-annihilation."[32] Here, Wagner's listeners instead recover the capacity to think clearly about concrete, demystified reality—a reality that includes themselves. Toward the end of the production—when the frame is joined by additional pieces that form its smaller shadow—Wilson presses the point. For those spectators sitting in the center of the orchestra section (Wilson's ideal audience, whose sight lines this neoclassicist always flatters), the receding frames look like a huge telescope or camera lens—as if at the upstage end of the nested lightboxes, from behind a windowlike square, someone were looking back.

Yet this *Lohengrin* is most interesting when such monitoring breaks down, and with it Wilson's efforts to control his landscape. In its final sequence, a production characterized by inevitability—in plot, emotional development, movement, and decor—is once again the image of uncertainty. The story has come full circle and we are again by the banks of the Scheldt. The lost brother returns. Brabant is promised victory over its enemies. Elsa's transgression brings its predicted punishment: An opera that began with Lohengrin's long entrance ends with his equally protracted exit. Yet, despite the narrative's conclusion, nothing looks resolved in Wilson's staging. After three acts in which the characters are wedged into ever smaller spaces and aggressively focus on one another, they now seem to elude all such constraints—as if to renounce attention itself.

Wilson suggests as much by his actors' gestures and placement. For the first time, Lohengrin faces away from the audience—staring across the riverbank into nothingness. The arrival of Elsa's brother breaks the frame again. One of his first acts is to point up at the sky—a radical event in a production that, from the moment the Judgment Oak descended, has kept our eyes on the ground. The object of his wonder—the dove— itself refutes the premise of Wilson's staging. Hovering weightless above the river, then soaring away from the characters, it is the antithesis not only of the earthbound swan but of anything that, in its proximity and visibility, suggests it can be known. Lohengrin confirms these doubts when he unburdens himself of his horn, ring, and sword. He too seems to be rejecting the whole world of materiality. The tangibility of these objects is deceptive. For Elsa and Gottfried they are images of loss; the longer one looks at them, the deeper one sees into emptiness. The obsessive extreme of such scrutiny is embodied by Ortrud, who ends the production by twisting Friedrich's burial shroud: It is the only object left her on a suddenly depleted stage. When all these actions are taken together, an opera staged to affirm principles of presence surrenders to the equally unequivocal fact of absence.

To emphasize the point, Wilson shuts off all but the smallest of his lightboxes in this scene. Presiding over a disabled frame, he once again resembles Poussin, now in his mode of expressing ambivalence about his art and, beyond that, skepticism about the possibilities of classical style. Just as Poussin resisted confinement in his final self-portrait, here Wilson himself worries about the power of vision. Can sight diminish what it touches, even as it seems to ensure significance—sapping things of the vitality they had when they were unmonitored? After all, Lohengrin and Elsa sustain their love only for as long as they don't look at one another: Under Wilson's direction, the singers often gaze just past one another, as if at an idealized double of their actual companion, or face the audience, seeming to recount their narrative even as they live it. When they do finally turn to one another, Wilson expects us to see in their subsequent fate a cautionary tale, and to ask what we ourselves distort, denature, or oversimplify in our own mode of attention.

Fairfield Porter once wrote that Cézanne "had a passion for fastening things down, a passion too neurotic to be called classical."[33] Yet Poussin and by extension Wilson seem to embody this same neurosis (if one must call it that), as if they recognized that such passion is what keeps classicism from degenerating into mere draftsmanship. Poussin came close to confessing the troubled sources of his style in a letter to his patron Cassiano dal Pozzo: "Nothing torments the spirit of men more than thinking of more than one thing at a time."[34] After doing what he could to relieve that torment in his art, he encouraged his viewers to continue the effort in the gallery. He was pleased when another of his collectors, Paul Fréart de Chantelou, hung seven small curtains in front of the seven paintings that make up the "Sacraments" series of 1644–48, enabling a visitor to look at—and think about—them one at a time. It wasn't the first time Poussin responded to theatrical form. At the earliest stage of planning a new work he built a small proscenium stage that corresponded to his envisioned landscape, equipped with wings, sliding pieces of scenery, and movable clay figures. The theatrical apparatus in the studio and later in the collector's gallery only emphasizes the mutability behind the work's apparent poise. As in performance, one imagines that the composition is invulnerable, and its energies unspent, only up to the moment Chantelou's curtain parts. Then it starts to decay, as if from the mere exposure to the air.

Robert Wilson, by working in a discipline that is both dependent on and victim to time's passage, of course brings a spectator closer to the transitoriness of classical form and proportion. Despite the confidence suggested by his analytic perception, he remains preoccupied at the end of *Lohengrin* by everything that *doesn't* fit his scheme. Wilson's second thoughts concern more than his use of space. As he ushers us beyond the proscenium and out of the landscape, hoping now that we'll follow Gottfried and Lohengrin's gaze, he looks beyond his production's temporal frame as well. Elsa and Ortrud sink into memory, hoping there to recover their lost companions. Lohengrin fills with anticipation of his return to Monsalvat. The stage now becomes a place for facing history, his actors' mere gestures and placement readmitting the past, and everything else edited out in the interest of securing an attachment to the material facts of the stage. There is always *more* happening than one can show, Wilson now concedes. After the soldiers' triumphalism, after the melodrama of Ortrud's defeat, even after the rapture of Elsa's suffering,

Wilson's production sounds a note of humility. His study of the varieties of vision ends by accepting that much remains out of sight, unsusceptible to his art. As with Poussin in the self-portrait, Wilson's embrace of classicism is especially poignant for his awareness that its promise of total control and reliable structure cannot be fulfilled. The world—vulnerable to chance, disordered by metaphysics and memory—is too much with him.

NOTES

1. Gertrude Stein, "Plays," in *Lectures in America* (Boston: Beacon Press, 1985), 131.

2. Gertrude Stein, "Portraits and Repetition," in *Lectures in America,* 199.

3. Gertrude Stein, "Pictures," in *Lectures in America,* 78.

4. Gertrude Stein, "Plays," in *Lectures in America,* 122, 125.

5. Richard Foreman, "The Life and Times of Sigmund Freud," *Village Voice,* January 1, 1970. Reprinted in Stefan Brecht, *The Theatre of Visions: Robert Wilson* (Frankfurt am Main: Suhrkamp, 1978), 425.

6. Ibid.

7. Brecht, *The Theatre of Visions,* 60, 79.

8. Edwin Denby, *Two Conversations with Edwin Denby* (New York: Byrd Hoffman Foundation, 1973), 1.

9. Leo Bersani, *A Future for Astyanax: Character and Desire in Literature* (Boston: Little Brown, 1976), 285, x.

10. Wilson quoted in Laurence Shyer, *Robert Wilson and His Collaborators* (New York: Theatre Communications Group, 1989), xvi.

11. Gertrude Stein, "Poetry and Grammar," in *Lectures in America,* 227. Also see Gertrude Stein, *Everybody's Autobiography* (London: Virago Press, 1985), 131, 152–53.

12. Paul Schmidt, introduction to *Robert Wilson: Dessins et Sculptures* (Paris: Musée Galliera, 1974), quoted in Trevor Fairbrother, *Robert Wilson's Vision* (Boston: Museum of Fine Arts, 1991), 40.

13. Craig Owens, "*Einstein on the Beach:* The Primacy of Metaphor," in *Beyond Recognition: Representation, Power, and Culture* (Berkeley and Los Angeles: University of California Press, 1992), 6; Jill Johnston, "Family Spectacle," in *Art in America,* December 1986; Bonnie Marranca also criticizes the policy of no-criticism surrounding Wilson in her essay "Robert Wilson, the Avant-Garde, and the Audience: *Einstein on the Beach,*" in *Theatrewritings* (New York: PAJ Publications, 1984).

14. Elinor Fuchs, *The Death of Character: Perspectives on Theater after Modernism* (Bloomington, Indiana University Press, 1996), 10, 173.

15. The program note is reprinted in Shyer, *Robert Wilson,* 57–58.

16. Quoted in an interview with Laurence Shyer: "Robert Wilson: Current

Projects" *Theater* 14, no. 3 (1983): 93. My reading of *the CIVIL warS* is indebted to this article, which outlines the projected structure of the entire production, and to John Rouse's discussion of the German section in "Robert Wilson, Texts and History: *CIVIL warS*, German Part," *Theater* 16, no. 1 (1984): 68–74.

17. The photographs and Wilson's comment are from Howard Brookner's film, *Robert Wilson and "the CIVIL warS"* (1985).

18. Quoted in Arthur Holmberg, *The Theatre of Robert Wilson* (Cambridge: Cambridge University Press, 1996), 79. Wilson's relationship to Cézanne is also briefly mentioned in "The Weight of a Grain of Dust" by Bice Curiger and Jacqueline Burkhardt, *Parkett* 16 (1988): 116. In 1989, Wilson made a short video based on (and titled after) Cézanne's *La Femme à la Cafetière*.

19. Johann Joachim Winckelmann, *Writings on Art,* ed. David Irwin (London: Phaidon, 1972), 73, 133.

20. Bonnie Marranca, "Hymns of Repetition," *Performing Arts Journal* 18, no. 3 (1996): 43.

21. William Hazlitt, "On a Landscape of Nicolas Poussin" (1821), in *The Essays of William Hazlitt,* ed. Catherine Macdonald Maclean (London: Macdonald, 1949), 172.

22. The drawing is reproduced and discussed in Richard Verdi, *Nicolas Poussin, 1594–1665* (London: Zwemmer and Royal Academy of Arts, 1995), 218–19. Although he doesn't mention Poussin, Holmberg cites Cézanne's famous letter to Emile Bernard directing attention to the recurring shapes in nature—cylinder, sphere, and cone (p. 76).

23. Quoted in Anthony Blunt, *Nicolas Poussin,* A. W. Mellon Lectures in the Fine Arts (New York: Bollingen Foundation/Pantheon, 1967), 222.

24. Quoted in Alain Mérot, *Nicolas Poussin* (New York: Abbeville, 1990), 311. This passage, excerpted from a letter to Sublet de Noyers, is also discussed in a chapter on photography in Henry M. Sayre, *The Object of Performance: The American Avant-Garde since 1970* (Chicago: University of Chicago Press, 1989).

25. Fénelon's dialogues are reprinted in Maria Graham, *Memoirs of the Life of Nicholas Poussin* (London: Longman, Hurst, Rees, Orme, and Brown, 1820), 156–78.

26. Quoted in Blunt, *Nicolas Poussin,* 372.

27. In "Stage Space: Statement by Robert Wilson," an interview by Ulrich Conrads (*Daidalos,* June 15, 1992, 100), Wilson says that his design was derived, in part, from Wagner's own sketches for the opera. (Wagner's first drawing shows only a horizontal river and two trees.) These are reproduced in Nicholas John, ed., *Lohengrin* (London: John Calder, 1993), 48, 80.

28. Quoted in Ernest Newman, *The Wagner Operas* (New York: Alfred A. Knopf, 1963), 127.

29. Charles Baudelaire, *The Painter of Modern Life and Other Essays,* trans. and ed. by Jonathan Mayne (New York: Da Capo, 1964), 117.

30. Rothko himself anticipated their theatrical connotations: "I think of my pictures as dramas," he said in 1947, and "the shapes in the pictures are the per-

formers. They have been created from the need for a group of actors who are able to move dramatically without embarrassment and execute gestures without shame" (quoted in Anna C. Chave, *Mark Rothko: Subjects in Abstraction* [New Haven: Yale University Press, 1989], 105). In all his productions, Wilson asks his own actors to meet the same criteria.

31. Robert Wilson, "The Architecture of the Theatrical Space," in *Theaterschrift* 2 (October 1992): 104.

32. Quoted in Eric Bentley, ed., *The Theory of the Modern Stage* (New York: Penguin, 1986), 300, and in Newman, *The Wagner Operas*, 127.

33. Fairfield Porter, *Art in Its Own Terms: Selected Criticism, 1935–1975*, ed. Rackstraw Downes (Cambridge, Mass.: Zoland Books, 1993), 151.

34. Quoted in Verdi, *Nicolas Poussin 1594–1665*, 238. The painter's desire to see things one at a time is echoed in Wilson's oft-repeated comment that "theater must be about one thing first, then it can be about many things." Chantelou's curtains, described below, are discussed on page 242 of Verdi's *Nicolas Poussin*.

Four

Redirected
Geographies

9

Staging the Geographic Imagination: Imperial Melodrama and the Domestication of the Exotic

Edward Ziter

Long before the term *Middle East* was coined, the geography had been created in the popular imagination in British exhibition halls and theaters. Throughout the nineteenth century, British audiences marveled at depictions of desert storms and harem dances as well as depictions of Nile steamers and colonial armies. With each year, new images reflecting the changing nature of British imperialism were incorporated into the theater's East. The features of this theatrical East attained a remarkable currency throughout British culture as a wide population became versed in a pictorial vocabulary that organized and interpreted the expanses east of Europe. As British involvement in the eastern Mediterranean grew more extensive, images of the colonial infrastructure came to dominate theatrical orientalism. New reproduction and communication technologies intensified this process, enabling the theater to provide increasingly detailed and up-to-date representations of the terrain, architecture, implements, and peoples purportedly encountered in the regions east of Europe. Trains, telegraphs, and steamships became as common in these depictions as Bedouin princesses and fantastic palaces.

Despite the wide range of often contradictory iconography, distinct phases in the manipulation and combination of orientalist imagery can be discerned. In this essay I will address a late phase of theatrical orientalism characterized by the representation of geographic context and its translation into three-dimensional stage environments. This process, I will argue, domesticated regions long associated with excess and transgression while simultaneously transforming a dizzying quantity of new geographic information into a coherent theatrical landscape. The challenge for theater managers was to provide an enveloping and readable view from the ground without sacrificing the claims of comprehensive mastery implicit in geography's view from above. If landscape is the artful *combination* of elements that reproduce the *essence of an area* and geography is the *delineation and arrangement* of elements that purportedly reproduce a *physical reality,* then theater managers sought to define themselves as both artists and draftsmen. They promised engaging Eastern landscapes that simultaneously clarified the wider colonial geography. All the resources of the stage—from script to publicity materials to lobby exhibitions—along with images from Romantic poets and illustrated dailies were commandeered for the project. Whether a production placed Ayesha the Desert Queen in a landscape of dunes and simooms or the British Camel Corps before the Suez Canal (and often productions combined such contrasting features), the theatrical landscape served to structure and disseminate a geographic imagination.

Context, Combination, and Colonialism

Theatrical orientalism's new emphasis on geographic representation reflected a significant epistemological shift in the period. Newspapers, exhibitions, and a variety of emerging academic disciplines elevated the significance of context—whether it was geographic or social—in the creation of meaning. Increasingly, notable events and objects were presented as "indicative" rather than "wondrous." Stage depictions of travel and communication in colonial regions were consistent with this shift. The theater compressed vast distances as the once obscure and magical East was integrated into the empire. In the process, the theater transformed the East into a safe, accessible, and familiar colonial interest.

New staging practices contributed to the emphasis on context. In lieu of backdrops and wings, designers now composed landscapes from practical "set pieces." Earlier, scene painting constituted an ornamental backing complete in itself. Now actors were integrated into three-dimensional environments that purportedly reproduced fragments of colonial space that extended beyond the proscenium. The once sublime vistas of Romantic scenography were replaced with built-out sand dunes and Islamic arches like those in the smoking rooms and cafés of better hotels. This new theatrical East resembled the snapshots sent back by growing numbers of journalists, tourists, and soldiers—a series of detailed fragments indicative of Eastern life.

Yet the theater retained the fantastic exotica that had long been a feature of orientalism. Exotic imagery recycled from past seasons was interspersed between these realistic snapshots. Dancing girls and odalisques, along with foreign journalists and colonial officers, inhabited settings equally indebted to Romantic poets and illustrated newspapers. The theater offered the modern East while still delivering landscapes of Romantic excess.

This new emphasis on context and combination lies at the heart of the shift from the antiquarianism of early-nineteenth-century scene painting to this new geographic mode. By the end of the nineteenth century, antiquarianism's engrossment in isolated objects had come to embody a dilettantism in contrast to the professionalism of the newly emerging academic disciplines. As Nietzsche famously wrote, the antiquarian is obsessed with "his ancestor's furniture" and all that is "small and limited, moldy and obsolete."[1] Similarly, antiquarian scene painters in the first half of the century transformed the theater into a picture gallery of distinct views, each featuring "correct" architecture or artifacts but disconnected from any sense of a lived past. Late Victorian scene designers replaced these complete, single-perspective views with a scenography of fragments that surrounded actors and combined with them to more fully realize the places and periods represented. Rather than provide audiences with a single focal point—a rendering of the Sphinx on the backshutter, for example—these designers arranged built-out pieces into a terrain that appeared to extend beyond the stage space. This was not a formally complete stage picture, but a space masquerading as a discrete segment of the larger terrains linking the East to the West. In this sense, the design of realist plays—like their subject matter—was devoted to the creation of plausible geographies.

In the late nineteenth century, theater managers increasingly depicted modern communication and transportation systems in the East in order to create such plausible geographies. In the process, the theater transformed once remote lands into a periphery closely tied to the London center. Melodrama, for example, no longer simply depicted the East but instead depicted Europeans who traveled to the East by steamer and transcontinental railway. Often, climactic scenes demonstrated that the safety of these Europeans depended on new communication technology. Even extravaganza and pantomime stressed the East's new proximity and position in a colonial economy, combining Romantic exoticism with images of colonial infrastructure, as when Kate Vaughn danced the "Suez Canal" scene in *Excelsior* in her familiar Lalla Rookh costume

(Her Majesty's Theatre, 1885). In the new theatrical East, geographic—rather than antiquarian—knowledge generated authority. Authenticity did not lie in the recognizable artifact or monument, but in the impression that the troop movements depicted on stage resembled the troop movements depicted in newspapers. The theater, like the journalism it emulated, presented a geography defined by European entrance and traversal. The theater, no less than the Conservative opposition, campaigned on the mastery of a foreign geography.

The new landscape of theatrical orientalism generated an aesthetic of artful combination that can be related to the logic of colonialism. This aesthetic was evident in the growing emphasis on stage composition, as well as in the frequent mixing of Romantic exotica with colonial references and "real" native products (not to mention "real" natives). While the persistence of Romantic imagery might appear anachronistic, the theater's emphasis on composition and combination showed its affinity to emerging disciplines such as anthropology and archaeology as well as new strategies of museum display. In theatrical and scholarly displays, objects created meaning through their presentation and relation, not simply as a result of their unique qualities. Theater, like the Victorian Arabists Edward Said describes in *Orientalism*, sought to make the Orient "totally visible" for an English public through a process of selection and combination. The Orient, Said explains, "would be reconverted, restructured from the bundle of fragments brought back piecemeal by explorers, expeditions, commissions, armies, and merchants into lexicographical, bibliographical, departmentalized, and *textualized* Orientalist sense."[2] The theater produced a *spatialized* corollary for Said's "*textualized* Orientalist sense." If orientalism forms, as Said argues, "a sort of imaginary museum without walls," then the theater reflected an attempt to embody the museum. The three-dimensional environments and integrated actor/ specimens of late Victorian theater constituted the literal reconversion and restructuring of those "fragments brought back" so as to reveal oriental systems of information and behavior. The meanings latent in the exotic landscape were only apparent through the careful manipulation and presentation of its features and monuments. All that was needed was a manager to arrange the stage.[3]

While the new landscape of theatrical orientalism with its encapsulation of geographic context is evident in scores of productions from the late Victorian period, the stakes for spatial representation were especially high in 1885. Throughout the previous year, newspapers carried daily reports on the progress of a seven-thousand-man British force as it made its way up the Nile and across the Sudanese desert to relieve the besieged city of Khartoum and the commander of its defense, Major General Charles Gordon. The fall of Khartoum and the death of Gordon and his men at the hands of Sudanese rebels led by the Mahdi produced an unprecedented public outcry. Gordon memorials were unveiled throughout England, Gordon Boys' Clubs opened, dozens of poems and songs eulogized the fallen hero, and the theater mounted an avid defense of imperialism in a series of highly successful military spectacles and dramas. Even ballet, music hall, and pantomime responded to the increased attention to the Middle East with literal depictions of Gordon and his men or more general paeans to the British presence in the region.

In the depiction of the Sudanese relief expedition, theater practitioners employed a range of strategies for disseminating an evolving colonial geography in the form of theatrical landscape. I will now examine these orientalist landscapes as drawn in two melodramas depicting the relief expedition—Drury Lane's *Human Nature,* by Henry Pettitt and Augustus Harris, and the production of *Khartoum,* by William Muskerry and John Jourdain, at Sanger's Grand National Amphitheater[4]—as well as the transformation of these landscapes in related entertainment venues. "War teaches us geography," one journalist wrote twelve days after the fall of Khartoum.[5] In its sustained focus on colonial warfare, the theater both taught a new geography and developed a new theatrical landscape.

The Technology of Travel in Imperial Melodrama

In highlighting the spectacle of colonial travel, imperialist melodrama departed from a pattern established in earlier exotic plays. The theatrical East, as defined in Romantic Eastern plays and the dramatization of oriental romances by poets such as Byron, Moore, and Southey, usually depicted struggles between natives.[6] Similarly, most early Eastern melodramas focused on struggles between pashas, sultans, pharaohs, and sorcerers, as well as Eastern usurpers and rightful heirs.[7] This East was obscure and remote and often featured supernatural events. When not specifically portrayed in the past, this East demonstrated a timeless quality. Those melodramas that featured Europeans were set entirely in the East; travel to the East was presumed but never depicted.[8] Whereas this early East suggested an imaginative landscape removed from a representable geography, the imperialist melodramas of the late Victorian period defined an East next door in which Europeans vied for mastery.

As Heidi Holder has noted, in the imperialist melodramas from the 1880s and 1890s, "the real battles [were] between Europeans, fought *within* a conflict with indigenous people."[9] The East had been transformed into an arena for European expansion—a hinterland in which good and evil (both European) fought, surrounded by a potentially treacherous landscape.

Imperialist melodramas perpetuated standard melodramatic devices within this new geography. These plays invariably began in England with familiar misunderstandings and false accusations, which ultimately motivate colonial travel. In *Human Nature* the hero mistakenly suspects his wife of adultery and so joins an expedition to relieve a "desert city" under siege by the "Mahdi." In *Khartoum,* the heroine learns that her husband, who is part of the expedition to relieve Khartoum, has been accused of forgery, and so she travels East to inform him of the libel. In both plays, the villain threatens the hero's physical and financial well-being, while menacing the heroine's purity. In *Human Nature* the French villain, Paul De Vigne, has made the English hero, Frank Temple, responsible for a huge financial loss when the Egyptian government backs out of an arms deal the two men had orchestrated at De Vigne's insistence. At the same time, the Frenchman ceaselessly attempts to seduce the hero's unsuspecting wife. In *Khartoum,* the Greek villain, Nicolas Mavrogordato, threatens to have the hero imprisoned unless the heroine submits to his lust. Both Frenchman and Greek are revealed to be the traitors who betray the desert city to the Mahdi's siege.

While these plays ultimately erupt into colonial warfare, the battle scenes are no more intrinsic plot elements than the avalanches and floods of Pixérécourt's melodramas. Such third-act cataclysms were, in the words of Peter Brooks, the "physical 'acting out' of virtue's liberation from the oppressive efforts of evil." These sensational scenes of battle, explosion, and natural disaster acted as the last gasp of a pervasive evil before virtue could be read as such and "be brought into the sphere of public recognition and celebration."[10] The potential dangers of colonial regions constitutes a refocusing of what Eric Bentley calls melodrama's "paranoid" vision[11] onto those peripheral regions where the future of the empire was being decided. Melodrama's traditional concern with the vulnerability of virtue was accompanied with a new concern for the vulnerability of empire. In the process, virtue and empire were conflated.

Imperial melodrama's most significant departure from the traditional structure of melodrama was also that feature most significant to defining a new geography: once providence interceded at critical junctures, but now the hero relied on telegraphs, steamers, and repeating weapons. Imperial melodrama, like colonial warfare itself, contributed to a popular fascination with new technologies that delivered daily reports and images from the East, enabled troop movement across vast terrain, and (usually) insured British victories against much larger native forces.[12] In all likelihood, audiences at *Khartoum* and *Human Nature* were especially conscious of the technology required to traverse and control Eastern terrain. From September 1884 to February 1885, the British public read daily reports on the "Gordon relief expedition." Newspapers described every facet of the transport, which was contracted out to the travel company Thomas Cook and Son, already well known for its tours of the Nile. Papers detailed the logistical and technological skills marshaled by industry and the military, explaining how the steamers were dragged over the first and second cataracts, and how a railway was constructed to convey stores to these points, accompanying these reports with maps and topographical sketches. In fact, from the time the weekly *Illustrated London News* began reporting on the expedition to the months after the fall of Khartoum, that paper published over 260 illustrations related to the expedition and its battles, some images covering two full pages. The British public was deluged with information on Eastern terrain and how its vast expanses had been mastered by British technology.

Both *Khartoum* and *Human Nature* gave considerable attention to the spectacle of travel, asking audiences to marvel at the military's ability to move large numbers of troops around the globe at remarkable speeds. Notably, both plays rewrote history; the race is won, the troops arrive in time to save the besieged city. *Khartoum* was produced less than two months after Gordon's death and one day after memorial services for Gordon were conducted at Saint Paul's Cathedral and Westminster Abbey, further demonstrating the increased accessibility of the East. *Khartoum* transformed the relief expedition into a lightning race out from England, up the Nile, and across the desert. The play opens at the Portsmouth Dockyard with laborers transporting supplies from the railway lines to a large practicable troopship. Midway through the scene a train appears carrying additional troops. They debark and the train pulls off, revealing "more troops massed behind" along with a crowd to see the soldiers off. The scene culminates with the troops marching onto the troopship, which slowly moves off as crowd and soldiers cheer. Later in the play, audiences witnessed a group of these soldiers at "the Cataract on the Nile" with their "nuggars," broad native boats that the British forces in Egypt towed behind steamers.[13] On stage, the British grenadiers repeatedly arrive in the nick of time. First they successfully relieve an advance column ambushed at "The Wells" (the only major engagement for the actual relief expedition took place at the Wells of Abu Klea when an advanced column of two thousand British soldiers defeated ten thousand dervishes), and then they press on to Khartoum, preventing its fall.

In *Human Nature,* British troops similarly relieve a "desert city" under siege by the Mahdi, an obvious reference to Khartoum.[14] *Human Nature,* like *Khartoum,* depicts desert camp, battle, and a scene in which the villain is finally defeated at The Wells. However, the play's most sensational scene was the soldiers' homecoming. Harris reproduced Trafalgar Square on the Drury Lane stage and drilled a giant cast representing soldiers and onlookers in what the *Era* described as "the most striking and stirring piece of realism the stage has known."[15] The production concluded with Frank Temple on horseback, leading a procession of soldiers home after their long Eastern tour.

Melodramatic Revelation and Communication Technology

In the spectacle of travel, communication technology could prove as dramatic as any departing steamer or railcar, and the theater was clearly aware of this fact. While reporting on the relief expedition, newspapers focused attention on the communication system that delivered descriptions of the East, just as they focused attention on the transportation system that opened this once remote region. Telegraph cables not only carried the news, they *were* the news. "Never was a break in telegraphic communication more tantalizing," the *Illustrated London News* announced when reporting that the line to Khartoum was broken and no news was forthcoming on Gordon's planned offensive.[16] Throughout the empire, a growing number of businessmen, diplomats, and soldiers relied on England's network of submarine and overland cables, as well as transit routes. British business, policy, and lives all depended on the free flow of information from the periphery, and when the network was threatened, papers made the most of the ensuing drama.[17]

The newest star in the imperial economy, the wartime-press artist or "special," was also dependent on this network of cables and steamers. Specials like Melton Prior of the *Illustrated London News* and Frederick Villiers of the *Graphic* had become celebrities in their own right. It was with some fanfare, as John O. Springhall notes, that the *Illustrated London News* informed its readers on September 13, 1884, that Prior was already on his way to the front. Prior was one of twenty British newsmen reporting on the relief expedition. The competition between papers and the resulting need to differentiate their star reporters from the pack was considerable. In addition to prominently mentioning Prior's name and discussing his sketches in reports on the expedition, the *Illustrated London News* even reported their receipt of Prior's telegraphic messages announcing that sketches were in transit.

The special was aided by new reproduction technology, in addition to steamers and telegraphs. Previously, the artist's sketch served merely as a guide for engravers who then recomposed the subject. However, by 1884 new photoengraving techniques made it possible to directly reproduce sketches. The *Illustrated London News* published an increasing number of facsimiles during the relief expedition, suggesting that readers demanded the immediate reproduction and the sense of authenticity suggested by the word *photoengraving*. Descriptions that accompanied these facsimiles drew attention to the speed with which they were produced, as when the *Illustrated London News* explained of a Melton Prior image: "This sketch, together with many others, was only received late on Tuesday last and was reproduced by Direct Photo-Engraving Process in ten hours!"[18] Though sketch artists were initially resistant to using hand cameras (dry-plate, fixed-focus photography had only recently been perfected), at least one soldier brought a camera on the campaign. The *Illustrated London News* thanked an unnamed soldier for sending a photograph of the British camel corps. Sketch artists would soon take advantage of the technology that would ultimately make them obsolete. When Frederick Villiers returned to the Sudan during the 1898 reconquest, he brought a movie camera and a bicycle, both emblems of modern revolutions in communication and transportation.

Communication technology made a previously remote and dangerous region safe and accessible. However, as melodrama liked to point out, safety hung on a thin telegraph line. The need to communicate across Eastern deserts, as well as the English public's need for instant reports on the East, is a pressing concern in *Khartoum*. In the play, the dilemma is repeatedly described by Walter Sketchley, a press artist sent by the general at Khartoum with vital information for the advancing relief expedition. As Sketchley explains, much more than the city's safety depends on his mission:

> Press correspondents now-a-days do not belong to the rosewater brigade—they are quite prepared to share the hard-

ships—aye, and the dangers of any campaign, provided that the British public can have its war news served up every morning at breakfast, fresh and hot, with rolls and coffee![19]

As the figure most associated with the modern communication network, Sketchley repeatedly finds ways to convey information when all avenues appear closed. When captured by the Mahdi's troops, he seizes an Arab's shield and improvises a "heliograph," flashing a message to the distant troops. Though hardly an example of advanced technology, the bills asserted that the scene depicted "English pluck . . . and modern science." As further proof, the bills included a quote from the *Scientific Review* explaining that the heliograph was a "recent discovery adopted in military tactics" which uses "the rays of a tropical sun" to flash a message to "a distant outpost, even when situated beneath the horizon." Later, when Sketchley reaches the advanced guard of the relief expedition, he again uses "modern science" to facilitate communication. The general's most recent message, "Khartoum all right—can hold out for months," is revealed to mask a dire warning when Sketchley holds the paper to a flame.

> [R]ead between the lines—the heat brings out the cipher, and in the faint, trembling characters, which every moment grow more distinct, you can trace the agony of the brave hand which penned them, the brave heart's despair, abandoned and alone,—a cry to England's faith and fealty. Listen! *(uncovering, reads through soft music)* "While you are eating, drinking, and resting at your ease—we and those with us—soldiers and servants—are watching by night and by day—treachery is abroad, and our hearts grow weary waiting for the succour which never comes. The end is not far off, when all will be—too late!"[20]

The reading of this letter no doubt caused a sensation in the theater, as it employed much of the actual language of Gordon's last letter to the British consul general in Egypt.[21] Blockaded in Khartoum and ignored by the Liberal government, Gordon becomes the typical melodramatic victim. In melodrama, cries for help and assertions of innocence go unheard until the final act.[22] The vastness of the empire and the vulnerability of communication systems (not to mention Gladstone's reluctant imperialism) become another of melodrama's silencing devices. In addition to the mute characters, gags, and elaborate misunderstandings common to traditional melodrama, imperial melodrama featured a geography that conspired against speech. Only modern communication technology could breach the perils of the East and reveal the truth obscured by villainy.

While the English characters in *Khartoum* were surrounded by elements of the new colonial infrastructure, some of the Arab characters seemed largely derived from earlier oriental melodramas and Romantic plays. Ayesha—ruler of the wild horsemen of Kordofan and known by friend and foe as "The Queen of the Desert"—resembles the noble Bedouins of earlier plays such as Dimond's *The Aethiop; or, The Child of the Desert* (Covent Garden, 1812), or the original prototype, Brown's *Barbarossa* (Covent Garden, 1754). In such plays, proud independence and a love of one's native terrain is indication of a pure and primitive nature and has no relation to the nationalist struggles that serve as a backdrop in imperial melodrama. Consistent with the atavistic nature of the Arab characters in *Khartoum*, Ayesha is scornful of the Mahdi's revolution. She explains, "Our home is in the desert. There our great mother Nature spreads her wide arms to take us to her ample bosom. Let us strike our tents and plunge into the wilderness, at peace with all men!" Like exotic characters in plays from the first half of the century, Ayesha refers to herself in the third person and occasionally slips into an antiquated form of English. On separating from the English officer whom she secretly loves, Ayesha requests the crucifix he wears as a pledge that "when in happier times, Cross and Crescent are once more at peace, Ayesha shall behold thy face again."[23]

Interracial love had been a common feature in orientalist plays from the first half of the century but was largely absent from imperial melodrama. Not surprisingly, then, Ayesha's love does not advance beyond a crush. What had been an element of fantasy in earlier plays was now a troubling possibility. Oriental sensuality was instead evidenced in a standard holdover from an earlier theatrical orientalism—the harem dance. At one point the Mahdi is entertained by a "Nautch Dance." The fact that an Indian dance has been transplanted to the Sudan demonstrates the persistence of a generalized Eastern exoticism that marked earlier plays. Even a play that aspired to a certain ethnographic realism—and *Khartoum* featured an elaborate scene in a Cairo bazaar with native dress and Arabic expressions—reverted to a generalized exotic in matters of sex.

Theatrical Geographers

Human Nature more consistently focuses on the vulnerability and eventual triumph of Britain's colonial infrastructure, largely avoiding the

devices of earlier theatrical orientalism still evident in *Khartoum*.
Though evident in the play's plot and dialogue, the change is most
clearly evidenced in Augustus Harris's strategies for promoting the production. His most original publicity move was to transform the Grand
Saloon of Drury Lane into an exhibition of "Egyptian and Soudanese
arms, accoutrements, and relics" that had been collected by the soldiers
and correspondents of the relief expedition. The *Era*'s article on the
exhibition named the individual officers and press artists who contributed the materials, as well as the battlefields from which they were
recovered.[24] As these same battlefields had been frequently represented
in sketches and maps in the illustrated papers, the assembled arms,
musical instruments, and utensils at the Grand Saloon had the effect of
tracing the British advance over hostile Sudanese terrain.

The display of original sketches by Melton Prior and Caton
Woodville, artists for the *Illustrated London News,* further clarified the
geography evoked by the exhibition. Presumably, some of these
sketches depicted the same battlefields represented by the displayed artifacts. The *Era* described these artifacts as ethnographic, being "illustra-
tive of African life and warfare." However, in the context of the exhibition's elaborate cross-referencing, the objects become significant for
their ability to represent geography as well. Press artists sat at the center
of this cross-referencing. Objects and illustrations that were lent by such
artist-celebrities as Charles Williams, Melton Prior, and Frederick Villiers shared the stage with the contributions of Admiral Hewett, Lieu-
tenant-General Graham, and General Wolseley. The press not only
described the East for the home audience, but also shared in the military's project of crossing, collecting, and claiming.

The theme of martyrdom colored Harris's depiction of communication systems within the empire. Even as the exhibition celebrated the ability to report back a coherent landscape from the periphery of the empire,
the repeated subject at the Grand Saloon was the tragic break in communications. Douglas H. Johnson has argued that once it became clear that
Khartoum would not be retaken, Gordon was transformed from a soldier
into a Christian mystic and martyr—the sacrificial victim of a government
that ignored his pleas.[25] The canonization of Gordon was already under-
way at the Drury Lane exhibition. Harris amassed an impressive array of
Gordon artifacts: a piece of carpet from Gordon's room in Khartoum, a
Sudanese Kourbash he had given as a present, a decoration he struck at
Khartoum, and finally a bust of the general. Even the *Times* referred to the
collection as the "relics of the martyr of Khartoum."[26]

In this treacherous landscape, communication came at a price. The exhibition echoed Sketchley's assertion that correspondents were "prepared to share the hardships—aye, and the dangers of any campaign." Among the objects in the glass cases in the center of the room was the revolver worn by John Cameron of the *Standard* when he was shot and killed at Gubat. The death of a correspondent was sharp indication of the vulnerability of communications. All of the correspondents that accompanied the relief expedition suffered at least minor wounds, two were killed, and Cameron's death and funeral were the subject of large newspaper illustrations. Audiences at the Exhibition circulated between artifacts and illustrations taken from a region that had dominated the press. "Real" objects combined with past accounts to powerfully evoke both a geography and the systems that delivered this geography. As such, the Drury Lane exhibition served as a compelling verification of the landscapes produced on the Drury Lane stage.

Harris consistently used the dramatization of Britain's colonial wars to assert the patriotism and educational value of his theater. As Michael Booth points out, between 1881 and 1902 six of Drury Lane's autumn melodramas depicted British battles in colonial wars—a military world tour covering Afghanistan, Egypt, Burma, South Africa, and the Sudan.[27] Other, nonmilitary, melodramas featured civilians overseas, and references to colonial wars were inserted into several of the Drury Lane Christmas pantomimes. As the *Times* explained in its review of *Human Nature*:

> It is the function of Drury-lane to give practical illustrations of the latest war in which this country may have been engaged. The Ashantee, the Afghan, and the first Egyptian campaign have in turn been dramatized. In this instance the late war in the Soudan furnishes the huge spectacular effects of which Mr. Harris's melodramas so largely consist.[28]

Harris positioned these "practical illustrations" of colonial wars as a service to the nation, bolstering Drury Lane's unofficial status as England's national theater at a time when some critics were calling for a subsidized theater precisely because of the fare available at West End theaters like Drury Lane. In Harris's estimation, "the function of [a national theater] was not so much the reproduction of the plays of the past as a representation of the deeds of the present," as he reportedly explained at the opening of the Soudan Exhibition.[29] Drury Lane was in fact the national theater, according to Harris, because it had abandoned Shakespeare and Sheridan for illustrations of colonial conquest.

The Soudan Exhibition was further proof of this fact. In these same opening remarks, Harris reportedly explained that "it had been suggested that the Government might have opened an exhibition of that kind; but as Drury Lane is looked upon as the National Theatre, [Harris] thought the same end was attained as if they had done so." In its project of familiarizing the London public with contested colonial regions, Harris presented Drury Lane as an extension of the government.[30] According to Harris, the theater was even responsible for military recruitment. In the preface to the catalog of the Soudan Exhibition, Harris reportedly asserted that "the drama may have some share in popularizing the profession of arms amongst the rising generation of Englishmen."[31] The Soudan Exhibition and the press it generated did not simply authenticate *Human Nature* but the entire colonial geography constructed at Drury Lane. When the national theater depicted Egypt, the Sudan, South Africa, or a host of other regions, audiences could be assured that the stage picture was produced in coordination with, and for the benefit of, the British military.

At Drury Lane, respectability was in part dependent on the authenticity of the depicted geography, so publicity materials often stressed the extensive knowledge of theater practioners. A preproduction article published in the *World* depicted *Human Nature*'s coauthor, Henry Pettitt, as a master of geography. The article describes Pettitt as a self-made man, who was first able to obtain a stable position when "his superior knowledge of geography . . . gained him an usher's desk at the North London Collegiate School." According to the article, Pettitt taught for six years, "taking the boys of North London in imagination all over Europe with the aid of Bradshaw, Cook's Circulars, and Murray's Guides."[32] No specific training or authorities are cited for the development of Pettitt's "superior knowledge of geography," and the article would suggest that Pettitt solely employed tourist publications as teaching materials. *Bradshaw's Railway Guide* (presumably the quote is not referring to the antiquarian, Henry Bradshaw), promotional circulars for a travel company, and travel guides enabled Pettitt to conjure the world in a classroom. The mention of these popular materials did not diminish Pettitt's authority, but rather celebrated his resourcefulness as a geographer and the new accessibility of geographic information.[33] Routes to the new geographic knowledge abounded, whether one studied guidebooks or the theater.

Even before *Human Nature* was produced, Pettitt was establishing himself as a popular geographer. At least four of his previous plays depicted Englishmen who made fortunes in exotic lands like India,

Flight of Mrs. Temple (Miss Isabel Bateman) with her child.

HUMAN NATURE at Drury Lane.

Captain Temple (Mr. Henry Neville) saves Paul De Vigne in the Soudan.

Human Nature by Henry Pettitt and Augustus Harris at Drury Lane, September 1885, *Illustrated London News,* September 26, 1885. (Photo courtesy of The Ohio State University libraries.)

Bolivia, and Australia, and Pettitt would continue to depict distant regions in his later plays. Many of his plays were partially or entirely set overseas. Pettitt's success was derived from his knowledge of colonial territories, just as his characters' wealth was generated in colonial territories. Pettitt's public image dovetailed with the story he repeatedly told: opportunities awaited the man who would know the exotic.[34] Both Augustus Harris and Henry Pettitt claimed respectability for the theater through the apparent accuracy of the geographies they created.

In defining themselves as geographers, playwrights and managers aped their subject matter; the actual officers and correspondents suggested by *Human Nature* and *Khartoum* were praised for their knowledge of Eastern geography and customs. Descriptions of Gordon often detailed his knowledge of geography. When Gordon was dispatched to the Sudan in January 1884, the *Illustrated London News* began its report by explaining that he had been lately occupied with archaeological and topographical studies of Jerusalem.[35] In a review for a published facsimile of Gordon's sketch of his route to Khartoum, the *Athenaeum* announced that "General Gordon lost no opportunity to add to our geographical knowledge."[36] Biographies of Gordon often gave considerable attention to his mapping of the Nile (although he once asserted that he did not care whether the Nile had a source or not). After Gordon's death, his knowledge of Eastern manners and terrain became legendary.

Late-nineteenth-century staging practices, when adapted to orientalist productions, further reinforced audiences' confidence in the accuracy of the geographies articulated by the theater. Theater managers went to great lengths to convince their audiences that the space behind the proscenium provided accurate three-dimensional reproductions of exotic space. The stage lent credibility to the entire geography mapped within the play. If the playwright and manager had fully mastered the contours of this portion of exotic space, it seemed likely that they similarly had mastered the much wider space that connected periphery to metropole, the place of the play with the place of the stage. The stage space, in this sense, acted as synecdoche for the geography created by the play. The stage stood in for the vast terrains through which the protagonist journeyed, and scenic design stood in for a range of geographic practices intended to make distant regions legible and available to the European audience.

Late Victorian theater managers claimed to present actual geographies as experienced by tourists, correspondents, and soldiers. The "exotic" stage was no longer viewed as a complete and self-contained landscape suitable for imaginative (and potentially transgressive) self-projection but was instead seen as the reproduction of a fragment in the "real" geography that linked London and the East. Whereas an earlier generation of poets had imagined the East as a space outside of modernity affording possibilities for sexual freedom and political revolt, late Victorian writers created an East contiguous with and subject to Europe. If sexual tyranny and a propensity to violent revolt persisted in the East, they were evidence of atavistic forces that needed to be contained and not an alternative to European modernity. The "exotic" was domesticated and connected to normative imagination, as imagination itself was restructured by new connections between home and colonial terrains. These connections were dramatized in the theater and in theatricalized exhibitions, helping to formulate and disseminate the modern geographic imagination.

NOTES

1. Friedrich Nietzsche, *The Use and Abuse of History*, trans. Adrian Collins (New York: Macmillan, 1957), 18. Phillippa Levine provides a thorough analysis of the decline of antiquarianism in *The Amateur and the Professional: Antiquarians, Historians, and Archaeologists in Victorian England, 1838–1886* (Cambridge: Cambridge University Press, 1986). My own understanding of the antiquarian impulse is indebted to the work of Stephen Bann, particularly *Romanticism and the Rise of History* (New York: Macmillan, Twayne, 1995).

2. Edward Said, *Orientalism* (New York: Vintage, 1979), 162, 166.

3. This focus on meaningful combination was a feature of Victorian historicism and not simply the province of those new disciplines that depended on the increased accessibility of the exotic. Historians, after all, placed a new value on the assessment and combination of multiple sources. In this light, Victorian historicism and colonialism can be seen as constitutive of the same epistemological shift. The historian's new role as arranger of source material was consistent with the growing faith in the superiority of Victorian culture. The professional historian mastered primary documents in order to accurately depict the distinctiveness of individual periods as well as the development and progress that linked periods. Victorians saw their society as the pinnacle of historical achievement, just as they saw England as the center of a world empire.

4. For analysis of how these productions relate to other imperial melodramas see Michael Booth, "Soldiers of the Queen: Drury Lane Imperialism," in *Melodrama: The Cultural Emergence of a Genre,* ed. Michael Hays and Anastasia Nikolopoulu (New York: St. Martin's Press, 1996); and Heidi J. Holder, "Melodrama, Realism, and Empire on the British Stage," in *Acts of Supremacy: The British Empire and the Stage, 1790–1930,* ed. J. S. Bratton et al. (Manchester: Manchester University Press, 1991).

5. *Illustrated London News,* February 14, 1885.

6. English Romantic poets wrote few dramas (Coleridge's *Remorse* and Byron's *Sardanapalus* being two orientalist exceptions). However, theater managers often adapted current poems to the stage, especially the highly popular oriental romances. Examples of these adaptations include *The Corsair* (Sadler's Wells, 1814), *The Bride of Abydos* (Drury Lane, 1818), *Thalaba, the Destroyer* (Royal Coburg, 1826, and Covent Garden, 1836), and *The Siege of Corinth* (Drury Lane, 1836). *Lalla Rookh* was adapted as *The Gherber; or the Fireworshipers* (Sadler's Wells, 1818), *The Veiled Prophet of Khorossan* (Royal Amphitheater, 1820), *Hafed the Gherber; or the Fireworshipers* (Drury Lane, 1824), and *Mokanna; or, The Veiled Prophet of Khorassan* (Cambridge Theater, 1843). In addition, *The Corsair* and *Lalla Rookh* inspired several dance adaptations.

7. Examples include W. Dimond's *The Aethiop; or, The Child of the Desert*

(Covent Garden, 1812), C. Farley's *The Spirits of the Moon; or, The Inundation of the Nile* (Covent Garden, 1824), W. Moncrieff's *Zoroaster; or, The Spirit of the Star* (Drury Lane, 1824), E. Fitzball's *The Earthquake; or, The Spectre of the Nile* (Adelphi, 1828) and W. Cooper's *Zopyrus, The Hero of Persia* (Theater Royal, Norwich).

8. Examples include W. Dimond's *The Seraglio* (Covent Garden, 1827), W. Dimond's *The Englishmen in India* (Drury Lane, 1827), and J. Haine's *The French Spy; or, The Siege of Constantina* (Adelphi, 1837). For a discussion of these and the aforementioned orientalist productions, see Edward Ziter, "The Invention of the Middle East in British Scene Painting and *Mise en Scène:* 1798–1853," Ph.D. diss., University of California, Santa Barbara, 1997.

9. Holder, "Melodrama, Realism, and Empire," 142.

10. Peter Brooks, *The Melodramatic Imagination: Balzac, Henry James, Melo-drama, and the Mode of Excess* (New York: Columbia University Press, 1985), 32.

11. Eric Bentley, *The Life of the Drama* (New York: Applause, 1964), 202.

12. Daniel R. Headrick convincingly argues that technological innovations shaped the development of nineteenth-century imperialism in *The Tools of Empire: Technology and European Imperialism in the Nineteenth Century* (Oxford: Oxford University Press, 1985).

13. In point of fact the commander of the relief expedition, General Garnet Wolseley, refused to use native boats and instead ordered eight hundred boats specially constructed in London to navigate the cataracts at low water. These ships proved too light and fragile to navigate the Nile rapids. Later in the scene, an explanation is provided for the often-reported capsizing of Wolseley's low boats; an Arab "fellaheen" cuts the nuggar free, and it is "borne by current . . . strikes rock and founders."

14. In fact, both the review in the *Times* (September 14, 1885) and in the *Athenaeum* (September 19, 1885) assume the play depicts the recent war in the Sudan.

15. *Era*, September 19, 1885.

16. *Illustrated London News*, March 29, 1885.

17. British newspapers were not alone in adapting real events to melodra-matic conventions. In her analysis of French nineteenth-century theatrical ori-entalism, Angela C. Pao argues that "if dramatic authors did indeed rely heavily, even exclusively, on dispatches and commentaries published in the daily papers for their plot outlines and composition of scenes, journalists just as consistently organized their reportage in terms of dramatic scenarios." *The Orient of the Boulevards: Exoticism, Empire, and Nineteenth-Century French Theater* (Philadel-phia: University of Pennsylvania Press, 1998), 123.

18. *Illustrated London News*, February 23, 1884.

19. William Muskerry and John Jourdain, *Khartoum! or, The Star of the Desert* (London: Samuel French, n.d.), 29.

20. Muskerry and Jourdain, *Khartoum!* 50–51.

21. The double letter also served to explain the apparent contradiction

between Gordon's last desperate letter and earlier dispatches that asserted the city could "hold out for years."

22. *Khartoum,* with its rescue of the city in the last act, was not the only work to adapt events to the melodramatic formula. When the British recaptured the Sudan in 1898, the victory was presented as Gordon's long-delayed rescue. The British victory at Omdurman in that year was commemorated with a medal inscribed "Khartoum." This second Sudan campaign concluded with a memorial service for Gordon. As one journalist wrote of the ceremony, Britain's "long-delayed duty was done. . . . We left Gordon alone again—but alone in majesty under the conquering ensigns of his own people." Quoted in Douglas H. Johnson, "The Death of Gordon: A Victorian Myth," *Journal of Imperial and Commonwealth History* 10 (1982): 304.

23. Muskerry and Jourdain, *Khartoum!* 17, 20.

24. *Era,* November 14, 1885.

25. As Johnson explains, the increased emphasis on Gordon's religious character is evidenced in a number of pamphlets and sermons published after his death. In them, Gordon is referred to as a "Christian Hero," "The Youngest of the Saints," a "Hero and a Saint," "England's Hero and Christian Soldier," "The Forsaken Hero," and "The Hero Sacrificed" ("The Death of Gordon," 302).

26. *Times,* December 1, 1885.

27. Booth, "Soldiers of the Queen."

28. *Times,* September 14, 1885.

29. *Era,* November 14, 1885.

30. The *Bat,* a journal that was critical of Victorian spectacular theater, linked its criticism of Harris's management to its criticism of the war:

> We ratepayers were charged about thirty millions sterling for the Soudan war. All we got for the money, a few swords, some Mahdi's uniforms, a shield or two, a coat of mail, and some wooden saddles have been handed over to Augustus Harris. And certainly we must be poor patriots indeed if we grudge that paltry sum to decorate the walls of the grand saloon of the National Theater.
>
> To those whose disgust that the course taken by England both with regard to Egypt and the Soudan does not destroy any interest in the relics, the show must be instructive and entertaining. And it is satisfactory to notice that the collection is much better shown and catalogued at Drury Lane than it would have been had it been exhibited by public authorities at a national museum. (November 17, 1885, 499)

31. *Era,* November 14, 1885.

32. Reprinted in the *Era,* September 19, 1885.

33. Pettitt lived well before tourism had become associated with passivity and cultural insensitivity. In fact, Gladstone himself would cite modern tourism as one of the great successes of Victorian society when responding to Ten-

nyson's famous attack on the decadence of contemporary culture, *Locksley Hall Sixty Years After* (1886). Gladstone asserted:

> Among the humanizing contrivances of the age, I think notice is due to the system founded by Mr. Cook, and now largely in use, under which numbers of persons, and indeed whole classes, have for the first time found easy access to foreign countries, and have acquired some of that familiarity with them, that breeds not contempt but kindness. (Quoted in Richard Shannon, *The Crisis of Imperialism, 1865–1915* [London: Hart-Davis, 1974] 201)

It is also worth remembering that Cook was lionized in the press for his efforts during the Gordon relief expedition. For example, the *Illustrated London News* asserted, "It is quite certain that without Mr. Cook's co-operation the expedition by the Nile would never have been carried out" (November 1, 1884).

34. A similar lesson was repeated in imperial melodrama. In *Khartoum,* lost honor is regained through colonial warfare. In *Human Nature,* fidelity is proved after tracking the villain across the desert. Edward Said has argued that in the English realist novel, colonial territories were depicted as realms of possibility, which, in turn, supported the domestic order. According to Said, "Whether it is Sir Thomas Bertram's plantation in Antigua [in *Mansfield Park*] or, a hundred years later, the Wilcox Nigerian rubber estate [in *Howard's End*], novelists aligned the holding of power and privilege abroad with comparable activities at home." *Culture and Imperialism* (New York: Knopf, 1993), 76.

35. *Illustrated London News,* January 26, 1884.

36. *Athenaeum,* February 28, 1885, 283.

10

Under the Brown Tent: Chautauqua in the Community Landscape

Charlotte Canning

Begun in 1904, the Chautauqua circuits, a descendant of the institution founded in upstate New York in 1874, were an accepted, eagerly anticipated, and highly celebrated part of the rural experience by the 1910s. The original institution focused on adult education and self-improvement primarily through lectures. The circuits followed this model while adding elocutionists, music, and lighter forms of entertainment. Audiences waited for the circuits, which came annually for three to seven days, to bring stimulation, ideas, and a rare opportunity to socialize with distant neighbors. "There was a great deal of excitement when the programme was announced and the posters put up in the store windows. . . . For weeks nothing was talked of but Chautauqua and it seemed as if everyone was planning to go."[1] There were many other tent entertainments that came to rural towns in the early part of the twentieth century and to commentators at the end of the twentieth century they all look much the same. To the Chautauqua audiences, however, there were huge differences. That brown tent going up in the large field near town was not a circus, a medicine show, or a traveling tent theater but a Chautauqua, and Chautauqua was a welcome sight.

Despite its relatively brief visit, the Chautauqua served its audience as a crucial link with and extension of both the rest of America and each other. Every year the circuit tent was erected in an appropriate location, usually a large field near a small town. Its coming was heralded with the transformation of the town by banners, window displays, and placards. For the duration performers of all kinds brought new music, information, images, and drama. At the end of Chautauqua the tent was struck and the banners shipped on to the next site. All traces disappeared. Impermanent though it may have been, many Chautauqua practitioners and commentators argued that Chautauqua and rural America were synonymous, that the existence of Chautauqua proved the superiority and strength of the rural West and Midwest as the most American part of America.[2] One site where these claims were made forcefully and literally was in the cartoons in Chautauqua journals. Two of these, "A Chance for Cultivation" (1913) and "Our Town" (1914), are remarkable depictions of the complex claims Chautauqua made about its importance to the communities it served and the urgent spatial, geographic, and physical assumptions that constructed, supported, and emerged from those claims.

The 1913 cartoon consists of two panels. The first—a "before"—depicts a chaotic, dark, and dying landscape where the trees are gnarled and bare, the brush matted and dense, and the setting sun weak and pale. In the center a young man, "The Pioneer," rolls up his sleeves, a hatchet close by, and prepares for action. The second panel—an "after"—shows the same pioneer, now an older man, standing in the same spot with his arm around his son gesturing toward what he has wrought. Gone are the dead trees and tangled brush, replaced by roses and orderly orchards, streetlights, and buildings. These buildings are labeled with their role, the last in the row a crisp tent marked "Chautauqua." The caption reads: "Let the son continue the father's work, the greatest inheritance is ambition."[3] The 1914 cartoon also is divided into two panels, this time to represent two options. A field with straight furrows is growing lush crops, each row is labeled to identify the fruit for harvest—"Schools" or "Chautauquas" for example. The alternative, also labeled "Our Town," shows the same field, but this barn is tumbling down, the field is overgrown with random weeds, and scattered signs read "low amusements," "vice," and "loafing" to name only a few of the threats that lurk in the uncultivated and neglected field.[4]

There are striking similarities in the landscapes depicted in both cartoons despite their different artists and dates. The labor of cultivation and the benefits of cultured civilization are analogized; the value and importance of Chautauqua is placed on the same level as other communal institutions, most notably schools and churches; and the precariousness of the moral and spatial gains of previous generations are foregrounded. As Simon Schama has argued, the landscape that "we suppose to be most free of our culture may turn out on closer inspection to be its

"CULTIVATION has changed the jungle into the garden. Cultivation has changed the bramblebrush into the Beauty Rosebush. Cultivation has changed the election by bullets into the election by ballots on the other side of the Rio Grande. STOP CULTIVATION and we revert to the jungles, brambles, bullets and bullfights."

"A Chance for Cultivation." (Photo courtesy of the University of Iowa Libraries, Iowa City.)

Cartoons by Ned Woodman

Cultivate or Degenerate—Which Shall it Be?

"Our Town." (Photo courtesy of the University of Iowa Libraries, Iowa City.)

product."[5] Both cartoons contend this with a vengeance by turning the supposition on its head—landscapes that are not the overt product of cultivation are dangerous, threatening, and, perhaps most important of all, nonproductive. Both cartoons, and by extension the Chautauqua, argue against land not radically shaped by human intervention and development. It is a "shaping perception that makes a difference between raw matter and landscape," and it was Chautauqua that made the difference between a useless void and a productive community.[6] The white pioneer's claiming of the West for farming is obviously and unquestioningly celebrated as the triumph of civilization over seemingly empty and wasted space. How better both to support and preserve that triumph than by supporting the institutions that signify stability and community? Thus the more desirable landscape contains the church, school, and Chautauqua. This makes two crucial points: that Chautauqua is as important as, and analogous to, products of community effort; and that Chautauquas are central to the survival and prosperity of the communities they serve. A third equally important point is made by these two cartoons: that Chautauqua is a permanent part of that landscape. It is as "rooted" as the crops, orchards, homes, schools, and churches.

Both "A Chance for Cultivation" and "Our Town" depict Chautauqua as first and foremost a spatial experience, as part of the familiar and typical landscape of any small rural town. Landscape is space transformed into "a unit of human occupation," which marks the labor and existence of the community.[7] These communities, under threat from the external forces of urbanization and industrialization, as well as from a decrease in the agrarian population, seized on Chautauqua as one weapon in the resistance against forces they could not control nor fully understand. In order to explore how the performances in the Chautauqua tent shaped, and were shaped by, spatial understandings, it is necessary to identify and examine two cultural spaces. The first is the space within which the Chautauqua operated, in other words, the ways in which rural America was constructed, empowered, and embattled during the first third of the twentieth century. The second is the space created by the Chautauqua tent itself. Both these spaces were metaphoric constructions. The tent was a metaphor for Chautauqua, and Chautauqua offered itself as a way for the community to understand itself as a metaphor for the United States. These powerful metaphors were the processes through which communities and Chautauquas could reciprocally construct their landscapes. If "landscapes can be self-consciously designed to express the virtues of a particular political or social community," then the presence of Chautauqua is a productive subject for examining spatial experience as an important constituent in the social, cultural, and performed constructions of experience and meaning.[8]

To understand how the circuits situated themselves within the community landscape, one must understand how that landscape was constructed politically, culturally, and socially by both national discourse and the Chautauquas. As the United States moved away from its early-nineteenth-century agrarian roots into the industrial power of the late nineteenth and early twentieth centuries, it had to redefine national geography. Urban centers increased in importance, and concomitantly, rural ones were dismissed or ignored. For the many people who lived rurally or were critics of the cities, these shifts were at best disturbing, at worst a harbinger of the accelerated decline of the nation. These worries often found their expression in discussions and debates about "community" and the belief that its very existence was threatened by these new developments. As one Chautauqua pamphlet titled *I Am What I Am* boasted about the circuits: "I fuse aggregations of individuals into communities."[9] Ronald Wiebe has noted that the nineteenth-century United States was a country of "island communities."[10] By the end of the century these communities were superseded by new social organizations based on "the regulative, hierarchal needs of urban industrial life" that were alien to those who lived outside these urban centers.[11]

Rural communities were the locus of this national uncertainty. Their experience—"to live in the countryside by 1900 was to have the sense that the nation was passing you by, leaving you behind, ignoring you at best, derogating you at worst"—was born in part from tremendous population shifts that fueled the growing urban domination.[12] From 1880 to 1930 rural population increased 150 percent, but during the same period the urban population expanded 500 percent. Another sense of this immense change in the spatial distribution of the population is that in 1880 only 26 percent of the population lived in towns with more than five thousand residents, but by 1936 urban dwellers were 56 percent of the population.[13]

> [A] majority of Americans would still reside in relatively small, personal centers for several decades [after the late nineteenth century, but] the society that had been premised upon the community's effective sovereignty . . . no longer functioned. The precipitant of the crisis was a widespread loss of confidence in the powers of community. . . . [C]ountless citizens . . . across the land sensed that something fundamental was happening to their lives, something they had not willed and did not want and they responded by striking out at whatever enemies their view of the world allowed them to see.[14]

Losing the belief that a community could and should have the "effective sovereignty" to control whatever occurred within its parameters, and seeing it replaced with the demands of national industrialization angered many who continued to commit to the lives they and their parents had fought to establish in the nineteenth-century expansion of the nation across the continent. Those struggles were too recent and too personal to be threatened by the abandonment of the farm by young people for big cities or of the general store by farmers for mail-order catalogs.

"Confidence in powers of the community" was not lost without a fight, as Wiebe indicates. Many in rural communities, as well as several commentators on the situation, believed "that the metropolises, with their congestion, hectic pace, lack of adequate air and space, and crime, violence and pollution, would destroy not only their residents but American civilization as well" and that they were fighting not simply for their community or way of life but for the survival of the nation.[15] Chautauqua offered itself as a place to stage the battle and as a medium for restoring the lost "confidence" in order to resituate rural communities as the center of American values, morals, and beliefs. According to the president of the Swarthmore Chautauqua, Chautauqua was "the medium through which the community may express itself at its best."[16] This sentiment was reiterated in every piece of Chautauqua literature and picked up by most of the contemporary articles that examined the phenomenon. As one circuit, expediently named the Central Community Chautauqua System, announced in its 1915 program, "Our Creed: We believe in our Community. . . . We believe that out of hopes and labors now will grow a community, democratic, prosperous and strong."[17] Community was seen as the inevitable outgrowth of the investment in "uplift," a Chautauqua watchword. No community could help but be improved by its association with Chautauqua: it "was charged with the vital essence that leads to higher life."[18] That "higher life" was a product of the strong communal bonds under attack. Community survival was a paramount concern, and the circuits appeared to be a very effective solution.

The circuits made strong claims to helping stem the tide of people leaving the farm for the city. A program for Keith Vawter's 1909 Chautauqua warned that the "greatest industrial problem in this country today comes from the congestion of population in the great cities, and corresponding scarcity of labor on the farms."[19] Vawter combines both threats to community: the departure of people to the cities and the dangers of the cities themselves. Arriving in the city, farm youth "generally speaking . . . land in the lowest stratum of the city's working class, and far too often, the city's criminal class."[20] The destruction of the community landscape posed huge risks—not only was it menaced by abandonment but also by moral and social decay. The strong presence of Chautauqua, however, was offered as a preventative.

> Here is the greatest of the many missions of the modern Chautauqua. It makes life in the country cities more enjoyable, if it furnishes a glimpse of the great outside world. . . , if it makes life in the country brighter and happier, and tends to keep a fraction of those young men and women at home. . . , then Chautauqua is worth all of the support and assistance you can possibly render it.[21]

In his program address, Vawter tried to sidestep a difficult contradiction within the issue. City life was, for many, more interesting and exciting than life in the country. Urban opportunities for employment, entertainment, and socializing were more diverse and numerous than rural ones. Chautauqua found itself imbedded in a challenging situation—it claimed to bring the benefits of city life (access to ideas, people, and developments) without the concomitant dangers (immorality, crime, congestion).

The crux of the problem was precisely that no matter how much communities inveighed against city life, its attractions could not be denied, and even the most strenuous critiques contained their own rebuttal.

> Fifty years ago fifteen percent of our population lived in the great cities. Today over fifty per cent . . . live in cities. . . . And yet Ambassador Bryce, who has been a close student of American life says that THE STRENGTH OF AMERICA IS IN HER RURAL COMMUNITIES, and that THE DANGER OF AMERICA IS IN HER BIG CITIES. If these rural communities are the bulwark of our power, then we must preserve and increase this power. . . . Men crave education, recreation, new ideas, growth! If these things are not taken to the youth of the community, the youth will leave the community.[22]

Addressing Vawter's audience five years later, this writer faced the same challenge of how to make country life attractive while acknowledging that the lure of the city was a legitimate one. The contradiction was seemingly insoluble: the city was "the danger of America," the country "the strength," yet the benefits the city offered (education, recreation, etc.) were undeniably positive and productive. While one might question why the cities were so dangerous if they provided such beneficial opportunities, Vawter, Kessinger, and their fellow rural boosters came to the same conclusion—the solution was to borrow the best of the city and bring it to the country. "Supplying the motive power" for this solution of "making the small town attractive and powerful" is the Chautauqua. The battle Chautauqua joined to fight on behalf of the small community was one of the land and its controlling metaphors. At stake is where the definition of "American" will reside and how the American landscape will be represented.

Whether the strength or danger of America was to be found in the country or the city, each term is connected through the powerful process of metaphor. This reductive movement played a controlling part in conceptualizing and utilizing the community landscape, as well as Chautauqua's place in it. Metaphor licenses materiality by defining how what can be seen is seen. It proceeds "by invoking one meaning system to explain or clarify another. The first meaning system is apparently concrete, well understood, unproblematic, and evokes the familiar. . . . The [second meaning system] is elusive, opaque, seemingly unfathomable without meaning donated from the [first]."[23] The "first meaning system" was the home landscape with which every Chautauqua spectator was familiar—their own town, village, or county—in other words, "Our Town." Circuit materials, as well as public discourse encouraged rural citizens to think of themselves and their community as America at its best. Exhortations similar to Kessinger's above, that the "strength of America is in her rural communities," were endlessly repeated in those communities. Given the economic and cultural developments of the period, however, it is clear that such pronouncements were as much to convince, as they were to describe.

The second meaning system, that which is "elusive, opaque," was the United States itself. Positioning the community landscape with its requisite Chautauqua as comparable to the entire nation was both reassuring and empowering. It reassured because it suggested that life and the nation had not, as described above, "passed them by," but that rural needs, concerns, and practices were still central to the United States. The metaphoric construction empowered audiences because it suggested that they should be able, through the contributions of Chautauqua, to improve and strengthen rural life, and that the entire nation would benefit and progress. Influential Redpath circuit manager Charles Horner wrote in his memoirs, "Chautauqua people are not likely to forget that their own community is part of America, and that the whole nation is a great family of neighborhoods."[24] Horner described precisely the substituting process of metaphorization. Those who were inculcated with greater knowledge and inculturation through Chautauqua conceived of their own experiences within their community landscapes as typically modeled throughout the United States. By comprehending their own tangible space, they comprehended the intangible space of the nation. But as Wiebe has noted, this effort was doomed, and many sensed it. As the United States moved away from such "sovereign communities," Americans, particularly rural ones, "tried desperately to understand the larger world in terms of their small, familiar environment. They tried, in other words, to impose the known on the unknown, to master an impersonal world through the customs of a personal society."[25] "Impos[ing] the known on the unknown" is a process through which the unknown is made approachable and familiar and subsequently stripped of its power to threaten. Ultimately these efforts would fail, but the struggles to counter the trend away from "sovereign communities" as materialized in Chautauqua demonstrate the power of the idea of community and the magnitude of the changes that occurred.

If Chautauqua was one metaphor that made the United States and its struggles over community concrete and familiar, then the tent was the metaphor that made Chautauqua familiar, local, and tangible. Everyone who wrote about Chautauqua used the tent to evoke its experiences. Books with titles like *Culture under Canvas* or *Strike the Tents,* and articles similarly identified, "Tents of the Conservative" or "Tent Universities," mark the tent itself as the synecdoche for Chautauqua. Promoting the tent was a crucial decision for the circuit managers. While they stressed Chautauqua's essential role in the community, in reality it was not produced from within the community, and the management allowed local people very little influence. The community, however, was expected to sign contracts guaranteeing a minimum return and to handle all ticket sales. The circuits presented the same program in town after town, with few allowances for local differences. Doing so aligned them, however, with other tent entertainments that came from outside the community and had little local interaction. In order simultaneously to convince local communities that Chautauqua was a stable and permanent constituent, and to resist efforts to categorize Chautauqua as yet another traveling tent show, the circuits embraced the tent as its identity, leaving no room for a critique that might use the tent against Chautauqua. In "A Chance for Cultivation" the cultivated rows of necessary institutions start with home, church, and culminate in the Chautauqua tent, flags proudly flying, seemingly as fixed in space as the buildings that preceded it. It is also clear that the Chautauqua is meant to be analogous to the other institutions. Certainly in "Our Town" the same analogy is made. The straight furrows are of equal size and value, making a visual argument for the equality among them. Two contentions were made to ensure these connections. The first was that the circuits were an essential part of the community—to forgo Chautauqua was to guarantee decline. The second was that they were similar to institutions familiar for their quotidian presence, and because of their essential and familiar presence they were not similar to other seemingly analogous but discredited tent entertainments. In other words, the circuits were education, religion, and community, but were not theater or any other morally suspect activity.

Circuit Chautauqua's comparison of itself to churches and schools, as typified in both "A Chance for Cultivation" and "Our Town," tapped into assumptions about and histories of their importance to newly established rural communities in the American wilderness that dated back to the mid–nineteenth century. Churches played a crucial role, not simply as weekly places of worship; they "provided consolation, celebration, and explanation . . . [and] were . . . major recreational centers in rural America. . . . Churches everywhere underscored neighborhood efforts to regulate behavior."[26] In identifying itself with the church the circuits recalled these various functions. Not only did the circuits remind their audiences of their unassailably moral and respectable offerings for Christian audiences, they also called up communal ties and commitments—productive associations for the circuits to elicit.

Public school education was not widely available until after the Civil War in part because citizens had to tax themselves to provide it.[27] But those costs came to be considered essential as, for example, "school activities such as declamations and spelling matches focused community pride and loyalty."[28] Between 1900 and 1920 an unprecedented number of rural communities did levy taxes on themselves to create or better their schools, as schools were seen as a central way to "improve their communities."[29] Circuits capitalized on the fact that people had made collective financial sacrifices for the greater communal good, reminding people that improvements did not come without selfless commitment.

In their advertisements and programs, the circuits were careful to emphasize the connections between the missions and purposes of churches and schools and the Chautauqua. On a sheet of suggested text for advertisements Lyman Abbott, respected minister and regular Chautauqua speaker, affirmed that the Chautauqua "was next to the church and the public school system among the forces that are making for the elevation and ennobling of the American people."[30] In the same vein, Charles Horner declared in his 1925 program: "The Chautauqua is determined to be the constant ally for these four great ideals of human achievement; the *Church,* the *School,* the *Home,* and the *Government.* No community can come under the lectures of this program without becoming more American, more law-abiding, more healthful and progressive."[31] In both these instances, typical of program and advertisement rhetoric, the circuits are positioned to share purposes and effects with other communal institutions—specifically the improvement and uplift of people for personal and civic enrichment. These elements are connected to the strength of the community and the country. These analogies bound communities closer to their Chautauquas by recognizing what the establishment of churches and schools meant to most communities—permanency and legitimacy—and that these changes were brought about by their own labor. Churches and schools, almost more than any other civic and public institutions, signified a permanent cultivation of the landscape and movement from pioneer to farmer or businessman. No longer wilderness, untouched and uncivilized, the landscape was organized around human, European-American institutions. Such intervention was recent enough in both historical and personal memory that invoking it allowed the circuits to bridge their outsider status by metaphorizing their labor and institution to those at the heart of community effort, investment, and history.

The comparison with church and school elided a crucial difference between them and the circuit Chautauquas. Churches and schools, on the one hand, were permanent buildings (or at least housed within them) that a community's citizens passed regularly as they navigated their landscape. Occupying a physical site, these buildings were constant spatial reminders of the many and complex roles the church and school played in the community. Tents, on the other hand, were not structures generally thought to be permanent, a seeming contradiction to the circuit's assertion of itself as solid, reliable, and familiar. Chautauquas came once a year, brought all their own materials, and removed all traces when they departed. Citizens might point to an empty field or pasture, but there were no continuous physical signs of the Chautauqua. Claiming to be integral to the landscape was tricky and needed strong arguments to buttress the claim.

The most practical argument was simply that few people could afford to travel to upstate New York to attend the original institution, so a version must come to the people. Touring was the only way to bring "Chautauqua advantages" to a broad spectrum of people.[32] Keith Vawter, architect of the circuit plan, described the impetus behind the circuits: "The people in general cannot go to the Chautauqua; it is too far away and too expensive a trip. I will take Chautauqua to them."[33] The stronger arguments admitted Chautauqua as transient but stressed its effects as permanent. What becomes central is the experience of Chautauqua and how it translates into communal change and improvement. While the physical reality of Chautauqua may be temporary, the effects of Chautauqua were understood as "an established and immovable institution in American life as vital as democracy itself."[34] Given this requisite character, its impermanency was transformed into permanency.

> This tent, with all its appurtenances . . . is a transient affair, come but a short time ago and due to fold and depart a few

hours hence. Yet it will all come again. And through the apparent transience of it all there is a pervading air of permanence. The chairs, at least, are firmly held, for in every one of them sits a man or a woman or a child. Around the fringes, leaning on or holding to tent poles and ropes, or standing grouped at the back of the main aisle, there are more people. They are all intently listening.[35]

The tangible aspects of Chautauqua are indicated (the "appurtenances"), reminding readers that while Chautauqua is in a town, it has a strong physical presence. The promise is in its cyclical nature. Like the spring it will return and bring with it growth and sustenance. The permanence, however, is not so much in its material appearance or properties as in its audiences. Those audiences are what makes Chautauqua permanent. Their desire for "uplift" and their need for Chautauqua to support their efforts at maintaining community in the face of political and historical changes place Chautauqua firmly in the community landscape. One observer noted, "Well, the tent went away and the talent vanished, but the spirit of Chautauqua remained. I saw what Chautauqua had done for our community. I heard men in the corner groceries discuss the lectures. I heard children repeat the games and stories taught and told them that week."[36] While it cannot always be seen, that is, outside of the few days of the year when the tent is actually present, during the time the Chautauqua is there, the community is able "to realize itself at its best." The tent would leave, but the audiences would stay. If the Chautauquas were indeed "firmly held" by their audiences who remained, then the Chautauquas were never truly absent and their tangible and visible effects, "what it has done for the community," would endure.

The biggest challenge to these assertions was Chautauqua's clear similarity to morally and culturally suspect traveling entertainment, specifically, other tent shows.

The circus, carnival, and traveling tent drama. . . , obviously were circuit practitioners. Chautauquans did not appreciate this association, however, and were at much pains repudiate any comparisons between themselves and other itinerant entertainers. It cannot be fairly said that this dislike proceeded from snobbery or self-righteousness. It arose rather from the conviction and fact that Chautauqua took an advanced position on public and private morals and desired the cultural and spiritual elevation of its following. The carnival connotation came usually from critics, whimsical or savage. . . , or from those who, confused by the similarity of the paraphernalia: tents, freight cars, gaily colored posters, assumed that the parallel was thus established between the circus and the circuit.[37]

This long quotation contains both the basic challenge facing the circuits and the assumptions made by the circuits about their differences from other tent shows. That the Chautauquas, at least outwardly, were little different from other tent shows was manifest to anyone who saw them. Those who were "confused" by the "outward paraphernalia" might be excused from being so—not only did all the tent outfits look much alike, but they also often had similar personnel appearing within the tents. Certainly the widespread use of tents to tour shows and the Chautauqua movement were concurrent cultural developments.[38] But of course the circuits had to refute such assumptions, as well as the critics who used the comparison to discredit the Chautauquas. That such a connection could discredit them demonstrates the lasting prejudices against theater and related entertainments in rural areas, long after such beliefs were thought to have disappeared from the American scene.[39]

That theater or other entertainments like circuses would endanger rather than strengthen the moral character and behavior of its audiences was a long-standing assumption among Chautauqua audiences. The circuits' "conviction and fact" that they were superior to other tent forms, not because they were "snob[s]" but because they assisted in the regulation of public and private behavior (that is their "advanced position on public and private morals") echoes their claims of similarity to the church's role in the community. Ida Tarbell, the famous investigative journalist who published her influential exposé of Standard Oil in 1903, discovered when she lectured on the Coit-Alber Circuit in 1917 that such assumptions about the dangers of other circuits and the benefits of Chautauqua were common among loyal audiences.

In several of the towns the women work hard to make the show a success . . . that they might have an antidote to the traveling carnival, . . . which in place after place I was told had done serious harm. They claimed it had encouraged boys in evil ways and unsettled their girls; and in some cases there were tragic tales of young girls enticed away from town, or of boys bitten by the desire to go with the show.[40]

Audiences shared the Chautauqua's contention that what they did was different from other tent outfits, and the assumption that the Chautauqua was an "antidote" also suggests that communities welcomed Chautauqua in ways that they did not other circuits. While the threat was often couched in moral terms—theater "encourage[s] evil ways and unsettle[s]"—there was also a threat to the constitution of the community. While the ill effects of the carnival were primarily discontent and dissatisfaction elicited among the younger residents, there were "tragic" instances of young people lured away from their homes, thus disrupting the community and threatening its survival. Chautauqua, as argued above, assured audiences that their offerings would strengthen and improve the community in order that such "tragic" events be avoided.

The Chautauqua tent did house entertainments similar to the ones found in other tent shows. Aside from the lectures by politicians, public figures, and experts in self, home, and community improvement, there were elocutionists, musicians, and comedians. After 1913, theater—first Shakespeare, then contemporary Broadway hits—joined the other offerings on the platform. The circuit managers fought all comparisons, however, with any ammunition they could find. Even the tent itself was marked as uniquely Chautauqua. As one manager wrote: "That was no circus or medicine show looming up there in the middle of the field. The brown tent . . . meant Chautauqua and nothing but."[41] This was because the "white tents of strolling entertainers aroused suspicion in the more puritan minds. . . . Therefore, by using brown canvas instead of white, Chautauqua promoters removed any chance of their being identified with 'show business'; brown canvas symbolized cultural inspiration— improvement of mind, body, and spirit."[42] The circuits did not intend to work as pioneers against theatrical prejudices, nor were they concerned with promoting theater for its own sake. The fact that "puritan minds" and women, as Ida Tarbell testified, were strongly opposed to theatrical entertainments meant that Chautauquas had to differentiate both themselves and what they did from theater and the diverse range of tent shows touring the United States during the beginning of the twentieth century. When community citizens saw the brown tent going up in their town or village, they could read that tent's presence as a realization of the community's hopes and proof of their continued existence.

Because "the literal place of performance or exhibition . . . plays a role in the cultural recognition of theater or art," Chautauquas worked to mark their "place of performance" as removed and differentiated as possible from theaters and other tent repertoires.[43] While the circuit tent had positive connotations—community, rural pride, traditional morals and values, patriotism—it also promoted negative ones: not theater, not circus, not urban. This reassured spectators and made audiences loyal and supportive. By the 1920s the circuits regularly presented theater and other urban-associated ideas, but by that time the meanings of the Chautauqua space had been determined and continually reinforced. Seeing theater or hearing about urban achievements was not as overtly offensive as it might have been earlier. Advance agents who preceded the Chautauqua in a given town to place advertisements, check ticket sales, and generally create excitement for the coming event were ordered in 1918, "Remember that it is the town's Chautauqua, refer to it as 'your' Chautauqua. Localize all the time."[44] This "localizing," reminding audiences over and over that the Chautauqua was a matter of civic pride and improvement, was a successful strategy to determine the space of Chautauqua, particularly the tent, as one of unquestioning benefit to the community that would bring improvement, strength, and survival.

On the cover of the 1929 New York–New England Redpath Program was a ringing endorsement from President Herbert Hoover: "This civilization is not going to depend so much upon what we do when we work as what we do in our time off." With the circuits beginning to close and the stock market crash only months away, this prophecy is simultaneously astoundingly blind and bizarrely prescient as it ironically foretells the beginning of the Great Depression. There were many signs of the coming depression that had been willfully ignored. That the president who would preside over one of the worst economic disasters in U.S. history would emphasize leisure time for the millions who would soon no longer have work is high historical irony. But at the same time, in the long term, Hoover was absolutely right.

The United States has largely become a nation where deciding what to do with the hours when one is not working has become an identity-defining choice and a multi-billion-dollar industry. Like the circuit Chautauquas, one significant aspect of that industry is based on selling the United States back to its citizens. Whether "visiting" colonial America by walking on the very streets our forebears are said to have walked on at Colonial Williamsburg and witnessing the very activities they participated in, by strolling down the fanatically and falsely nostalgic "Main Street USA" at Disney World, or communing with nature in one of the many government-run national parks, U.S. citizens are still invested in and compelled by representations of their communal landscapes.

In a time of political, social, and cultural transformation nationally, the circuit Chautauquas proposed and embodied metaphors that "assist[ed] in reducing the unfamiliar to the familiar, [and] reinscribe[d] the unfamiliar event, experience or social relation as utterly known."[45] The nation, with help from the circuits, could be viewed not as a threatening heterogeneous space of factories, immigrants, and social unrest but a homogenous "great family of neighborhoods."[46] The tent, concomitantly, did not house iniquity and evil but community improvement and empowerment. This spatial framing sanctioned previously suspect performance as necessary to community survival. The lectures, music, and drama helped both to articulate and define the community landscape not through content, but by their presence in the space constructed by the brown tent. Americans have continued to transform empty space into landscape and community. The aging pioneer's achievements and the well-cultivated fields of the desirable version of "Our Town" reminded their contemporary audiences that the brown tent and all that happened within it were part of those transformations. The relationship between the circuit Chautauquas and the communities within which they worked demonstrate ways of understanding how performance and the political, social, and cultural meanings produced by and within it participate in the primarily spatial struggles of national definition. Who and what will be the "most American thing in America" is yet to be resolved and is still performed and struggled over in contemporary sites of leisure.

NOTES

1. Gay MacLaren, *Morally We Roll Along* (Boston: Little, Brown, 1938), 8.

2. Theodore Roosevelt is often credited with calling Chautauqua "the most American thing in America," and it was one of the most repeated and quoted phrases about Chautauquas. There is, however, significant doubt about who actually said it. See Alma Ellerbe and Paul Ellerbe, "The Most American Thing in America," *World's Work,* August 1924, 441; and Robert Louis Utlaut, "The Role of the Chautauqua Movement in the Shaping of Progressive Thought in America at the End of the Nineteenth Century," Ph.D. diss., University of Minnesota, 1972, 2.

3. Colby, "A Chance for Cultivation," *Lyceumite and Talent,* May 1913, 24.

4. Ned Woodman, "Our Town," *Lyceum,* May 1914, 24.

5. Simon Schama, *Landscape and Memory* (New York: Vintage, 1995), 9.

6. Schama, *Landscape and Memory,* 10.

7. Schama, *Landscape and Memory,* 10.

8. Schama, *Landscape and Memory,* 15.

9. *I Am What I Am* (Swarthmore Chautauqua Association, n.d.), n.p.

10. Ronald H. Wiebe, *The Search for Order, 1877–1920* (New York: Hill and Wang, 1967), viii.

11. Wiebe, *The Search for Order,* xiv.

12. David B. Danbom, *Born in the Country: A History of Rural America* (Baltimore: Johns Hopkins University Press, 1995), 134.

13. U.S. Department Commerce Bureau of the Census, *Historical Statistics of the United States, Colonial Times to 1970* (Washington, D.C., 1975), Series A 57–72 and A 73–81.

14. Wiebe, *The Search for Order,* 44.

15. John Whiteclay Chambers II, *The Tyranny of Change: America in the Progressive Era, 1890–1920* (New York: St. Martins Press, 1992), 111.

16. Albert E. Wiggam, "Is Chautauqua Worth While?" *Bookman,* June 1927, 403.

17. Central Community Chautauqua System, program, September 1915, np.

18. Na, *Vandalia Leader,* n.d., n.p.

19. Keith Vawter, introductory remarks, Redpath-Vawter Chautauqua program, 1909, n.p.

20. Vawter, introductory remarks, n.p.

21. Vawter, introductory remarks, n.p.

22. Harold C. Kessinger, "What the Small Town Must Do to Be Saved," *Lyceum,* April 1914, 12.

23. Neil Smith and Cindi Katz, "Grounding Metaphor: Towards a Spatialized Politics," in *Place and the Politics of Identity,* ed. Michael Keith and Steve Pile (London: Routledge, 1993), 69.

24. Charles F. Horner, *Strike the Tents: The Story of Chautauqua* (Philadelphia: Dorrance, 1954), 90.

25. Wiebe, *The Search for Order,* 12.

26. Danbom, *Born in the Country,* 92.

27. Steven J. Diner, *A Very Different Age: Americans of the Progressive Era* (New York: Hill and Wang, 1998), 196.

28. Danbom, *Born in the Country,* 93.

29. Danbom, *Born in the Country,* 164.

30. "Chautauqua—Community Development Page," *Lyceumite,* June 1914, 17.

31. Charles F. Horner, introductory remarks, Redpath-Horner Chautauqua program (1909), n.p.

32. W. Frank McClure, "Under the Big Tent," *Independent,* June 1915, 503.

33. Harrison John Thornton, "Chautauqua in Iowa," *Iowa Journal of History* 50, no. 2 (1952): 106.

34. Truman H. Talley, "The Chautauquas: An American Achievement," *World's Work,* June 1921, 184.

35. Talley, "The Chautauquas," 172.

36. Frances D. C. McCaskill, "Chautauqua in a New England Community," *Lyceum,* June 1919, 16.

37. Thornton, "Chautauqua in Iowa," 104.

38. "Reference to tent touring companies is rare before 1885." William L.

Slout, *Theater in a Tent: The Development of a Provincial Entertainment* (Bowling Green, Ohio: Bowling Green University Popular Press, 1972), 49. By 1885 independent Chautauquas had begun to spring up across the country, although tent Chautauquas would not appear until 1904.

39. For a discussion of these prejudices, the Chautauquas' fight to place productions of dramatic literature on the platform, and the use of theater practitioners long before their professions were acknowledged see my "The Platform versus the Stage: Circuit Chautauqua's Antitheatrical Theatre," *Theatre Journal* 50 (October 1998): 305–20.

40. Ida M. Tarbell, "A Little Look at the People," *Atlantic Monthly*, May 1917, 608.

41. Harry P. Harrison (as told to Karl Detzer), *Culture under Canvas: The Story of Tent Chautauqua* (New York: Hastings House, 1958), 96.

42. Slout, *Theatre in a Tent*, 40.

43. Loren Kruger, *The National Stage: Theatre and Cultural Legitimation in England, France, and America* (Chicago: University of Chicago Press, 1992), 12.

44. Redpath-Vawter, "Bulletin to 9-Day Advance Men," 1918, n.p.

45. Smith and Katz, "Grounding Metaphor," 69.

46. Horner, *Strike the Tents*, 90.

11

Artaud in the Sierra Madre: Theatrical Bodies, Primitive Signs, Ritual Landscapes

Julie Stone Peters

It is September 1936. Artaud has been withdrawing from heroin for twenty-eight days.[1] After days on horseback, he has reached the village of Norogachic, high in the Sierra Madre, "one of the last places in the world where the dance of healing by Peyote still exists" (*PD*, 46–47), the territory where "there is a race of pure red Indians called the Tarahumara" (*PD*, 3). This is, Artaud writes, one of the last regions in which a "primitive people" has been preserved from the attacks of "interbreeding, war, winter, animals, storms, . . . the forest," and, above all, "civilization" (*PD*, 3). Artaud is on a "Mission" both to protect the Tarahumara from the colonizing Mexicans and to "rediscover" and "revive" the "vestiges of the ancient Solar culture."[2] There, in the heart of the Sierra Madre, with this "anachronistic" and "Primeval Race," this "primitive people" (*PD*, 3) in whom the "Great Ancient Myths" come back to life, Artaud's voyage to Mexico will find its purpose. There he will participate in the "erotic Peyote rite" (*PD*, 5)—the ritual of *Ciguri*—led by the "ritual . . . sorcerers" (*PD*, 53). In these mountains, where "the rocks all ha[ve] the shape of a woman's bosom with two perfectly delineated breasts" (*PD*, 15), he will "become immersed in the original mythic arcana," "enter . . . into the Mystery of Mysteries" (*PD*, 20), "rediscover an idea of sacred theater" (*OC*, 4:146).

In the writings that led up to Artaud's Mexican journey in 1936, one can find the intertwined themes of his era. Among these perhaps paramount is the modernist primitivism that was produced in the fraught encounter with the first decades of the twentieth century, in the search to escape both the progressivist mythologies of the nineteenth century and its nostalgia for a preindustrial paradise lost, in recognition of the limits and failures of empire and in the wake of the devastations of a world war that showed just what "progress" could become.[3] By the time of his voyage to Mexico, Artaud had broken with most of the "'isms" of his generation, most notably surrealism and mainstream European Marxism (just another example of "Barbarie Européenne," he wrote from Mexico [*OC*, 8:126]). But he carried on, throughout the 1920s and 1930s, a romance with what he saw as ancient, primitive cultures that was very much of a piece with that of his theatrical contemporaries and most of the rest of the European intellectual avant-garde of his era. Michel Leiris, for instance, was writing about the phantom Africa. Georges Bataille was planning ritual sacrifices in the streets of Paris in the late 1930s. Revolutionaries, aesthetes, ethnographers ambivalent about their chosen missions—those engaged in what James Clifford famously termed "Ethnographic Surrealism"—were steeped in a vitalist primitivism that was vehemently antiprogressivist and violently anticolonial (with all the paradoxes of an anticolonialism that recognized its own dependence on the aesthetics of colonial exchange).[4] Like them, Artaud was seeking voyages (real and imaginary) beyond the bounds of sickly, dying Europe and toward an Orient understood as preserving, in its ancient cultures, the essence of the primitive and, in its rituals, the origins of theater.

As early as 1922, Artaud had seen the Cambodian dancers at the Colonial Exhibition in Marseille. He began to grow increasingly preoccupied with the Far East in the years that followed, writing two letters, the *Address to the Dalaï-Lama* and the *Letter to the Schools of Buddha,* in 1925 (*OC*, 1, pt. 2: 42–43). By the early 1930s he was reading the Upanishads, the Tibetan Book of the Dead, the Bhagavad-Gita, and books on tantric and hatha yoga, making extensive notes on Oriental, Greek, and Indian cultures (*OC*, 8:101–26, 354–55). In the series of poems on which he began working during these years, he drew on the work of historians of ancient pagan religions such as Ernest Renan, whom he consulted (among dozens of other sources) for material on the ancient Syrian sun cult that he used in *Héliogabale ou l'anarchiste couronné.* He looked to Charles Fossey, whose *Assyrian Magic* (1902) was later to show up in the glossolalia of *The Return of Artaud the Mômo,* and such ethnographers as Carl Lumholz, the specialist in the tribes of the Sierra Madre, reading these alongside Jung and Freud.[5]

Unsurprisingly, he shared some of the most basic assumptions of early twentieth-century ethnography: its high-minded anti-ethnocentrism; its reverence for primitive culture; its universalism. He could identify with the ambivalently protective and recuperative projects of ethnography: the ethnographers' struggles to protect the dying primitive against the encroachments of modernity, even while they recognized their own perplexing complicity with modernity. He could identify with their attempts to record and reproduce rituals in their pure form, before it would be too late—to capture the pretextual, lived, enacted essence of culture so that it could be offered up for European consumption, even while they reviled the fashionable buying and selling of primitive culture. Artaud could applaud the 1931 surrealist slogan, *Ne visitez pas l'Exposition Coloniale* (Do not visit the Colonial Exhibition) but happily attend the performances of the Balinese dancers there, discovering in them the key to his developing aesthetic. He worried that such icons of primitivist exchange as the mask (adopted as fashionable items for the boudoir or for photographic arrangements) were in danger of becoming (as he wrote) "a collection of outworn imageries from which the Age, true to its own system, would at most derive ideas for advertisements and models for clothing designers" (*PD,* 58). But primitivism, with its masks and totems, was a spiritual quest for him: "All true culture," he wrote in the preface to *The Theater and Its Double,* "relies upon the barbaric and primitive means of totemism whose savage, i.e. entirely spontaneous, life I wish to worship."[6]

The Ritual Theater and the Conquest of Mexico

Artaud's encounter with the Cambodian and Balinese dancers and his extensive reading of Oriental, Greek, and Indian texts (and anthropological literature generally) suffuses the texts he wrote between 1931 and 1935, after the failure of the Théâtre Alfred Jarry and leading up to the Mexican trip. Among these were those he later collected for *The Theater and Its Double.* It should come as no surprise that *The Theater and Its Double* and the texts that emerged from the Mexican journey have a shared set of preoccupations. Artaud submitted the collection for publication shortly before he left for Mexico. Its title came to him on the boat. He was revising the Mexican material at the same time that he was revising the *Theater and Its Double* essays. The aesthetic developed in these essays even before his trip certainly shaped his perceptions of Mexico and what he experienced among the Tarahumara. But, in a sense, that aesthetic also produced in him the *need* for the Mexican geography: the

longing to identify a source and an objective cultural and spatial correlative—and a broader and more open landscape—for the metaphysics
(manifest in primitive form and symbol) that the true theater was to
reveal.

In the essays leading up to the voyage, then, it is not difficult to see
Artaud seeking, in his particular version of the primitivist aesthetic,
what he eventually came to feel he could find only in Mexico: in the soil
from which the blood of the ancient races still took its life and in the
land and mountains where the "hieroglyphs of their gods" (as he was to
write [*OC*, 8:131]) were not yet extinguished. The Theater of Cruelty
was to reflect "the ideas of the archetypal, primitive theater" (*TD*, 50).
Like the Balinese theater, it was to be "at the service of age-old rites"
(*TD*, 58), producing the kind of "religious terror" that had seized the
crowds watching the Balinese dancers at the 1931 Colonial Exposition
(*OC*, 8:172–73). "Enormous masks" (*TD*, 97) could render in concrete
terms the exchange of individual psychology for the metaphysical representation of human consciousness. They could stand in for the break-
down at once of the boundaries between life and death, among the
human and the animal and the spiritual, between individual and collective consciousness. Hieroglyphs drawn from "magic cultures" (*TD*, 12)
were to form the expressive language of the new theater, "a new physical language, based upon signs and no longer upon words." By making
the unconscious manifest through symbols and images (*OC*, 5:17), the
hieroglyph could express "secret attitudes inaccessible to thought" (*TD*,
54). In identifying with "age-old rites" that had, at the same time, a kind
of "mythical immediacy" (*TD*, 116)—in expressing the hieroglyphic
unconscious—one could recapture "the true purpose of the theater"
(*TD*, 116): to "free *us*, [into] a Myth in which we have sacrificed our little human individuality" (*TD*, 116), into the collective realm of the
spirit.

The concern for the role of ritual and primitive religious terror as a
vehicle for a return to primal myth and symbol, the transcendence of
individual psychology by collective consciousness accessible through
mass spectacle, the various forms of symbolic writing offering direct
access to the symbolic realm—all these converge in Artaud's dramatization of *The Conquest of Mexico*. Artaud began writing *The Conquest of
Mexico* in conjunction with the essays eventually published in *The Theater and Its Double*, publishing a fragment of it as part of the "Second
Manifesto of the Theater of Cruelty" in 1933 and offering the full version
in a formal reading early in 1934.[7] The manifesto declares, at the outset,
The Conquest of Mexico's anticolonial intent. But Artaud immediately

casts the political question of colonialism as an exploration of the "genius of a race" and its ties to particular forms of civilization:

This subject has been chosen:

1. Because of its immediacy and all the allusions it permits to problems of vital interest for Europe and the world. . . .
2. By posing the alarmingly immediate question of colonization and the right one continent thinks it has to enslave another, it questions the real superiority of certain races over others and shows the inmost filiation that binds the genius of a race to particular forms of civilization. (*OC*, 5:18; *TD*, 126–27, trans. modified)

In *The Conquest of Mexico*, then, Artaud casts Cortez's conquest of Mexico and the death of Montezuma not only as a political war: between European-Christian civilization and Aztec-pagan civilization; between a society whose revolution had failed and one "which knew how to feed all its members and in which the Revolution had been accomplished from the very beginnings." He also casts it as a spiritual war: between "the disorder of the European monarchy" and "the organic hierarchy of the Aztec monarchy established on indisputable spiritual principles"; between the "dynamic but misguided conception of life of the so-called Christian races" and the "static conception of life of the inward races, . . . contemplative and marvelously hierarchized" (*OC*, 5:19); between "the tyrannical anarchy of the colonizers [and] the profound moral harmony of the as yet uncolonized" (*TD*, 127). It is the task of *The Conquest of Mexico* to represent "the ever active fatuousness of Europe" in order to "deflat[e] . . . her idea of her own superiority." The spectacle will "underlin[e] with burning emotion the splendor and forever immediate poetry of the old metaphysical sources" on which natural religions "much older . . . than Christianity" are built (*TD*, 126).

The (racially marked) "organic hierarchy" of Aztec political life brings with it all the spiritual qualities that Artaud identified primarily with the Oriental in the early 1930s, but comes to identify, around the time he is writing *The Conquest of Mexico*, with "the ancient races," the "indigenous," the living primitive.[8] The Aztec race is static, contemplative, harmonious, imbued with magic. It has secret access to the double through its access to "the poetry of the old metaphysical sources." In a sense, here, Artaud merely transfers the stage of his spiritual imagination from East to West. In this transfer, from East to West, from the Orient to the New World, however, he transforms his use of the sign, moving it into the broader landscape. What crucially differentiated the Balinese theater from the Occidental was that it used the concrete language of the theater to manifest ideas in space by objectifying them into gestures, dances, pantomimes, rites, symbols, images, hieroglyphs. *The Conquest of Mexico,* similarly, realizes cosmic history symbolically in space. Montezuma's internal struggles, for instance, are shown "in an objective pictorial fashion" (*TD,* 127): "Montezuma himself seems split in two, doubled; . . . with many hands coming out of his dress, with expressions painted on his body like a multiple portrait of consciousness. . . . The Zodiac [roars] with all its beasts in the head of Montezuma" (*OC,* 5:22; *TD,* 130, trans. modified). The opening "tableau of Mexico" is made up of "warning signs": "objects, music, stuffs, lost dresses, shadows of wild horses pass through the air like distant meteors, . . . the signs of the zodiac, the austere forms of the firmament" (*TD,* 129). But where the Balinese use of the symbolic object occurs in a geographical vacuum, in *The Conquest of Mexico,* space begins to take on a definite geographical form.

The Mexican landscape represented in the opening "tableau"—with "its cities, its countrysides, its caves of troglodytes, its Mayan ruins" (*TD,* 128)—plays a crucial role here. It is the representational space, the sensate ground against which the symbolic takes its meaning: "a landscape which senses the coming storm." At the same time, it is an animate agent of symbolic expression: "lightning on the horizon brimming with mirages, as the wind pitches wildly along the ground in a lighting prophecying torrential, violent storms" (*TD,* 129). Toy landscapes come into contact with the broader scene to remind the audience of landscape's symbolic role. Cortez is represented by "a *mise en scène* of sea and tiny battered ships," shown beside Cortez himself and his men "larger than the ships and firm as rocks" (*TD,* 129). Objects come onto the stage, evoking "on a grand scale . . . those bizarre landscapes that are enclosed in bottles or under glass bells" (*TD,* 128). The tools of theater are harnessed to produce the Mexican landscape unconsciously, so that what the audience perceives is not only landscape representing events, but half-seen images and half-heard sounds evoking an invisible landscape: "The cities, monuments, countryside, forest, ruins and caves will be evoked—their appearance, disappearance, their form in relief—by means of lighting. The musical or pictorial means of emphasizing their forms, of catching their sharpness will be devised in the spirit of a secret lyricism" (*TD,* 128).

Both humans and events here are functions of the landscape, as Artaud's rhetoric implies when it casts in spatial terms his antihumanist intent: "Humans will come in their place (*à leur place*)" (*OC*, 18; *TD*, 126). In the rush of metaphors of sublime nature that alone seem sufficient to express the sublime violence of cataclysmic historical events as they unfold in space, the human and natural landscapes become indistinguishable. "Space is stuffed with . . . horrible faces, dying eyes, clenched fists, manes, breastplates, and from all levels of the scene fall limbs, . . . heads, stomachs like a hailstorm bombarding the earth with supernatural explosions" (*TD*, 130) until, in the finale, "like a tidal wave, like the sharp burst of a storm, like the whipping of rain on the sea, the revolt, . . . with the body of the dead Montezuma [and] the cornered Spaniards . . . squashed like blood against the ramparts" (*TD*, 132). In the intermingling of body and landscape we can see Artaud's general erasure of the divide between the realm of (human) symbolic agency and the nonintentional realm of objects (natural or otherwise). The human body itself is part of the cosmic symbolic system: Montezuma's, for instance, split in two, hands emerging from his body, and surrounded by the zodiac. Through the ecstatic dehumanization of the individual, the body, representation of cosmic cruelty, bearing ideas "like stigmata" (*TD*, 127), may liberate itself into the symbolic realm.

Toward Mexico

We do not know when, precisely, Artaud decided that he wished to substitute this landscape of the imagination with the real Mexico, nor do we know what the immediate triggers for the trip were. But his letters and notes from this period are consumed with images of the voyage: of ships and ports (associated with Artaud's childhood in Marseille, and perhaps with his mother's far-off birthplace in Smyrna),[9] of imaginary symbolic landscapes. In a letter to Juliette Beckers (written around the time he completed the first version of *The Conquest of Mexico*), he describes the "mountain" he saw in her hand, which gave him a vision. "A violent landscape," with sands blowing in the desert winds, a Greek temple, the evening light unfurling itself, a sense of despair. "The entire landscape seems like a skeleton wearing an immense hieroglyph, in which the signs are where they should be, but a secret force has scrambled their meaning" (*OC*, 7:355). In fragments of a letter written to the painter André Derain in 1935, he describes the music of the "rigging" on the ships in Derain's paintings next to "a strangely lit patch of land" that "responds with a glimmer like a sign," a "rocky landscape, completely gray, with tongues [of] white light" and "luminous streaks like precious liquid filaments"—making up a "veritable hieroglyph" (*OC*, 7:371–72).

In the essays of this period, ships are menacing but magical and liberatory. European vessels become capable of mysteriously transmitting previously unknown diseases—shingles, influenza, grippe, rheumatism, sinusitis, polyneuritis—to the native inhabitants of the islands they pass (*TD*, 9). The significantly named *Grand-Saint-Antoine* carries the Oriental plague to Marseille in 1720 (*TD*, 15) (like Artaud himself, as he liked to think of himself, vehicle of a redemptive and sanctified scourge).

As if he could no longer bear to be confined to the theater proper anymore (with its frustrations, its failures, its airless confinement of his visions), at some point in 1935 Artaud began to make plans for the voyage to Mexico. There were numerous reasons to direct his general imaginative longings toward Mexico. The new revolutionary government under Lázaro Cárdenas seemed to offer the prospect of a real revolution, an alternative to that in the Soviet Union, with which the European Left was growing increasingly disillusioned. Sergei Eisenstein, for instance, had traveled to Mexico in 1931 to direct *Que Viva Mexico!* his (ultimately unrealized) "Film-Symphony" of its contrasting landscapes, ending with a banner with the words "Towards Revolution. . . . Towards a New Life!"[10] But for Artaud, Mexico had come to take on a different importance, as his writings over the course of the year preceding his trip suggest. In Mexico, there was "a naturalism in full magic," he wrote to Jean Paulhan on July 19, 1935, "a sort of natural efficacity scattered here and there in the statuary of the temples, in their forms, their hieroglyphs, and above all in the subsoil of the earth and in the still moving avenues of the air" (*OC*, 8:286–87). The blood of the Maya race was beginning to speak again, he explained in an essay called "Mexico and Civilization" (probably written in August 1935). "Neither the images of their thundering poems, . . . nor the hieroglyphs of their gods, still armed, still thundering, have exhausted their spirited ascendancy; it is the same blood that continues to speak." European culture was dead. There were, it was true, other civilizations that still held onto their ancient forms of life: Tibet, for instance, toward which his early attention had been turned. But Tibet was for the dead only, India was asleep in a dream of liberation, China at war, and the Japanese had become the fascists of the East. Only Mexico remained, its ancient blood pulsing in the earth and its occult life still to be found in its landscapes. One day, he wrote, the ancient Mexican races would dominate civilization. It was the place predestined to preserve the culture of the world (*OC*, 8:131, 186–87, 210–11, 168, 218).

For Artaud, then, the Mexican Revolution seemed at once to announce this destiny and to promise a reinvestiture of political life with the sense of mystery and reverie that the surrealists had lost. In Mexico, the revolution would not be conceived primarily in economic and political terms, but in spiritual terms: revolution was to serve cosmic spiritual redemption. The surrealists had accused Artaud, in 1929, of "not wanting the Revolution to consist of anything but a transformation in the interior conditions of the soul," what they characterized as a "detestable mixture of dreams, vague affirmations, gratuitous insolences and manias."[11] Mexico was, for Artaud, a way of redeeming the claims that had isolated him from those with whom he had worked in the 1920s. In Mexico, he could prove to them that dreams *were* revolution. The youth of Europe, he wrote to the Mexican minister of education, had their eyes turned toward Mexico. They "believe with all their might that contemporary Mexico wants to unleash an original revolutionary idea of man and culture, opposed to European ideas of progress." What had been lost through so-called progress was "the science of the profound and the knowledge of Man in relation to the forces of the whole universe." "We expect from Mexico, in sum, a new concept of Revolution, and also a new concept of Man, which will serve to nourish, to feed this last form of Humanism with its magical life" (*OC*, 7:373, 195). In seeking original Mexican culture, original Mexican medicine, that "buried treasury of archaic images" that could still be found in Mexico, he was seeking to understand the original powers of life (*OC*, 8:216–17, 228, 230). Seeking a concept of revolution that could save sickly, rotten, dying Europe (*OC*, 1, pt. 2: 43; 8:161, 186), he was also on a mission to save the indigenous soul, a sort of reverse conquest of the Americas that would return it to its pre-Cortesian state. "In a word, we believe that the Mexican revolution is a revolution of the indigenous soul, a revolution for reconquering *the indigenous soul* as it was before Cortez." His task was to help Mexico realize its unique civilization—to change the unconscious dreams of the primitive into reality (*OC*, 8:195, 212, 230).

Artaud set sail from Antwerp on January 10, 1936, arriving in Mexico City on February 7, where he spent the next months lecturing at the National Autonomous University of Mexico, the Alliance Française, and other venues, writing articles for *El Nacional Revolucionario,* and spending the rest of his time in Mexico City's flophouses and drug dens.[12] Very shortly, he discovered that the real revolution was not in the least about the magic-imbued return to the indigenous past he had envisioned. In buying into the humdrum delusions of Marxist materialism—the vulgar attention to the prosaic needs of the body—it had turned against its own deep spiritual consciousness: "I am afraid there may be an anti-Indian movement in Mexico," he wrote (*OC*, 8:196). By June

1936, he could describe his own fantasies of the spiritual promise of the Mexican Revolution with a degree of self-mockery, as he did in an article in *El Nacional* called "First Contact with the Mexican Revolution": "Europe is, at the moment, in full phantasmagoria, prey to a species of collective hallucination. It's almost as if they see today's Mexicans, dressed in the costumes of their ancestors, in the midst of *actually* sacrificing to the sun on the steps of the pyramid of Teotihuacan. I assure you that I am barely joking" (*OC*, 8:195). But he nonetheless held onto something much like this "phantasmagoria," simply displaced from Mexico City into the far-off mountains, where there lay the "vestiges of the ancient Solar culture" (*OC*, 8:314), and tribes who still worshipped peyote (*OC*, 8:260), and a "Nature" that, "as if responding to the ever-more despairing cry of man," sculpted the signs of traditional magic "with an obstinate and mathematical rigor in the forms of her rocks" (*OC*, 8:262).

Distressed that the Mexican government had turned out to harbor the real colonizers, with its perpetual assault on Indian religious practices, Artaud turned his attention to the defense of the indigenous populations (to the Mexican government's irritation). He was later to claim, truthfully or not, that the Tarahumara had asked for his help in overcoming government resistance to their rites (*PD*, 25). In any event, as summer came, he began to plan a trip into Tarahumara country in the Sierra Madre: his "Mission" to protect the Tarahumara from the Mexicans. Just as he had projected the symbolic landscape of the "countrysides, caves of troglodytes, . . . Mayan ruins" (*TD*, 128) into *The Conquest of Mexico* long before he saw Mexico itself, in Mexico City he projected the symbolic landscape of the "red earth" infused with Maya blood into the Sierra Madre long before he saw them. The voyage to the land of the Tarahumara would be a voyage to the last place on earth where the culture was "based on blood and the magnificence of land" (*OC*, 8:159), he wrote (in disturbingly familiar 1930s rhetoric). There, the "blood of the Maya race"—of the "red man" (*PD*, 4)—could truly speak, speaking through the red earth itself (*OC*, 8:131). The Mexican landscape of the 1930s had inspired others with a visionary sense of the supernatural. When Eisenstein went to Mexico in 1931, he could see only triangles and grew to feel that a "supernatural consciousness" was dictating that "primal form."[13] For Artaud, it was here that the true theater could be found. If theater was an art of space (*OC*, 8:165, 194), made up of revelatory symbolic form, the kind of organic culture to be found among the Tarahumara was theater unmediated—already based in space (*OC*, 8:164), already made up of the most ancient symbols. "I have something precious to find," he wrote to Jean-Louis Barrault of his impending voyage into the mountains. "When I have it in hand, I will be able automatically to realize the *true* drama" (*OC*, 8:312–13).

The Mountain of Signs

Toward the end of Artaud's journey on horseback, in agonies of withdrawal, speaking neither Spanish nor the language of the Tarahumara, translating for himself from the landscape around him, everywhere he looks he sees "magical signs." "The land of the Tarahumara is full of signs, forms, and natural effigies which in no way seem the result of chance" (*PD*, 12), he writes in "The Mountain of Signs."[14] Some are familiar: the Rosicrucian cross (*PD*, 85). Others are mysterious and illegible: the hieroglyphs he draws in a letter to Jean Paulhan with "triangles, crosses, dots, circles, teardrops, and streaks of lightning" (*PD*, 87). These are "intelligent and purposeful signs" (*PD*, 16). It is "as if the gods themselves, whom one feels everywhere here, had chosen to express their powers by means of these strange signatures" (*PD*, 12). The trees that Artaud sees along his journey are doubles: like the theatrical double in the Balinese theater (*TD*, 54), they "manifest the essential *duality* of things" (*PD*, 16). The hieroglyphs in the landscape (reminiscent of those in *The Theater and Its Double*) are "universal signs" (*PD*, 61), objective proof of the authenticity of the Tarahumara's link to the secret forces of life. Just as peyote will soon revive in his "nervous system the memory of certain supreme truths by means of which human consciousness . . . regains its perception of the Infinite" (*PD*, 21) (he writes, in an echo of Jung),[15] nature here awakens strange memories in him. He suddenly remembers that there were once "Sects which inlaid these same signs upon rocks," and he begins to think that "this symbolism conceals a Science," one that the Tarahumara "actually possessed . . . well before the appearance of the Legend of the Grail, or the founding of the Sect of the Rosicrucians" (*PD*, 17).

The Tarahumara themselves are part of this system of natural signs containing the deep history of the race. Through their instinctive sense of the land, they are connected to the beginnings of human history. "To watch them unswervingly follow their course," he writes, "through torrents, ground that gives way, dense undergrowth, rock ladders, sheer walls, I cannot help thinking that they have somehow retained the instinctive force of gravitation of the first men" (*PD*, 4). The race and its geography are one, unified through nature's inscriptions (nature's "voice"): "it is over the whole *geographic expanse of a race,* nature *has chosen to speak*" (*PD*, 12). They breathe the land of the "Tara-humara" (signifying, in Artaud's hyphenated spelling, the earth, *la terre*, and the future tense of *humer*, to inhale [*PD*, 98]). Taking up in the Sierra Madre the antihumanism already implicit in *The Conquest of Mexico*, Artaud identifies humans and landscape as the product of the same intelligent but impersonal forces: "Just as [this nature] evolved men, she evolved rocks" (*PD*, 13). The Tarahumara *are* their landscape, even while they perform their landscape: "They are made of the same substance as Nature," an "authentic manifestation[ ] of Nature" (*PD*, 8); "nature has produced the dancers in their circle just as she produces corn in its cir-cle and the signs in the forests" (*PD*, 63). Integrated with nature, the Tarahumara are free of the Occidental entrapment in individual con-sciousness.[16] As they perform their rites, they are performing the collec-tive voice of nature. Ritual offers a translation of the laws of the earth (*OC*, 8:187), but it is not so much that the landscape is translated by the Tarahumara in their rituals, as that Tarahumara ritual and landscape obey the same deep laws: "The forms of the landscape are repeated by the Tarahumara in their rites and their dances. And these dances are not the result of chance but obey the same secret mathematics, the same concern for the subtle relations of Numbers which governs the entire Sierra region" (*PD*, 16). The dances "imitate the movements of external nature—wind, trees, an anthill, a rushing river," but they "take on a cos-mogonic meaning" (*PD*, 67). The rites and the landscape (changing before him as the light changes) together perform the symbolic forms of this "secret mathematics," the "true theater" that Artaud is seeking.

In Artaud's description of the peyote rite itself, one can see the familiar tropes of *The Theater and Its Double:* the ritual "oriented in space" (*PD*, 385), laid out in a "physical arrangement of cries, tones, steps, chants" (*PD*, 57); the hieratic, ritual, sacerdotal gestures (*PD*, 53); the mysterious alphabets; the Chinese and Mosaic symbols that Artaud now sees in the Tarahumara's dress and the arrangement of their hair (*PD*, 8); the ever-present "Double." The *Ciguri* ritual is to be performed in order to appease the double of a man of the tribes who has died (*PD*, 48). (The Tarahumara are aware of their Double at all times, since "it is the loss of their Double which they dread above all," and "not to be aware of what one's Double is, is to risk losing it, . . . a kind of abstract fall, beyond physical space" [*PD*, 10]). The priests write hieroglyphs with their feet in the sand ("something that resembled the limbs of a let-ter, an S, a U, a J, a V" [*PD*, 32]). On a branchless tree trunk that has been carved in the shape of a cross, the lungs and hearts of two goats that have just been killed tremble in the wind (*PD*, 52). Here, "geometric

Mountain in the Sierra Madre. (Photo by Richard Speedy.)

space is alive" (*PD*, 10), pregnant with signs. But the landscape takes over as the ground of symbolic action. On the slopes of the enormous mountain descending toward the village there is a circle drawn on the ground (*PD*, 50). On the side where the sun rises, there are ten crosses of unequal height but arranged in a symmetrical pattern, and to each of these crosses is attached a mirror. Inside the circle, at the foot of each sorcerer, is a hole covered by an inverted basin representing "the Globe of the World" (*PD*, 52) and containing the peyote plant, with its "hermaphroditic roots" in "the shape of the male and female sexual organs combined" representing the hermaphrodite Nature whom the Tarahumara worship (*PD*, 7). While the inverted basin covering the peyote represents the Globe of the World, the circle on the mountain represents the cycle of history. "The history of the world, . . . compressed between two suns, the one that sets and the one that rises" is delineated "in the circle of th[e] dance" (*PD*, 51). As the dancer enters and leaves the circle, he enters and leaves the daylight (like the Double in the Egyptian Book of the Dead), enacting "a descent in order to REEMERGE INTO THE DAYLIGHT" (*PD*, 52). The ritual is a voyage, across the globe of the world and through the cycle of time that constitutes the history of the cosmos.

If Artaud's description of the *Ciguri* ritual translates the symbolic space of *The Theater and Its Double* into the landscape, it equally transforms the role of the body. In *The Theater and Its Double,* the body is an agent of symbolic space. Here, the body is at once an agent of symbolic space and the object of nature's complex intentions, subject to its compelling forces. The ritual circle drawn on the mountains is magical, dangerous: "it is told that birds who stray into this circle fall, and that pregnant women feel their embryos rot inside them" (*PD*, 51). As his consciousness becomes a kind of "inner landscape" (*PD*, 47), Artaud begins to imagine his own body as inseparable from the mountains. It is "a vast landscape of ice on the point of breaking up" (*PD*, 46). It is a "piece of damaged geology, [i]nert, as earth with its rocks can be," with "all those crevices that run in sedimentary layers piled on top of each other," "friable" like the mountain itself (*PD*, 45). Like the rocks, his body begins to emit signs: "The things that emerged from my spleen or my liver were shaped like the letters of a very ancient and mysterious alphabet" (*PD*, 36–37). He cannot determine whether it is he himself or the mountain that is "haunted" (*PD*, 13). The Theater of Cruelty is transferred into the rocks, as he begins to see, in the mountains, human dismembered shapes: a naked man with nothing but a huge hole, "a kind of circular cavity," for a head (*PD*, 14); an "animal's head carrying in its jaws its effigy which it devoured" (*PD*, 15); "drowned men, half eaten away by stone" (*PD*, 15); "truncated statues of human forms." "Not one shape . . . was intact, not one body . . . did not look as if it had emerged from a recent massacre" (*PD*, 15). The burned peyote plant, whose image he sees in the hills, is "a man whom you have castrated, . . . a red and mutilated member" (*PD*, 27). There is a tortured man whom Artaud repeatedly sees in the rocks ("dismembered" like the castrated peyote). "The dismembered form of man is answered by the forms of the gods who have always tortured him," he writes (in a phrase that overlays what might be a motto of cubist aesthetics over the recurrent castration imagery in his account). "A theme of death emanates from them" (*PD*, 13).

Ritual Visions

If the rocks reflect visions of violence reminiscent of those evoked by the Theater of Cruelty, an encounter between Artaud and one of the priests enacts that violence through a masculine initiation rite of sorts, which Artaud must undergo before he can be shown "the way of Tutuguri" (*PD*, 18). The head priest, "the *Master of All Things*," awakens him on a Sunday morning "with a prick of the sword between the spleen and the heart" (*PD*, 19). Retreating three or four steps, designating a circle in the air behind him with his sword, the priest then "rushed forward and leaped at me with all his strength, as if he meant to destroy me. But the point of his sword barely grazed my skin and drew only a tiny drop of blood" (*PD*, 19). The sword, here, prefigures the all-important curved, phallic rasp, which plays a central part in the peyote ritual—an instrument in which "the whole secret of these savage Indians resides" (*PD*, 5). "In this wand that is held out and withdrawn," writes Artaud, a wand that "has absorbed the secret salts of the earth" (*PD*, 55), lies the curative power of this rite" (*PD*, 55). If the rasp is curative, the sword is symbolically preventative: wielded by a Master who comes to represent, through his masculine authority, the figure of the father. The rite is "a rite of humiliation" (*PD*, 18) that enacts a castration averted. It is a protection against becoming the "castrated" peyote, or the dismembered man whom Artaud sees in the rocks. In a sense, it presages the "miracle" that Artaud later sees in the rocks: "By I know not what . . . miracle, the [tortured man] remained whole" (*PD*, 13). In touching the son with the sacred sword, in a bloodletting that leaves him intact, the father passes on the power of the sword to the son. After the ritual, Artaud feels "filled with a light" (*PD*, 20). This light is a kind of annunciatory illumination, revealing the true identity of the "Master of All Things": the priest has allowed him "to look upon the face of . . . THE FATHER MAN [WHO] CREATED ALL THINGS," and thus to recognize those whom he has touched as "manifestations of the Word of God, or of his Logos, that is, Jesus Christ" (*PD*, 20). The ritual of entry into manhood, the ritual of castration averted, is a ritual of entry into divinity in human form.

The sword initiation rite—in which the "father man [who] created all things" anoints his son—is followed by a vision Artaud has just before the peyote ritual is to begin. This vision reiterates the terms of the rite (the anointing by the father, the initiation into Christ-like divinity) but casts them symbolically as a birth, transferring them into traditional Christian narrative:

> As the daylight faded, a vision confronted my eyes. I saw before me the Nativity of Hieronymus Bosch, with everything in order, . . . the fire of the Infant King glowing, . . . the scattered farms, and the shepherds, . . . the kings, with their crowns of mirrors on their heads and their rectangular purple cloaks on their backs. . . . And suddenly as I turned around, [I saw] my sorcerers coming down the mountain, . . . and mirrors that glittered like segments of sky, . . . and at the sight of this beauty at last realized, . . . I felt that my effort had not been in vain. (*PD*, 49–50).

Part of Artaud's purpose, here, is to identify the Tarahumara legend of three kings who traveled toward the polestar with the story of the three Magi (*PD*, 60). But at the same time he identifies the cosmic cycle of history that the ritual circle represents with the cycle of Christian narrative, beginning with the birth of Christ. The vision of the Bosch nativity, then, serves to represent the broader return to the birth of human history (to a race identifiable with the "first men" [*PD*, 4]). Importantly, however, Artaud misremembers the Bosch painting, imagining the Magi on the right (rather than the left, as in Bosch) and thus placing himself in the position of the infant Jesus, looking to his right at the kings bearing gifts (an image reproduced, later in the ritual, when Artaud describes himself lying "on the ground at the foot of that enormous beam on which the three sorcerers were sitting" [*PD*, 57]). In his reversal of the Bosch painting, Artaud casts his return to the origins of humankind (to a "Primeval Race" in the ancient mountains [*PD*, 3]) as, in the end, a symbolic return to a nativity imagined as his own. In traveling into the Sierra Madre, in seeking (as he writes) "the primitive people of the Tarahumara tribe, whose rites and culture are older than the Flood" (*PD*, 17), Artaud is seeking his own origins.

If the Magi represent a triadic version of the figure of the father (anointing the son, like the Master of All Things), the nativity takes place in the bosom of Mother Nature herself, whose great breasts begin to surround Artaud in the rock formations around him: "And I saw that the rocks all had the shape of a woman's bosom with two perfectly delineated breasts" (*PD*, 15). Imagining himself enveloped in the breastlike hills, he identifies the Sierra Madre with the archetypal mother: Mother Nature in her most primitive form. If the primitive *is* the feminine (in the habitual modernist equation), the voyage west (away from the Orient, from Smyrna, Artaud's real mother's birthplace)—the voyage to the site of human origins and to the nativity—has turned out, in fact, to be a voyage back to the mother. Frustrated by his separation from the mountain ("this terrible mountain which . . . had raised barriers against me to prevent me from entering [her]" [*PD*, 45]), in a fantasy of still deeper regression than that figured in the nativity, he longs to reenter her. Seeking to undo the tragic separation that initiates individuated consciousness, he will return, through the ritual, to his prenatal self: "I felt . . . that I should go back to the source and expand my pre-consciousness to the point where I would see myself evolve and *desire*" (*PD*, 75). He imagines that, as he loses the sense of his body in peyote, he will be carried on an "effervescent wave" (in another version of that "oceanic feeling" that Freud had described six years earlier),[17] happy to belong to the limitless (*PD*, 36), to "an immense void . . . painted gray and pink like the shore of the sea" (*PD*, 37). "Transported by Peyote," he writes (in a switch of tenses that situates him back in the womb), "I saw that I had to defend what I am before I was born" (*PD*, 75).

Instead of providing the safety of a return to the oceanic preconsciousness, however, the ritual culminates in an act of exposure, one that offers the nativity its natural narrative completion. After he has heard "the piercing cries of the dancer," seen the dance, like an "epileptic pendulum, . . . the crosses with their mirrors in which the distorted heads of the sorcerers alternately swell and disappear into the flames of the fire," felt "the rite, . . . the fire, the chants, the cries, the dance, and the night itself" turn over him "like a living, human vault" (*PD*, 56–57), Artaud imagines that he can, at last, understand the ritual's purpose. Like all true ritual, it demands a sacrifice—an act of ritual cruelty—and the sacrifice is him: "Greater than all this and beyond it, there was concealed something else: *the Principal*" which can "serve precisely by *my crucifixion*" (*PD*, 58). Artaud's crucifixion, this hieroglyph for the Theater of Cruelty, at once announces the universal apocalypse and serves as a figure of salvation. "To this [crucifixion] I knew," he writes, "that my physical destiny was irrevocably bound. I was ready for any burning, and I awaited the first fruits of the fire in view of a conflagration that would soon be universal" (*PD*, 58). In January 1944, incarcerated in the Rodez asylum, without sufficient bread, reeling from electric shock treatments, descending into a confused memory of heroin withdrawal and peyote, he could write that peyote "is given by Jesus Christ" (*PD*, 74), that the story of "the Great Celestial Healer . . . is the true Story of Jesus Christ," that "behind the sacred memory of those Rites which I know not what paganism has overlaid, the Tarahumara of the modern age . . . recognize their Initiator" (*PD*, 72–73). A decade later, he may have dismissed "my delirium . . . on the subject of Christ" (*PD*, 43) as the result of shock treatments and visits from the asylum priests. But, throughout his narrative, even in his more lucid descriptions of the rocks and hills, he sees figures of his own "perpetual crucifixion" (*PD*, 46) everywhere in the landscape. The "Man quartered in space, Man with his arms extended to the sides, invisible, nailed to the four cardinal points" represented in the crosses that surround the Tarahumara villages (*PD*, 9) prefigures the "naked man . . . being tortured, . . . nailed to a rock" (*PD*, 13) whom Artaud sees repeatedly in the hills. And this image becomes, in full hallucination, Jesus Christ whose cross is both projected on the mountains and part of Artaud's own body:

> And I saw, on the mountains of Mexico, . . . the glowing flames of a Great Bleeding Heart, . . . and in this Flaming Heart a Form in which I could not help recognizing JESUS CHRIST [and] the entire Cross, incorruptibly spread[ing], at the Cardinal Points. [And] internally replaced in the stature of my limbs, I saw the Cross of Calvary appear like a bloody rending of organs. (*PD*, 77–78)

Artaud's images of the crucifixion seem, in one sense, to reiterate the theme of the initiatory sword rite, with its affirmation of phallic inheritance. The sword rite enacts "a Myth of reawakening, then of destruction, and finally of resolution" (*PD*, 19) clearly identifiable with the Christ narrative. The Master of All Things has struck him and made him bleed, Artaud explains, so that he might "dissolve and be reborn" (*PD*, 19). The sword rite wounds the body, but the body is miraculously preserved from harm, rendered invulnerable ("By I know not what . . . miracle, the [tortured man] remained whole" [*PD*, 13]). The Father exposes the Son to the violence of the world, but ultimately enacts the Son's resurrection. This is the salutary crucifixion: crucifixion as the power of resurrection. But the crucifixion is also terrifying, a form of torture and slow death. And this aspect is repeatedly associated with the maternal presence in the mountains: the breastlike rocks on which "the naked man [is] tortured," on which the "drowned men" are "half eaten away by stone" (*PD*, 15) and all the "truncated statues of human forms" appear as if they had "emerged from a recent massacre" (*PD*, 15). If the rock formations are intentional, produced by an "intelligent and purposeful" (*PD*, 16) Mother Nature, their intention is torture. As an act of torture, however, the crucifixion is also an erotic act: there is "nothing more erotically pornographic than Christ" on the cross (writes Artaud), "ignoble sexual materialization of . . . magical masturbation" (*PD*, 44). Noting the Aztec spring ritual in which a boy or girl was nailed to the cross to pacify the goddess Cinteotl, Jung had claimed that all crucifixion served symbolically as a union of the son with his mother: the son was hung on the tree of life.[18] If the crucifixion figures a union of Artaud with the Sierra Madre (the landscape that he seeks to reenter), it is simultaneously erotic and horrifying, product of a "masturbat[ory]" fantasy in which the naked and bleeding body of the Son is exposed by, to, and on the very body of the terrifying Mother.

Perhaps Artaud had read Jung's *Symbols of Transformation*, with its sections on "Symbols of the Mother and of Rebirth," "The Battle for Deliverance from the Mother," and "The Sacrifice," and its images of Earth Mothers eating their children and infants being sacrificed to the Mother-Cross. Whether or not there are echoes of Jung here, the Tarahumara writings track—and transform—some of the most insistent of the psychic strains in Artaud's work. Artaud was, throughout, preoccupied with incest—in *Héliogabale*, *'Tis Pity She's a Whore*, *Les Cenci*, "Metaphysics and the Mise en Scène." At the same time, his writings of the period are suffused with insistently gynophobic expressions of sexual horror. In *Jet of Blood*, there are scorpions swarming from the vagina of a wet nurse (*OC*, 1, pt. 1: 76). In "The Theater of the Seraphim" (written in Mexico City) the "Feminine" is (Artaud writes) "thundering and terrible, like the baying of an incredible mastiff, squat as the cavernous columns, dense as the air that immures the gigantic vaults of the underground cavern" (*OC*, 4:143). The air in this underground cavern closes around Artaud, and he screams, "but with this stricken scream, to scream I must fall. I fall into a tunnel and I cannot get out, I can never get out. Never again *into the Masculine*" (*OC*, 4:143). In the Tarahumara writings, the terrifying cavern of "the Feminine" is transposed into the landscape, into the engulfing mountains. These rise up in the form of sexually voracious phantasms that pursue him, like a chorus of harpies. He is afraid of being swallowed up by "the whole series of lustful fan-

Entrance to cave in the Sierra Madre. (Photo by Richard Speedy.)

tasies projected by the unconscious" (*PD*, 37), the "shameless fantasies" to which the "unhealthy mind" may "abando[n] itself," and in which it may "dissolv[e] completely" (*PD*, 39). In an attempt to escape from the "sin" of sexuality (to avoid "sink[ing] into the void," he seeks, "beyond the cross, . . . the Virgin of the Eternal" (*PD*, 79) (the sexual mother purified) and emerges understanding "the law of Purity": "Be chaste or perish" (*PD*, 79), he writes. But pursuing "chastity" in the Sierra Madre, he is persecuted by "that infernal coalition of creatures who have taken over and polluted our consciousness" (*PD*, 77).

This fear of "the Feminine" (the voracious figure of the maternal) permeates his characterization of the peyote rite. The rite is an expression of the essential war between "the Male and Female principles in Nature"—a war represented in Tarahumara headdress (*PD*, 11), the hermaphrodite peyote (*PD*, 11), the trees and rocks, and finally the dances themselves. At its center is a dance, for instance, that figures the creation of man and woman (in a parody of God's animation of Adam and Eve, in which the priest expels his breath and, "under the influence of this pulmonary vibration, the man and woman simultaneously came to life" [PD, 31]). But what begins as a creation story turns into a grotesque enactment of cannibalistic human copulation:

> The male, mouth open, gums smacking, red, flaming, bloody, as if lacerated by the roots of the teeth . . . , the female, toothless larva, molars filed down, like a she-rat in its cage, imprisoned in her own heat, shifting and turning in front of the hirsute male; and it was also clear that they were going to collide, smash frantically into one another, [and] finally intermingle. (PD, 31)

The sex act *is* the war between the male and the female, a carnivorous act in which the individuated self is finally ingested by the other: the male, bloody-gummed, lacerated by the teeth; the woman, her *vagina dentata* appearing toothless but with molars ready to bite, "like a she-rat in its cage," ready to perform the castration already figured in the rocks. The war between the male and female issues in a series of images that pervert the nativity theme into one of death and decay: "a story of childbirth in war," which Artaud sees in the rocks (PD, 15); "the figure of death . . . in its enormous left hand [holding] an infant" (PD, 85) carved beside it; and one, in particular, that haunts Artaud, a naked child, "his face literally devoured by pus" (PD, 88).

Years later, locked up in Rodez, finishing his revision of *A Voyage to the Land of the Tarahumara*, Artaud is fixated on the loss of one of the possessions he acquired on his travels: a small sacred sword, twelve centimeters high, in a red leather case, "an object known to all Initiates" (PD, 96). Insofar as the sword is still associated, in his mind, with the initiation rite, its loss seems to represent the failure of that rite—a failed coming into manhood, symbolized in a symbolic castration (the twelve-centimeter-high sword encased in the blood-colored case). A few years later, he begins writing and rewriting a dissociated poem on the Mexican rites, "Tutuguri: The Rite of the Black Night," in which the Tarahumara ritual of crosses involves a series of attempts at purgation (washing, dressing in clean white garments [PD, 101]) but (writes Artaud) the sun-god will not forgive "the sin of man" (PD, 101). The poem culminates in an apocalyptic image of a runaway horse with a naked rider, "the sawed-off torso of a man," who holds aloft

> not a cross,
> but a staff of ironwood,

attached to a giant horseshoe
that encircles his whole body,
his body cut with a slash of blood,
and the horseshoe is there
like the jaws of an iron collar.
                    (*PD*, 104–5)

Clamping the man to the runaway horse (for Artaud, as for Jung, a symbol of the libido unleashed), the horseshoe is a set of iron jaws, an image that associates it not only with Artaud's incarceration but also with the mouth of the cavernous Feminine, the molar-filled mouth of the sexually voracious she-rat. It is a violent instrument that has cut the man's body "with a slash of blood." Like the staff of ironwood (an amputated cross), the man is nothing more than a sawed-off torso (in a reiteration of the castration imagery of the earlier writings). He is bereft of the cross (and thus of its promise of resurrection), forever attached to the imprisoning horseshoe, which encircles him "like the jaws of an iron collar," never to get out, "Never again *into the Masculine*" (*OC*, 4:143).

Artaud had to come to the Sierra Madre to complete the erasure of the body, its dissolution into pure consciousness, undivided from the life force. He had imagined himself entering into the cosmos through the landscape—and, in the peyote ritual, finding the essential theater. In the eating of peyote (as in the Mass), "Man, by eating the flesh of a man who *wanted* to sacrifice himself to death" could "eat his own disappearance and affirm his contempt for the duration of things, for *their form,* and for their effigies" (*OC*, 7:224). There, where the body could dissolve into the mountains, "the idea of matter" could be "volatilized" (*PD*, 31). But the open landscape carried him back to the ultimate space of enclosure. A year after his return to Paris in November 1936, Artaud entered the asylum in Quatre-Mares, Sotteville-lès-Rouen. He spent most of the rest of his life in a series of asylums, confined, his organs wasting as he pronounced mystical poems about the horrors of the body and its dreamed-of liberation, scrawling incantations against the demons, writing and rewriting (in "Tutuguri," "La Culture Indienne," "Ci-Gît") the great symbolic landscape of the Sierra Madre. But if his last years represented the failure of those liberatory visions, one could argue that the most expansive impulses of the theater that followed took their inspiration, at least in part, from Artaud's Mexican voyage and the transformed sense of the theatrical project that emerged from it. The ritualized theater of the 1950s, the hallucinogenic happenings of the 1960s drug culture, the experiments in theater anthropology that emerged in the 1970s, the various interpretations of environmental theater drew on his vision of theater transcending its narrow houses, expanding into the far corners of the earth, and, at the same time, freed from those secular halls, reaching into the deepest sources of sacred experience.

NOTES

1. Antonin Artaud, *The Peyote Dance,* trans. Helen Weaver (New York: Farrar, Straus and Giroux, 1976), 45. All subsequent references will be noted in the text as *PD.* For the sake of compression, I have given all quotes in English, providing the original French only where necessary.

2. Antonin Artaud, *Oeuvres complètes* (Paris: Gallimard, 1979–), 8:314. All subsequent references will be noted in the text as *OC.* Translations from the *Oeuvres complètes* are mine, unless otherwise noted.

3. For helpful discussions of the development of the primitivist aesthetic in the context of contemporary ethnographic writing, see James Clifford, *The Predicament of Culture: Twentieth-Century Ethnography, Literature, and Art* (Cambridge: Harvard University Press, 1988); Marianna Torgovnick, *Gone Primitive: Savage Intellects, Modern Lives* (Chicago: University of Chicago Press, 1990); and Sieglinde Lemke, *Primitivist Modernism: Black Culture and the Origins of Transatlantic Modernism* (Oxford: Oxford University Press, 1998).

4. See Clifford, *The Predicament of Culture,* 141 (on Bataille's plans for a sacrifice) and 117–51 (on "Ethnographic Surrealism").

5. On the use of Fossey, see Ronald Hayman, *Artaud and After* (Oxford: Oxford University Press, 1977), 133. On the use of Lumholz, see François Lartigue, "Les Tarahumaras mis à l'ombre," in Odette Virmaux and Alain Virmaux, *Artaud vivant* (Paris: Nouvelles éditions Oswald, 1980), 146.

6. Antonin Artaud, *The Theater and Its Double,* trans. Mary Caroline Richards (New York: Grove, 1958), 10. All subsequent references will be noted in the text as *TD.*

7. The translation in *The Theater and Its Double* (126–32) combines the original draft of the first section (published as part of the Second Manifesto and appearing in *OC,* 4:122–24) with the expanded version, given a reading by Artaud at his friend Lise Deharme's house on January 6, 1934, but not published until 1950. I follow, here, principally the revised 1934 version (appearing in *OC,* 5:16–34), indicating where my translation departs, due to textual divergences, from that in *The Theater and Its Double.*

8. See Eric Sellin, *The Dramatic Concepts of Antonin Artaud* (Chicago: University of Chicago Press, 1968), for a discussion of the Oriental in Artaud (identified with the lunar: feminine, static, mysterious) and the New World influences (identified with the solar: masculine, revolutionary, cruel).

9. See the discussion in Florence de Mèredieu, *Antonin Artaud Voyages* (Paris: Blusson, 1992), especially 10–11.

10. S. M. Eisenstein, *Que Viva Mexico!* (London: Vision Press, 1972), 73.

11. Hayman, *Artaud and After*, 64 (quoting "Le Surréalisme en 1929," a special issue of *Variétés* containing minutes of a meeting at the Café le Prophète).

12. See J. M. G. Le Clézio, *The Mexican Dream; or, The Interrupted Thought of Amerindian Civilizations*, trans. Teresa Lavender Fagan (Chicago: University of Chicago Press, 1993), 166. Martin Esslin, *Antonin Artaud* (Middlesex: Penguin, 1976), 42–45; and Bettina L. Knapp, *Antonin Artaud, Man of Vision* (Chicago: Swallow Press, 1980), 131–52 offer useful brief summaries of his trip to Mexico and relations with the Mexican government.

13. Knapp, *Antonin Artaud*, 140.

14. The essays that make up Artaud's *Les Tarahumaras* were written between October 1936 (when Artaud was still in Mexico) and February 1948, a month before his death, when he composed the last version of *Tutuguri: The Rite of the Black Sun*. He continued to revise the texts throughout his life (he was planning the texts as a collection just before his death, though the collection was published only in 1955). Thus, it is difficult to distinguish segments written close to the events, and in a relatively coherent state of mind, from memories of the voyage long after the fact, but I have tried to do so where relevant.

15. See, for instance, "The Concept of the Collective Unconscious," first delivered as a lecture in 1936, in C. G. Jung, *The Archetypes and the Collective Unconscious*, 2d ed., trans. R. F. C. Hull, in *Collected Works of C. G. Jung* (Princeton: Princeton University Press, 1953–), vol. 9, pt. 1: 42–53.

16. For Occidentals, writes Artaud, "only our own ideas remain in the field of consciousness, and the rest automatically vanish. And our self, when we question it, always responds in the same way: like someone who knows that it is he who answers and not another. It is not like this with the Indian" (*PD*, 24).

17. For Freud on the "oceanic feeling," see Sigmund Freud, *Civilization and Its Discontents*, trans. James Strachey (New York: W. W. Norton, 1961), 11–21.

18. Jung, *Symbols of Transformation*, especially 263–64, 423–24 (*Collected Works*, vol. 5, par. 400, 659) (and see Knapp, *Antonin Artaud*, 139). *Symbols* was first published in 1912, but frequently republished in the 1920s and 1930s. Jung identifies the mother, here, as Cinteotl, actually the name for a group of Aztec maize deities and for one of the male gods in this group (though his mother—the "Earth-mother," called Teteoinnan, Mother of the Gods, or Tocitzin, Our Grandmother, was also sometimes referred to by the name Cinteotl).

12

Bayreuth, Disneyland, and the Return to Nature

Matthew Wilson Smith

The Technological Transfiguration of the Romantic Dream

> Shows there will certainly be in great variety in the modern
> civilization ahead, very wonderful blendings of thought,
> music and vision; but except by way of archaeological
> revival, I can see no footlights, proscenium, prompter's box,
> playwright and painted players there.
>
> —H. G. WELLS, *A Modern Utopia*

By the mid–nineteenth century, a reasonable German might well have concluded that the Romantic dream of an aesthetic state had ended in failure. The answer to the old Romantic query, *why has Goethe not been able to do for the Germans what Homer did for the Greeks?* seemed no longer that Goethe was a lesser talent but that modern society simply had no place for a new Homer. Where Schelling and the Schlegels had enthusiastically anticipated the rise of a unified Germany, a new mythology, and a modern synthesis of aesthetics and daily life, Germany had proven tenaciously resistant to such attempts. Society from the standpoint of 1850 might well have looked like a realm in which regionalism had triumphed over unity, and cold, hard "realism" over mythopoesis.

What our hypothetical German would never have predicted was the resurgence of the Romantic dream of an aestheticized nation, and the new form that this resurgence would take. Wagner's prescience lay largely in this, that he saw the resurgence, and understood its form.

However obliquely, Wagner understood that Goethe was not born too late but too early, his failure not of talent nor of will, but of media technology. In the wake of the collapse of the 1848 revolution, Wagner held not only to the dream of remythologizing society but, crucially, understood the importance of a mechanized total theater to the fulfillment of this project. The founding of Bayreuth would change the nature of the question, though the worst effects of Wagner's innovation would take a little over fifty years to be realized. By 1933, the old query was fully transformed, and the new question could read, *why has Wagner been able to do for Germany what Homer did for the Greeks?* How has a new mythology taken hold, how have politics been reinvented as sacred ritual, how have the masses become aestheticized? And if one turns ahead another fifty years, to 1980 perhaps, then the question undergoes yet another permutation. *Why has Disney been able to do for America what Wagner did for Germany?* For if Hitler was a child of Bayreuth, then Reagan was surely the same of Disneyland, and if the two are alike in anything, they are alike at least in this, that they are creatures of an altogether new mode of performance.

Bayreuth

The wound is healed only by the spear that caused it.

—*Parsifal*, ACT 3

Echoing a widely held belief of the German Romantics, Wagner believed that an original, Edenic state of being existed among the ancient Greeks, who fashioned art that spiritualized nature rather than resisting it and molded themselves into a true folk rather than splintering into separate classes. This, he held, was *true* culture, far from the degraded forms of modernity that go by that name. But with the collapse of the Hellenic city-states came the collapse of humanity's receptivity to nature, and the emergence of this "culture" that serves as little more than a marker of our alienation. The situation only worsened with time, as art was increasingly swept aside in favor of mere fashion and luxury. Humanity's redeemer came, now, in the form of the *Gesamtkunstwerk*, which marked a return to the totality of nature for which the restless spirit longs. It brought with it an age in which man's self-differentiation from nature would be overcome, genuine community and true, spontaneous culture rediscovered. The *Gesamtkunstwerk*, then, was not merely a great synthesis of the arts, but also the marker and the means of a new synthesis between nature and humanity.[1]

The theater as an architectural site played a crucial role in this project. Once again turning to the Greeks, Wagner found the pinnacle of architecture in Hellenic temples and theaters. It is in the temples that "we recognize the form of Nature, but spiritualized by human Art," and the grandest temple of all, because it belonged to the people, was the theater.[2] The theater harmonized man and nature by spiritualizing nature as human art; as such, it was no mere site of performance but an extension of the *Gesamtkunstwerk* itself. Accordingly, its disappearance marked the decay of "common bonds of life" and a rise of that "Egoism" which alienated man from his fellows, from nature, and from himself (1:159). Wagner hoped that Bayreuth would reverse this process, and do so by fundamentally restructuring the relationship between the German people and the German land.

The choice of the site was counterintuitive: his royal sponsor Ludwig II preferred Munich, and generous offers were made for the cash-strapped Wagner to locate in Berlin and even Chicago. Moreover, Bayreuth was an unknown, out-of-the way town, hardly a candidate for any cultural map. But the reasons behind Wagner's selection reveal both the practical and mythmaking sides of the artist. On the practical side, Wagner appreciated that the town fell within Ludwig's kingdom, that it boasted a large opera house (which Wagner had originally considered using), and that it was far enough from Munich to avoid the machinations of friends and enemies alike. On the mythmaking side, Wagner saw in "little, out-of-the-way, forgotten Bayreuth" (5:328) the antithesis of all that Munich, Berlin, and Chicago represented: an affirmation of nature over culture. In a letter to Liszt, Wagner insisted that the *Ring* could not be performed in a city for a metropolitan audience; its proper setting should be some "beautiful quiet place" far from "the smoke and disgusting industrial smell of our urban civilization."[3]

Bayreuth's location near the center of the German states also appealed to Wagner, who considered the town's geographical centrality to be symbolic of the aspiration of the *Gesamtkunstwerk* itself. It was an essentially German land that Bayreuth occupied, a "vast Hercynian wild, in which the Romans ne'er set foot."[4] Indeed, the town was so profoundly German that we might "paint a picture of the German character and history, a picture which enlarged would mirror back the German realm itself" (5:330). The town symbolized Germany despite, and perhaps even because of, the fact that the residents of Bayreuth were not particularly "pure" in their Germanic heritage. Wagner pointed with enthusiasm to the fact that many of its first residents were Slavs, that "many local names still bear alike the Slavic and Germanic stamp," and that "Bayreuth was not left without Romanic culture" (ibid.). Bayreuth's strength lay in its peculiar ability to assimilate multiple cultures into a single German spirit: "Here first were Slavs transformed into Germans, without a sacrifice of idiosyncrasy, and amicably shared the fortunes of a common country. Good witness to the German spirit's qualities!" (ibid.). Similarly, the influence of Italian culture was one of assimilation rather than fundamental change, as exemplified by the fact that the town acquired a grand rococo opera house but the local Bürgermeister still insisted upon speaking "honest *German*" to visiting Italian nobility (ibid.). In short, Wagner held Bayreuth to be the mirror and microcosm of Germany at its most essential and a crucible in which the non-Germanic would be Germanized. As such, the town foreshadowed the function of the theater house, a house that would mirror Germany back to itself at the same time that it threw open its doors to non-Germanic peoples, initiating the wider world into the collective German myth.

Finally, Bayreuth enjoyed the advantage of isolation, which forced visitors to make special, often devotional, journeys to the *Festspielhaus* and so furthered the site's aspiration to become a cultic center. The distance between Bayreuth and urbanized Germany, Wagner hoped, would necessitate a pilgrim's progress, one that would prepare the visitor to enter into the mythic space and time that Bayreuth offered.[5] By making his theater a pilgrimage site, Wagner intended to return Germans' sense of their landscape from a modern to a medieval form.[6] It is a strategy we might term *retro-mapping*—that is, attempting to return a society to an antique form of marking the landscape. By this strategy, Wagner also helped to break down the barrier between audience and spectacle, for the *Volk* who reembodied this ancient way of being in the landscape would help to realize the more natural society which was the aim of the *Gesamtkunstwerk* itself. Pilgrims to Bayreuth became essentially visitor-actors, participants in a single, great drama of reawakening.

If the *Festspielhaus* attempted to reconcile humanity and landscape in the journey to the theater, then this attempt was doubled *within* the theater, by the performance of the operas themselves. A largely neglected aspect of Wagner's dramaturgy is the importance he attached to landscape painting in the production of his operas. With typical enthusiasm, Wagner called Romantic landscape painting and the natural sciences "the only outcomes of the Present which, either from an artistic or a scientific point of view, offer us the smallest consolation in our impotence, or refuge from our madness."[7] Unlike the painting styles that preceded it, landscape painting restored the broken bond between man and nature and, as such, was capable of lifting her sister arts out of their present state of degeneracy. Wagner was particularly interested in the redemptive power that landscape painting might have over architecture, and expected that landscape painting would "broaden Architecture out to a full and lifelike portraiture of Nature" (1:176). Turning his attention to the stage, Wagner concluded,

> Landscape-painting, as last and perfected conclusion of all the plastic arts, will become the very soul of Architecture; she will teach us so to rear the *stage* for the dramatic Artwork of the Future that on it, herself imbued with life, she may picture forth the warm *background of Nature* for *living,* no longer counterfeited, *Man.* (1:181)

In sum, Wagner's dream might be rendered thus: landscape painting, highest of the plastic arts, will redeem the theater, pinnacle of architecture, and together they will set the stage for the music-drama of the future. The fact that Wagner broke with theatrical tradition by hiring a landscape painter to make his sets for Bayreuth is almost beside the point: for Wagner, the whole opera, as realized within the *Festspielhaus,* functioned as a single landscape painting in sight, sound, and motion.

The *Festspielhaus* opened on August 13, 1876, to the sound of an E-flat so low that the double basses had to tune their E strings down a semitone to achieve it. In the fifth bar three bassoons entered on B-flat; the fundamental tone is joined by its dominant. Original Being, peaceful yet static, had been interrupted and transformed, giving birth to the dynamic, harmonious state of nature that Wagner called "the world's lullaby." The curtain rose to reveal a vista of this Edenic world:

> Greenish twilight, brighter towards the top, darker below. The upper part of the stage is filled with swirling waters that flow relentlessly from right to left. Towards the bottom, the waters resolve into an increasingly fine damp mist, so that a space a man's height from the ground seems to be completely free of the water, which courses like a drain of clouds over the dusky bed. Craggy points of rock rise everywhere from the depths and mark the confines of the stage. The whole river bed is broken up into a craggy confusion so that nowhere is it completely flat, and on all sides, in the dense darkness, there seem to be deeper gorges. . . .

When the curtain rises, the watery depths are in full flood. In the center of the stage, around a rock whose slender point reaches up into the brighter area of densely swirling water, one of the Rhinemaidens is circling with a graceful swimming motion.[8]

The elaborate detail, the attention to shades of color and degrees of motion, the use of both stark and subtle contrasts, the volcanic dynamism of the scene: altogether, a paradigmatically Romantic landscape. With one important qualification: the scale of nature here, though grand, was not so large as to overwhelm the actors within it. We are not in the world of, say, an Albert Bierstadt painting, with its towering trees, mountains, and ravines, and isolated, passive observers. On the contrary, Wagner's landscape was built to human proportions: the space beneath the Rhine is "a man's height from the ground," and the slender rock at center stage is just wide enough for a Rhinemaiden to swim around. Other scenes too emphasized the harmonious relationship between man and landscape. Take for instance Hunding's house at the opening of *Die Walküre*. In the middle of the house stands "a mighty ash tree," which, according to Wagner's description, stands almost entirely *within* the great house, indicating a tree of less-than-sublime size. Moreover, the interweaving of tree and house is a graceful one: the openings in the roof "exactly fit" the tree branches, and the walls of the house, made of rough-hewn wood, blur the distinction between nature and artifice. This rather modest rendering of nature was echoed in the design model for the original production.[9]

While Wagner's settings echoed Romantic landscape painting in many respects, they did not push the sublimity of the landscape so far that nature became truly overwhelming to humanity. And just as the sublimity of the landscape was tempered to a human scale, the characters who inhabited Wagner's stage rose to superhuman dimensions. Powerful but not overwhelming nature meets heroic, plus-sized humanity on the Wagnerian stage.

Though spectators could not literally walk through the mockmedieval landscapes depicted in Wagner's operas, they could travel across them in their imaginations, and so participate, at least vicariously, in the mythic age of German romance. In *Parsifal*, the only opera written expressly for the Bayreuth stage, this strategy of retro-mapping was rendered more forceful by the central role of pilgrimage in the opera itself. In the original 1882 production, Wagner sought to create the illusion of

Richard Wagner's *Die Walküre,* Bayreuth, 1876. Reconstructed stage model, 1927, by Josef Zehetgruber. (Photo courtesy of Richard-Wagner-Stiftung.)

Gurnemanz and Parsifal's journey into the shrine of the Grail, so that the audience might be "led quite imperceptibly, as if in a dream, along the 'pathless' trails to the Gralsburg."[10] The journey consisted of a pilgrim's progress (through the woods), a liminal crossing (marked by a rising passageway, a gateway, rising trombone tones, and ringing bells), and a transformation in space and time from profane to sacred (Gurnemanz to Parsifal: "Du siehst, mein Sohn, / zum Raum wird hier die Zeit" [You see, my son, here time becomes space]). Scenically, the effect of this pilgrimage was produced by means of four long moving dioramas, which were spooled into rollers and gradually unraveled to simulate movement through the forest and into the shrine. Essentially, a four-part, moving Romantic landscape-painting was designed in a manner that trumped even the popular diorama-theater techniques of Louis Daguerre.[11] The effect of this mechanized landscape painting, at least on enthusiasts, is typified by Felix Weingartner's reactions to the first performances:

> When Gurnemanz was ready to accompany Parsifal to the Grail
> castle, I was seized by a slight dizziness. What was happening?
> It seemed to me that the theater with its entire audience began
> to move. The scene had started to change by means of moving
> the backcloth. The illusion was complete. One did not walk, one
> was carried along. "Here space was one with time."[12]

Parsifal's pilgrimage to Monsalvat doubled the audience's own pilgrimage to the *Festspielhaus,* thus reinforcing a medieval sense of the German
landscape as well as an identification of Bayreuth with the long-lost castle of the Grail.

The recovered unity that the *Gesamtkunstwerk* seeks to forge rests,
however, on two new bifurcations, one of them revealed, the other quite
hidden. First the revealed one. Nowhere before Bayreuth was the audience so rigorously separated from the spectacle; most of the architectural innovations of Bayreuth, not to mention the aesthetic innovations
of the operas themselves, are intended to serve this separation. The
darkening of the houselights during performance, the sparse adornment
of the theater house, the elimination of box seating, the sunken orchestra pit: all of these elements removed the audience from the theatrical
spectacle and enforced a strict division of realms, audience versus performance (in Wagner's terms, "reality" versus "ideality"). The "mystic
gulf" between audience and stage separated the two zones by "making
the spectator imagine [the scene] quite far away,"[13] and thereby reinforced the illusion of a distant dreamworld on stage, entirely removed
from the contingencies of everyday life. At the same time, the techniques
of the *Gesamtkunstwerk* were intended to so entrance the audience that
the fundamental distance between spectator and spectacle would be
overcome. The mystic gulf thus separates the real from the ideal in order
to cause the real to realize itself, its real self, in the ideal: the
audience/spectacle opposition at Bayreuth is enforced only for the sake
of its elimination.

But this reconciliation between reality and ideality, audience and
spectacle, rests upon another, unresolved bifurcation, one that must be
repressed in the interest of totality. The split may be rendered roughly as
follows: on one hand, the *Gesamtkunstwerk,* on the other, the machine.
Along with its concomitants—production, labor, technology, industry—the machine is the *Gesamtkunstwerk*'s unassimilable element and
its necessary other. A point largely missed by scholars is that Wagner's
prose writings reveal an odd penchant for using technological phrases to

refer to opera production.[14] Here, for example, is Wagner writing on the importance of hiding the orchestra:

> To explain the plan of the festival theater now in course of erection in Bayreuth I believe I cannot do better than to begin with the need I felt the first, that of *rendering invisible the mechanical source of its music, to wit the orchestra;* for this one requirement led step by step to a total transformation of the auditorium of our neo-European theater.[15]

The technological appellation of the orchestra here ("the mechanical source of [Bayreuth's] music") is placed right beside the injunction that the orchestra must be "render[ed] invisible." A connection is implied between orchestra-as-mechanical and the necessity of concealment, a connection that is expanded upon in the passage that follows:

> The reader of my previous essays already knows my views about the concealment of the orchestra, and, even should he not have felt as much before, I hope that a subsequent visit to the opera will have convinced him of my rightness in *condemning the constant visibility of the mechanism for tone production as an aggressive nuisance.* In my article on Beethoven I explained how fine performances of ideal works of music may *make this evil imperceptible* at last, through *our eyesight being neutralized, as it were, by the rapt subversion of the whole sensorium.* With a dramatic representation, on the contrary, it is a matter of *focusing the eye itself upon a picture; and that can be done only by leading it away from any sight of bodies lying in between, such as the technical apparatus for projecting the picture.* (Emphasis added)

What Wagner is describing here, essentially, is a vast performance machine. And it is, more precisely, a performance machine ashamed of its status *as* machine. Thus the "mechanism for tone production" becomes an "aggressive nuisance" and an "evil" that must be rendered "imperceptible," and whose "constant visibility" must be "condemned." That the mechanical nature of the *Gesamtkunstwerk* should be a source of discomfort for Wagner follows from the stark dichotomy he makes of nature and culture. Wagner argues in *Artwork of the Future* that "the mechanical" is "Fashion's invention" and culminates in "the Machine," whereas "the artistic" springs from "*Nature's* self" and culminates in art.[16] The antithesis of art and machine echoes that of nature and modern culture. "The Machine," writes Wagner, is the cold and heartless ally of luxury-craving men. Through the machine have they at last made even human reason their liege subject; for, led astray from Art's discovery, dishonored and disowned, it consumes itself at last in mechanical refinements, in absorption into the Machine, instead of in absorption into Nature in the Art-work. (1:85)

Wagner's point here is trenchant: both the machine and the *Gesamtkunstwerk* have "absorption" as their aim, but the machine aims to absorb the audience into culture, while the artwork aims to absorb it into nature. The fact that the *Gesamtkunstwerk* relies so much on mechanics, then, is no small problem for Wagner. The problem is neatly captured by his statement that "the technical apparatus for projecting the picture" is impeded by "any sight of bodies lying in between." Though the purpose of this "technical apparatus" is the reconciliation of humanity and nature, this reconciliation is blocked by the sight of actual living bodies—specifically, by the bodies of the people who operate "the mechanism for tone production." For nature and humanity to be reconciled, such producing bodies must be hidden; for the *Gesamtkunstwerk* to succeed, Wagner must rely upon nature's antithesis.

The business of the *Gesamtkunstwerk* is never complete. The more it aims to realize nature, the more it must utilize the machine, a vicious circle that produces a multiplication of blinders. It is often forgotten, for instance, that the two prosceniums Semper designed to enclose the mystic gulf actually gave birth to a series:

> Now, to mask the blanks immediately in front of our double proscenium, the ingenuity of my present advisor [Semper] had already hit on the plan of throwing out a third and still broader proscenium. Seized with the excellence of this thought, we soon went further in the same direction, and found that, to do full justice to the idea of an auditorium narrowing in true perspective toward the stage, *we must extend the process to the whole interior, adding proscenium after proscenium until they reached their climax in the crowning gallery, and thus enclosing the entire audience in the vista, no matter where it took its place.* (5:336; emphasis added)

Wagner's account shows how the imperative of concealment produces a multiplication of blinders amid a fear of contamination of the natural by the mechanical. But it suggests, too, that the *Gesamtkunstwerk*, logically extended, places the audience "on the other side" of the proscenium. To

The Rhinemaidens from Wagner's *Das Rheingold,* onstage and below, Bayreuth, 1876. Production photo and drawing of machines. (Photos courtesy of Richard-Wagner-Stiftung.)

enclose the audience "in the vista, no matter where it took its place" is to take another step toward the total disappearance of the spectator/spectacle dichotomy. The audience, Wagner suggests, might now be located *within* the spectacle itself. Wagner, who foresaw so much, may also have anticipated this: that the disappearance of the theater constituted the culmination of his own project. "After creating the invisible orchestra," he remarked after the opening of Bayreuth, "I would now like to invent the invisible theater."[17]

Disneyland

> I've always wanted to work on something alive, something that keeps growing. I've got that in Disneyland. Even the trees will grow and be more beautiful every year.
>
> —WALT DISNEY

At first glance, Walt Disney would appear to share little ground with Richard Wagner. Outside of the innumerable differences of time and place, they would seem to hold quite different notions of "nature" and "culture." While Wagner gravitated toward Teutonic *Ernst* and *Wille,* Disney tended to associate the natural with a sense of childlike glee and simple silliness. On this account, two more disparate sensibilities would be hard to come by: the artist of the monumental sublime, one might say, meets his antithesis in the showman of the monumental ridiculous. Similarly, whereas Wagner's attacks on modern culture entailed strong critiques of the role and form of high art in European society, Disney rarely if ever directed attacks against high art per se. The relatively peripheral role of high art in American culture allowed Disney to avoid the confrontation altogether; thus he could set the "Dance of the Hours" to dancing hippos wearing tutus—a move that would have appeared downright dadaist if staged in Europe—with little fear of being branded an iconoclast. Wagner and Disney differed substantially, too, in their understanding of the relationship between modern culture and capitalism. Unlike the early Wagner, Disney linked the evils of "modern culture" not with capitalism, but rather with capitalism's seedy underside, its sad but "avoidable" traces: the urban slums and the fashionable elite, the filthy sidewalks and the phony hucksters, the rat-race competition and the depressing lack of play.

And yet. Disney's sense of nature, like Wagner's, was of a thing at once mythic, real, essentially, timeless, spontaneous, naive; his sense of modern culture, like Wagner's, was of a thing corrupt, fake, overly intellectualized, antagonistic, heartless. It is this connection—and its implications for performance—that warrants further examination.

By the early 1930s, Mickey Mouse had emerged as the central symbol of nature as seen through the Disney lens, a figure, like Wagner's Parsifal, of the eternal child. "[Mickey is] a clean, happy, little fellow who loves life and folk. . . . He is Youth, the Great Unlicked and Uncontaminated," wrote Disney in 1933.[18] People are drawn to the mouse, Disney continued, because Mickey represents them at their most essential:

> The Disney audience is made up of parts of people, of that deathless, precious, ageless, absolutely primitive remnant of something in every world-wracked human being which makes us play with children's toys and laugh without self-consciousness at silly things, and sing in bathtubs, and dream and believe that our babies are uniquely beautiful. You know . . . the Mickey in us. (Ibid.)

Mickey Mouse exemplified, for Disney, all that culture *could* be. Unlike some of his associates, who hated the term *culture* (Disneyland's general manager, for instance, insisted straightforwardly that "culture will kill you"),[19] Disney distinguished between two types of culture, a good one and a bad one. "At times," Disney admitted,

> I've even caught myself viewing the word "culture" with suspicion—it seems to have an un-American look to me—sort of snobbish and affected. Actually, as I understand it, culture isn't that kind of snooty word at all. As I see it, a person's culture represents his appraisal of the things that make up life. And a fellow becomes cultured, I believe, by selecting that which is fine and beautiful in life, and throwing aside that which is mediocre or phony. . . .
>
> Well, how are we to recognize the good and beautiful? I believe that man recognizes it instinctively. . . .
>
> I believe that you will find this spontaneous reaching out for the fine and beautiful in all mankind; it is man's indestructible and godlike quality, and the guarantee of his future.[20]

Like Wagner, Disney balanced his suspicion of "culture" with an appeal to another definition of the term, one rooted in instinct and spontaneity, and realized by the masses.

By the late 1940s, Disney was already developing plans for an amusement park that would house his characters but would also provide a vision of America's legacy and promise. Disneyland was originally conceived as Disney's answer to Coney Island, the Brooklyn amusement park that typified, for many, the corruption of modern urban life. Spatial disorganization, litter, traffic, poor crowd control, "carny" atmospherics—the hardboiled grit of Coney Island was, for Disney, a particularly virulent form of a national disease. As John Hench, one of Disney's closest associates and a chief designer of Disneyland, noted:

> In modern cities you have to defend yourself constantly and you go counter to everything that we've learned from the past. You tend to isolate yourself from other people. . . . You tend to be less aware. You tend to be more withdrawn. This is counter-life . . . you really die a little. . . . I think we need something to counteract what modern society—cities have done to us.[21]

Disneyland was intended as a counterspace to the modern city and an antidote to modern alienation. Like Bayreuth, Disneyland was countercultural, so to speak, from its origin.

In 1952 Disney hired the Stanford Research Institute to locate a suitable place for his park. The institute eventually settled on Orange County as the best site, since land (most of it orange groves) was cheap, the terrain was flat, and a new freeway would make the area easily accessible from Los Angeles. After two long years of negotiations with the twenty families who owned the site, the newly founded Walter Elias Disney (WED) Enterprises had quietly bought up 160 acres of property. WED Enterprises bulldozed the land, burning orange, walnut, and eucalyptus trees, in order to create a stage upon which to manufacture an entirely new landscape of hills, valleys, and lakes. "No distinguishable landmark remained," one Anaheim official remembered; "the neighborhood was obliterated."[22] Once the stage was set, any incursions by the outside world were to be repelled. Disney erected a fifteen-foot-tall earthen bank around Disneyland so that nothing of the surrounding environment could be seen from within, negotiated with the town council to prevent tall buildings from being erected within sight of the park, buried high-tension lines, and tried to prevent airplanes from flying overhead. The land would be, truly, a world apart, in this sense more reminiscent of American utopian communities than American amusement parks. "I don't want the public to see the world they live in while they're in the park," Disney said. "I want them to feel they're in another world."[23]

The center of that world was to be Cinderella's Castle, a soaring confection modeled on Ludwig II's Neuschwanstein. Cinderella's Castle had much the same symbolic resonance in Disney's day that Neuschwanstein had for Wagner's Dream King, emphatically evoking a fairy-tale world of fantasy over against the disenchanted workaday

Aerial view of cleared Disneyland site, prior to development. (Photo courtesy of the Anaheim Public Library.)

world of modern life. With time, a visit to the Mouse and the Castle assumed the character of a pilgrimage. The anthropologist Margaret King writes that the Disney parks "serve as Meccas, sacred centers, to which every American must make a double pilgrimage, first as a child [and] later as an adult with his own children."[24] King's observation of the cultic nature of Disneyland is expanded upon by anthropologist Alexander Moore, who describes the Magic Kingdom as a "bounded ritual space and playful pilgrimage center."[25] Visitors to the kingdom, he writes, come from afar, leave their cars behind, and

> enter a giant limen, a replica of a baroque capital, whose central avenue is the symbol of the dominant cultural form of nineteenth century America, Main Street. Passage through each

attraction takes the form of mini-phases of separation, transition, and reincorporation as the passenger journeys past electronically manipulated symbols evoking well-known myths.

As with Bayreuth, the pilgrimage to Disneyland has a particularly nationalistic cast. While proposing to represent something essential in all humanity, Disneyland, like Bayreuth, links this natural, universal state of being to a particular cultural identity. This linkage is particularly evident in a site like Main Street USA, where Disney's nostalgia for his hometown of Marceline, Missouri, returned with a vengeance. At story sessions for this segment of Disneyland, Disney would reminisce for hours about the old Main Street of Marceline. The final plan aimed to recreate the barbershop, the dry-goods store, and the post office of that town as well as its overall look and feel. Disney's rosy memories of the town were essentially performative from the outset: "this is scene one, this is scene two and this is scene three and they have this relationship," Disney used to say, describing Main Street.[26]

In Disney parlance, Main Street is the "center stage" of Disneyland, the route through which one must travel to enter the various mythic zones that spiral off in all directions. The nationalistic, and at the same time the quite personally nostalgic, rhetoric of this design is clear enough, and is further reinforced by a large plaque in the Town Square at the end of Main Street, which reads:

TO ALL WHO COME TO THIS HAPPY PLACE:
WELCOME.
DISNEYLAND IS YOUR LAND. HERE AGE
RELIVES FOND MEMORIES OF THE PAST . . .
AND HERE YOUTH MAY SAVOR THE CHALLENGE
AND PROMISE OF THE FUTURE.
DISNEYLAND IS DEDICATED
TO THE IDEALS, THE DREAMS, AND THE HARD
FACTS THAT HAVE CREATED AMERICA . . .
WITH THE HOPE THAT IT WILL BE A SOURCE OF
JOY AND INSPIRATION TO ALL THE WORLD.

The connection made here between Disneyland and America is so close that the former becomes virtually metonymic for the latter. "Disneyland is your land," the sign proclaims, echoing the words of Woody Guthrie about America (absent, of course, Woody's sly irony). By the end of the inscription, the reader is left somewhat confused: does the pronoun "it" in the final phrase signify Disneyland or America? The answer would seem to be either, or both.

Along with this nationalistic aspiration came the ontological claim that Disneyland was more real than "the outside world." A good example of Disney's thinking in this regard may be found in a confrontation between Disney and the evangelist Billy Graham. After touring Disneyland, Graham referred to it somewhat dismissively as "a nice fantasy," to which Disney replied,

> You know the fantasy isn't here. This is very real. . . . The park is reality. The people are natural here; they're having a good time; they're communicating. This is what people really are. The fantasy is—out there, outside the gates of Disneyland, where people have hatreds and people have prejudices. It's not really real![27]

Disney's belief, or something similar to it, is echoed throughout his organization. The Imagineers who designed Adventureland's Jungle Cruise ride, for example, were aware that the scenery depicted a "Hollywood jungle" rather than a real one, but described this romanticized depiction as "a *concentrated form* of nature" (71). This sense of Disneyland as "concentrated" nature is termed "Disney realism" by the corporation, a phrase used to describe the "really real" of Disneyland, the "natural" behavior of people within it, and the corresponding phoniness of the world "out there." "What we create is a 'Disney realism,' sort of utopian in nature" one Imagineer said, "where we carefully program out all the negative, unwanted elements and program in all the positive elements."[28]

"Disney realism" dominates the park, aiming to unify spectacle and spectator in a single, idealized reality. As at Bayreuth, this reality is located in a mythic time that encourages nostalgia, hope, and fantasy while discouraging present consciousness. One Disney publicist put it this way: "In Disneyland, clocks and watches lose all meaning, for there is no present. There is only yesterday, tomorrow and the timeless world of fantasy."[29] Here time, one might say, becomes space; and yet a critical difference exists between this "timeless world" and Wagner's: in Disneyland the spectator can actually move *within* the idealized landscape of the theater. The spectator at Disneyland originally had a choice of four mythic "lands," each one announcing itself as a distinct landscape within an overall mythic world: Frontierland, Fantasyland, Adventureland, and Tomorrowland. These four lands are connected by the central thoroughfare, Main Street. The existence of these zones, each of which is marked by its own miniature journey and itinerary, recalls once again the medieval understanding of the landscape, and the Bayreuth strategy of retro-mapping. But a significant development has been made from Bayreuth, for at Disneyland the active involvement of the audience in the interior of the theater is greatly increased. Not only the journey to Disneyland, but the journeys between the lands *within* Disneyland became active spatial stories, and the spectators essentially actors in the spectacle itself.[30]

The existence of different magic lands, however, creates at least one problem for Disneyland that Bayreuth avoids. Unlike Bayreuth, Disneyland must prevent the increased audience agency within the theater from subverting the totality of the *Gesamtkunstwerk*. The solutions developed at Disneyland are various and complex. To begin with, the zones themselves are of a piece with a single, overarching myth, one tightly modeled on Disney's brand of conservative, postwar American romanticism. The choice of mythic zones is really a selection between permutations of a single zone, a master zone already fixed with the imprint of its creator. This uniformity of spectacle is reflected in Disney parlance, in which the various "lands" are referred to collectively as "the show," with performances beginning in the "outer lobby" (the parking lot), passing through the "inner lobby" (the main entrance), and culminating on "center stage" (Main Street USA).

Getting consumers from the lobby to center stage was one thing; getting them to play their parts correctly once there quite another. In order to properly script the performance of the audience, the interactive landscape of Disneyland had to be carefully planned. Main Street USA was central to this strategy of crowd control. Main Street leads the visitor-actor to the Plaza, which functions as a large hub from which the other "lands" radiate outwards. A major landmark distinguishes each theme area and acts as a beacon to draw spectators into the area. Within the theme areas, smaller patterns of circulation were created, each of them leading back again to Main Street USA. In order to minimize the sense of social control on the visitor-actors, these lesser pathways were carefully planned to seem natural: the Imagineers made no walkways for the opening days of the park, in order to see where people would naturally walk, and then laid down permanent paths along those routes. Literary critic Susan Willis refers to this "erasure of spontaneity"[31] as a central feature of Disneyland, but it is an erasure of spontaneity, oddly enough, in the interest of a return to spontaneity.

Much like Wagner, Disney understood the machine to be central to his theatrical project; unlike Wagner, Disney was openly enthusiastic about at least the *myth* of technology. A *Buck Rogers*–like notion of techno-wizardry can be seen most clearly in the zone of the park called Tomorrowland, which features various corporate-sponsored attractions intended to convince visitors that "tomorrow can be a wonderful age."[32] Of these attractions, the "General Electric Carousel of Progress" was the most elaborate and possibly the most telling. The drama was essentially a march through time, from the 1890s to the 1960s, depicting the improvement of the lives of successive generations of a middle-class American family through the wonders of technology. The actors in the play were Disney's famous "Audio-animatronics," lifelike robots that appear throughout the park. Critic James Bierman notes of the performance that

> at first, [the Audio-animatronics'] movements are just stiff and jerky enough to call attention to the fact that they are automata. As the play progresses in time, the movements become more fluid until, in the present-day scene, they appear almost human.[33]

The progression of the robots' performance from "stiff and jerky" to more "fluid" is, in fact, an allegory of the mass-cultural *Gesamtkunstwerk* itself. Utilizing the mechanical (in this case, robotics) to realize the natural (in this case, a happy domestic scene), the total work of art becomes gradually more convincing with the advancement of technology, until, in the end, it appears "almost human." The irony here is that the real technological wonders of Disneyland lie not in the evocations of the robots but in the robots themselves, and, moreover, in the vast mechanical array that underlies Disneyland and is kept permanently out of sight. Despite Disney's technophilia, the essential fear of the *Gesamtkunstwerk*—the fear of the exposure of its own means of production—remains.

This fear permeates the park. It gives rise, for example, to the rigorous process of "theming," which may be defined as the incorporation of a uniformity of style throughout the Disney landscape so as to ensure a unified audience experience. The process of theming often involves a translation of signs of labor into elements of landscape, such that electric outlets at Disneyland are themed to resemble the bark of living trees, garbage bins themed to look like animals, water nozzles themed to look like rocks. In fact, the *Gesamtkunstwerk* itself can be understood as one vast project of theming, music to drama to stage design to costume to text. And at Disneyland, not even workers are left out of the total experience. As Disney executive Dick Nunis explained, "when we hire a girl [as a worker at Disneyland], we point out that we're not hiring her for a job, but casting her for a role in our show. And we give her a costume and a philosophy to go with it."[34] Nunis's use of theatrical terms to refer to labor is hardly idiosyncratic; it is, in fact, a required aspect of Disneyspeak. At Disneyland University, workers and managers are taught to substitute the word *cast member* for *worker, costume* for *uniform, audition* for *job interview, backstage* for *restricted area,* and so forth.[35]

By means of their theatrical training, Disney employees are alienated not so much from the product of their labor as from the fact that they labor at all. Such alienation further conceals the realities of production, as the employees do not really labor, but merely "act natural." Still, training several thousand employees to whistle while they work is a difficult task, one that can be largely avoided if the employees are simply replaced with robots. Enter, again, the Audio-animatronics. Whole attractions—the Carousel of Progress or Great Moments with Mr. Lincoln, for example—are nothing more nor less than journeys through elaborately staged Audio-animatronic worlds. Management considered such robots to be superior to employees because, as one Imagineer remarked, "I've seen actors when they're better at times than they are at other times. But these figures perform the same way every time! They're reliable, and they don't belong to unions, and they don't go on strike, and they don't want more money."[36]

Finally, and most importantly, the Audio-animatronics were considered actors par excellence at Disneyland because each is a *Gesamtkunstwerk* in miniature. "Walt has often described the 'Audio-Animatronics' as the grand combination of all the arts," reads a Disney press release. "This technique includes the three-dimensional realism of fine sculpture, the vitality of a great painting, the drama and personal rapport of the theater, and the artistic versatility and consistency of the motion picture."[37] Left out of this description is the additional art of music, which almost unfailingly accompanies an Audio-animatronic exhibit, as well as the art of industrial design that animates each creation. Each Audio-animatronic is therefore a microcosm of the great artistic unity that is Disneyland itself; the robots are, in a sense, not only the ideal actors, but also the ideal inhabitants of this mechanized utopia.

A generational leap in Disney's hallmark combination of landscape and technology came with Disney World and the later parks. By the mid-1960s, Disney had become dissatisfied with the way in which the environment around his Anaheim theme park had become contaminated by the signs of modern urban life; despite his best attempts to keep them at bay, restaurants, hotels, and other attractions rapidly surrounded the perimeter of his land. The problem was that Disney owned less than two hundred acres, beyond which he exercised little control. For the new park in Florida, Disney was determined to do things differently. "The one thing I learned from Disneyland," he said, "was to control the environment"[38]—and control it he did. Operating in great secrecy so as not to drive up land prices, WED proceeded to buy up territory in central Florida. Disney wanted enough land, he said, "to hold all the ideas and plans we can possibly imagine" (279), and also to provide a sufficient buffer zone between his new park and the surrounding world. Eventually 27,443 acres were purchased for Disney's "total destination vacation resort," and WED began to exercise its considerable new power within local politics. Its primary desire was an enormous and utterly unprecedented one: WED wanted more or less complete autonomy within the state of Florida. After considerable debate, the Florida State Legislature granted extraterritorial status to the "Reedy Creek Improvement District" (the somewhat deceptively titled Disney land-acquisition organization) in 1967, and today, in the words of one Disney executive, Disney World "basically . . . operates as a country."[39]

The heart of Disney World was essentially a replication of Disneyland, consisting of an almost identical landscape of mythic lands linked together by Main Street USA. As such, Disney World was the first in what would become a series of mechanically reproduced worlds modeled on the original Magic Kingdom of Disneyland. Here, too, Disney blazed new ground in the mechanized production of nature. Treating his idyllic world as an industrial design prototype, Disney severed the link between utopian landscape and geographic place; henceforth the Magic Kingdom could appear, in remarkably similar form, almost anywhere: Orlando, Tokyo, France. Within one of these kingdoms, the problem is not so much that "there's no there there"; there is emphatically a "there there," but one that has little or nothing to do with the actual place one happens to be. It is only a step beyond this plan to design, as Disney did, an urban utopia the form of which could be replicated across the globe. Such was his "Experimental Prototype City of Tomorrow," which, though never realized in the form that Disney imagined it, was the inspiration behind such recent creations as Celebration, the Disney "real-life" town in central Florida.

The literally unique political, legal, and territorial freedom that WED enjoyed in its construction of Disney World was married to its new science of "depth-computerization." Everything in this new World would be planned from the very beginning around a nexus of integrated electronic monitoring systems, a process that is referred to by Disney management as a "Total Systems Approach." One of the main aspects of the Total Systems Approach was the Automatic Monitoring and Control System, which, according to one WED executive, "gives Disney at one center and many other places the ability to monitor, and be aware of, really . . . the total status, everything that goes on within the confines of the park, in so far as it is measurable" (278). Based on a system originally developed to monitor nuclear missiles, the AMCS allows Disney World to operate as a total theater by constantly testing the site for disturbances. "These are quite small computers that are hooked up literally to thousands and thousands of individual sensors in the park" (278), explained an executive.

Another aspect of the Total Systems Approach at Disney World is a vast network of tunnels beneath the show. The tunnels were in fact the first sites constructed at Disney World, and were located at ground level; they were then covered over with the soil dredged from an artificial lake, and Disney World was placed atop them. Dubbed "utilidors," the miles of tunnels house storage facilities, staff cafeterias, laundries, dressing rooms, and vast pneumatic tubes designed to "whisk refuse away like magic,"[40] and thereby "keep the magic in the Magic Kingdom."[41] In addition to housing such backstage functions, the utilidors also provide a means for characters to leave one mythic zone without passing through another. Thus a space-suited actor from Tomorrowland can make his way to the parking lot while still in costume without having to cross through Frontierland, and a "Frenchman" from EPCOT's France can avoid being seen in Mexico or Canada.[42] In this way the utilidors serve not only as a means of sweeping away the refuse of the "outside" world, but also of preventing contamination of one mythic zone by another. Finally, the utilidors function, spatially and temporally, as an inverse of the mythic zones above. If the cartography of Disney World is pseudomedieval, then that of the utilidors is decidedly modern in the Disney sense of the word: that is, geometric and utilitarian, devoted to time and decay. Unlike the land above, the utilidors are organized in straight lines between points, and identified by numbers. Here space reverts to units of feet and yards and miles, and time to the motions of a clock. Whereas time becomes space in Disney World, in the utilidors time and space become unbuckled again; in the utilidors lies the chronology, the distance, and the production that appears in the upper world as spatialized myth.

If the utilidors of Disney World are a latter-day evolution of the sunken orchestra pit of Bayreuth, then their far greater size and range of function is mirrored in a greater concern for their concealment. Though Disney promotional material is rich in depictions of all aspects of the parks, one must search far and wide for a map, photograph, or design sketch of the utilidors. Disney now runs a tour of the tunnels, but photographs of them are strictly forbidden. If a tourist should take such a picture, company policy is strict: her camera is confiscated, her film developed, and only the unrestricted photographs are returned.[43] To expose the utilidors is, according to Disney management, to shatter the magic of the park.

From Brunelde to Oklahoma

> The Great Theater of Oklahoma calls you! Today only and never again! If you miss your chance now you miss it forever! If you think of your future you are one of us! Everyone is welcome! If you want to be an artist, join our company! Our Theater can find employment for everyone, a place for everyone!
>
>   —KAFKA, *Amerika*

Near the end of Kafka's early, unfinished novel *Amerika,* the young hero Karl is kidnapped and forced into servitude to a gargantuan, slothful ex-diva named Brunelde. The event represents the nadir of Karl's luckless American adventures. Made to sleep on a heap of velvet curtains in a corner of her crumbling apartment, Karl must listen to Brunelde make love upon a couch she rarely leaves, and he is soon kicked out to the terrace like a dog. Karl attempts to escape, is thwarted and beaten unconscious, and soon thereafter the chapter abruptly ends. We never learn how Karl makes his way out of his particular Wagnerian nightmare—all we know is that the next we see him he is on a street corner, viewing an advertisement for "The Nature Theater of Oklahoma." Swept up by its promise that "everyone is welcome," Karl is off to find a place in the new theater. He soon discovers that it is "on a much larger scale than he could have conceived possible,"[44] as all around him stand hundreds of actors, perched on separate pedestals, dressed as angels in white robes with great wings on their shoulders, blowing through gold-glittered trumpets. The placard did not lie: the Nature Theater does indeed offer employment for all. Though he considers himself unsuited to be an actor, Karl eagerly takes a job behind the scenes as a technical worker. A new job, a new community, a new place in the "limitless" spectacle of the New World: for the first time in the novel, Karl seems to have found a home. Nor does he need to worry about the future: "it's an old theater," an angel tells him, "but it's always being enlarged" (280).

The concluding, unfinished chapters of Kafka's novel come close to an illustration of the development of the mass-cultural *Gesamtkunstwerk,* from the velvet draperies of Brunelde to the Nature Theater of Oklahoma, "the biggest theater in the world" (279). Our analysis suggests something of the character of this theater as well as its enlargement. Whatever their differences, the theaters of Wagner and Disney both have the reunification of nature and humanity as one of their central aims. The form of *Gesamtkunstwerk* that they share attempts to forge the reunification by its performance in the "real" exterior as well as the "fantasy" interior landscape. Its performance in the exterior landscape is primarily one of retro-mapping by means of pilgrimage, while its performance of the interior landscape is primarily one of absorbing the audience into a spectacle of the desired natural state, a theatricalized form of nature more natural than the nontheatricalized world. To affect this absorption in nature, both Bayreuth and Disneyland must turn to the machine, a reliance that must be concealed from the spectator. As the size and scope of the reliance grows, so too do the strategies of occlusion. Moreover, as the spectator becomes capable of exercising a degree of choice within the theater, more pervasive yet subtle controls must be brought to bear over spectatorship. Finally, through all of the above means, Bayreuth and Disneyland have become significant tools in the formation of modern conceptions of nationhood.

This particular, mass-cultural evolution of total theater is one that may now be found across the American, and increasingly the global, landscape. One indication of this trend is the recent proliferation of books by business advisors and economists arguing that providing goods and services are no longer enough for today's corporations to compete; today's corporations, the current thinking goes, must create carefully staged, unified aesthetic experiences in order to attract consumers.[45] The unification of media in the theatricalization of capital is a proliferating phenomenon, spreading far beyond amusement parks to resorts, malls, shops, hotels, restaurants, and urban design. Certain movies, too, are inseparable from this trend, especially if they can be linked to cultic sites: consider the group of *Star Wars* fans who camped out for six weeks in front of Mann's Chinese Theatre ("the ground-zero of movie fandom") to see the next installment of a saga that one fan described as "a life-defining moment," another as "a cultural icon," and a third as a "modern American mythology that transcends every race, religion, generation, class."[46] Once they had viewed *The Phantom Menace* together—and together, in effect, with much of America—the group were to take a celebratory trip to Disneyland, after which they would attend the premieres of the film in Sydney, London, and Paris. The story may give a clue to the next frontier of the mass-cultural *Gesamtkunstwerk:* namely, the interfacing of multiple total theaters within a single global nexus, a neomedieval landscape under the sign this time not of Christ but a mechanized Bacchus.

NOTES

1. Though expressed most fully in writings from his Zurich years (1849–57), this position was one to which Wagner remained faithful, in its essentials, throughout his career.

2. Richard Wagner, *Prose Works,* trans. W. Ashton Ellis, 8 vols. (London: Keagan Paul, Trench, Trübner, 1895–96), 1:159.

3. Quoted in Frederic Spotts, *Bayreuth: A History of the Wagner Festival* (New Haven: Yale University Press, 1994), 33.

4. Wagner, *Prose Works,* 5:329.

5. This religious character of Bayreuth reached its apex with the Wagner cult of the Third Reich, but it has by no means passed away—consider Frederick Spott's recent account, quite typical, of his visit to the *Festspielhaus:* "There was something oddly religious about the day—a shared experience of deep meaning, like-minded participants, everyone familiar with the ritual and equally moved. . . . The music and the staging, a long and famous tradition, the theatre itself, the civilized way of doing things, the 'island' atmosphere—do these add up to the mystique that surrounds the Festival and that for a century has drawn millions on what even today retains the character of a pilgrimage?" (Spotts, *Bayreuth,* 28.)

6. Michel de Certeau offers one of the clearest distinctions between modern and medieval landscapes when he distinguishes between modern maps of "geographic form," which are born "of modern scientific discourse" and medieval maps, which "[mark] out . . . itineraries (performative indications chiefly concerning pilgrimages)" (Michel de Certeau, *The Practice of Everyday Life,* trans. Steven Rendall [Berkeley and Los Angeles: University of California Press, 1988], 120). These two different notions of space also imply two different notions of time. In the modern geographic form, space is mapped separately from time, such that one speaks of miles or kilometers that may be traversed at varying speeds; the medieval map, on the other hand, was organized around "distances calculated in hours or in days, that is, in terms of the time it would take to cover them on foot" (120). Distance, in the medieval map, was made a unit of travel time and social function of place rather than abstract measurement. Moreover,

since the medieval map was largely organized around pilgrimage sites, the diachronic time of travel was inextricably linked to the synchronic time of ritual space. This last point becomes clearer if de Certeau's understanding of the medieval map is read alongside Mircea Eliade's distinction between sacred and profane time. Profane time is the realm of "ordinary temporal duration, in which acts without religious meaning have their setting," whereas sacred time is "a primordial mythical time made present," and is particularly associated with festivals and pilgrimage sites (Mircea Eliade, *The Sacred and the Profane* [New York: Harcourt Brace Jovanovich, 1987], 68). Medieval mapping, then, organized space according to performative itineraries that particularly stressed the assumption of profane time into sacred time.

7. Wagner, *Prose Works,* 1:180.

8. Wagner, *The Ring of the Nibelung,* trans. Andrew Porter (New York: W. W. Norton, 1977), 3–4.

9. In this case, Wagner's emphasis on harmony rather than sublimity differs from that of even the most "faithful" of latter-day designers. Take, for example, the ash tree designed by Günher Schneider-Siemssen for the 1962 production at Covent Garden, in which the tree slammed through the roof like an obelisk, did not branch off until well above the house, and then did so horizontally. This massive, alien tree was itself dwarfed by the hulking vegetation of the 1975 Met production, in which only the base of the trunk was visible, the rest rising up into the gloaming. Such latter-day designs, though hardly radical, evoke the towering redwoods of Bierstadt's California paintings, with their roots as thick as men, more than the aspirations of the Wagnerian landscape. For photographs of these designs, including a model of the original stage design, see Charles Osborne, *The World Theatre of Wagner* (New York: Macmillan, 1982), 116, 137, 147.

10. Wagner, *Prose Works,* 6:309.

11. For a full account of this scenic illusion at Bayreuth, see Evan Baker, "Richard Wagner and His Search for the Ideal Theatrical Space," *Opera in Context,* ed. Mark Radice (Portland, Oregon: Amadeus Press, 1998), 269–78.

12. Quoted in Baker, "Wagner and His Search," 277.

13. Wagner, *Prose Works,* 5:334–35.

14. My discussion here is inspired by Theodor Adorno's *In Search of Wagner,* in which Adorno argues that the occultation of production is "the formal law governing [Wagner's] works" (85). Though Adorno examines this occultation in Wagner's libretti and musical compositions, he does not comment on Wagner's prose writings, scenography, or theater architecture. See *In Search of Wagner,* trans. Rodney Livingstone (New York: Verso, 1981).

15. Wagner, *Prose Works,* 5:333; emphasis added.

16. In this light it is also revealing to read, e.g., Wagner's attack on Berlioz in *Opera and Drama,* in which he accuses the Berliozian orchestra of being fundamentally "*un*-natural" because it attempts to bring "supernatural wonders" to a "gaping public" through "the wonders of mechanics" (*Prose Works,* 2:76). Behind this attack one senses the fear of a double.

17. Spotts, *Bayreuth,* 76.

18. Walt Disney, "The Cartoon's Contribution to Children," *Overland Monthly and the Out West Magazine* 91, no. 8 (1933): 138. Disney was not alone in viewing his creation as a global icon. One of Mickey's original animators, Ub Iwerks, noted that Mickey's shape recalls Jung's archetypal symbols of wholeness, and audaciously described his neotenized form as "a trinity of wafers." See Paul Jerome Croce, "A Clean and Separate Space: Walt Disney in Person and Production," *Journal of Popular Culture* 25, no. 3 (1991): 97.

19. John Findlay, *Magic Lands* (Berkeley and Los Angeles: University of California Press, 1992), 86.

20. Robert D. Feild, *The Art of Walt Disney* (New York: Macmillan, 1942), 283–84.

21. Findlay, *Magic Lands,* 67.

22. Findlay, *Magic Lands,* 75.

23. John Schultz, "The Fabulous Presumption of Disney World: Magic Kingdom in the Wilderness," *Georgia Review* 42 (summer 1988): 276.

24. Margaret J. King, "Empires of Popular Culture: McDonald's and Disney," in *Ronald Revisited: The World of Ronald McDonald,* ed. Marshall Fishwick (Bowling Green, Ohio: Bowling Green University Popular Press, 1983) 117.

25. Alexander Moore, "Walt Disney World: Bounded Ritual Space and the Playful Pilgrimage Center," *Anthropological Quarterly* 53 (1980): 214.

26. Karal Ann Marling, ed., *Designing Disney's Theme Parks: The Architecture of Reassurance* (New York: Flammarion, 1997): 60.

27. Findlay, *Magic Lands,* 70.

28. Alan Bryman, *Disney and His Worlds* (New York: Routledge, 1995): 102.

29. Findlay, *Magic Lands,* 54–55.

30. The spectators became participants, too, in a nationwide television show. Originally conceived as a promotional piece for the theme park, ABC's *Disneyland* broadcast old Disney movies and new productions alongside footage from the theme park. The synergy between theme park and television show was part of Disney's plan from the early days of construction, with ABC purchasing a third of the shares of Disneyland, Inc. in order to finance the building of the park. See Richard Schickel, *The Disney Version* (Chicago: Ivan R. Dee, 1997), 313.

31. Susan Willis, "Disney World: Public Use/Private State," *South Atlantic Quarterly* 92, no. 1 (1993): 123.

32. Disney quoted in Bryman, *Disney and His Worlds,* 134.

33. James Bierman, "The Walt Disney Robot Dramas," *Yale Review* 66 (December 1976): 226.

34. Bryman, *Disney and His Worlds,* 110.

35. Findlay, *Magic Lands,* 75–77. In addition to their theatrical training, aspiring workers at Disneyland University also receive a crash course in the mythology of Walt Disney. The example of Disney's life and the wisdom contained in his utterances are reinforced throughout the training procedure. A 1987 study gives evidence that this initiatory system is so successful that many

Disney "graduates" react very negatively to perceived deviations from the "Disney way." As a result, the labor pool becomes largely self-regulating. See R. C. Smith and E. M. Eisenberg, "Conflict at Disneyland: A Root-Metaphor Analysis," *Communication Monographs* 54 (1987): 367–80.

36. Bryman, *Disney and His Worlds,* 119. Disney himself added to this list that robots "don't have to stop for coffee breaks and all that kind of stuff" (120). See also Bierman, "Walt Disney Robot Dramas," 231.

37. Schickel, *The Disney Version,* 335.

38. Schultz, "Fabulous Presumption," 279.

39. Anthony Haden-Guest, *Down the Programmed Rabbit-Hole* (London: Hard-Davis, 1972), 277.

40. Quoted in Alexander Wilson, *The Culture of Nature* (Oxford: Blackwell, 1992), 176.

41. Quoted in Haden-Guest, *Programmed Rabbit-Hole,* 297.

42. EPCOT is the acronym for Disney's Experimental Prototype City of Tomorrow project discussed above, and the current EPCOT Center is another legacy of that dream. EPCOT Center opened in October 1982 and is one of the three theme parks that make up Disney World (the other two are the Magic Kingdom and Disney-MGM Studios). EPCOT Center itself is divided into two parts: Future World and the World Showcase. The latter is a series of pavilions representing different nations organized around a central lagoon.

43. Willis, "Disney World," 134–35.

44. Franz Kafka, *Amerika,* trans. Edwin Muir (New Directions, New York: 1946): 274.

45. See, for instance, Michael Wolf, *The Entertainment Economy* (New York: Times Business, 1999); B. Joseph Pine II and James H. Gilmore, *The Experience Economy: Work Is Theatre and Every Business a Stage* (Boston: Harvard Business School Press, 1999); Bernd Schmitt, *Experiential Marketing: How to Get Your Customers to Sense, Feel, Think, Act, and Relate to Your Company and Brands* (New York: Free Press, 1999).

46. Todd Purdum, "With the Force, in the Movie Line," *New York Times,* April 29 1999, A18.

13

Bordering Space

W. B. Worthen

. . . being American today means participating in the draft-
ing of a new cultural topography.

—Guillermo Gómez-Peña,
Warrior for Gringostroika

Mais zoot alors. Je comprends maintenant, mais oui, merde!
Je suis Argentin-Canadien! I am a post-Porteño neo-Latino
Canadian! I am the Pan-American highway!

—Guillermo Verdecchia,
Fronteras Americanas

As Carmelita Tropicana remarks, "Identity really depends on where you
are at, it's so much about geography."[1] In many ways, Latino performance—like the category "Latina/o" itself—illustrates both the dialectical mobility of identification in the production of contemporary ideologies of "America," and the role of the performative in the fashioning of
national and/or ethnic "identity." An unusually volatile ethnic marker,
Latina/o is applied to persons of Latin American origin or descent, as
well as (among other striking anomalies) to Puerto Ricans (U.S. citizens), and to Chicanos (many of whom trace their ancestry to the settlement of the Southwest before its appropriation by the United States),
and signifies mainly within North America. As an available ethnic positionality within the discourse of contemporary U.S. nationalism,
"Latina/o" arises in response to a now-protracted crisis in the imagining
of national identities in the United States.[2]

The term—*Latina, Latino*—like all terms that nominate agents of
social action—operates as a point of identification, and so implies an
inherently dialectical and spatializing activity: it points to an agency
directed both within and without the subject, a citational act, a claim of
likeness *with* a positionality in order to become identified *as* a subject, *to*
a larger community or culture.[3] The performance of "identity" is never,

as Judith Butler argues, entirely sovereign; when bodies are used rhetorically, asserting an identity through claims of likeness, they necessarily engage in an elaborate process of citation, evoking the "regulatory norms that govern their materialization and signification," and dramatizing "the reiterative power of discourse to produce the phenomena that it regulates and constrains."[4] At the same time, this reiteration is public and makes sense in the relational topography of social space, in the "actually lived (and socially produced) space of sites and the relations between them."[5] As Edward W. Soja argues, this space—like the prepositional dynamics of identification *with* and *to*—is experienced and produced as at once symbolic and physically given, an "actually lived and socially created spatiality, concrete and abstract at the same time."[6] An overdetermined practice, at once expressive and regulated, a mode of action and a mode of experience, the "moment of identity and identification" is performative, engaging the body as the interface of the subject's public articulation, as "a variable boundary, a surface whose permeability is politically regulated, a signifying practice within a cultural field."[7]

The politics of *latinidad* in the United States point to the impact of political geography on the process of subjection-qualification, the ways in which a "*frontera* imaginary" marks the necessity to identify with(in) the nation.[8] Identification involves a complex performance, the negotiation of available positionalities, "moment[s] of identity and identification," so to speak, and the playing of them, a dialectical process of subjection that renders the subject a recognizable agent, "qualifies" him or her for action in the social field; "performing skills laboriously works the subject into its status as a social being."[9] In the United States, the dialectical subjection-qualification of Latina/o identification is characteristically—indeed, almost uniquely—marked as a consequence of the national border, the passage from a now largely irrelevant national space (outside or inside the United States) to an ethnic space here. As Suzanne Oboler's informants testify, emigration to the United States is experienced as a replacement of national with ethnic identifications that is registered primarily as a transformation of *class* identity (often as a consequence, of *race*).[10] Insofar as this formation embodies fluid internal and external national and political dynamics, its characteristic forms of subjection/qualification—"identification" as both identifying *with* and identifying *to*—are multiple and divided.[11] *Latina/o* seems less to point to Anthony D. Smith's traditional account of ethnic identification—"a collective proper name," "a myth of common ancestry," "shared historical memories," "one or more differentiating elements of common culture," "an association with a specific 'homeland,'" and "a sense of solidarity for significant sectors of the population"—than to an assimilation crisis at the juncture of ethnicity and nationalism per se, a crisis in the imagining of subjects and citizens, territory and nation.[12]

Latino/a points to a "'war of position'" in the imagining of the space of América, as the advent of new ethnicities, new positionalities puts pressure on all other positions, transforming the lived space—*l'espace vécu*—of national and social identification.[13] In many respects, autoperformance seizes this juncture between metaphor and metonymy, identification *as* and identification *to,* framing identification as an elision that necessarily produces difference, and that produces the subject relative to a contiguous space: contiguous with technology (Laurie Anderson), with oppressive patriarchy (Carolee Schneeman, Karen Finley), with compulsory heterosexuality (Tim Miller). Anna Deavere Smith's well-known series of performance works—including *Fires in the Mirror: Crown Heights, Brooklyn, and Other Identities,* and *Twilight: Los Angeles, 1992*—undertakes a related strategy, as Smith's celebrated efforts to imitate the subjects of her interviews might be said to cause her to disappear, leaving only the contiguities between ethnic identities remaining. Tim Miller demonstrates in *My Queer Body* that the space of performance is occupied by the audience as well as the performer; the rigorous work of performance art often involves unseating the "absent" voyeur of film and realistic theater in order to stage the audience as a constituent subject, a participant in the spectacle. In such performance, identity positionalities (race, ethnicity, sexuality) emerge "not as a fixed singular essence, but as the *locus* in which economic, gender, sex, and race contradictions converge."[14] Addressing the audience, hailing the spectators (sitting in their laps in Miller's case), performance displaces the representation of identity—of ethnic, national identity—from the screen of representation *there* to the practice of representation *here,* the performance of identity between and among us. How does the performance of "new ethnicities" onstage imply a reterritorialization of the space of performance, use the space to perform—and so to theorize—the possibility of new positionalities, new forms of national identification?[15]

Latino/a performance articulates its "subjects," both represents and interpellates ethnopolitical agents, by framing the space of performance through an experiential mapping of ethnic and national positionalities. Works like Carmelita Tropicana's *Milk of Amnesia/Leche de Amnesia* or Guillermo Verdecchia's *Fronteras Americanas* enact Fredric Jameson's sense that the shift from modernist to postmodern cultural production involves a shift in our ways of experiencing self and culture, a shift from "categories of time" to "categories of space."[16] One sign of this shift is the interplay between narrative and spatial modes of identification, the ways in which the performers stage ethnic identification, telling the history of a return to origins as a spatialized act of performance, a multiplex portrayal of alternate identities that Joseph Roach has called *surrogation*—"the doomed search for originals by continuously auditioning stand-ins."[17]

In *Milk of Amnesia/Leche de Amnesia,* Carmelita Tropicana (Alina Troyano) stages an elaborate allegory of "the larger exilic project of staving off a mode of assimilationist forgetting that plagues exiles."[18] The performance frames an interplay among the characters Troyano plays in the piece: the unseen voice-over of the Writer, whose upbringing in the United States has instilled a systematic forgetting, isolating her from "Mi Cuba querida" (99); Carmelita Tropicana, "baptized in the fountain of America's most popular orange juice, in the name of Havana's legendary nightclub" (98), and now suffering from amnesia in a Cuban hospital; and Pingalito Betancourt, "the Cuban Alastair Cooke" (95), who rescues Carmelita and visits her in the hospital.[19] Although the performance begins by marking the Writer and Carmelita as different characters, they gradually blend together and are fused in the final moments of the show, when the Writer's recovery of her Cuban past is played as Carmelita's reawakening: "My amnesia is gone. After so many years in America, I can drink two kinds of milk. The sweet condensed milk of Cuba and the pasteurized homo kind from America" (109–10). To traverse the "border" between the United States and Cuba is not only to cross a geopolitical line dividing a common culture (as it does in some, though not all, areas along the southwestern United States–Mexico border), but to cross a strait that enforces and defends an economically inflected (capitalism vs. Marxism) politics of identity. Throughout *Milk of Amnesia/Leche de Amnesia,* "identity" is performed not merely as tourism, but through the discourse of objects, commodities. The Writer, waiting in her hotel, sees the lipstick she gave to a girl on the street: "who do I see coming in, Pinta Labios, Revlon #44 looking good with a man. What is she doing with that man and my lipstick? . . . I'm pissed, but with a swig of beer reconsider: maybe the lipstick got her a steak dinner" (102). Yet the Writer herself has been the vehicle for the commodification of *cubanidad* as the seductive "Pinta Labios," returning to Cuba like a vacationing Cuban, her hat loaded with U.S. products, "a walking Cuban department store. Tampons and pearls, toilet paper, stationery supplies" (102). This linkage between political and economic colonization seems to be the burden, too, of two other narratives: the

story of the Spanish conquest (told by Cortés's horse, Arriero) and the
history of the U.S. economic embargo of Cuba, told by a pig raised
secretly in an apartment for slaughter. The surrogations of performance
return the Writer to Cuba, but the "identity" she finds—and assumes—
there is a complex moment of nonorigin, traced in the commodified
imaginary of five centuries of colonial politics, the densely overdetermined persona of "Carmelita Tropicana."

Guillermo Verdecchia's *Fronteras Americanas* stages an analogous
interrogation of the space of ethnicity, from a different location: the
Anglo-Canadian borderland to the north of the United States. Born in
Argentina and raised in Canada, Verdecchia places the question of
latinidad in a more broadly North American context—"Where and what
exactly is the border? Is it this line in the dirt stretching for 5,000 kilo-
metres? Is the border more accurately described as a zone which includes
the towns of El Paso and Ciudad Juárez? Or is the border—is the border
the whole country, the continent?"[20] Like Carmelita Tropicana, Verdecchia's performance takes the form of a personal quest; his Alastair Cook
is "Wideload," a stereotypical reflection of the Anglo imaginary who
fuses the borders of barrio and nation: "I live in the border—that's Queen
and Lansdowne for you people from outta town. Ya, mang, I live in de
zone—in de barrio" (24). More than Pingalito Betancourt, Wideload
stakes his identity across another border, the border with the audience,
"you people" (25), and sees ethnic identification itself as a function of a
mobile politics of position. Much as the social border—in 1993
Toronto—is the barrio marked by Queen and Lansdowne streets, Verdecchia takes *Latino* to mark a mobile ethnic borderization, producing social
"others" from an unmarked Anglo perspective: "[D]e term Latino could
include people as different as right-wing Cubans living in Miami, exiled
Salvadorean leftists, Mexican speakers of Nahuatl, Brazilian speakers of
Portuguese, lunfardo-speaking Koreans in Buenos Aires, Nuyoricans
(dat's a Puerto Rican who lives in New York) and den there's de
Uruguayans—I mean dey're practically European" (27).

Verdecchia presents the problems of Latino identification in a
wider, global context. Discovering his "identity" involves figuring out
"the moment that I first discovered I was lost": "En France," he finds
himself "étranger, un anglais, un Argentin-Canadien, un faux touriste,"
and travels from France to Canada to Chile to Argentina. He also moves
through a stream of history that allies personal and public geographies,
mixing "the night Bolívar burned with fever" and the "Zoot Suit Riots"
(71) with personal memories of a red snowsuit and "la machine queso,"
of a gang of Spanish-speaking boys who stole his leather jacket (and

"who taught me I could be a long-lost son one minute and a tourist the next" [72]). Like Carmelita Tropicana's, Verdecchia's performance of ethnicity involves him in a complex act of geographical and historical surrogation, the citational replaying of hegemonic identifications as stereotypes: Carmelita, Pingalito, Wideload.

In *Fronteras Americanas,* as in *Milk of Amnesia,* the cultural "other" is only accessible through its representations. Yet these often stereotypical characters are not merely citations of ethnic otherness. In the theater, these stereotypes structure and sustain the relationship between performer and audience. Verdecchia's Wideload might be described as a kind of reflexive parody. Something like the "characters" assumed in the stand-up routines of Richard Pryor or Eddie Murphy, Wideload appears to resist or resignify the dominant stereotypes of Latino others. Verdecchia uses Wideload, though, less to reflect overt racism than to ethnicize Anglo identity, to dramatize how white/Anglo/"Saxon" social power is naturalized, and rendered normative, in the act of ethnic discrimination. Wideload can adopt an authoritative critique of Anglo attitudes because he stayed with a nice "ethnic family"—the Smiths—when he arrived in América del Norte, and "got a really good look at de way dey live. I mean sure at times it was a bit exotic for me, you know de food for example" (34).

Exoticizing América, Wideload becomes the ethnographer of "Saxon" ethnicity. He surveys its physical performance ("I think you Saxons are some of de most interesting dancers on de planet. . . . like nothing gets in your way: not de beat, not de rhythm, nothing" [40]), its traditional costumes ("you guys wear very funny shoes for dancing—I mean dose giant running shoes with built-in air compressors and padding and support for de ankles and nuclear laces" [41]), and the fantasies that inform its reading of others ("the Exotica Factor. De Latin Lover Fantasy" [41–42]). Indeed, part of Wideload's work here is to mark the practices of Anglo culture: "I have de greatest respect for your culture . . . and you know every culture has its own fertility dances, its own dance of sexual joy"; while "we have de mambo, de rumba, de cumbia, de son, son-guajiro, son-changui, de charanga, de merengue, de guaguanco, de tango, de samba, salsa," "you people hab de Morris Dance" (42). Rather than merely estranging whiteness or Anglo ethnicity, Verdecchia uses Wideload to put a dizzying spin on Homi Bhabha's account of colonial mimicry: Anglo identity emerges as a moment of ontological collapse, the failure of imitation ever to *be* the other it attempts to reproduce.[21]

"So what is it with you people? Who do you think you are? Who do you think we are?" (75). Implicit in these performances is the transaction of identity, the use of performance to render visible the troping of place and its mapping of identities. In the past decade, Guillermo Gómez-Peña has developed a body of performance work that takes the reciprocal relationship between national, ethnic, and theatrical borders as its subject, and as its means of performance. Gómez-Peña's critical writings and performances are preoccupied with the impact of the national border on the fashioning of identity, and this "'borderness'" characteristically arises through a spatial imagining of the politics of ethnicity: "I am Mexican but I am also Chicano and Latin American. At the border they call me *chilango* or *mexiquillo;* in Mexico City it's *pocho* or *norteño;* and in Europe it's *sudaca.* The Anglos call me 'Hispanic' or 'Latino.'"[22] Internalizing a contested social and political geography, Gómez-Peña registers the dispersal of identity enforced by the political hegemonies of border and nation. In his critical writing, Gómez-Peña explores this shifting subjectivity in a series of mobile terms (*mestizaje,* hybridity, syncretism, postmodernity, intercultural performance), each of which puts a different spin on the process of identification.

Though Gómez-Peña frequently disclaims the term *postmodern* as "ethnocentric and insufficient," in many respects the spatialized dimension of his performances articulates well with the critical politics of postmodern geography (46). Calling for "a new terminology for new hybrid identities and métiers constantly metamorphosing: sudacá, not sudaca; Chicarrican, not Hispanic; mestizaje, not miscegenation; social thinker, not bohemian; accionista, not performer; intercultural, not postmodern," Gómez-Peña insists that "all cultures and identities are open systems in constant process of transformation, redefinition, and recontextualization" (43, 48). The hybrid poetics of the border—a *rasquachi* aesthetics arising from specific material, economic, social, and cultural history—sorts strangely with the dehistoricizing pastiche that marks postmodern aesthetic production. Gómez-Peña's "border citizen" seems to resist assimilation to a regressive transnational identity, one that would blunt the mobilizing of political action with the fantasy of a global freeplay of identities.[23] Gómez-Peña's border marks the relational, heterotopic, dimension of social space, the way identities and their playing emerge at the interface between given spaces or positions: "the border was not a straight line; it was more like a Möbius strip. No matter where I was, I was always on 'the other side,' feeling ruptured and incomplete, ever longing for my other selves, my other home and tribe."[24]

Gómez-Peña's performances typically work to produce this otherness, this sense of being on the other side; these strategies are most visible in his collaborative works, such as *Two Undiscovered Amerindians*

Two Undiscovered Amerindians Visit Madrid, site-specific performance by Coco Fusco and Guillermo Gómez-Peña. (Photo by
Peter Barker.)

Discover . . . (with Coco Fusco) or the more recent *El Naftazteca* (with
Roberto Sifuentes) and *The Mexterminator Project* (with Roberto
Sifuentes, Sara Shelton Mann, and others). Despite the fact that *Two
Undiscovered Amerindians* and *The Mexterminator Project* might be characterized as installations or environmental theater, in which the audience crosses the border into the space of the performance, these works
sharply and surprisingly limit the ways the audience might interact with
the performers. The purpose of the film *The Couple in the Cage,* which
both documents the live performances of *Two Undiscovered Amerindians*
and constitutes a new video work, seems to be to display the spectators'
take on Fusco and Gómez-Peña. While it is difficult to get much sense of
the rhythm and duration of Fusco's and Gómez-Peña's performance, the
film's emphasis on the audience's reaction suggests that the onstage performance is only an instigation, a way of rendering another mode of
identification—the audience's—visible, performed. As Diana Taylor has
asked recently, "who is positioned where in this most uncanny, postmodern drama of cultural encounter?"[25] *The Couple in the Cage* implies
that *Two Undiscovered Amerindians* refuses to incorporate the audience

into the performance in order to *stage* the spectators' performance of identity-as-difference.[26] Despite Coco Fusco's rather narrow reduction of the range of these responses to a kind of racism (they are often, though hardly simply, that) in her celebrated article "The Other History of Intercultural Performance," what emerges from the film is a vividly localized series of performances framing identity within its social and political geography: the complacent midwesterners at the Field Museum of Natural History in Chicago; the black-tie art crowd at the New York gala and the performance art aficionados at the Walker Art Center in Minneapolis; the ironic and urbane businessmen in the plaza in Madrid. This "othering" of the audience dramatizes the work of "borderization" and is surprisingly characteristic of Gómez-Peña's live solo performance work as well.[27] Rather than assuming that the space between identities can be readily crossed, Gómez-Peña's performance stages that space as ideologically saturated, already laden with opportunities for the enactment of power.

Border Brujo uses performance space both to analyze the impact of borders on subjectivity and to represent—indeed to enact—this bordered process of subjection. In the performance, Gómez-Peña adopts the role of "Border Brujo," yet the word *role* is misleading, implying as it does in conventional theater (and in many performance artworks, including *Milk of Amnesia/Leche de Amnesia* and *Fronteras Americanas*) a single presence, a "character." Nor is it quite accurate to say that he plays a series of roles, several "characters" in sequence, along the lines of Anna Deavere Smith's or Danny Hoch's work. In the course of the performance, the "Brujo"—a sorcerer, healer, magician, witch—is less a character than a zone traced and transgressed by a series of voices, fleeting, evanescent signals of "subjects" that appear and disappear, flickering across and through Gómez-Peña's/the Brujo's body. Much like Gómez-Peña's *rasquachi* costume—a border guard's jacket layered with hundreds of buttons (political buttons, sheriff's badges, Batman logo), banana necklace, various hats, wrestling mask—these voices seem more accretions than individual subjects. Gómez-Peña's performance briefly clothes each in a local habitation, without quite providing a name.[28]

The performance opens with the Brujo lighting the candles that illuminate a kind of kitsch/folk/popular altar, mumbling audibly but indistinctly in an "Indian dialect" (76).[29] The sense of the Brujo as a figure loosed from history and geography is immediately confirmed by his first address to the audience, via megaphone, in which he urges the "dear audience" to "feel at home / this continent is your home" (76). Yet

Guillermo Gómez-Peña as the Border Brujo, with Emily Hicks in
Tiaguana–Niagara, on the United States–Canada border, 1988.
(Photo by Biff Hendricks.)

while the continent is our home, the Brujo immediately moves into
another key:

> dear foreign audience
> it's January 1st, 1847
> & the U.S. hasn't invaded Mexico yet
> this is Mexico carnales!
> there is no border
> we are merely divided
> by the imprecision of your memory
>
> (76)

Border Brujo isn't a personalized memory-performance. Much as
Gómez-Peña's costume signals the unavailability of the authentic behind
the kitschy productions of commodity culture, so the notion of a single
authentic Latino identity proves evanescent, a mode of address but not
an address. But beyond that, our own identities are cast here as well, as
the space of border encounter is staged not as a neutral space, but as a
space already "filled with politics and ideology."[30]

What's most powerful about *Border Brujo* is the way it forces the
audience to ride its own roller-coaster on the Möbius strip of border
identification. Though part of the verbal texture of the script ("dear
audience"), this hailing is enacted in performance, as a variety of other
voices speak to the audience from the physical "space" of the Brujo.
Immediately after the Brujo's introduction, for example, a rowdy, Anglo-
accented voice declaims drunkenly,

> you're just a border-crosser
> a "wetback" with amnesia
> who the hell invited your ancestors
> to this country anyway?
>
> (77)

Throughout *Border Brujo,* Gómez-Peña moves from voice to voice.
Sometimes these voices are marked by costume changes: he removes the
elaborate jacket, keeping only the banana necklace, bandolier, and various amulets for the speech beginning, "I speak Spanish therefore you
hate me"; he puts on a panama hat advertising Corona beer and sunglasses for the "welcome to the Casa de Cambio" section (80); he returns
to his original costume, wearing a fedora (instead of a sombrero) for the
chant beginning "Cyber-Bwana" (80).

More often the Brujo's voices shift with little warning, insinuating a range of relationships with the audience. The audience is also "cast," addressed as illegal Mexican immigrants, as tourists, as performance art patrons, by the voices that circulate through the Brujo: the smooth-talking deejay ("It's me, the Mexican beast / we are here to talk, to change, to ex-change" [82]), the various Anglo-accented "redneck" voices ("whatever happened to the sleepy Mexican / the smiley guy you met last summer / on the 'Amigou Country' cruise, remember" [87]), perhaps the voice of Gómez-Peña, performance artist ("can anyone document me please?" [87]), the barking voice of the critic ("not experimental enough / not inter-dizzy enough" [89]), the border-patrol voice that points the flashlight at the (art museum) audience asking us "a few questions" (92), and the stylized *pachuco* voice of the conclusion:

> we are finally in the same room
> even if only for an evening
> we are truly conversing right now
> in your language
> but conversing after all
> so I mean to ask you
> where is the threshold of your desire?
> (94)

In the policed space of the border, and of this theater space, the performance of "identity" happens across the political fracture of power: in the borderland, "identity" is not chosen, but negotiated, across a terrain where the maps are constantly in flux. This experience, as C. Carr suggests in a review of the live performance, can be disorienting. Carr is at first impressed by the speed of Gómez-Peña's "Transitions from one character or caricature to the next—from undocumented Chicano to obnoxious gringo to the seedy *bandido* of a Saturday morning cartoon," transitions that "seemed to happen mid sentence, almost imperceptibly, like one more sneaky border crossing."[31] The adjective "sneaky" here is an odd one, the residue of dominant attitudes toward border crossing active elsewhere in Carr's review. The contradictory phrase "undocumented Chicano" points to Carr's misprision of the realities of Chicano experience (as U.S. citizens, Chicanos *need* no documents, but rightly fear being mistaken for "undocumented" Mexicans and summarily deported), as does her reduction of Gómez-Peña's performance to comic stereotypes (what *bandido* are we talking about here? Speedy Gonzalez? the Frito bandido?). Gómez-Peña's performance seems implicitly to stage its audience across the fracture of border politics, constituting the space of the "border shaman" as a space of transgression, of infiltration.[32] Carr's experience seems momentarily—and uncomfortably—one of identification with a kind of hegemonic nationalism, in which "others" are identified as seedy stereotypes, misrecognized as foreigners, stealthily occupying "our" space.

Carr, of course, understands that Gómez-Peña means to stage "a border situation in which the audience members became visitors to his 'performance country,'" and describes a notable transformation of subject positionality: "Watching this border guard, who occasionally addressed us through a bullhorn, I felt moments of irritation and anxiety at not understanding words and references. (I don't speak Spanish.)" Yet, "listening to it a second time on tape, I realized that most of the performance had been in English. Annoyance with the linguistic Other had distorted my perception. I'd been, perhaps, alienated. And this was the point, of course."[33] Carr describes this "alienation" as a reflex avant-gardism, "the point, of course." Yet as Brecht recognized, "alienation" is never in general, never "of course"; it uses a specific mode and moment of production as a means of alienating the subject, estranging those moments of innate "desire" to produce the possibility of different modes of identification with(in) the state. José David Saldívar remarks that Gómez-Peña's "Deleuzian-Guattarian riffs on postmodern Tijuana" imply that "we can no longer conceptualize the U.S.-Mexico border self as 'alienated' in the sense that Marx defined it, because to be alienated in the classic sense presupposes a coherent self rather than a scrambled, 'illegally alienated' self."[34] But while Saldívar takes Gómez-Peña's "videotext" as a means of othering Tijuana as *el otro lado,* the other side, the anxiety that the live performance raises for Carr—and in my experience, to many viewers of the video as well—appears to summon the multiple "alienation" of the border subject: the inability to choose a stable position, the constant sense of forcible interpellation, of being hailed (as *Norteamericanos,* as racists, as tourists, as *compadres*) through the bullhorn.

This threshold of desire—the desire to situate ourselves, to define ourselves by fixing the Brujo's many "others"—is contested in Gómez-Peña's final raplike chant, applying face makeup while he extinguishes himself before the flames. The fluid subject that Gómez-Peña articulates as performance, the voices that speak from different psycho-geographical-political spaces, defines the ritual space of performance we share with him—whoever *we* are. The subjects constituted in performance, in relation to these voices, are by turns oppressive and just ignorant, complicit in their desire to see and fearful of what seeing might mean. If performance constitutes a divided subject here, it does so not merely by representing one—the Brujo seems more like a screen than like a divided self—than by articulating the variety of relations of power and subjectivity that can be constituted by the performance itself.

Despite Gómez-Peña's resistance to an aestheticized postmodernism, *Border Brujo* recalls Fredric Jameson's familiar account of the Gehry house in Santa Monica as "the new postmodern space, which our bodies inhabit in malaise or delight, trying to shed the older habits of inside/outside categories and perceptions, still longing for the bourgeois privacy of solid walls (enclosures like the old centered bourgeois ego)."[35] Jameson's sense of "the strange new feeling of an absence of inside and outside, the bewilderment and loss of spatial orientation in Portman's hotels, the messiness of an environment in which things and people no longer find their 'place,'" approximates the feel of Gómez-Peña's performances.[36] At the same time, though, *Border Brujo* works to politicize this sensibility, to locate this disorienting process of subjection as a consequence of social and political history. Both in his own enactment, and in his engagement with the audience, Gómez-Peña insinuates an experience of decenteredness, in which the relationship between place and identity—the solid walls of the bourgeois ego, shored up by the impermeable borders of the nation—is not so much suspended as shaped and reshaped. While Gómez-Peña's performances may be disorienting, they do not evoke the affectless euphoria of late capital, but have an edgier feel: on the border, it's important to know where you stand, because where you stand may determine who you can claim to be.

Border Brujo participates in a specifically performative rethinking of narrative, location, power, and identity. In *Border Brujo,* as in his other performance pieces, Gómez-Peña's performance is "tactical" in de Certeau's sense; it operates in the social "space of the other" and so must "play on and with a terrain imposed on it and organized by the law of a foreign power."[37] These performances cite the differences imposed by hegemony, a citation that is also a kind of resistance through resignification, a "*disordering* of difference from its persistent binary structuring and the reconstitution of difference as the basis for a new cultural politics of multiplicity" that we might take to be a part of the "development of radical postmodernism."[38] *Border Brujo* takes the stage not as a place for forgetting, but for remembering, for seeing the richly overdetermined meaningfulness of space and place. Staging the relational contours of ethnicity, of nation, of history, *Border Brujo* charts the ideological landscape of the deceptively "empty space" of performance.

NOTES

I would like to thank both colleagues and students in the International Centre for Advanced Theatre Studies, Finland, and the seminar participants at the American Society for Theatre Research annual meeting in Pasadena in 1996 for their helpful comments on earlier versions of this essay.

    1. David Román, "Carmelita Tropicana Unplugged," *TDR* 39, no. 3 (1995): 90.

    2. Suzanne Oboler notes that the use of "the term *Latino* began to emerge among grassroots sectors of the population, coined as a progressive alternative to the state-imposed bureaucratic label Hispanic." See *Ethnic Labels, Latino Lives: Identity and the Politics of (Re)Presentation in the United States* (Minneapolis: University of Minnesota Press, 1995), vii. As Oboler's study argues, in a variety of ways immigrants to the United States from Latin America discover that national identity—Peruvian, Brazilian, Mexican—is irrelevant to the formation of ethnicity in the United States. Taking a group of Peruvians traveling by air, land, and sea to the United States as exemplary, Oboler remarks that once across the U.S. border, "to their eventual surprise, they also discovered that their newly asserted national identity was of little relevance to the society at large. Instead, they found out that they were now U.S. 'Hispanics,' a term whose meaning(s) and social value, *as these have evolved in this country,* they were expected to learn and assimilate" (xii).

    3. Neil Smith and Cindi Katz develop an excellent reading of the metaphoricity of *position* in studies of ethnicity:

> Location may be no more than a zero-dimensional space, a point on a map. "Position," by contrast, implies location *vis-à-vis* other locations and incorporates a sense of perspective on other places, and is therefore at least one-dimensional. "Locality" suggests a two- (or more) dimensional place, an area within which multiple and diverse social and natural events and processes take place. The appeal of these concepts as source domains for metaphors obviously lies in the precision and fixity they impute to the target domain. Notions like subject position, social location and locality borrow this concreteness of spatial definition to impose some order on the seemingly chaotic *mélange* of social difference and social relations. "Social location" gives differentiated social subjects a place to stand, rendering them at the very least visible in their differences. "Subject position" takes up the question of the standpoint and the relativity of social location as a place of seeing and acting: different social actors, by virtue of their distinctive identities, are particularly located *vis-à-vis* other actors and therefore enjoy a distinctive perspective from which they construct different social meanings. The metaphor of locality, finally, suggests that social location is less an individual than a multi-dimen-

sional experience, a collective engagement of mutually implicated identities.

See "Grounding Metaphor: Toward a Spatialized Politics," in *Place and the Politics of Identity,* ed. Michael Keith and Steve Pile (London: Routledge, 1993), 69.

4. Judith Butler, *Bodies That Matter: On the Discursive Limits of "Sex"* (New York: Routledge, 1993), 2. Moreover, as Kenneth Burke argues, identification operates by asserting likeness in the face of difference; by claiming likeness, acts of identification both specify and constitute difference as a precondition of identity; see *A Rhetoric of Motives* (Berkeley and Los Angeles: University of California Press, 1969), 19–29. Burke's discussion of identification is relevant here, especially his sense that "Identification is affirmed with earnestness precisely because there is division. Identification is compensatory to division" (22). As Scott Michaelsen and David E. Johnson observe, "Chicano identity is inscribed, as is every other identity, within the horizon of the politics of opposition." See "Border Secrets: An Introduction," *Border Theory: The Limits of Cultural Politics,* ed. Scott Michaelsen and David E. Johnson (Minneapolis: University of Minnesota Press, 1997), 19.

5. Edward W. Soja, *Postmodern Geographies: The Reassertion of Space in Critical Social Theory* (London: Verso, 1989), 17.

6. Soja, *Postmodern Geographies,* 18. Lisa Lowe suggests that this construction is specific to the formation of nationalist identification, and her reading echoes Soja's account of the transformation of space by capital: "capital, with its supposed needs for 'abstract labor,' is said by Marx to be unconcerned by the 'origins' of its labor force, whereas the nation-state, with its need for 'abstract citizens' formed by a unified culture to participate in the political sphere, is precisely concerned to maintain a national citizenry bound by race, language, and culture." See *Immigrant Acts: On Asian-American Cultural Politics* (Durham, N.C.: Duke University Press, 1996), 13.

7. I am adapting Judith Butler's reading of the mapping of sexual identity onto the body to a reading of ethnic identification; her remarks in full are these: "the body is not a 'being,' but a variable boundary, a surface whose permeability is politically regulated, a signifying practice within a cultural field of gender hierarchy and compulsory heterosexuality." See *Gender Trouble: Feminism and the Subversion of Identity* (New York: Routledge, 1990), 139. Una Chaudhuri argues that "the construction of cultural otherness"—an otherness necessarily constructed as an effect of identification, the assertion of sameness—"is also a *mapping of the world,* a fact that contributes powerfully to the literalization of accounts of ethnic difference." See *Staging Place: The Geography of Modern Drama* (Ann Arbor: University of Michigan Press, 1995), 3.

8. José David Saldívar, *Border Matters: Remapping American Cultural Studies* (Berkeley and Los Angeles: University of California Press, 1997), xii.

9. Judith Butler, *The Psychic Life of Power: Theories in Subjection* (Stanford:

Stanford University Press, 1997), 119. Göran Therborn argues that the "reproduction of any social organization, be it an exploitative society or a revolutionary party, entails a basic correspondence between subjection and qualification.
Those who have been subjected to a particular patterning of their capacities, to
a particular discipline, qualify for the given roles and are capable of carrying
them out." See *The Ideology of Power and the Power of Ideology* (London: Verso,
1982), 17. This reading of Louis Althusser is given a more energetic reading in
Judith Butler's account of Althusser's "Ideology and Ideological State Apparatuses," where she argues that it is the performance of attributed skills that brings
the subject into social being: "This performance is not simply *in accord* with
these skills, for there is no subject prior to their performing; performing skills
laboriously works the subject into its status as a social being. There is guilt, and
then a repetitive practice by which skills are acquired, and then and only then
an assumption of the grammatical place within the social as a subject" (*Psychic
Life of Power*, 119).

   10. One of the most fascinating dimensions of Oboler's study is her record of
the transformation of ethnic ("whiteness") and class markers among middle-
and upper-class Latin American immigrants. What is perceived as a "prevalence
of class over race in organizing the social hierarchies of Latin American soci-
eties" (*Ethnic Labels, Latino Lives,* 100) is generally reversed in the United States,
to the extent that middle- and upper-class individuals who formerly were likely
to identify themselves in *class* terms are identified principally in the minoritiz-
ing discourse of *race* when they enter the United States: "while white, middle-
and upper-class Hispanics might be able to attribute an *ethnic* status to themselves, others would assign to many 'non-white Hispanics' a *minority* status
based on class and racial considerations" (99). As one of Oboler's informants, a
"very fair skinned" (156) island-born Puerto Rican man, put it, "White people
have a name for everybody else" (155); he recognizes that "in this society, and
insofar as his nationality and his race *are* conflated, his identity as a Puerto
Rican is not 'white'" (156). As another informant asked of the census questionnaire, marking the different mapping of race in the United States and in her
native Colombia, "'how could someone who is really black but speaks Spanish
write down that he's black?" (156). Diana Taylor notes that while most Latin
Americans identify more along national than hemispheric lines (as Mexicans,
Chileans, Peruvians, rather than as "Latin Americans"), any sense of collective
identity that *is* felt "stems less from a history of shared community than from
the shared history of *opposition to* the colonial powers." See "Opening
Remarks," in *Negotiating Performance: Gender, Sexuality, and Theatricality in
Latin/o America,* ed. Diana Taylor and Juan Villegas (Durham, N.C.: Duke University Press, 1994), 9. See also Angie Chabram-Dernersesian's reading of the
discourse of "whiteness" in Chicana/o representation, involving a similar "passage from *país* (country) to *cultura* (culture)," in "On the Social Construction of
Whiteness within Selected Chicana/o Discourses," in *Displacing Whiteness:*

Essays in Social and Cultural Criticism, ed. Ruth Frankenberg (Durham, N.C.: Duke University Press, 1997), 125.

11. Norma Alarcón remarks that a "bi- or multi-ethnicized, raced, and gendered subject-in-process may be called upon to take up diverse subject positions which cannot be unified without double binds and contradictions." See "Conjugating Subjects: The Heteroglossia of Essence and Resistance," in *An Other Tongue: Nation and Ethnicity in the Linguistic Borderlands,* ed. Alfred Arteaga (Durham, N.C.: Duke University Press, 1994), 136.

12. Anthony D. Smith, *National Identity* (Reno: University of Nevada Press, 1991), 21.

13. On "war of position," see Stuart Hall, "The Meaning of New Times," in *Stuart Hall: Critical Dialogues in Cultural Studies,* ed. David Morley and Kuan-Shing Chen (London: Routledge, 1996), 237; I am also much indebted to Hall's foundational essay "New Ethnicities," in the same volume, 441–49. On lived space, see Soja, *Postmodern Geographies,* 18.

14. Lowe, *Immigrant Acts,* 26.

15. By "hailing," I have in mind Louis Althusser's classic, and controversial, discussion of *interpellation.* See Louis Althusser, "Ideology and Ideological State Apparatuses (Notes towards an Investigation)," in *Lenin and Philosophy and Other Essays,* trans. Ben Brewster (New York: Monthly Review Press, 1971), 127–86.

16. Fredric Jameson, *Postmodernism; or, The Cultural Logic of Late Capitalism* (Durham, N.C.: Duke University Press, 1992), 16. Soja considers this temporal-to-spatial dynamic at length in the first chapter of *Postmodern Geographies;* see also his comments on posthistoricism, post-Fordism, and postmodernism (61–62).

17. Joseph Roach, *Cities of the Dead: Circum-Atlantic Performance* (New York: Columbia University Press, 1996), 3.

18. José Esteban Muñoz, "No es fácil: Notes on the Negotiation of Cubanidad and Exilic Memory in Carmelita Tropicana's *Milk of Amnesia,*" *TDR* 39, no. 3 (1995): 77.

19. In my discussion, I rely as well on a performance of the work at San Francisco's Theatre Rhinoceros, October 16, 1997. Although in many of her interviews and in personal appearances Troyano appears as Carmelita Tropicana, it is difficult to characterize the several personae in play in the performance of *Milk of Amnesia/Leche de Amnesia* without recourse to the figure of Troyano, even if only to label the visible performer who gives voice to the Writer and who changes costume onstage to perform both Pingalito and Carmelita.

20. Guillermo Verdecchia, *Fronteras Americanas* (Toronto: Coach House Press, 1993), 21.

21. Verdecchia's use of dance to resignify the ethnicized body recalls Richard Dyer's searching account of his own body-in-dance in *White* (London: Routledge, 1997), 6. See also Homi K. Bhabha, "Of Mimicry and Man: The Ambivalence of Colonial Discourse," in *The Location of Culture* (London: Routledge, 1994), 85–92.

22. Guillermo Gómez-Peña, *Warrior for Gringostroika: Essays, Performance Texts, and Poetry* (St. Paul: Greywolf Press, 1993), 37.

23. Angie Chabram-Dernersesian has recently argued that it's possible to understand "transnational identity" as a "regressive" mode of political identification, one that places ethnic subjects "within a series of multiethnic constructions that purposefully stop right where our emergent and oppositional agencies begin." See "The Spanish Colón-ialista Narrative: Their Prospectus for Us in 1992," in *Mapping Multiculturalism,* ed. Avery F. Gordon and Christopher Newfield (Minneapolis: University of Minnesota Press, 1996), 228. As Deborah Paredez suggests in "Blood and Salsa: That's the Nature of the Relationship," (a paper presented to the American Society for Theatre Research, Pasadena, November 1996), Gómez-Peña's sense of the fluidity of identity depends—as it does not for a Chicano confined by economic and social barriers to East L.A., or to rural New Mexico, or to Eagle Pass, Texas—on his access to a range of geographical and geopolitical contexts, a range of scenes in which to perform "difference." *Rasquachi* is sometimes translated as "underdog"—as when El Teatro Campesino's *La carpa de los Rasquachis* appears as "The Tent Show of the Underdogs"—but *rasquachi* also suggests the making-do, improvisation, and resourcefulness necessary in the daily life of oppressed groups. Jorge Huerta suggests "funky," "unsophisticated," and "humble" as translations in "Contemporary Chicano Theater," in *Chicano Studies: A Multidisciplinary Approach,* ed. Eugene E. García, Francisco A. Lomelí, and Isidro D. Ortiz (New York: Teachers College Press, 1984), 142.

24. Gómez-Peña, *The New World Border,* 63. Judith Butler's reading of the function of melancholia in the constitution of the subject engages the question of power and subject-formation more broadly than Gómez-Peña does here, but her account is nonetheless striking in its evocation of his experience: "The inaugurative scene of interpellation is one in which a certain failure to be constituted becomes the condition of possibility for constituting oneself. Social discourse wields the power to form and regulate a subject through the imposition of its own terms. Those terms, however, are not simply accepted or internalized; they become psychic only through the movement by which they are dissimulated and 'turned.' In the absence of explicit regulation, the subject emerges as one for whom power has become voice, and voice, the regulatory instrument of the psyche. The speech acts of power—the declaration of guilt, the judgment of worthlessness, the verdicts of reality—are topographically rendered as psychic instruments and institutions within a psychic landscape that depends on its metaphoricity for its plausibility" (*Psychic Life,* 197).

25. Diana Taylor, "A Savage Performance: Guillermo Gómez-Peña and Coco Fusco's 'Couple in the Cage,'" *TDR* 42, no. 2 (1998): 172. See also Barbara Kirshenblatt-Gimblett, "The Ethnographic Burlesque," *TDR* 42, no. 2 (1998): 175–80.

26. *The Couple in the Cage: A Guatinaui Odyssey,* dir. Coco Fusco, Authentic

Documentary Productions, 1993. See also Coco Fusco, "The Other History of Intercultural Performance," *TDR* 38, no. 1 (1994): 143–67.

27. On the night I attended *The Mexterminator Project* in San Francisco, for example, spectators were required to request a "script" from a "docent" if they wished to enter the elevated "stages" where the cyber-stereotypes Gómez-Peña and Sifuentes were performing (*The Mexterminator Project*, performed by Guillermo Gómez-Peña, Roberto Sifuentes, and Sara Shelton Mann, San Francisco, March 1998). Many aspects of this performance have changed significantly over time and are documented in Lisa Wolford's excellent reading of the piece, "Carnival Apocalíptica: *The Mexterminator Project*." I am grateful to Professor Wolford for sharing an unpublished version of this article with me. See also Samira Kawash, "Interactivity and Vulnerability," *PAJ* 21, no. 1 (1999): 46–52. Much of *Mexterminator* has been incorporated into *Borderscape 2000: A Spanglish Lounge Operetta,* performed by Guillermo Gómez-Peña, Roberto Sifuentes, Sara Shelton Mann, Juan Ybarra, and Gustavo Vazquez, which I attended at the Magic Theatre, San Francisco, March 13, 1999. Unlike *The Mexterminator Project, Borderscape 2000* was (on this occasion, at least) performed on a proscenium stage, before a seated audience; it is the third and final part of a performance trilogy, including *The New World Border* and *Dangerous Border Games.*

28. I am indebted here to José David Saldívar's reading of the piece (*Border Matters,* 151–57), as well as to Claire F. Fox's useful study, which carefully locates *Border Brujo* as a turning point in Gómez-Peña's career, marking a shift from his preoccupation with the U.S.-Mexico border, to a sense of global "borderization" that nonetheless remains dependent on the notion of national borders; see "Mass Media, Site Specificity, and the U.S.-Mexico Border: Guillermo Gómez-Peña's *Border Brujo* (1988, 1990)," in *The Ethnic Eye: Latino Media Arts,* ed. Chon A. Noriega and Ana M. López (Minneapolis: University of Minnesota Press, 1996), 233, and passim. Both Saldívar and Fox treat *Border Brujo* as a video and dwell largely on its video apparatus; my effort here is to use the video as a kind of evidence for the live work of Gómez-Peña's performance. The two works, as Fox carefully explains, are not equivalent: not only does the camera work of the video constitute *Border Brujo* as less local, less preoccupied with the Tijuana–San Diego border, but it omits several forms of critique, both of Anglo culture and of certain strains of Chicano cultural nationalism.

29. Throughout my discussion, I refer to the video *Border Brujo,* prod. Isaac Artenstein, Sushi Gallery, and Cinewest Productions, 1990. This performance cuts considerable portions of the text published in Guillermo Gómez-Peña, *Warrior for Gringostroika: Essays, Performance Texts, and Poetry* (St. Paul: Greywolf Press, 1993). When specific spoken passages are cited, I refer to the published script, *Border Brujo,* in *Warrior for Gringostroika,* 75–95. On occasion—as when Gómez-Peña changes the text's "January 1st, 1847" to 1848—the words spoken in performance differ from the published text.

30. Michael Keith and Steve Pile, "Introduction Part 1: The Politics of Place," in Keith and Pile, *Place and Politics of Identity,* 4.

31. C. Carr, "Guillermo Gómez-Peña, Dance Theater Workshop," *Artforum* 27, no. 5 (1989): 119.

32. This is Miriam Horn's evocative phrase, in "The Art of Ethnic Tensions," *U.S. News and World Report,* December 30, 1991, 79.

33. Carr, "Guillermo Gómez-Peña," 119.

34. Saldívar, *Border Matters,* 158.

35. Jameson, *Postmodernism,* 115.

36. Jameson, *Postmodernism,* 117–18.

37. Michel de Certeau, *The Practice of Everyday Life* (Berkeley and Los Angeles: University of California Press, 1984), 37.

38. Edward Soja and Barbara Hooper, "The Space That Difference Makes: Some Notes on the Geographical Margins of the New Cultural Politics," in Keith and Pile, *Place and Politics of Identity,* 187.

Five

Out of Space

14

Landscapes of the Unseen: Turn-of-the-Century Symbolism from Paris to Petersburg

Daniel Gerould

Un paysage au théâtre, qu'était cela? On ne voyait pas les paysages réels, tels qu'ils s'élargissent par les temps de soleil ou de pluie.

[What was a landscape in the theater? We never saw real landscapes, as they stretch before us in rain or shine.]

—EMILE ZOLA,
Le Naturalisme au théâtre, 1880

Pour trouver l'Idéal, il faut d'abord passer par le royaume des taupes.

[To find the Ideal, we must first pass through the kingdom of the moles.]

—VILLIERS DE L'ISLE-ADAM,
L'Eve future, 1886

Edison's Underground Eden

Emile Zola and Villiers de l'Isle-Adam propose radically different concepts of theatrical landscape. Champion and interpreter of his friends the impressionists, Zola makes eyesight the measure and cocreator of reality. Preexistent scenery in the perceptible world of nature—constantly distorted by the conventions of the stage—must be made directly accessible to human vision.[1] Zola proclaims the reign of the scenographic milieu. The invasion of nature that has gradually taken place over the past two centuries, Zola argues, provides a frame for humanity. The characters of drama are no longer abstract or alone; they exist as integral parts of a landscape formed by the natural world. What was formerly only background or decor now is foreground shaping and advancing human actions.

Even as Zola was hailing the advent of "real landscape" on the naturalist stage, his contemporary Villiers de l'Isle Adam, mentor and prophet to a new generation of poets, was preparing the artistic counterrevolution that would usher in symbolism and create a new landscape of the mind. For Villiers, obsessed by epistemological questions, the illusory nature of the phenomenal world made the positivists' claims to scientific knowledge of truth a crude delusion. Only dross dots the surface of pseudoreality; treasure lies buried deep. Uncovering what is hidden means descent into the earth, into the darkness, into the labyrinths of the mole kingdom. Deprived of sight, the magus-mole burrows into the subterranean realm of the unseen—to discover the ideal.

In symbolist ideology blindness becomes a badge of insight. "I believe only in what I cannot see," declared the painter Gustave Moreau.[2] Not observation, but the mechanism of reflection—the mirror and what lies behind it—offers a window on the unknown. Hidden in the mysteries of night, first and last things, origins and endings, genesis and eschatology remain forever beyond the visible.

In the theater, this radical new poetics that rejected the naturalist perception of the world led to innovative reconfigurations of stage space as the organizing principle of drama and to the discovery of darkness and shadow as the very matter out of which the work of art could be sculpted.

In act 5 of Villiers's grandiose protosymbolist drama *Axel* the proud aristocratic protagonist moves backward in time—out of the hated nineteenth century to an imagined age of honor and chivalry—by seeking refuge in his ancestral estate, "The gallery of tombs in the underground vaults of the castle of Auersperg."[3] Identifying with the earth and taking as his allies the roots of trees, Axel descends into the crypts to meet his demonic soul-mate Sara amid "the secular silence of the statues" in the mausoleum of his forebears.[4] There, deep beneath the mountain, Axel brings his rebellion against reality to a head.[5]

"Drop those hangings, Sara; I have seen enough of the sun," Axel commands, undoing the work of creation with his inverted *fiat lux*.[6] The clear daylight of naturalism is excluded, plunging the world into the primeval, fertile chaos of night. As in subsequent symbolist drama, movement through the landscape of Villiers's *Axel* is predominantly vertical, dispelling any sense of forward motion and producing an effect of deeply layered stasis. Heights and depths provide constant points of reference, but the direction being taken remains a matter of perspective. The deeper hero and heroine descend the higher they seem to rise. "Is there still any up or down?" Nietzsche asks in *The Gay Science* (written at almost exactly the same time as *Axel)*, reformulating Mephistopheles' "Up or down, it's all the same" from Goethe's *Faust*, Part II.[7]

In *The Future Eve*, Thomas Alva Edison, spokesman for scientific pragmatism, sets out to demonstrate the superiority of artifice over nature. Brandishing a perpetual cigar and offering his friend Lord Ewald lights from strange mechanical devices, the "Wizard of Menlo Park" is a modern Prometheus bringing humankind electricity. A daring rival of God the Father, he creates a new Eve, an android, in his underground laboratory, formerly a cave used as burial grounds of the Algonquin tribes, and now "our lost Eden, rediscovered" in America.[8]

In this Avernus to which the questing heroes must descend in a special electrical elevator, the "artificial paradise" consists of bogus vegetation and flowers that wave in gusts of sham breezes. Mechanical birds groom themselves and smooth their fake feathers with artificial beaks, while a recorded nightingale's song plays and a hummingbird on display is capable of reciting all of *Hamlet*. The novel has been projected a few years into the future, and inventions still to come—the cinema (in color and with sound!)—are included among Edison's accomplishments and described in detail.

In the "Wizard of Menlo Park's" subterranean electrical realm of antinature, where man-made machinery has replaced natural landscape, the human imagination is liberated to create its own universe. Inspired partly by memories of Jules Verne's *Journey to the Center of the Earth* (1864) and partly by the bizarre inventions designed for King Ludwig of Bavaria's grotto in his fantastic castle, the android's underground residence is an immense hall whose vaulted ceiling, lit by a luminous globe at its apex, simulates the vault of the sky.[9]

Edison, who starts the novel as a ruthless and pragmatic technician, is revealed to be the Faustian director of a *theatrum mundi* actually controlled by invisible higher powers. According to Villiers's theory of illusionism, the power of theatrical machinery to generate images exposes the trompe-l'oeil of "natural" landscapes and enables us to penetrate to what lies beyond, behind, and beneath. The vulgar world of "simple reality" yields to the magical space of artificial Edens, where the entire boundless universe can be reflected in a sealed subterranean antechamber.

The invention of modern electric lighting by Villiers's "Wizard of Menlo Park" opened the way for the creation of complex effects of light and dark that proved essential in the staging of symbolist drama. The new stagecraft—in large part a product of electric lighting—also exerted a major influence on the writing of plays, liberating the theatrical imaginations of turn-of-the-century writers and directors.[10]

Cracks in the Castle Walls

However, it was not the Frenchman Villiers but the Belgian Maeterlinck who, with his early short plays and especially with *Pelléas et Mélisande,* established the first important landmarks of symbolist drama on the topographical map. In his essay on *paysage* in the European theater, the theater sociologist Jean Duvignaud suggests that countries like Belgium and Ireland (he could have added Poland), with distinctive regional dramatic traditions distanced from the universalizing aesthetic promulgated by the French, produce legendary topologies, obsessional psychic landscapes that lend themselves to poetic visualization.[11]

Maeterlinck's meetings with Villiers in 1886 proved decisive for the Belgian as he prepared to embark on his career as playwright. From Villiers's example, Maeterlinck learned the dramatic intensity of sheer inwardness, the endless fascination of the dream, and the theatrical power of prolonged waiting. Like his mentor, Maeterlinck would oppose the real world to an ideal world of one's imagining.[12] But whereas the superheroes Axel and Sara consciously waged an antinature campaign and sought to stage—through histrionic bravado—their own alternative reality, Maeterlinck's wanderers, literally or figuratively blind, are lost in a universe whose coherence they cannot grasp; they remain locked in their own interiority, solitude, and silence.

Pelléas et Mélisande is set in a psychic landscape of disconnections and fractures, a country of amnesia where the characters' powers of recognition have grown impaired. No master plan controlling events is readily discernible to those being most cruelly buffeted. In this land of forgetting one can neither recall what came before nor foresee what lies ahead. Scattered pieces of past, present, and future dot the landscape, without coalescing or taking any firm shape. Mélisande cannot remember where she has come from, who she is, or where she is going. A victim of time, she finds her inner experiences captive to her lapses of memory. Mélisande cannot hold onto her ring, which falls into the pool—in the same way that her identity slips her grasp.

The natural world in Maeterlinck furnishes signs that both characters and spectators must decipher if they are to "read" what destiny has in store. Almost imperceptible noises acquire mysterious resonance. In act 4 of *Pelléas et Mélisande,* the terrified Mélisande says, "I heard the crackling of dead leaves"; shortly thereafter Golaud discovers the lovers kissing and kills Pélléas.[13] The crackling of dead leaves trampled underfoot is the "sound of time," a symbolist topos—recurring in artists as diverse as Wyspiański (*November Night*), Beckett (*Waiting for Godot*), and Fellini (*Amarcord*)—that translates a seasonal metaphor into an animist setting.

All theater deals, in varying degrees and fashions, with the revelation of what is hidden, but Maeterlinck was the first playwright to make penetration into the depths of consciousness the essential, and sometimes the sole, dramatic event, finding strange equivalencies between topography and the psyche. This penetration takes the form of an excursion or journey, often downwards. The landscape of *Pelléas et Mélisande* is riddled with labyrinthine corridors, passageways, and stairs leading down to crypts, caverns, and abysses. As is the case with Maeterlinck's dialogue, only what lies buried below the surface is truly significant.

The visit of the young lovers to the grotto in act 2, scene 3 is a descent into the innermost landscapes of spiritual awareness. The path is narrow, passing by dangerous places between two lakes whose depths have yet to be plumbed. There are shipwrecks and secret passageways to the sea (Maeterlinck's repository of destiny). As in *Axel*, great treasures are hidden somewhere within the cavern, which has never been fully explored. Amid the blue shadows are stalactites resembling plants and men, in an ambiguous interchange between animate and inanimate.

As the sound of silence grows oppressive, the moon suddenly comes out, illuminating the entrance to the grotto and permitting the visitors to catch sight, at a depth, of three old beggars with white hair leaning upon each other, asleep against a boulder. This perspective on human frailty and mortality offered by the hidden enclosure—like a circular insert in the illustration of a medieval illuminated manuscript—becomes a nonrecognition, a missed epiphany, a deflected revelation for the doomed lovers.

The use of chiaroscuro, the beam of light through the shadows, the figures caught in the bright circle—all these effects anticipate the cinema and the cinematographic. The rise of the symbolist aesthetic in theater coincides with the birth of the film (in its fantastic, "trick" phase), and it is worth noting that two symbolist playwrights, Saint-Pol-Roux and Béla Balázs, became film theorists.

The second underground scene, in act 3, scene 3 of *Pelléas et Mélisande,* takes place in a setting riven by the cracks that divide the brothers. As Golaud and Pelléas make the treacherous descent into the subterranean vaults of the castle, their fears of falling into the abyss and their unspoken jealousies come close to the surface and then recede. The immediate danger is surmounted, but the scent of death rising from stagnant waters that have poisoned the castle remains strong in the nostrils. Golaud comments on the precarious position of the crumbling castle in danger of disappearing into the morass.

> The cavern containing this stagnant water should be walled up. It's time anyhow to inspect these underground passageways. Have you noticed the cracks in the walls and in the pillars of the vaults? There's something mysterious going on here that we haven't suspected; and the whole castle will be swallowed up one of these nights if nothing's done about it. . . . There are strange cracks in many of the walls.[14]

The classical scholar and critic J. W. Mackail has suggested that Maeterlinck's theatrical landscape may in part be drawn from the actual Flemish countryside with its fortresses, towers, canals, and nearby sea.[15] But each of these real elements is transformed into metaphor through parallels to literary or legendary analogues. For example, the "sick" castle in *Pélléas et Mélisande* derives its dangerously fissured subterranean caverns and stagnant waters giving off the stench of death from Edgar Allan Poe's "House of Usher" and other tales of the grotesque.[16]

In order to dramatize the interior life—"those mysteries lying half-hidden below the surface of existence, those meanings inhabiting the silence and the darkness"[17]—Maeterlinck created a secret language and a mysterious landscape in which silhouettes furtively and fearfully move among shadows.

Falling Azure Snow in the Evening

Maeterlinck's aesthetic underwent a variety of transformations when it was transplanted—in this case to Russia and Poland—and crossbred with native traditions and artistic temperaments of a different order. Serving different cultural and national purposes, the symbolist paradigm in eastern Europe became subject to drastic revisions. In the first decade of the twentieth century the whole of Russia was astir with theatrical experimentation and innovative stage design. Symbolism found a warmer welcome in the theaters of Moscow and St. Petersburg than in those of Paris. Maeterlinck was the most discussed and influential new foreign dramatist in Russia at the turn of the century. Interested in the Belgian writer since the mid-1890s, Chekhov only months before his death persuaded Stanislavsky to present the three early one-acts, but did not live to see the production. Vakhtangov, Kommissarzhevskaya, and Meyerhold all staged Maeterlinck.

The outstanding Russian symbolist poet of the second generation, Alexander Blok, was critical of Maeterlinck, considering his work monotonous and judging the texture of his theatrical landscape thin. Although he translated the Belgian's short plays in 1908 (the same year that he published his own *Lyrical Dramas*), Blok was hostile to the dominance of western European influences and preferred native Russian talents.[18] He considered Chekhov a greater symbolist than Maeterlinck. Acting by "intuition alone," Chekhov, in Blok's opinion, "eliminated from Russian drama what Maeterlinck eliminated from European drama."[19] This innovative purification consisted of ridding the stage of the bric-a-brac of naturalist mimesis and letting the poetic imagination create new forms.

For the setting of his lyrical drama, *The Stranger,* Blok turned not to Maeterlinck's vague primeval forest or timeless interiors, but rather to the seedy outskirts of St. Petersburg, as presented in the novels of Dostoyevsky. The play is a descent into the nocturnal labyrinth of the tentacular, spectral city where real and phantasmagoric intersect.

The Russian poet applied the new symbolist principles of spatial organization to a modern urban landscape, where he could accentuate the breakup of spatial coherence and homogeneity and set multiple viewpoints against one another. Petersburg was a striking locus of modern instability and anxiety. According to legend, the imperial metropolis was courting disaster, its elegant masklike facades resting on the shaky foundations of swamps littered with the corpses of workmen sacrificed during its hasty building at Peter the Great's insistent orders.

In the form of a triptych, *The Stranger* presents, instead of scenes, three parallel "Visions" of the urban landscape: tavern, street, and salon. We can find on a map precisely where the sleazy tavern of the First Vision is located—on the corner of Geslorovsky Lane and Bolshaya Zeleninaya Street, not far from where Svidrigailov committed suicide in *Crime and Punishment.* Blok found "the real Russia" not in the snobbish central Petersburg of Nevsky Prospect, but in the outer working-class districts where he went for long strolls and dropped in at bars, cinemas, and circuses. It was in this poverty-stricken, debauched Russia of thieves, prostitutes, and drunkards (and their banal counterparts in a fashionable salon) that Blok's drama of transcendental aspirations is played out.

The Stranger is a star who, in response to the Poet's longings, has fallen from heaven to earth where she becomes a fallen woman. They meet on "a dark deserted bridge" in a landscape of falling snow and mystical encounters, but speaking different languages, they fail to understand one another. Unity of personality disintegrates; doubles proliferate. Forever splitting in two (as does the scenery, revealing new perspectives), the Stranger is half Madonna, half harlot. The Poet divides into Azure, his spiritual alter ego, and the Astrologer, his earthly antiface; all three—Azure, Astrologer, and Poet—find an antipodal double in the Gentleman in the Derby, a cynical man-about-town, who deftly whisks the Stranger off for the night.

The setting undergoes comparable metamorphoses. The closed space of the tavern breaks open: "The walls fly apart. The ceiling, tilting all the way, reveals the sky—wintry, blue, cold."[20] The ships on the wallpaper in the tavern—sailing endlessly in a drunken storm with foam at their prows—become the boats drowsing on either side of the bridge in the Second Vision, which is another "real" place in Petersburg: the bridge across Karpovsky to Krestovsky Island.

When the Poet is transformed into Azure during the snowstorm and gradually vanishes, Blok's stage directions indicate the power of light and color to produce magical effects.

> Azure drowses in the pale light. A ray shines against his dark cloak, as though he were leaning on a sword . . . Azure's cloak undulates and disappears beneath the falling snowflakes. . . .
> There is no more Azure. A bluish pillar of snow has spun around and around, and then on that spot there appears to be no one at all.[21]

The First and Third Visions—the low-life beer hall and the fashionable salon—are mirror images. Circularity of structure and endless repetition characterize the fallen world of *The Stranger*. Despite a tormenting sense of déjà vu, chronic forgetfulness of transcendent origins prevents the Poet from recognizing the beautiful Stranger when he meets her for a second time in the salon. Signs are everywhere to be read; the Poet tries to grasp the thread but fails. His tragic nonrecognition causes the Stranger to vanish, mysteriously returning to her starting place in the sky. The circle is closed; the end repeats the beginning.

The Stranger is composed in different tonalities of blue and azure, which are contrasted with the darkness of the night sky. Color is the dominant element in Blok's evocation of landscape, defining its mood. Blue, according to Goethe, arouses anxiety and nostalgia. For the fin de siècle it was the color of art and artists, of dreams and dreamers. Azure defines the sphere of beauty and the limitless world of the ideal. In establishing grotesque parallelism between disparate worlds, the Russian poet uses a mode that is pictorial and painterly.

The terrestrial and the supraterrestrial in *The Stranger* fail to find a common scenic language. Once traditional perspective and spatial coherence break apart, protocubist clashing planes replace narrative dramatic structure. According to the director and filmmaker Grigori Kozintsev, *The Stranger*'s three "Visions" reveal "the simultaneous existence of different spatial dimensions and the impossibility of reconciling one with the other."[22]

During the exceptionally snowy winter of 1907–8, Blok had been reading *The Birth of Tragedy,* as well as rereading Dostoyevsky; Nietzsche's concept of eternal recurrence informs the landscape, serving to generate horror at the aimlessness of existence and the senselessness of time. The play's entire meaning resides in the estranged, yet circular relationships of three spaces of the urban landscape—tavern, bridge, salon—where the endless, empty repetitions of everyday life are set against the bluish falling snow that covers both streets and characters beneath the circling stars in the eternity of night.

Zones of the Soul

Like Blok, Andrei Bely claims that Chekhov is more of a symbolist than Maeterlinck. In Chekhov's plays, Bely argues, reality splits apart, revealing the world beyond—a formulation that could be aptly applied to the plays of Blok or those of Bely himself.[23]

"The coming of the Antichrist under the mask of Christ" is the subject of Andrei Bely's two fragments of a planned mystery: *The Jaws of Night* (1898) and *He Who Has Come* (1903).[24] The "sensation of the abyss" is the hallmark of Bely's apocalyptic landscapes. Dread, doubt, and satanic laughter subvert joyous anticipation of the Second Coming. Before the glow of a new dawn comes the glacial darkness ushered in by the reign of the Antichrist, the appearance of false messiahs, and the return to primordial chaos. Here, the subterranean has been projected onto the entire cosmos.

In these two short fragments of Bely's planned Antichrist drama (which was to be his *Faust*), the entire universe—heavens above, hell below, earth poised precariously between—grows animate. Constellations and comets, sky, surf, wind, precious stones, and flowers—as well as sudden bursts of light creating strange epiphanies—express psychic states of spiritual illumination, and its opposite, deprivation of divine light. Through a display of visual and auditory effects, Bely evokes feelings of cosmic wonder and dread in the face of the boundless expanse of the universe.

Except for interminable waiting for the Redeemer—who may be no redeemer, who may never come, or who may already have come unnoticed—Bely's plays have no action. Their magical poetic texture consists of a symphony of shapes, colors, and sounds. Rather than working as a detachable background, the metaphysical landscape setting itself becomes the drama.

Jaws of Night is a drama of eschatological premonitions, played out in indeterminate time and murky interstellar space. Since the sun has been extinguished and all entities subjected to the power of negation, night and day are no longer distinguishable. Darkness prevails in this battle between spiritual enlightenment and benightedness; the action is condensed into the light given off by different objects and personalities. But all the signs are ambivalent, and the inability of both dramatis personae and audience to determine which are true luminosities and which deceptive will-o'-the-wisps results in agonizing dilemmas.

The opening stage directions paint a landscape of deep abysses and mysterious radiances.

> The corner of a plateau in the mountains, the last refuge of the Christians, cut off from the rest of the world by deep abysses. It is dark. The lace formed by the stars is pale and misty. To the right, the edge of a cypress grove. To the left, enormous rocks. The mountain plateau comes to an abrupt end in a steep precipice that plunges down to the depths.[25]

On a forbidding mountain plateau cut off from the rest of the world by a deep abyss, illuminated by the pale light of the moon, a band of Christians bewail the apparent extinction of the sun and await with dread, apprehension, and prayer the imminent attack of the "black hosts," which will herald the end of the world. The Christian women begin to glow with a mysterious incandescence as they approach the stone railing over the abyss. But it is the mysterious old prophet who grows illuminated and then loses his radiance. When he smiles, it "seems as if a sudden bolt of lightning had licked the mass of rocks." The cypresses whisper like murderers awaiting execution. When he rises up to oppose the evil forces, "Bright beams fly off his body and shafts of light stream forth from his illumined head."[26] The holy elder is multiplied throughout the sky. There appear, shining like fireflies or precious stones, luminous spots, each containing a venerable old man at their center. In a hallucinatory play of shapes, colors, and lights, luminous little flowers blossom and go out.

A mother begins to suspect that the old man has misled them and doomed their children to death and destruction with his magic spells. All are plunged into total darkness, and a voice full of despair is heard to cry, "Woe." A strong wind blows and the clump of cypresses moans like a host of souls in torment. Could the prophet, whose dried-up right hand emits a dry crackling, be the Antichrist?[27]

In *Notes of an Eccentric,* Bely locates the source of his Antichrist plays in a visionary landscape that he saw in church during Holy Week: "It was as if one wall of the church opened into the void. I saw the End (I don't know of what—my life or the world's), but it was as if the road of history rested upon two domes—upon a Temple; and crowds of people thronged toward it. To myself, I called the Temple I saw the 'Temple of Glory,' and it seemed to me that Antichrist was threatening this Temple. I ran out of the church like a madman. . . . In the evening, in my little room, I drafted the plan for a mystery drama."[28]

For his drama of the abyss, Bely envisages an arena expressive of the boundless expanses of the universe, a landscape that opens out onto infinity. In its cosmic locus, *Jaws of Night* stands midway between the allegorical wooded island of Maeterlinck's *The Blind* and the primeval chaos of Artaud's *Spurt of Blood.*

Pulsating intensities of light and the refraction of radiance become the dramatic action, replacing psychology and plot. The play abounds in strange optical effects. The Prophet passes his dazzling palm over the child's white hair, causing lilac-colored electric sparks to shoot forth. Sometimes the venerable old man grows dimmer and dimmer until, like the Cheshire Cat, he fades out except for a faint afterglow; sometimes his image becomes reduplicated in a whole series of tiny bubbles of light.

Luminous Little Flowers Blossom on the Ground
in Exploding Flashes of Light

In *Jaws of Night,* Bely creates a weather map of the mind. He gives the soul its own geography and topography, he assigns appropriate climate to the spiritual states of the psyche. In the character of the ambiguous prophet, Bely anticipates his future feelings about Rudolph Steiner, whose disciple he would become from 1912 to 1916. According to Bely, Steiner possessed a strange affinity with landscape, "according to which

he could 'multiply' himself so as to turn up everywhere, be present
everywhere." The Doctor—as Bely called Steiner—had many personalities (or doubles) and existed on all different climatic levels of the soul,
moving freely "in the zones of the tempests as well as on the flowering
meadows. . . . From the dimension of storms he threw lightning bolts, he
gathered flowers on the meadow."[29]

In composing his mystery as a theatrical synthesis of light, color,
movement, and shape, Bely drew inspiration from Arnold Böcklin's *Isle
of the Dead,* of which he wrote: "We are struck by the correspondence
among the human figure (enclosed in a white robe), the cliffs, the
cypresses and the dark, gloomy sky."[30] In *Jaws of Night* we encounter
just such a correspondence between figure and landscape, achieved
through the use of sound, movement, shape, and color. By multimedia
techniques, Bely—who believed that the human eye can never capture
the essential image—depicted what he called the "sound of space."[31]

An Island Theater in the Park

In Poland, where Maeterlinck's plays had first been staged in the 1890s,
the symbolist aesthetic was quickly absorbed and given a strongly political dimension. The joining of symbolist poetics with historical and
mythological themes in the service of national goals produced in the
plays of Stanisław Wyspiański a breadth and depth of dramaturgical
inventiveness scarcely foreseeable from the muted, quasi-abstract
Maeterlinckian model. While Maeterlinck's characters move slowly
amid an indirection of moods, half-shades, and nebulous anxieties; total
tragedy strikes Wyspiański's heroes like bolts of lightning. His protagonists from Polish history do not have time to "read"—or even "mis-
read"—the signs embedded in the landscape; totally possessed by the
hidden forces of destiny, they must immediately act out these imperatives and embrace their fate.

There is nothing vague in Wyspiański's notations of time or space.
In his "Dramatic Scenes" about the first great Polish uprising against
czarist oppression, *November Night,* the landscape corresponds with
strict topographical accuracy to existing locations, which, however, lose
their particularity and acquire the broadest mythic and political resonances. The time is the night of November 29, 1830, and the place is
Warsaw's Łazienki Park, where the uprising starts. The opposing forces
are headed by the Russian grand duke Constantine, governor general of
Poland, and the Polish Cadets Corps, who spearhead the rebellion. At the
same time a second set of characters is ever-present: the statues of Greek

gods and goddesses in the park who come down from their pedestals to direct the modern heroes in the reenactment of an eternal drama.[32]

The events and characters of the insurrection assume the lineaments of the ancient myth of Demeter and Persephone (the essential sacred drama advocated by the playwright and theorist of mysticism, Edouard Schuré). Through juxtaposition and syncretism, the nineteenth-century Polish soldiers become Greek warriors, playthings in the hands of the Homeric gods, and the 1830 uprising turns into an Eleusinian mystery of vegetation.

In his 1919 essay "The Collapse of Humanism," Blok talks of the two orders, the mundane and the musical. "There exist two times and two spaces; one historical, corresponding to the calendar, the other musical, escaping from all evaluation. The first time and the first space are invariably present in the civilized consciousness; we only live in the second time and the second space when we feel ourselves close to nature, when we abandon ourselves to the musical wave which emanates from the orchestra of the world."[33] In the best turn-of-the-century symbolist drama, these two times and two spaces coexist in creative tension. Inheritor of the symbolist legacy, Tadeusz Kantor would continue this type of cultural syncretism whereby different historical, mythical, and personal layers are conflated.

As a professional painter and the director/designer of a number of his own plays, Wyspiański was accustomed to working directly with light and shadow. His extensive stage directions transform his plays into theatrical scenarios and lighting scores, which utilize cinematic devices, including moving light projections. From his four years of artistic apprenticeship in Paris in the early 1890s, Wyspiański had grown familiar with early precinema and the technology for creating an illusion of moving pictures, from the magic lantern through Edison's kinetoscope and Lumière's cinematographe.[34]

Stage directions in Polish artist's work exist on an equal plane with the dramatic text. They are written in verse in the same poetic style as the dialogue and constitute a theatrical score that is to be enacted. The Aristotelian hierarchy is inverted; spectacle in Wyspiański is more important than plot or character.

In *November Night* the moment is once more night, a magical time of dreams, memories, and associations reaching back to the roots of consciousness. The principal place, to which the action constantly returns, is a windswept autumnal park where the conspirators meet to launch their ill-fated revolt. In this ominous setting, dead leaves—the ground cover of symbolist landscape (introduced by Maeterlinck in *Pelléas et*

Mélisande)—are given a speaking voice as they swirl under the feet of the doomed officers who will win no other laurels.

The nocturnal landscape itself undergoes striking metamorphosis. The desolate park becomes transformed into the borderland between Earth and Hades where the goddess Demeter says farewell to her daughter Persephone, who every year must descend into the underworld—only to return each spring, bringing hope of deliverance from pain and death. As the immortals converse, the two dialogues—human and divine—become intercut, the Polish cadets taking up the words of the mythic litany without realizing that they are entering into the occult world and reenacting the Eleusinian rites. The seasonal death of nature (and its longed-for resurrection)—embodied in the withered leaves—is the eternal mystery confronting the officers who await their destiny in the autumnal park.

In Wyspiański's visionary mythopoetic awareness, past times and present times, Greek myth and modern history coexist in an eternal moment. The park is now the underworld: the trees with their bare branches darkly outlined, the whirling leaves underfoot. Scene 9, occurring within this nether world setting, is a remarkable instance of symbolist metatheater. The action takes place before King Stanisław August's eighteenth-century outdoor theater located on an island in a small lake within the park. All the characters are either dead or immortals from the panoply of Greek gods. As Charon sails toward the island, his bark loaded with dead cadets being wafted to the other world, the deities of tragedy watch from the small stage.[35] The ancient funeral rites are celebrated in a theater-in-the-theater; high theatrical artifice is juxtaposed to the "natural" outdoor setting.

A new concept of staging follows from the premise advanced by symbolists like Wyspiański that the elements of decor (colors, shapes, light and shadow) are primary in the total theatrical experience. Only the dominant artist-director can organize these elements and give coherent form to such a painterly, pictorial theater.

Epilogue

The symbolist landscape—always in danger of imploding—was capable of considerable variation in shape and design, but it was inevitably drawn to blackness, because somber tonalities best represented states of mind. Speaking of his compositions done in charcoal, which he called his "noirs," the graphic artist and painter Odilon Redon said, "Black is the essential color. . . . Black should be respected. Nothing prostitutes it.

It does not please the eye and does not awaken sensuality. It is the agent of the spirit much more than the splendid color of the palette or of the prism."[36]

In 1907, Konstantin Stanislavsky, who felt that the Moscow Art Theatre had reached an impasse, sought a way out of the dead end of realism by experimenting with techniques of abstraction. In search of new theatrical forms, he created a black velvet background "which, like a piece of black paper, could give the stage the appearance of having only two dimensions, width and height, for with the presence of the black velvet, which would cover the whole stage, its sides, its ceiling and its floor, the third dimension would disappear entirely, and the velvet would pour itself into one plane. On such a tremendous black sheet one could draw in various paints and lights all that the human mind could conceive."[37]

Symbolist directors—like Meyerhold in his production of Maeterlinck's *Sister Beatrice* at Kommissarzhevskaya's Theatre in 1906—had already shown a preference for a scenic two-dimensionality that, like ancient icons, could evoke the imminent, eternal, and numinous. Contraction of perspective and flattening out of represented space resulted in stress on frontilization of image and suppression of detail. Flatness led to Byzantine incorporeality and decorativeness; characters were freed of fleshy solidity and commonplace manifestations of sex and personality. Lack of spatial recession imparted timelessness to the picture.

Leonid Andreyev's *Life of Man* proved to be the right play to test Stanislavsky's new methods of staging. Andreyev himself resisted categorization, refusing to be enrolled in any camp, but his best work, like *The Life of Man,* represented a powerful blending of symbolist techniques with naturalist assumptions about the human condition. The resulting pictures of man's existential isolation, in both society and the universe, lacked even a briefly glimpsed transcendence, but evoked a powerful Goyaesque atmosphere of the grotesque and macabre.

In act 1 the entire stage is plunged in "profound darkness;" in act 4 "Night looks in through the windows."[38] Because the life of man "can take place only in gloomy blackness, in deep and fearsome endlessness," Stanislavsky made his characters "appear unexpectedly on the forestage and disappear in the endless space of the darkness in the background."[39] In this fashion, the darkness of night became the principal compositional element in Stanislavsky's mise-en-scène. In his production of Andreyev's play, the Russian director realized Appia's ideal of the poet-musician painting his picture with light.

Landscape in symbolist drama is participatory, drawing performer, director, and designer into imaginative complicity that allows the collective enactment of inner states. Spectators too must make contributory acts. Writing of the Renaissance Neoplatonic pastoral, Richard Cody comments that landscape traditionally evokes less a place than a state of mind, leading into rather than out of the self-conscious mind—a reflexive process he calls "inscaping."[40]

The turn-of-the-century symbolists seem intent on retelling and revising Plato's parable of the cave, one of the earliest "landscapes of the mind." Superior to the real objects outside the cave, the shadowy figures on the wall are our best guides to a higher reality. The bright sun outside can be dispensed with. A system of projection by electric light casts the shadows eternally. The flowering of symbolist dramaturgy and the birth of cinema coincide.

The outer world, which naturalists had claimed could be fully known and accurately depicted, was revealed by the symbolists to be pure illusion—a veil of fleeting appearances behind which were hidden deeper truths. It was these inner worlds buried in the psyche that the symbolist playwrights sought to reveal.

Embarking upon voyages toward an unknown world lying outside everyday experience, these playwrights created a new time and new space rather than copy existing models. In this dramatic universe, seemingly odd-shaped and lacking in proportion to the untrained eye, consciousness met cosmos. Natural and supranatural intersected, merged, and dissolved. The stage became neither an imitation of the external world, nor a conventional playing area, but magical space. An extension of the human mind, such invented space was fluid and multilayered, existing along shifting planes and given to undulation and pulsation. In apparent violation of the law of theater that mandates only one unchanging point of observation between spectator and represented reality, magical space could accommodate close-ups and long shots at one and the same time, as well as two or more simultaneous actions, as in film or medieval mystery plays. Internal landscapes, revealing the creative powers of the individual soul, engulfed the stage, as boundaries between subjective and objective, self and universe were annihilated.

NOTES

1. William J. Berg, *The Visual Novel: Emile Zola and the Art of His Times* (University Park: Pennsylvania State University Press, 1992), 31–39.

2. Gustave Moreau, *Notebooks* IV, 20 in the Moreau Museum, quoted in Julius Kaplan, *Gustave Moreau* (Los Angeles: Los Angeles County Museum of Art, 1974), 35.

3. Villiers de l'Isle-Adam, *Axël*, ed. Pierre Mariel (Paris: La Colombe, Editions du Vieux Colombier, 1960), 213. English translation, *Axel*, trans. June Guicharnaud (Englewood Cliffs, N.J.: Prentice-Hall, 1970), 152.

4. *Axël*, 222; *Axel*, 159.

5. See Jean Pierrot, *L'Imaginaire décadent 1880–1900* (Paris: Presses Universitaires de France, 1977), 91–92.

6. *Axël*, 248; *Axel*, 182.

7. Nietzsche, *The Gay Science,* trans. Walter Kaufmann (New York: Vintage Books, 1974), 181. Goethe's *Faust,* Part II, act 1, ll. 1668–69, used by Villiers as the epigraph to book 3, chap. 1 of *The Future Eve.*

8. Villiers de l'Isle–Adam, *L'Eve future* (Paris: José Corti, 1977), 156. The English translation is called *Tomorrow's Eve,* trans. Robert Martin Adams (Urbana: University of Illinois, 1982). Maurice Ravel admired *The Future Eve* and planned to make it into an opera. It was adapted and staged in France in the 1980s.

9. For the sources of Villiers's novel, see Jacques Noiray, *Le Romancier et la machine: L'image de la machine dans le roman français (1850–1900),* vol. 2: *Jules Verne—Villiers de l'Isle Adam* (Paris: José Corti, 1982), 279–80.

10. For Villiers, Edison was the first cinematographer-magus who practiced the black arts with moving images. See Felicia Miller Frank, *The Mechanical Song: Women, Voice, and the Artificial in Nineteenth-Century French Narrative* (Stanford: Stanford University Press, 1995), 143.

11. Jean Duvignaud, *L'Almanach de l'Hypocrite* (Brussels: De Boek, 1990), 59–64.

12. A.-W. Raitt, *Villiers de l'Isle Adam et le mouvement symboliste* (Paris: José Corti, 1965), 384–88.

13. "J'ai entendu craquer les feuilles mortes . . ." Maeterlinck, *Pelléas et Mélisande,* act 4, scene 4, in *Théâtre,* vol. 2 (Brussels: P. Lacomblez, 1904), 90.

14. Maeterlinck, *Pelléas et Mélisande,* act 3, scene 3 (2:56). In the standard English translation, Richard Hoving confuses *lézards* (lizards) with *lézardes* (cracks): "Have you noticed those lizards on the walls and pillars of the vaults? . . . There are strange lizards in many of the walls."

15. Katherine Worth, *The Irish Drama of Europe from Yeats to Beckett* (Atlantic Highlands, N.J.: Humanities Press, 1978), 29.

16. Marcel Postic, *Maeterlinck et le symbolisme* (Paris: A.-G. Nizet, 1970), 44.

17. James McFarlane, "Intimate Theatre: Maeterlinck to Strindberg," in *Modernism,* ed. Malcolm Bradbury and James McFarlane (Harmondsworth: Penguin, 1976), 516–17.

18. Avril Pyman, *The Life of Aleksandr Blok* (Oxford: Oxford University Press, 1979–80), 1:153, 255, 304, 2:174.

19. Blok, "O Drame," in *Sobranie Sochinenii,* vol. 5 (Moscow: Pravda, 1971), 152.

20. Blok, *Neznakomka,* in *Sobranie Sochinenii,* vol. 4 (Moscow: Pravda, 1971), 78. English translation, *The Stranger,* in *Doubles, Demons, and Dreamers,*

trans. Daniel Gerould (New York: Performing Arts Journal Publications, 1985), 154.

21. Blok, *Neznakomka*, 80, 83, 84; *The Stranger*, 156–17.

22. Grigori Kozintsev, *King Lear: The Space of Tragedy*, trans. Mary Mackintosh (Berkeley and Los Angeles: University of California Press, 1977), 98.

23. For a discussion of Bely on Chekhov, see Laurence Senelick, *Russian Dramatic Theory from Pushkin to the Symbolists* (Austin: University of Texas Press, 1981), xli–xlii.

24. Bely, *Na Rubezhe dvukh stoletii* (On the brink of two centuries) (Moscow: Zemlya i Fabrika, 1930; rpt. Letchworth: Bradda, 1966), 401–2.

25. Bely, *Past' nochi, Zolotoye runo* (1906), 62. English translation, *Jaws of Night*, in *Doubles, Demons, and Dreamers*, 171.

26. Bely, *Past' nochi*, 66, 68; *Jaws of Night*, 174, 177.

27. Although there is no evidence that *Jaws of Night* was ever produced, it could only have been staged by the use of the most advanced lighting technology. The writing itself indicates that Bely was aware of the special effects that could be achieved by electrical lighting and had incorporated some of these into his drama; more particularly, he seems to have emulated the magic of early trick films.

28. Bely, quoted in Konstantin Mochulsky, *Andrei Bely: His Life and Works*, trans. Nora Szalavitz (Ann Arbor, Mich.: Ardis, 1977), 24. The passage appears in *Zapiski chudaka* (Notes of an eccentric), written in 1912 and first published in 1922.

29. Andrei Bely, "The Man, Rudolf Steiner," trans. Maria St. Goar, *Journal for Anthroposophy* 25 (spring 1977): 52–53. Bely's reminiscences of Steiner, written in 1928–29 and first published as *Verwandlung des Lebens* (Basel: Zbinden Verlag, n.d.), appeared in Russian as *Vospominaniya o Steinere* (Paris: La Presse Libre, 1982).

30. Bely, "Formy iskusstva," in *Simvolizm kak miroponimaniye* (Moscow: Respublika, 1994), 105. Originally published in *Mir Iskusstva*, 1902. For Bely's high estimate of Böcklin, see Aleksandr Vasil'evich Lavrov, *Andrei Bely v 1900-e Gody: Zhizn' i literaturnaya deyatel'nost'* (Moscow: Novoye Literaturnoye Obosreniye, 1995), 62–63 n. 108.

31. Bely, *Na rubezhe*, 169–70; "Magiya slov," in *Simvolizm*, 430.

32. Adam Grzymała-Siedlecki, *O twórczości Wyspiańskiego* (Cracow: Wydawnictwo Literackie, 1970), 60–62.

33. Blok, "Krushenie gumanizma," in *Sobranie Sochinenii*, 5:460.

34. Antonina Maria Terlecka, *Stanisław Wyspiański and Symbolism*, Ex Antemurale, 27–28 (Romae, 1985–86), 110.

35. Grzymała-Siedlecki, *O twórczości Wyspiańskiego*, 163–66.

36. Odilon Redon, *To Myself: Notes on Life, Art, and Artists*, trans. Mira Jacob and Jeanne L. Wasserman (New York: George Braziller, 1986), 103. The entry is dated January 1913, for a lecture given in Holland on the occasion of an exhibition of his works. In *Downcast Eyes: The Denigration of Vision in Twentieth-Cen-*

tury French Thought (Berkeley and Los Angeles: University of California Press, 1993), Martin Jay offers an analogous argument that since the symbolists, there has been a mounting current of anti-ocularcentrism in French perceptions of the world.

37. Constantin Stanislavsky, *My Life in Art,* trans. J. J. Robbins (New York: Meridian, 1957), 490–91.

38. Leonid Andreyev, *Zhizn' cheloveka,* in *P'esy* (Moscow: Sovetskii Pisatel', 1991), act 1, 93, act 4, 120.

39. Stanislavsky, *My Life in Art,* 494–95.

40. Richard Cody, *The Landscape of the Mind: Pastoralism and Platonic Theory in Tasso's Aminta and Shakespeare's Early Comedies* (Oxford: Clarendon, 1969), 45–51.

15

The Sonic Landscapes of
Robert Ashley

Arthur J. Sabatini

> With opera there's always some notion of landscape. It
> seems to me that the sound, that is the verbal meaning and
> the sound of the opera, besides evoking character also
> evokes landscape . . . I think that when you put characters
> in a landscape, that's opera.

—ROBERT ASHLEY[1]

For nearly five decades, Ashley has been creating music theater performances that revolve around stories of American lives in specific places and landscapes. A composer and performer, his uniquely theatricalized operas and other music/video performance art represent landscape in relation to its sonic, visual, historical, social, and allegorical dimensions. Ashley accomplishes this through a compositional style and an intermediated performance practice that "evokes" landscapes thematically, sensually, and conceptually. The stagings and narratives within his operas elucidate his ideas about the rhythmicity of landscapes and how they "effect the action of the perceiving mind," leading us toward a sense of our "connectedness."[2]

Thematically, the experiences of Ashley's characters are inseparable from the landscapes they inhabit and traverse. Their very consciousness, Ashley intimates, is partially composed by the motions and vibrations of everyday life in farmlands, river valleys, or the desert. These characters retain vestigial memories both of how their regions evolved and how natural phenomena and forms of knowing implicate each other: "[P]rincipal events, like majestic mountains *in the landscape* / Of time, are marks of origin *or destination* / For the form we take now," postulates a character in Ashley's *Perfect Lives*.[3] In this sense, although the location of his work is topographically the Americas, Ashley's texts and music inevitably refer to imaginary landscapes in ancient and mystical traditions.

When he speaks of putting "characters in a landscape," Ashley means both the character/performers and those who are in the theater or concert hall. In performance, the singers and musicians, led by Ashley, tell (that is, sing) long, multivoiced and intricately linked narrations accompanied by live music, electronic audio mixes, and, since the 1970s, onstage video monitors. The immediacy of performances, especially when augmented by video, situates the experience of his work in a "landscape of the moment," which is our mediated world. Ashley creates an experience that leads audiences toward acknowledging that outside of the theater—close by—there are parks, roadways, and towns where these stories are happening.

Ashley's work is not conventionally developmental or linear. He creates dense technologically enhanced environments on stage. Perceptually, audiences selectively switch focus from music to voiced text to moving images, then construct the relationships among all the elements in the mise-en-scène. In this respect, as Gertrude Stein recognized, theater and landscapes are analogous.

> The landscape has its formation and as after all a play has to have formation and be in relation one thing to the other thing and as the story is not the thing as any one is always telling something then the landscape not moving but always being in relation.[4]

Ashley's attention to landscape can appear Steinian, but his ideas and artistic practices derive from heterogeneous sources. He has been a figure in experimental performance world since the 1960s, and his work inevitably reflects currents in theories of culture, language, and consciousness. Landscape, a term he has always used, is fundamental to his aesthetic. In each phase of his development, landscape comes into focus in relation to musical forms, experimental performance practices, and advances in media and technology.

In what follows, I will present Ashley's "notions" of landscape, with the intent of framing how his thought has progressively expanded. I refer to his writings, librettos, audio and video recordings, and interviews and briefly discuss the four musical works of *In Memoriam* (1963), and the video opera, *Music with Roots in the Aether* (1976). The last part of the essay centers on a series of large-scale operas, which I refer to as the *Perfect Lives* trilogy. Begun in the late 1970s, the *Perfect Lives* trilogy is an integrated twenty-four-hour production in various parts that traces the lives of Americans from the East Coast through the Midwest to the Hispanic Southwest. It represents Ashley's richest meditation on music, performance, and landscape.[5]

Ashley's thoughts on language, consciousness, music, and land-scapes are elaborate. For him, music is a trope for perception in general and how we understand space and temporality in particular. That is, sound, as wave forms passing through landscapes, is recognized as significant by humans, something we often name "music." As the Narra-tor in *Perfect Lives* explains, "Endless thunder on the rolling plains comes back / To us in town like news / It's bigger than we thought. The pressure drops . . . Wyoming to the Mississippi" (*PL*, 79). In other words, not unlike Stein, Ashley speculates that the phenomenology of thought is entangled with landscape and environmental conditions and events.

Characters in Ashley's work habitually discuss and reference Amer-ican geography and history. They are equally consumed with reflections on mythical and imaginary landscapes. In *Improvement (Don Leaves Linda)*, Linda sings about "Some islands / GONE NOW," by which she means the lost continent of Atlantis. Other characters imagine them-selves in relation to historical figures or places (e.g., Giordano Bruno, the Sargasso Sea). Characters' sense of place is often keyed to distinctive landscapes. "She goes down to The River when she can . . . The Holy River where the notes came up from New Orleans," thinks Rodney, in *Perfect Lives* (*PL*, 75). With Ashley, this allusiveness and imagery implies that human beings live through repeating cycles of actions in places that have similar landscapes. (In the concluding section, I discuss this as sonic allegory.)

The human voice and language-as-music are Ashley's primary com-positional materials. In performance, solo voices may begin a song or narration but, often, other voices join in chorus. Voices are electroni-cally amplified, layered, or treated. Stylistically, Ashley's texts are con-versational and emphasize the American vernacular. Ashley writes the texts himself, and, although they range from anecdotal remarks to epical monologues to choral segments, he simply calls them songs. For each production, the songs—and music and images—accumulate. Like James Joyce or William Faulkner, Ashley presents a complex interweaving of narratives and verbal shiftings from direct to indirect discourse. On stage, performers gesture and occasionally change positions, but "action" is narrated, while video monitors show previously recorded dramatic sequences.

Ashley draws on and has contributed to performance concepts and practices common to the experimental theater tradition. He often relies on the same core performers, and the set locations of his works are invariably represented in live performances and on recordings.[6] Impor-tantly, when published as texts and books, musical notation is omitted, and Ashley's librettos typographically resemble long poems or play-scripts. These publications, along with the visual material accompanying his recordings are, in effect, cartographic signifiers of the landscapes that concern him. The endpapers of *Perfect Lives: An Opera* are white-on-black road maps of Illinois and Iowa; the composite photo on the CD for *Improvement (Don Leaves Linda)* depicts a woman in the foreground of a treeless, high-desert landscape. Thus, while the history and landscape of America are the source of his works thematically, the collaborative performance situations he participates in, and state of technologies required to represent place and geography, contribute to the design of his productions and related work.[7]

Ashley is well known for musing on subjects as diverse as Renaissance cosmology and theatrical practice, Tibetan spirituality, and architecture. He is mindful of how music and landscape are fundamental to the representational processes and historiography of opera. Recalling Wagner, his music-theater is mythic, albeit with a range of expression that is more localized and idiomatic (that is, in the way that the Mississippi differs from the Rhine). In sum, Ashley's songs, video images, and performances repeatedly insist that opera—not just theater—is, to use his term and his irony, *perfect* for imaginatively representing social life, transhistoric consciousness, and landscape. This aesthetic proposition embraces issues of perception and epistemology as well as an artistic gloss on allegorization, occult knowledge, and mystical paths to understanding.

Of Places and Landscapes in New Music, 1950–1970

Ashley (b. 1930) studied at the University of Michigan in the 1950s. By then, aspiring composers were investigating the legacies of Charles Ives, Henry Cowell, and Harry Partch.[8] There was also constant experimentation with magnetic tape and electronic sound technologies. Influenced by John Cage (*Silence* appeared in 1960), doors and ears were open for music and "organized sound" to be heard, seen, and played in nontraditional musical environments and outdoors.

In Ann Arbor, Ashley and his friends associated with a multimedia artist named Milton Cohen. He encouraged production of extended events in what was known as "The Milton Cohen Space Theater."[9] Eventually, Ashley and others organized an annual new music and performance festival called the ONCE FESTIVALS (1961–69).[10] The counterparts to the ONCE FESTIVALS were happenings, Fluxus performances, and the art scene in the San Francisco renaissance. All featured dance and theater where American artists often celebrated regionalism and local traditions.

Ashley, a pianist and composer, was attracted to electronic sound and all American musical forms. Music, he said, "had to be stories from your culture. I came to think of music as being a metaphor for stories— local stories, *real* stories, images from your life."[11] Growing up in a small Michigan town, some of the earliest stories he recalls were about local jazz musicians and Big Band era radio. While many Big Bands had national reputations, there were "territory bands" who played nearer to their homes or purposely cultivated the musical styles of cities such as Kansas City or St. Louis.[12] Musicians, like those in Count Basie's bands, were encouraged to convey stories of places and social life. Popular swing numbers had landscape connotations: *Down South Camp Meeting* and *Chattanooga Choo-Choo*. Duke Ellington, who said he composed with landscapes in mind, wrote pieces titled *East St. Louis Toodle-oo* and the Harlem-inspired *Happy Go Lucky Local*. He added *Serenade to Sweden,* the *Far East Suite,* and more after traveling abroad. Ellington was keenly conscious of his musicians' lives. His band, Ashley remarks, was "a collection of characters" (*PL,* 186).

Throughout his career, Ashley has conscientiously re-created a sense of place and personal musical identity through compositional practice. His scores and rehearsal process demand that musicians create "characters." For example, two characters in *Perfect Lives* are musicians. One is Raoul de Noget and the other is Buddy, "The World's Greatest Piano Player." Raoul wears wraparound sunglasses and maintains the detached air of a cool, urban jazz musician. Buddy, described as a Mexican or "brown fellow," dresses in a nightclub-style spangled sports jacket, and his playing is flamboyant and emotionally charged. As for the other characters in *Perfect Lives,* the awareness of the landscape informs who they are. In the first moments of *Perfect Lives,* Ashley sings, "these are stories about some of the people in the Corn Belt, or on it." The phrase "or on it" is represented in the *Perfect Lives* video imagery by an animated graphic of an open road surrounded by farmlands, as seen from the front seat of a car or pickup truck. The hypnotic, repetitive musical material conveys the sense that the stories will unfold with the minimalist stillness of the landscape of farmlands and cornfields in (or on) the American Midwest. By implication, the folks of *Perfect Lives* are as low-key, orderly, and subtle as their landscape.

Some of Ashley's earliest compositions are centered on social and geohistorical themes. He wrote pieces titled *Christopher Columbus Crosses to the New World in the Nina, the Pinta, and the Santa Maria Using Only Dead Reckoning and a Crude Astrolabe* (1959); *The Fourth of July* (1960); and, *Kitty Hawk: An Antigravity Piece* (1964). Rather than connote visual images of specific landscapes, these works are conceptual. They argue that music and performance in America are experienced with a consciousness that is conditioned by the country's' history, regions, and inevitable technologization. Thus, *The Fourth of July* employs continuous electronic sound punctuated by errant noise. Like the music of Ives that references the outdoors (e.g., *Central Park in the Dark*), *The Fourth of July* erupts with voices and the sonic textures of American celebrations.[13] As for Columbus's journey and the Spanish in the Americas, Ashley's *Now Eleanor's Idea* relates the history of the continent from an Hispanic perspective.

Ashley's early work included live performances, music, electronic sound, sets, and slide and film projections. With them, he and his collaborators intended to demonstrate that the chamber music and concert hall tradition inherited from Europe is artificial for American audiences. The acoustics of America's varied landscapes construct ways of listening and shared cultural experiences that require different musical environments for performances. Being from the Midwest, Ashley apprehends America by looking westward, across the Great Plains and toward the Southwest and California. Viewed this way, the sonic and musical underpinnings suitable for audiences are, arguably, not to be found in urban and European-influenced musical forms or orchestrations. Instead, Americans favor sounds in relation to open landscapes and the informal events that occur in them. (Similarly, Ives championed the sounds of picnics and parades.) Music, for Ashley, emerges from people rather than formal institutions like symphony orchestras. In *Perfect Lives*, after the Sheriff and his wife converse, the narrator comments: "such as the music is, such are the people of the commonwealth" (*PL*, 104). A note on setting indicates that the "landscape is mainly manmade, and the small town (gossip) always symmetrical" (*PL*, xvi).

Whether as gossip, stories, or songs, performances of oral texts can be shaped by natural phenomena and the physical properties of landscapes. Speaking of an episode in *Music with Roots in the Aether*, Ashley remarks, "You speak differently in a strong wind"—or in the sunlight, which is important to Ashley. In many scenes, images of the sun are pronounced.[14] *Perfect Lives* begins in the morning and ends precisely at "Nautical twilight, until the sun is up to twelve degrees below the horizon" (*PL*, 146). But the sun, or a river or mountain, are not merely iconic for Ashley. He is concerned with effects on consciousness. "Imagine the great curved plane, the plains, / And all its markings," a character says about the spacious Midwest farmlands. Accordingly, the music contains seemingly disconnected electronic material. "*Perfect Lives* is just the great Midwest, and no story has a beginning or an end. It's all digressions," Ashley comments, adding that midwesterners' speech is characterized by brief utterances (*PL,* 172).[15]

Ashley's views are similar to those of musicologist Wilfrid Mellers, who assesses the history of American music in relation to landscape. In *Music in a New Found Land,* Mellers discusses the Puritans, who "although at first did no more than sing the music they sang at home, they increasingly came to sing it in ways that were changed by the wilderness."[16] Puritan services included unison singing, but at home and, presumably, outdoors, the tunes were harmonized. Naturally, Mellers continues, "as the traditional skills were forgotten in the urgent necessity of keeping [the songs] alive, the music began to acquire some of the barbarity of the land." However, by building on technical mistakes, aided by forgetting, untrained singers laid the groundwork for new musical forms. Thus, as Mellers suggests, these "were not mistakes at all, since they were the creative manifestations of their identities" (7). Of course, it took well into the twentieth century for American composers to break free from European influences on tonality or even consider African, Asian, and other non-European music.

For Ashley, historical and social consciousness are inseparable from the experience of landscapes. Musical form and a reception aesthetics follow from geographic characteristics as perceived by individuals and the socius. Thinking about these issues in the 1960s led Ashley to compose works based on European musical forms: the quartet, concerto, symphony, and opera. He began with the assumption that Americans were aware of current events and political ideology in eighteenth- and nineteenth-century Europe. What, he asked, were the social and historical conditions present in North America during this time, and how would these musical forms be interpreted in such a radically different landscape?[17]

Ashley's response became four musical "portraits" based on the lives of men from diverse environments. He wanted to illustrate how their actions could be conceived as representative of disparate musical forms. The works are *In Memoriam . . . Esteban Gomez, In Memoriam . . . John Smith, In Memoriam . . . Crazy Horse,* and *In Memoriam . . . Kit Carson.* Esteban Gomez, Ferdinand Magellan's chief officer, acted like a string quartet's dominant member by coordinating the courses of four ships at sea. John Smith was an individualist who, Ashley imagines, had to function as a concerto soloist in contest with large social institutions (like the orchestra). By contrast, Crazy Horse acted as a "conductor." He conducted the great orchestral forces of American Indian tribes in a multisectioned symphony of resistance. Kit Carson's life played itself out as opera. Each nontraditionally notated composition allows for ample freedom for musicians. Thus, the decision-making processes required in order to creatively structure and realize each performance becomes analogous to the social interaction demanded in the context of the specific geohistorical places.

The four *In Memoriam* works move from the Northeast to the Plains to the Southwest. The series is slyly provocative. Without titles, it is unlikely that a listener could determine that a composition is about John Smith or Crazy Horse. Nor could musicians or listeners visually reference New England or Arizona on the basis of the sonic material alone. Arguably, the same could be said of any music that attempts to describe places. Beethoven's *Eroica* Symphony, for example, follows the triumphs of Napoleon through France to the streets of Paris. But such a journey could only be understood with both culturally shared geographical knowledge and an awareness of musical conventions. This is exactly Ashley's point. American music needs its own shared vocabulary and conventions. Toward that end, Ashley carefully selects the terms to describe his work. He calls the *In Memoriam* series *portraits* and *landscapes*. Within a few years, he adopts terms such as *dramatic music* and *music theater*, then, simply, *opera*.

Musical Portraits and Opera for Television: The 1970s

Ashley synthesized his ideas about music, theater, technology, and landscape through the 1970s. During that period, experimental performance was often "site-specific" and intent on integrating sonic, physical, or environmental qualities of places. John Cage's "general approach was to define a 'territory' and use all of the sounds within that territory as material for a composition."[18] Cage's *Birdcage* (1972), for example, used bird songs to define the performing space. Composers also explored the resonant frequency of spaces or, as in Ashley's *Wolfman,* tested the effects (and politics) of extreme amplification.

Ashley, like many artists, researched sources and artistic genres that could be definitively American. Like William Carlos Williams or Charles Olson, he traced the geographies and mythic histories of America's coasts. With attention to musical nuances, acoustics, and architecture, he examined regional accents, male and female voices, and idiosyncratic singing styles. In the spirit of the folk revival, he considered country music. Keyboardist "Blue" Gene Tyranny notes that the ONCE artists had a "fascination with the 'deep' culture of the States, and the states in people as being representative of various ancient cultures." Ashley's *Perfect Lives* trilogy had its beginnings, Tyranny recalls, in pieces like *In Never Changing Light (Dreams of Ancient Californians)*.[19]

Building on the *In Memoriam* series, Ashley developed his concept of "musical portraiture" by using video as a musical medium in order to present the voices of actual persons in specific landscapes. The result was *Music with Roots in the Aether*, a fourteen-hour "music theater piece in color video." It is based on interview-like conversations with Ashley and seven composers, including Philip Glass, Pauline Oliveros, and David Behrman. Each section, which also features a musical performance, is titled, "Landscape with . . ." The composers and Ashley meet in landscapes selected to inform, influence, if not guide their conversations. In order to accent environmental effects and the fundamental importance of place in musical processes, the camera runs continuously.

In one landscape, Ashley and Terry Riley sit outside Riley's farm in northern California's Sierra Nevada. Riley, who grew up in the region, remarks on his spiritual connection to its sounds. In another episode, Gordon Mumma plays an amplified cross-cut saw in an amusement park at dawn.

Although landscape is not the sole theme in every interview, questions about place are repeatedly asked, or implicitly staged. Composer Alvin Lucier, for example, stands in a canoe and practices casting with a fly-fishing rod. His movements create fluctuations in pitches generated by an oscillator. During an exchange on landscape, technology, and sound, Lucier's response to Ashley is the following:

> I don't think of technology as technology. I think of it as landscape. We're born and brought up in a landscape, and there's not much I can do about the fact that there are EEG amplifiers. . . . [A] composer in the nineteenth century or in any other century is talking about the landscape that he's in—the trees and the poetry—I'm just doing that.[20]

Music with Roots in the Aether has been screened in installation format and broadcast on European television. In program notes, Ashley comments that "the visual style for showing the music being made became the 'theater' (the stage) for the interviews." Stein might have agreed. She always wondered about "the question which comes first or which is first, reading or hearing or seeing a play."[21]

Operas for Stage and Television:
Perfect Lives *from 1978 to 2000*

"In my mind music and television are the perfect couple," Ashley wrote about the time he began, *Perfect Lives: an opera for television. Perfect Lives* was conceived as a live musical performance with video projections and multiple monitors. Begun in the 1970s, the trilogy, Ashley says, attempts to represent "the history of our consciousness as Americans." Sonically, narratively, and topographically the landscape of the *Perfect Lives* trilogy is specific to North America. Images of landscapes are visible both in on-stage videos and through lighting and minimal set design (boulders and cacti appear in *Now Eleanor's Idea*). For Ashley, the North American landscape excited the imaginings of early European settlers. It also incites and evokes acts of memory of actual, mythic, and transhistoric locales for all inhabitants or travelers. "Miami (Cuba)/Chicago (Germany)/Hollywood (Aztlan)" characters chant in *Improvement (Don Leaves Linda)*. Within this framework, and throughout *Perfect Lives,* American places also become a reference point for Ashley's larger metaphysics and allegorical design. The Mississippi River, for example, corresponds to the Nile; the Tennessee Valley Dam is likened to the pyramids. For Ashley, similar landscapes (valleys, deserts) affect human perception and actions in analogous ways. "People of the river," he says, think more or less alike. Moreover, Ashley, as I will explain, draws on the precepts of Renaissance Neoplatonism and selects particular landscapes to illustrate the "connectedness" of human consciousness.

As landscape is a prominent theme in the *Perfect Lives* trilogy, allusions to places are omnipresent visually on stage and in song throughout performances. Farmlands, highways, and horizons appear in video sequences, often on multiple monitors. The stage in *Now Eleanor's Idea* is divided by a winding road. Furthermore, the overarching story of *Perfect Lives* invites the audience to envision a journey across North America. The music conveys a sense of being transported, as if the audience were sitting in a car or train compartment. The electronic drone, 72 beats per minute tempo, extended modal patterning, and repetitive piano figures throughout *Perfect Lives* contribute to this effect.

In performance, Ashley strives for dreamlike settings that suggest the American surreal: Edward Hopper, Flash Gordon, Elvis, and Robert Wilson. His crisp, stylized mise-en-scène becomes oddly comic at moments. Characters, wearing shiny outfits or flowing dresses, appear like glossy magazine images "staged" or pasted onto the landscape. The singers are vocally expressive and lighting is designed to underscore shifts in the musical structure or texture, rather than theatrical movement. "Droll and detached" are words reviewers have used to describe performances. During its most intense moments, Friedrich Kittler's description of Wagner's operas as "acoustic hallucinations" is apt.[22]

Each opera in the *Perfect Lives* trilogy revolves around the experiences of ordinary Americans whose actions, relationships, and inner lives quietly reverberate in their own landscapes. Among other places, there is an Illinois town, highways in the Southwest, the New Mexico desert, and a college campus in California. As in Wagner's Ring Cycle, stories overlap and episodes are retold, both in musical and video images. Interestingly, Gertrude Stein's observation about her landscape plays elucidates the interwoven patterning of *Perfect Lives*. She wrote,

> Something is always happening, anybody knows a quantity of stories of people's lives that are always happening . . . In the country it is perfectly extraordinary how many complicated dramas go on all the time.[23]

The *Perfect Lives* trilogy is in three parts, the last of which is divided into separate operas based on different characters' lives in the Southwest. The operas are *Atalanta (Acts of God), Perfect Lives,* and *Now Eleanor's Idea. Now Eleanor's Idea* is a tetralogy that includes *Improvement (Don Leaves Linda), Foreign Experiences,* and *Now Eleanor's Idea.*

The elaborate and convoluted plot of *Perfect Lives* unfolds gradually. Ashley and four to seven singers deliver lengthy songs. As in epic poetry, action is simultaneously narrated, explained, and analyzed. There is little dialogue, although some song sequences include responses or choral commentaries. The songs have the texture of psychonarrations, and, on the video tape, multiple image systems amplify, metaphorize, and supplement the sung texts.[24] One monitor, for example, may show a single tractor in a field while another pans a downtown street and a third displays an aerial view of the earth. The imagery is not all literal. Animation, graphic inserts, documentary footage, and electronically altered tintings appear. Thematically, these images further inform and pluralize the realm of "connections" that contribute to the cosmos, both real and imaginary, that Ashley constructs.

Summarizing the trilogy can elucidate how Ashley elaborates his conception of landscape. *Atalanta (Acts of God)* consists of "anecdotes, or moral fables" by three men who sing to the mythical huntress Atalanta. The men are Max, inspired by the surrealist Max Ernst, Bud, the be-bop pianist, Bud Powell, and Ashley's uncle, Willard, who is referred to as a "shaman storyteller." The second opera, *Perfect Lives,* is a seven-part comedy about small-town life. Several stories are intertwined, at the center of which Gwyn, a bank teller, and her sweetheart, Ed, elope while the town is diverted by a phony bank robbery. During the "robbery," two musicians visit the town and a flying saucer hovers in the bank. The aliens in the saucer, coincidentally, are related to Max, Bud, Willard, and Atalanta's race. Offhandedly, we learn that they may be responsible for the mystical, life-transforming experiences of all the female bank tellers.

The last opera, *Now Eleanor's Idea,* recounts the stories of the female tellers, as each one of them quits and travels westward. In *Improvement (Don Leaves Linda),* Linda is left by her husband, Don, "at a roadside turnoff vista somewhere in the Southwest." She reflects on her life and incidents in airports, European cities, and, on the lost continent of Atlantis. In the libretto, the imagery of the opera is described in one word, "Landscape." *Foreign Experiences* takes place in the Southwest and on a campus in El Dorado (i.e., California). In *Now Eleanor's Idea,* Eleanor moves to New Mexico, becomes a television broadcaster, and develops a close relationship with the local Chicano low-rider community.[25]

Ashley often discusses the correlations between song, storytelling, and landscape. The *Perfect Lives* trilogy begins, he says, with a mythic and European reference system. In *Atalanta (Acts of God),* the anecdotal songs are remembrances by characters who live or have lived in Europe. The setting then advances to the Midwest for *Perfect Lives.* Americans, Ashley says, crossed

> the Appalachians. And when you come out the other side, you come down into the valley of the Midwest. You actually detach from anecdotal history. Realistically, you *lose* it. You can't keep telling the story about coming from Germany if you live in Illinois. You can be German, you can be Swedish, but if you say that you are, everyone laughs at you because you have lost it by coming across these mountains. There is a long flat place, which is *Perfect Lives.* (PL, 171)

The next site of passage for Americans are the Rocky Mountains and, then, you arrive in California. There, Ashley contends, you feel sadness.

> You can jet-set all around L.A., you can go to the great restaurants, and drive eighty-thousand-dollar cars, and you feel this

Atalanta (Acts of God), by Robert Ashley, Walker Art Center, Minneapolis, 1985. (Photo courtesy of Performing Artservices, Inc.)

sadness in your mind. Because you are here to stay. You aren't cut off from Berlin, you aren't cut off from the great civilizations of Europe, but you're cut off from Chicago, you're cut off from New York. The last four operas, *Now Eleanor's Idea*, are all about that feeling. . . . The thing that saves it is when you get to L.A. you meet the guys who came around the other way. The Spanish people. (*PL*, 171–72)

For me, the significance of these observations—as well as those on language, acoustics, and consciousness—is that they inform Ashley's artistic practice and provide clues about his intentions and tone.

In what follows, I want to isolate a prominent feature of Ashley's landscapes, the road, and explore it in relation to the mise-en-scène, themes, and allegory of the *Perfect Lives* trilogy. The road is a recurrent textual trope and visual image in Ashley's operas. Roads go by many names: paths, courses, tracks, passages, streets, lanes. Roads lead everywhere and nowhere. They are integral to our maps, both printed and

Video image from *Perfect Lives,* by Robert Ashley.

mental. In literature and theater, roads can be cited as grand metaphors ("the journey of life") and in relation to specific cultural places. The setting for *Waiting for Godot* is "A country road. A tree." Jack Kerouac's *On the Road* incited a generation to travel on Route 66.

But roads are more than signifiers of pilgrimages or transitions. In "Roads Belong in the Landscape," geographer John Brinckerhoff Jackson insists that "they are places."[26] Roads are markers of commerce, borders, ideology, and technological presence (e.g., telephone poles and powerlines). Roads are sites of work and leisure. Railroads, racetracks, and the information superhighway are types of roads.

In the *Perfect Lives* trilogy, roads are indispensable to the narrative, character's lives, and the operatic structure. After each manifestation of a road, it accrues ever denser significations. Roads reflect cultural, historical, and personal values. They also become portentous sites for Ashley's allegory of the repeating cycle of human actions. Thus, in *Atalanta (Acts of God),* the mythos of the road and its relation to civilizing impulses is established. In *Perfect Lives,* roads leading in and out of the small town define the characters' lives. The road becomes crucial for consideration of social and marital arrangements in *Improvement (Don Leaves Linda)*. More complexly, a mystical revelation in *Foreign Experiences* happens on a desolate road. Finally, roadways are central to the lives of the Chicano Low Rider community in *Now Eleanor's Idea.*

The ur-road for Ashley is the race course on which, in the Greek myth, Atalanta ran her famous and curious race. Atalanta, a virgin huntress, lived in the wild. She rebuffed her father's attempt to arrange marriage for her by agreeing to wed a man who could outrun her in a foot race. Those who lost were killed. A judge, Hippomenes, fell in love with Atalanta and decided to race her. He plotted with Aphrodite to drop three golden apples on the ground during the contest, and, as we know, Atalanta was diverted by the apples and Hippomenes won.[27] Ashley, like some scholars, interprets the story in terms of its implications for loss of wilderness and the domestication of women. As important, for him, is the geometrical shape of the race course, which marks the natural landscape either through a straight line or circular or oval track. Inscribing patterns on the land or dividing it into parcels, Ashley notes, is fundamental to such civilizing processes as farming, architecture, and the demarcation of the polis from the wild.

Here and elsewhere, Ashley's connections are elliptical, but fascinating. For the Boetians, Atalanta was a goddess of vegetation. As recorded in Hesiod's *Works and Days,* their region experienced a conflict over government encroachment. Protracted wars were fought over "the subdivision of lands, the dispossession of small landowners, and the progressive indebtedness of the peasants."[28] Ashley incorporates this sense of conflict in episodes in *Atalanta (Acts of God)*.

Willard's songs in *Atalanta (Acts of God)* describe an imaginary conversation between "Miss Atalanta and the Tennessean." The allusion is to controversies surrounding the building of the Tennessee Valley Authority dam in America during the 1930s. At the time, southern "Agrarian movement" writers saw the dam as destroying the wilderness and the region's rural way of life. In Ashley's allegorizing, the Atalanta myth encapsulates the conflict between nature and culture, with special reference to architecture and technology. A video, *Atalanta Strategy,* contains graphics and photographs (used in live performances) to show the similarities between the geometry of the TVA dam and Egyptian pyramids. Blueprint drawings become visible on screen and are traced over with white sight lines and perspectival triangulations that highlight the architectural relationship between the dam's structure and an inverted pyramid set in the middle of the river. Ashley also reminds us that along the Mississippi River there are cities named Memphis and Cairo and that Americans in the nineteenth century regarded it as the Nile of the New Land. Both the TVA and Hoover dams were frequently referred to as America's pyramids. In short, the landscape surrounding huge rivers, whether in Egypt or North America, provokes conflict between the wilderness and the demands of civilization, abetted by technology. When disharmony arises, it is resolved by myth (Atalanta), or through religion and mystical beliefs (Egypt), or with political and economic action (the TVA). We should be aware of how landscapes affect human life, but, as Willard might say, "We are invisible to ourselves."[29] Hence, the stories of past places need to be retold and performed.

In Ashley's version, Atalanta's story is told by individuals who remember European history and mythology. By the next opera, *Perfect Lives,* such myths have disappeared in the consciousness of everyday folks. Nevertheless, the effects of civilization and its reconstruction of landscapes—in the form of roads—are everywhere.

Roads abound in the *Perfect Lives* video imagery (which was used in live performances). The camera zooms in on highways, driveways, and streets; aerial maps fill the screen; cameras follow tractors crossing from roads to fields. There are also numerous pans of an empty downtown street shot from the front seat of a slow-moving vehicle. When staged, these images appear on multiple monitors. They provide the audience with a sense of a flat landscape where paths intersect and where the lives of individuals spin outward in different directions.

For Ashley, the road and landscapes are palpable sources of song and music. Of filming a sequence that captured a wedding in a small park, he said that he wanted "to make the piano playing look like the landscape, and . . . to make the landscape look like the person singing" (*PL,* 157). The piano keyboard, preeminently, becomes a sign for the road, travel, and movement. It reappears in dozens of video sequences and is magnified, rotated, multiplied, and overlayered with dissolves and fades. It resembles a road being crossed and crisscrossed, with the pianist's hands as vehicle. Musically, the repetitive chordal patterns suggest continuous driving. A drone implies the hum of the engine and the constancy of tires on the road. In several sections, songs and choruses echo 1950s rock and roll oldies playing on a scratchy AM car radio.

Yet, for all the roads in *Perfect Lives,* and despite the episode about a couple who elope, people do not go anywhere. Thus, *Perfect Lives* contains an ironic proposition. Amid the bounteous landscape of the Midwest corn belt, Americans seem to live perfect lives. But, as outsiders, we must ask: what does it mean to have perfect lives? As an allegorist (and

Neoplatonist), Ashley appears to affirm that all lives are perfect because human life as a whole is, like the universe and music and the spirit, of its own time and space: it is perfection. However, Americans do not think this way, even though the "connections" among places and histories inhabit their unconscious. We can, perhaps, find ways to deepen our understanding and spirituality, Ashley intimates, through musical theater and the songs evoked by our landscapes.

In any case, an argument can also be made that things were amiss in the heartland. After all, the women bank tellers all leave after the incident at the bank (or was that a result of the aliens' influence?). Their fate is followed in the operas in *Now Eleanor's Idea,* where roads, along with other elements in the landscape, again play a role. Linda, in *Improvement,* is left by her husband on the roadside; an hallucinatory recollection by a character in *Foreign Experiences* occurs during a near collision with a truck on a desert road. In *Now Eleanor's Idea,* Low Riders in New Mexico cruise in cars so lowered to the road that, as the locals say, the snakes are jealous.

The road and the entire Southwest landscape are richly represented in *Now Eleanor's Idea.* The set for productions include abstract flat, white cacti and rock formations scattered around a wavy two-lane highway. (There is no video material for *Now Eleanor's Idea.*) Serene white and yellowish lighting flood the stage. In a performance of *Now Eleanor's Idea* in Santa Fe, New Mexico, in 1995, two Low Rider cars and their owners were on both sides of the stage. Recorded voices of car owners and people from the community were integrated into the sound for performances. During the weekend performance, a Low Rider car show was held in the theater parking lot.

Low Rider cars represent an alternative narrative about the meaning of roads, landscapes, community, and values. The cars and their Chicano owners also disclose the mythic and historically complex desert landscape—and its current politics—through a baroquely paradoxical economy of images and practices. Low Riders remodel older cars into spectacular, personalized vehicles. Each car self-reflexively maintains its own history, and owners often carry photo albums of previous paint jobs and other alterations. The cars contain sacred and secular iconography as well as chronicles related to family and local events. Extravagantly ornamented, cars may have crucifixes, images of the Virgin of Guadeloupe, and various ethnic symbols. Low Rider cars occupy the road as shrines, asserting that the car itself is a special place. Automobiles are not mere means of transportation. Low Riders purposely drive "low and slow" through town. When a car is stopped, a hydraulic lift system elevates the body in a parody of the horizontal plane of automobile travel. Left and right side lifts are alternately pumped, causing the cars to literally jump in place. In the desert landscape, the cars affirm sociopolitical differences between the Chicano community and Anglo culture. Each Low Rider car reflects the aesthetics and obvious labor of its owners. Anglos value automobiles for their practicality and as a sign of status. By contrast, for the Low Riders, driving the roadways become a personal, blessed, and radiantly decorated celebration of the beauty of the desert landscape.

Ashley's choice of the Low Riders in New Mexico as the thematic, visual, and geographic center of his last work completes his allegory of the Americas. In Española, Eleanor, a descendant of northern European immigrants, encounters the families and descendants of the southern Europeans, or the Spanish. For Ashley, the "discovery" of America and its subsequent colonization, in the North by the English Protestants and through Mexico by the Spanish, represents a rift between mind and body, practicality and beauty, individual versus familial values, and other dualisms. Connecting Eleanor with the Low Riders, a reconciliation can lead to "a relinking of destinies" and, potentially, in Ashley's allegory, a renewal of one cycle of human life.[30] It is crucial that this happens in the desert that is invoked in various mythologies as a place of renewal and origins. Hermits, mystics, and shamans retreat to the desert; and, of course, in the Bible, numerous transformations occur in the desert. Native peoples of the Southwest and Central America also refer to desert wanderings in their myths. (Ashley, however, does not address indigenous American history.)

Theatrically, the musical and dramatic structure of the *Perfect Lives* trilogy elaborates itself as dream and echo. American places and their imagined and mythic references appear as if in an intricate and mathematically precise, yet floating apparition. But Ashley freely acknowledges other sources for the architectonics of *Perfect Lives,* including Dante's *Inferno* and the Tibetan Book of the Dead which, like *Perfect Lives,* is in seven parts. "Perfection" is cited in Tibetan Buddhist thought as attainable after great learning. In that respect, all of *Perfect Lives*— including the visual design of the video—invokes musicated imagery of vast spaces, relational worlds, distinct regions, multiple geohistories and consciousnesses. This is because, as Willard sings, "Everywhere, everywhere speaks."

Everywhere, son of everywhere speaks.
What is everywhere all about?

Where does it come from?
Answers follow.
Deep down in the deep-downness of where it comes from.

(*Atalanta,* 18)

This is a reference to what Ashley calls the "connections" and what I theorize as his sonic allegory.

Landscape and Sonic Allegory

Correlations among opera, landscapes, the pastoral, and allegory resonate in the theory and practice of music theater. Nietzsche, Wagner,
and Walter Benjamin, among others, have investigated the dramaturgical aspects of opera and approached the entangled subjects of myth,
song and speech, and music and meaning. Ashley is well aware of historical precedents regarding the aesthetics of opera and has worked to
achieve a version of the genre suited to this era and his own sensibilities
(i.e., "opera for television"). But, in addition to his technical use of electronic media in performance, his work also draws upon various strains
of thought in order to create what I describe as a *sonic allegory.* That is,
Ashley's work represents an example of the "allegorizing turn of mind"
in modern theater that has been elucidated by Elinor Fuchs. In her
assessment, a new "intersection" of myth, theater, and landscape has
been emerging in certain types of performance.[31] Ashley combines the
aesthetics of twentieth-century experimental music and performance
with adapted Neoplatonic concepts of imagination and theatrical production. His allegory derives from his intuitions and study of the relationships that coalesce when landscape, perception, music, and performance are considered together. He attempts to allegorize the American
past and its mythologies by dramatizing the effects of landscape on perception and consciousness. As he says in an interview, "You only know
who you are depending on *where* you are."[32] Ashley's allegorical scheme
begins with American places and their sounds. Song then "connects"
characters and audiences to mythic and transhistorical landscapes, past
lives, and the cyclical nature of existence.

Ashley's allegory is sonic on two levels: it is transmitted through
song and it affirms a conception of the universe as musical. Moreover,
making music means making "connections" that reveal the mystical "perfection" of life. Perfection, which also figures in Buddhist metaphysics, is
a key concept in the Neoplatonic tradition begun by Plotinus. Neoplatonism is important to Ashley as a philosophy, but it also provides a
framework for constructing allegorical relationships in his operas. "Since

this is allegory," he says, "all the cast has allegorical connotations, and the material, more or less comes from every reverberation, every resonance of my reading of Frances Yates" (*Guests*, 111). Yates writes about Neoplatonism, and Ashley ingeniously weaves her ideas on theater and history into his work. But before discussing Yates and Neoplatonism, it is worth considering how theater, opera, and landscape have been examined critically and how Ashley relates to this history.

A recurrent debate in opera and theater history converges on the matter of visuality versus aurality, or, more broadly, the experience of theatrical versus musical performance. Stein considers the rift between hearing and seeing from the perspective of the audience.

> And now is the thing seen or the thing heard the thing that makes most of its impression upon you at the theatre, and does as the scene on the theatre proceeds does the hearing take the place of seeing as perhaps it does when something real is being most exciting, or does seeing take the place of hearing as it perhaps does when anything real is happening or does the mixture get to be more mixed.[33]

As a musician and composer, Ashley attends to sound and aurality first. He privileges sonic rather than semantic aspects of speech to the point of suggesting that language and music are equivalent. Nevertheless, his texts, whether originating in inner speech or overheard utterances, are inseparable from visual aspects of landscapes and events. As he works on the mise-en-scène for performance, there

> is always the fascination of landscape. When the piecing together of imagery becomes so intense that one is aware of its rhythms, in effect the action of the perceiving mind, "opera," or the communication of those rhythmic forms, arises naturally.[34]

"Piecing together" is Ashley's term for creating "density" in his works. He uses the word *opera* to be provocative, but also because he associates density with opera rather than theater. Ashley reminds us that, historically, opera has been a controversial and innovative art form. There is a critical tradition that disparages opera for being musically simplistic and dramatically weak. Early critics considered opera as little more than light entertainment and a "low" form of spectacle that blurred genres. The pastoral and fantastical themes and settings of operas were dismissed as frivolous. Nevertheless, opera has had a significant impact on theater because of the often extravagant aesthetic and technical requirements for performance. For serious producers and artists, opera led to a reevaluation of acting, staging, vocal training, as well as a rethinking of stage design and theater architecture.[35]

European operas dating from the 1550s presented challenges to the stage owing to their settings and themes. Drawing on Greek mythology or Ovid's *Metamorphoses,* many works explicitly invoked wild or imaginary landscapes, complete with gods and monsters in their habitats. Marco da Gagliano's *La Dafne* (1597) opens in Arcadia, where nymphs and shepherds are fleeing a fire-breathing dragon. Monteverdi's *Ariadne* takes place on Naxos, "a wild rocky place in the midst of waves," as the score indicates. In many operas, music intentionally denoted actual and fanciful places. In *Orfeo* (1607), Monteverdi states that pastoral scenes should be introduced with recorders playing local melodies. In other contexts, the Underworld is signaled by cornets and sackbuts; the harp or flute imply Paradise or the Elysian Fields.

This is not the place to review the history of music and representation. But it should be mentioned that music, myth, and landscape also provide the theme for many operas. The Baroque madrigal tradition of pastoral poetry set to song is cited as a forerunner of opera. Composers from Gluck to Stravinsky have used the myths of Orpheus and Eurydice. Unquestionably, the most elaborate thought about the subject is found in the music and writings of Richard Wagner, for whom Germanic consciousness, myth, and landscape are commingled. In the theater at Bayreuth, which he designed, his music-drama is inexplicable without reference to specific geographic regions. Wagner's audiences knew that the *Ring* cycle begins under the Rhine, that *Tristan and Isolde* progresses from Ireland to Cornwall to Brittany, and that Nüremberg is the setting for *Die Meistersinger.* Wagner's work sparked other composers into consideration of landscapes and site-specific settings, especially when their music touched on nationalistic themes.

Ashley follows this tradition, except that his concern is for an Americanized rendering of opera in the media age. It is essential, he contends, to consider the situation of performance, architecture, and the cultural expectations of audiences. The aesthetics of people attending operas at La Scala, he quips, are not those of fans going to a baseball stadium. Thus, "there is no reason for an American opera to sound like Verdi." In fact, he archly declared that *Perfect Lives* was designed to resemble "televised baseball, which is elegant because of the space around the players . . . a very beautiful relationship between the person and the space" (*PL,* 180).

With operatic history in mind, Ashley is conscious of mythologies, both classical and across cultures. The *Perfect Lives* trilogy begins with the myth of Atalanta, absorbs the American myth of "manifest destiny," and concludes with the Chicano Low Riders' legends of their families. Like Ives, Partch, and even Aaron Copland, Ashley seizes on the close connections between mythmaking and music. Nietzsche writes on this very subject in *The Birth of Tragedy from the Spirit of Music,* where he declares that music strives for the exalted power of myth. Music speaks to desire, rapture, and a yearning for the earth. All music retains "a hankering for the idyll."[36] Furthermore, Nietzsche argues that the consummate authority of music is in song, which emanates from primitive folk rhythms evoked by pastoral landscapes. Since opera privileges music over language, it, too, unleashes a longing for natural places. Wagner, of course, unites this version of pastoralism with Germanic myth and the search for love and salvation. Nietzsche initially praised Wagner, but later rejected his work, claiming that it departed from pure song and became too theatrical.

A musician himself, Nietzsche valorized music to the point, according to Herbert Blau, that "perception of the deepest kind was finally a matter of the *auditory,* a reversion of the visual to its primordial state of sound."[37] In *The Audience,* Blau explores this "ideological burden of sight and sound" in various histories of theater and culture. Clearly, theater involves a total sensory response. But, the perceptual and cognitive processes involved in seeing, as Stein also reasoned, potentially conflict with those of hearing. There is an argument to be made, Blau admits, for acknowledging the "incommensurability of the showable and the sayable." Regardless, sound is, ultimately, the more dominant phenomenon in the context of the theater experience: knowledge and the word are united, even if language is audible only in the brain. Blau highlights "the word *audience* itself, the visible tracing of an acoustical truth that for all the materiality of theater is nowhere to be seen, most of all if there is an echo" (53). For Ashley, this rings true. The sound of words can disrupt our grasp of precise meanings, except for certain words—particularly those used in prayer or swearing—which are "slowed down" to the point of being thoroughly meaningful. "Hopefully," as Max in *Atalanta (Acts of God)* sings, most words "coincide with what's going on anyway in / the network of the connections between us" (21–22), which is why we have to continue talking and making music.

In different periods, recognition of the disparity between sight and sound has led to performance genres or styles that stress one sensory experience at the expense of the other. In Jacobean masques and the German Baroque *Trauerspiel,* visuality and spectacle preempt language and dramatic representation of plot and character. Action and realism are replaced by flamboyant costumes, embellished scenography, and little motion. In his study of the *Trauerspiel*, Benjamin characterizes movement on the *Trauerspiel* stage as emblematic, frozen. He writes of the exaggerated style of oral delivery, its torrent of voices, and the tension between sound and meaning in performance. More pertinently, he notes that the "enormous artificiality of expression [thus] has its roots in that same extreme yearning for nature in the pastoral plays."[38] Similar observations have been made about the twentieth-century "theater of images," from Stein's plays to the work of Robert Wilson. In these overly visualist conceptions of performance, different landscapes appear and allegories emerge, or as Fuchs prefers, the works become "allegorical" or conditioned by "allegorisis."[39] In this sense, Ashley's allegorisis is sonic and it is elaborated by his reading and theatrical use of Neoplatonist ideas.

Ashley has discussed Neoplatonism with particular reference to Frances A. Yates's books, *The Art of Memory, Giordano Bruno and The Hermetic Tradition,* and *Theatre of the World.*[40] Yates's studies encompass cosmology, music, memory theaters, the occult, and numerology. She examines the architectural and theatrical concepts of Vitruvius and Inigo Jones, among others. Ashley is attracted to Yates's spiritual and philosophical history of Neoplatonist commentary as well as her approach to the semiotics of theatrical space. "I've been reading Yates for ten years like the Bible," he said in 1984. "She's trying to explain the idea of being able to attach meanings to something that is outside of you, that you only get through your perceptions, something you see or hear" (*Guests,* 117). For Ashley, landscapes contain meanings, and our perceptions, through language and music (as heard), lead to a richer and deeper epistemology.

In Yates's writing, theater is a signifying system wherein any gesture, sound, utterance—for example, "the world is a stage"—refers to a moment in time, a location, the speaker, listeners, the semiotics of the performance situation as well as greater cosmological and transhistorical dimensions. Shakespeare's Globe Theater, Yates argues, "was a magical theater, a cosmic theater, a religious theater, an actors' theater, designed to give the fullest support to the voices and gestures of the players as they enacted the drama of the life of man within the Theater of The World."[41] For Robert Fludd and Inigo Jones, working in the theater demanded knowledge of archaeology, land surveying, theater design, and acoustics. Jones's theater models incorporated such notions as the geometry of the zodiac to the layout of the monuments of Stonehenge.

In my view, Ashley's rethinking of Neoplatonism involves affirming sound and music as the dominant signifying system when evoked by the specific geographies and landscapes of North America. In the *Perfect Lives* trilogy, his allegorical scheme proposes that the consciousnesses of all human beings are linked. Landscapes that have persisted throughout all time are to be found, literally, in the Americas. When we traverse or live in certain landscapes, we only need listen to ourselves and others close by to recognize that we share similar understandings and that we are all "connected."

Neoplatonism, Ashley notes, "is sort of like holography: the idea that the whole thing is contained in the smallest detail"(*Guests,* 118). Thus, any moment in *Perfect Lives* is meant to convey to the audience an awareness of how landscape invades and affects consciousness. Consider the first part. The town is Galesburg, Illinois, "down from Des Moines" (*PL,* 11). Raoul de Noget sits in a motel room thinking about a nearby downtown park and two men on benches. The "park graces the courthouse of the county . . . . The park has sidewalks, fences, trees, grass . . . a statue of a man and a horse at war" (*PL,* 13). Raoul tries to focus on the image, but it slips away, as in a fog. His thoughts drift and the text and music shimmer with poetic, stream of consciousness looseness. *Fog* has one g and there are "Two gees in eggs," Raoul thinks. This reminds him to order breakfast. The men on the park bench converse "about permanence and impermanence" (*PL,* 14). Human existence is impermanent; the "permanent side" is characterized as space, by which they mean connections. The act of talking and making music increases connections. In this instance, Raoul's inner speech, shaped by having traveled to the motel through the corn belt region on this summer day, is a form of imaginative activity in chorus with the men on the bench. The slowed-down music/language of Raoul's thought connects to speech of the old men sitting on park benches. This is, we realize, a landscape precisely made for floating conversations and rumination. The old men's dialogue is necessarily about space and time (including "attainment . . . aging, and coincidence" [*PL,* 14]) because the expansive American Midwest impels people to contemplate time and timelessness, the character of its landscape, and the land's significance in Euro-American history.

Landscapes retain visible and invisible voices, histories, and memories. The effects of the sounds of the natural world and the voices of generations of inhabitants and travelers continue. In the musical metaphysics and sonic allegory of Robert Ashley, the songs human beings have sung—and are singing—preserve and recall "connections." In *Atalanta (Acts of God),* a character explains the connections in terms of landscape:

We are all connected, or there would be no more of us.
It would be vast and empty, and the beaches would
stare back at the stars, and there might be other
things, but there would be no more of us.
Exit us, if there were no connections . . .
Now those connections have to be watched over,
apparently . . .
So, to protect those connections, which are our
Sargasso Sea— . . .
—we have to talk to slow things down.

(Atalanta, 19–20)

In his operatic, media-rich performances, Ashley's sonic allegories create intense recognition of the mythic, imaginary, and "deep-downness" of the human experience. Such "slow-downness is our salvation," Max sings (22), and Ashley asks us to accept.

NOTES

Acknowledgments: Many thanks to Elinor Fuchs, Christian Herold, Daniel Lentz, Susan Morrell, and Merilyn Jackson. I also want to thank Bob Ashley, Mimi Johnson, and Lovely Music, LTD for generously providing me with unpublished interviews and other assistance.

1. Thomas Holmes, "Interview with Robert Ashley," *Recordings of Experimental Music* 4, no. 2 (1982):13.

2. "Perceiving mind" is from Robert Ashley, "And So It Goes, Depending," in *Words and Spaces: An Anthology of Twentieth Century Musical Experiments in Language and Sonic Environments,* ed. Stuart Saunders Smith (New York: University Press of America, 1989), 5. "Connectedness" relates to Ashley's conception of Neoplatonism.

3. Robert Ashley, *Perfect Lives: An Opera* (San Francisco: Burning Books and Archer Fields, 1991), 113–14. Future references indicated parenthetically with *PL.*

4. Gertrude Stein, "Plays," in *Last Operas and Plays* (Baltimore: Johns Hopkins University Press, 1995), xlvii.

5. Audio and video recordings available from Lovely Music, Ltd. New York, NY.

6. Ashley insists on collaboration and unfailingly credits videographers and other technicians. His core performers are keyboardist "Blue" Gene Tyranny and vocalists Joan La Barbara, Jacqueline Humbert, and Thomas Buckner. Video collaborators for *Perfect Lives* were John Sandborn and Dean Winkler. See Lynette Taylor, "Sanborn and Winkler: The Making of *Perfect Lives,*" and "Sanborn and Winkler On-Line," *Artcom* 6, no. 3 (1985): 25–26, 27–29.

7. This is especially the case as he began actively touring and recording.

8. Charles Ives (1874–1954), who recognized the importance of folk and popular music, responded to the American social, geographical, and environmental experience. His *Housatonic Bridge* and *Three Places in New England* sought to capture emotional recollections of those places. Many contemporary composers also address landscape and the environment. R. Murray Schafer, Alvin Lucier, and Annea Lockwood have produced a rich body of landscape-conscious music.

9. Of Milton Cohen, Ashley wrote that his studio had a "dome shaped area with rotating light projection apparatus at the center and multichannel sound around the outside." Unpublished.

10. Cofounders were composers Gordon Mumma, Alvin Lucier, George Cacioppo, Roger Reynolds, Donald Scarvada, and Bruce Wise, architects Harold Borkin and Joseph Wehrer, and artists Mary Ashley and Milton Cohen.

11. Robert Ashley, interview by William Duckworth. Unpublished interview, 1985, shared by William Duckworth with the author.

12. Gunther Schuler explores "territory bands," regionalism, and big bands in *The Swing Era: The Development of Jazz, 1930–1945* (New York: Oxford University Press, 1989).

13. Ashley's music is not like Ives's music. Ashley is not interested in mimetic representations of landscape or actual sounds, although recorded sound is occasionally mixed into performances.

14. *Perfect Lives* contains extended ruminations on time and motion.

15. Also see Peter Gena, "Everything Is Opera," *Formations* 2, no. 1 (1985): 42–51.

16. Wilfrid Mellers, *Music in a New Found Land* (New York: Hillstone, 1964), 6.

17. Walt Whitman had similar thoughts. In "Italian Music in Dakota," he hears opera that is "strangely fitting even here, meanings unknown before, / Subtler than ever, more harmony, as if born here, related here, / Not to the city's fresco'd rooms, not to the audience of the opera house." *Leaves of Grass*, ed. Sculley Bradley and Harold Blodgett (New York: W. W. Norton, 1973), 400.

18. Joel Chadabe, *Electric Sound: The Past and Promise of Electronic Music* (Englewood Cliffs, N.J.: Prentice-Hall, 1997), 82. Chapter 4 focuses on music and environment.

19. "Blue," Gene Tyranny, unpublished ms. 2000, photocopy. For a parallel history of American folk music in the 1950s and Neoplatonism, see Greil Marcus, *Invisible Republic: Bob Dylan's Basement Tapes* (New York: Henry Holt, 1997), 95ff.

20. Transcribed from *Music with Roots in the Aether: Landscape with Alvin Lucier*, Lovely Music, Ltd. The series is beautifully realized by director and cameraman Philip Makanna, video engineer Jerry Pearsall, and audio artist Maggi Payne. After this essay was completed, a transcription of interviews from the series were published (Robert Ashley, *Music with Roots in the Aether*, Cologne: MusikTexte, 2000).

21. Stein, *Last Operas and Plays*, xxx. Incidentally, *Music with Roots in the Aether* was produced in Oakland, California, Gertrude Stein's childhood hometown, while Ashley was at Mills College.

22. Friedrich Kittler, "World-Breath: On Wagner's Media Technology," in *Opera through Other Eyes*, ed. David Levin (Stanford: Stanford University Press, 1993), 225.

23. Stein, *Last Operas and Plays*, xliv. Ashley plays with simultaneity in *Perfect Lives* when the entire plot is repeated in a two-minute video montage.

24. On Ashley's orality, see David Bailin, "Space and Time in the World," *Formations* 5, no. 2 (1985): 1. On his use of language, see Arthur J. Sabatini, "Performance Novels: Notes Toward an Extension of Bakhtin's Theories of Genre and the Novel," *Discours Social/Social Discourse* 3, nos. 1–2 (1990): 135–45.

25. For *Now Eleanor's Idea*, Ashley researched the region and cast local performers, including singer and translator Marghreta Cardero. For a fascinating analysis of *Now Eleanor's Idea* and Cardero, see Christian Herold, "The Other Side of the Echo: The Adventures of a Dyke-Mestiza-Chinca-Marimacha Ranchera Singer in (Robert) Ashleyland," *Women and Performance* 9, no. 2 (1997): 162–97.

26. John Brinckerhoff Jackson, "Roads Belong in the Landscape," in *Landscapes in Sight: Looking at America* (New Haven: Yale University Press, 1997), 249–54.

27. Eventually, the couple consummate their marriage in Aphrodite's temple. The goddess, jealous, then turns them into leopards, which, according to legend, are incapable of reproduction.

28. Marcel Detienne, *Dionysos Slain,* trans. Mireille Muellner and Leonard Muellner (Baltimore: Johns Hopkins University Press, 1979), 16. Detienne also says that "myth entertains a relationship to environment, to the ecological or social given, to the history of a group," 15.

29. *Atalanta (Acts of God)*, Lovely Music CD 3301, 1985. Booklet, 26. A video of the opera, entitled *Atalanta Strategy*, is also published by Lovely Music.

30. Herold, "Other Side," 167.

31. Elinor Fuchs, *The Death of Character: Perspectives on Theater after Modernism* (Bloomington: Indiana University Press, 1996). See "Pattern over Character: The Modern Mysterium," and "Another Version of Pastoral."

32. Melody Sumner, Kathleen Burch, and Michael Sumner, eds., *The Guests Go into Supper: Interviews with John Cage, Robert Ashley, Yoko Ono, Laurie Anderson, Charles Amirkhanian, Michael Peppe, K. Atchley* (San Francisco: Burning Books, 1986), 117. Future references indicated parenthetically as *Guests*.

33. Stein, *Last Operas and Plays*, xxxiv–xxxv.

34. Ashley, "And So It Goes," 5. Ashley "pieces" his work together by using musical materials as a basis for structuring visual and video concepts (a wedding, a girl sitting on a tractor), in order to create "rhythms." As each opera

evolves, new images and music are added. Thus, as in mythic traditions, Ashley's work reveals itself piecemeal through continuous variations.

35. Joseph Kerman, *Opera as Drama* (New York: Vintage, 1956).

36. Friedrich Nietzsche, *The Birth of Tragedy* and *The Genealogy of Morals,* trans. Francis Golfing (New York: Doubleday, 1956), 114.

37. Herbert Blau, *The Audience* (Baltimore: John Hopkins University Press, 1990), 99.

38. Walter Benjamin, *The Origin of German Tragic Drama,* trans. John Osborn (London: NLB, 1977), 210.

39. Fuchs, *The Death of Character,* 39.

40. For Ashley's comments on Neoplatonism, see Sumner, *The Guests.* For analysis of Ashley's Neoplatonism, see my dissertation, "Mikhail Bakhtin and Performance," Department of Performance Studies, New York University, 1994.

41. Frances Yates, *The Theatre of the World* (Chicago: University of Chicago Press, 1969), 189.

16

E-scapes: Performance in the Time of Cyberspace

Alice Rayner

A Fugitive Space

Cyberspace, variously known as the Internet, the Web, or an interactive digital technology, offers more than a new landscape for performance; it challenges the very meaning of "space." The technology of Internet communication shapes a landscape whose space is constituted neither as a latent, geometric arena, ready and waiting for action, nor as the vista of an earthly terrain. Neither a container nor a concept, "cyberspace" nonetheless tries to locate spatially events created by the interaction of digital codes and human desire. The landscape of digital interactions, furthermore, is not simply a metaphor for some social scene that lies elsewhere, outside technology. Rather, space itself is a metaphor for the social scene constituted by digital actions and exchanges on bulletin boards, chat rooms, e-mail, web pages, or in virtual reality. Cyberspace is entirely dependent upon technological equipment, to be sure. But that equipment demands a kind of use that undermines the adequacy of "space" to explain its operations.

The consequences for theater, coming from this technological shift into a new spatiality, are both radical and mundane. In this essay, I suggest that the technological shift into cyberspace is just one aspect of an epistemological shift in the culture that finds its way into theater not via drama or exciting new equipment, but by way of *performance* and theories of performance. I want to consider some ways in which performance aligns with digital technologies to resist landscapes and geometric space, and to resituate space in the fugitive dimension of time. Philosophically and culturally, the shift has been anticipated by any number of poststructuralists, though the harbinger appears in modernism itself. Baudelaire writes, "By modernity I mean the ephemeral, the fugitive, the contingent. . . . This transitory, fugitive element, whose metamorphoses are so rapid, must on no account be despised or dispensed with. By neglecting it, you cannot fail to tumble into the abyss of an abstract and indeterminate beauty."[1] The difference between cyberspace and Baudelaire's modernism, however, lies in the fact that the conceptual field, and its social imperatives for representation of the "transitory," has materialized in technological equipment. Material use of the equipment concretely creates the new spatiality. The pairing of performance and cyberspace is not about any sort of influence of one on the other. Rather, I am claiming they both belong to what Foucault might call the twenty-first-century *episteme*[2] in which the ordering of human relationships is not found in three-dimensional space but in the fugitive dimension of time.

The corporeal analogue to space, of course, is substance, with mass, weight, volume, and extension. Cyberspace has none of those aspects and thus has no substance, either materially or metaphorically. Its landscape is made of computational operations that have no substance, no body, no weight, no mass, and no boundaries. At most, it is a set of potentials. Against the disorienting lack of space and substance, a spatial world is supplied by a compensatory vocabulary. One speaks of *worlds, rooms, domains, fields, environments, architectures:* words that help to conceive computational reality in the familiar terms for definable spaces. Such spatial terms, promising enclosures, offer the comfort of boundaries within the homelessness of cyberspace. They serve to allay the vertigo of spacelessness. But these words are only part of the story.

There is also an expressive vocabulary. Words related to travel and movement discount the need for comfort and mock the habits of enclosure. Roads, highways, travelogues, and trips appear as the organizing images for cyberspace sites that in themselves have no place. With the adventurousness of explorers seeking the ever new, we speak of the nomad, of borders and boundaries, networks, liquidity, fluidity, visitors, and sites. Tourism and visiting, the consumption of spaces by moving through them, is a mode of being. The road is a site of motion where the substance of the land constantly dissolves and disappears. In cyberspace the road replaces the vista as a model of perception for technological pathways and connections. This landscape is not of the world but of circulation, modeled more on brain power than physical objects. Digital technology approximates a mindscape of neural potentials. It is a landscape in transit, passing data in the form of images (sounds, signs, sensations) but needing no placement, residing no *where*, not even an "elsewhere." In adapting to digital technology one needs to conceive of movement itself as a landscape that has neither land nor perspective. This vocabulary expresses the adventurous sense of traveling with the hopes of digital technology.

Finally there is the technical vocabulary. Abstract words for the spaceless dimension enter the cultural vocabulary as users become more at ease with computers. It is familiar now to speak of the disembodied, mathematical actions of cyberspace: *system, intensity, fractal, monad, information, matrix, noise, event, feedback, iteration, entropy, algorithm, emergence, interface.* Offering neither comfort nor hope, these words demand relatively rarefied, abstract thought precisely because they are not bound to the orientations of bodies in space or a human psychology. Most importantly in terms of understanding the landscape of cyberspace, these words have no visual analogue; there is no viewing distance from which to take a perspective on such space. These are words for events whose physical analogues are at a neurological level, active but unseen, sensed but unfamiliar.

Consider the ubiquitous word *site.* The word announces the compression of physical space into abstract placement. Sites are where perspective gives way to "mapping," and human relations are mediated by codes. As the cyberspace paradigm emerges into the culture, *site* becomes a dominant, if unexamined, term. *Site* is abstract, like a point on a line, yet specific. Its usage marks a conceptual change from an orientation based on vision and perspective to one based on a mathematics of position. *Site* articulates a strategic analysis of a landscape that is mathematical, pragmatic, and abstract. At the same time, the word linguistically, sonorously, restores the very thing that is absent from its sense: a terrain, an object, and a vision. A site is a creation, not a discovery, and it eludes the visible, cumbersome materiality of objects that embody space. It denatures the landscape of visual perception and implicates another pun: site as citation, the quotation of a constantly deferred real (substantive) place. Cyberspace images are themselves citations, visual quotations of particulars, representatives of codes that cannot be visualized.

These three kinds of vocabularies, the compensatory, the expressive, and the abstract, all mark the absence of materiality in cyberspace interactions, whether on the Internet or in virtual reality. The lack of material substance leaves cyberspace with the somewhat uncanny combination of equipment, imperceptible digital operations, and visual hallucinations. Visibility is the mode in cyberspace, but whatever is visible is a transformation of code and equipment into hallucinatory images of people, products, information, or fantasy. Those images are not of the world as much as they are the surplus of the world. That is, they depend on old habits of representation in which one thing stands in for the real thing, but in fact those images are not substitutes for the real. They are indexes that point to the simultaneity of the real and its image.

Hallucinatory Pleasures

Cyberspace, conveniently, has an historical origin that underlines its unique character as an hallucinatory reality. William Gibson, who coined the word in his 1983 novel, *Neuromancer,* described cyberspace as "A graphic representation of data abstracted from the banks of every computer in the human system. Unthinkable complexity. Lines of light ranged in the nonspace of the mind, clusters and constellations of data. Like city lights, receding."[3] When films try to give images of cyberspace, they often resort to the purely sensory image of multicolored lines of light rushing toward the viewers. The imaginary of cyberspace has no visual analogue except for these rushing colors, even though cyberspace itself is filled with visual images, images that are simply screen images that have no necessary connection to the digital operations that create them.

From Kubrick's *2001: A Space Odyssey* to Wim Wenders's *Until the End of the World* or the teen movie *Hackers,* those rushing, hallucinatory lines of colored light are a common filmic trope for entering the mind-space without form. In *2001,* as "Dave" rushed to "Jupiter and Beyond," his inner and outer space presumably became identical as he traveled into the speed of light. The Disney film *Tron* was another attempt to visualize abstract computer space as a multidimensional grid, where some coordinates opened up mazes in ever-deepening levels (like computer games), and others block the pathways for the speeding bits of code, represented by Jeff Bridges and David Warner on very fast, computer-generated motorcycles. Such images are attempts to visualize something that in fact has no substance and, hence, no space. In other words, there is no visual correspondence between the image (what is seen) and the object (the substance of what is "there" to be seen), since the film tries to visualize the time of computer codes as though they occurred in space. In representing cyberspace there can be nothing like a representational realism since what is "there" is nothing to be seen. The film images of computer space, then, are hallucinatory translations of speed and force.

The hallucinatory substrate of cyberspace tends to erase the contradictions between the real and the representational in the cyberspace environment. This erasure is in fact a nonspace where desire operates, or where desire performs, which is to say where desire occurs in the temporal, not spatial, contradictions of presence and duration.

There is perhaps no better evidence for the emergence of a new performative landscape out of Gibson's fiction than the "jennicam." The jennicam has become a generic name for the personal webcam phenomenon that puts daily life on the screen. With views on anything from Jenni's room, Times Square, or Dave's office, to Mars, real-time webcams play out complex interactions of performance, serial narrative, voyeurism, exhibitionism, travelogue, global economy, and time. The welding of those pleasures in a technology-driven sphere of social interaction represents, in many ways, the triumph of a new performance space. Although Jenni is hardly unique, she is one sign of Joyce's prophecy, "Here comes everybody." In cyberspace, everybody is a performer, and there is room for all because there are no rooms.

Jennifer Ringley started her personal website in 1996 and became a national celebrity, attracting fans via the Internet to the real-time images of her room at college and later of her apartment in Washington, D.C. She announces her definition of the "jennicam" as "a real-time look into the real life of a young woman" and "an undramatized photographic diary for public viewing esp. via internet."[4] On the site there are connections for members, who at present pay fifteen dollars a year to see rapidly changing photos of Jenni's daily life, and for guests, who may see a new image every twenty minutes for free. Making other connections on the site, one can read her biography, her journal, her poetry, and her dream recollections, learn about her favorite books and music, about her love of Winnie-the-Pooh, her "nutty cats," or past versions of the biweekly "JenniShow" and images archived from previous months. She was at one point the subject of a show at the New York Museum of Modern Art entitled "Fame after Photography," was a guest on several talk shows, and written about in *Time* magazine. In her archived show "Entrails and Ladybugs," she notes that she has found out her name is often the generic term (the "jennicam") for others setting up a webcam in their homes. Although the buzz of fame has already diminished, there are plenty of personal camera sites that follow her example.

Other personal webcam sites are created by more self-conscious artists. The "anacam" is "a window into my house, into my life . . . a picture updated every 5 minutes showing what i'm doing right now. . . . Sometimes i might be just staring (i'm really good at that). Sometimes i'll be surfing the net. Sometimes i'll be dancing wildly about my house to some disco music." She further warns the visitor to be prepared for "weirdness" or for just watching her sleep, because it is "not a 'show' . . . remember it's my life and i don't owe you anything." In answer to her own question about why she made the website, Ana writes:

> i feel i have a lot of fun things to share and being able to communicate to a worldwide "audience" in a totally spontaneous and immediate way from the comfort of my home appealed to me since I'm actually an introvert and prefer to be alone. i want to keep expanding myself in the different ways i can communicate to people. i'm an artist through and through. and this is a terribly arty self-indulgent thing to do, so i just had to do it, it was such an intense idea. and i like intense and i like to push boundaries of what people think a woman is and isn't. because i am in "showbiz" people always want to know about me and they usually get it all wrong and try to put me in a neat little compartmentalized package for mass consumption. . . . HERE I AM IN ALL MY MUNDANE AND SPECTACULAR GLORY. GO AHEAD AND ANALYZE THE CRAP OUT OF IT":) you want Ana? you got Ana!!!!!!LOL! :)[5]

It is tempting to answer the challenge to "analyze the crap out of it," or to account for the mixture of shame and aggression in the posture of the language and to discuss the apologetic smile signs [:)] after the taunting statements and LOL (Laughing Out Loud). One might ask how there is an "audience" but no show. But those factors may be no more than youthful markers in a youthful mood. (Ana gives her birthday as April 18, 1966, but declines to give her age, which she says is "totally meaningless! i've never felt any particular age at all." Math, perhaps, is not her thing.)

Ana explicitly articulates characteristics of the new space, however. The website is a place to be alone *and* to expand communication, to be introverted and on worldwide display, to display aggressively and deny understanding, to be intense and comfortable, to push boundaries without leaving home, to seek love and acceptance without knowing rejection. The public intimacy of Ana's site clearly identifies the new distribution of communicative power that Raymond Williams traces in his book *Television*. He points to the social factors shaping the changes in communication technologies: from the military use, with telegraphic or telephonic technology enabling person to person messages specific to an order, to the phenomenon of broadcasting in radio and television technologies, where central operations could send out "various mes-

sages to a general public." Cyberspace sites not only further decentral-
ize broadcasting centers, in Williams's terms, they allow every local terminal to be sender and receiver, maker and consumer, creator and
receiver of what Jacques Atalli called "noise." As Williams points out,
"radio and television were systems primarily devised for transmission
and reception as abstract processes, with little or no definition of preceding content. . . . It is not only that the supply of broadcasting facilities preceded the demand; it is that the means of communication preceded their content."[6]

The mundane intimacies of the personal website argue for the next
step in understanding technological space as a means that precedes content. In this step, I would suggest that cyberspace communications conform precisely to the "abstract processes" of the digital highway precisely because their content is "real time." So-called content—words and
images of Jenni or Ana—is of less interest than immediacy. Though the
sites also always offer the hopeful possibility that Jenni or Ana will be
undressing, masturbating, or having sex, there are plenty of other sites
that will guarantee sexual images, so Jenni et al. seem to offer a more
complex kind of titillation. In real time, "live" time, you take your
chances between a scene of inanimate furniture and sexual excitement.
The sites offer the Real[7] in the form of fortuitous intersections between
viewers and viewed. The accident of checking in while the room is dark
and Ana sleeps is just part of the wager with reality in real time. The digital technology gives new opportunities for chance encounters. The flow
of digital information that characterizes cyberspace communication
calls for a content that flows, a Real that cannot be consumed by the
medium but can be displayed.

 ·   Thus the daily routines and mundane activities of Jenni and Ana
(and countless others) suit the medium because the medium is not representative, does not signify, and does not select out meaning from the
flow of time. Cyberspace calls for the mundane content in a way that the
mundane does not call for cyberspace since it already operates in the
realm of the Real. Cyberspace is an aesthetic space to the extent it gives
the Real a technological forum, though "forum" is too spatial an image
for what it is doing. The cyberspace forum is a space made of speed.

In a digital occasion, only the speed of processors and the size of
memory matters; so-called content is incidental filler. The effect of technological speed on the culture has been remarked upon at least since the
Industrial Revolution.[8] Paul Virilio elaborates on the way that speed has
become an aesthetics, not simply in the way the futurists celebrated it,
but in the way that it conditions an "aesthetics of disappearance."

No need any longer for preliminary exposition of facts and places, so important in theatrical work. . . . with acceleration, to travel is like filming, not so much producing images as new mnemonic traces, unlikely, supernatural. . . . train, car, jet, telephone, television . . . our whole life passes by in the prostheses of accelerated voyages, of which we are no longer even conscious . . . the need for peregrination has led to the establishment in displacement itself of the very fixity of life.[9]

The "aesthetics of disappearance" describes the particular hallucinatory pleasures of cyberspace. The speed of digital communication makes it possible for Ana and her voyeurs to be present ("live") in the space of the screen. The screen divorces the image from the body, as does a photograph. But unlike the photograph, it puts the image, the body, and the viewer in the same moment, disappearing together in the moment, ready at any moment to be archived. This appearance/disappearance makes the images of the website especially ripe for hallucinatory projections of desire, not unlike the Romantic devotion to the pursuit of the pursuit. In her way, Ana confirms the hallucinatory projections of individual fantasies onto her site.

> . . . i'm coming to the conclusion that this site isn't about me at all it's about YOU!! yes, anacam seems to be a giant ink blot that people project their own psyche upon. it's about PROJECTION what do YOU see here? What do YOU think this site is about? And what does that say about YOU? :) what does it say about your ideas, morals, ethics, boundaries, state of mind . . . when you feel and think about this site? That is my question to you . . . i am your mirror, it seems. that's how I feel about this site so far. . . .[10]

In spite of the wealth of information I have about Ana, and the relative stability of the site, the temporal intersection in the present diverts the kind of intersubjective tension (two subjects, two objects) that relies on the space of delay and dilation, or of the negotiation of differences. In spite of the possibilities of multiple connections between people on-line, there is a also significant isolation and privacy, as noted by Ana, which makes individual fantasy the arbiter of "meaning" to an unprecedented degree. The details of Ana's site oddly lead to a sense of my failure to know her. Her public display is strangely private because it is hallucinatory and the hallucination is mine. Her presence on my screen is uncanny. In spite of her presence there, I know I am missing her, am missing an encounter with her even though I also know we both belong to a live moment (the Real of Now), which is always a missed encounter.[11]

When Gertrude Stein looked down on America from the airplane, she saw a Picasso,[12] recognizing his cubist analysis passing below, its abstract geometric shapes comprising the landscape. Picasso and Stein provided a defining image for twentieth-century modernism: a patch-work of abstractions, disjunctions, and images that changed along with position and viewpoint. The subjectivity of the eye created images that were both absolute, with respect to the individual perception (i.e., unar-guable because it is mine), and relative, with respect to position (i.e., in a different place I would see something differently or different). But however relative, the landscape was at least something to be seen, visi-ble to the eye. Physical distance determined perspective, and the mod-ernist landscape came about via the position of a viewer. In cyberspace, the crude reliance on the body's sensory organs, like the eye, is refined to the level of information or data. The exchange of data dismisses both the absolute of an individual perception and the relativity of place.

If the images and live pictures in cyberspace are seen as hallucina-tory rather than representational, the position of the viewer can never be wholly divorced from the image. That is, the images cannot enter the dimension of the Symbolic (in a Lacanian economy). The cyberspace image is not a substitution for a real object because the real is main-tained. It is total surplus, with largely surplus value. The material, bod-ily reality of Jenni and Ana is not erased by their images on screen, for their images are dependent upon their reality, yet it is those images that are the media of exchange. Digital images of cyberspace are less about mediating and distinguishing between a real and a representation, than they are about becoming surplus reality in themselves. Jenni is not exactly herself on the screen, but she is also "not not herself." There is no fictional space (narrative, for example) to buffer any difference because the "space" is technological and immediate. There is only the live, mutual presence or else the dead present, archived in digital stor-age. Jean Baudrillard's related notion of the simulacrum, the imitation without an original, does not account for the way in which time enters the cyberscene and dissolves the medial zone between now and then (*parole* and *langue*), real and representational. The simulacra of cyber-space images come from the tempos of computer systems that collapse distances and throw distant spaces into the temporal dimensions of *now*. The importance of the difference between the hallucinogenic and the representational is fundamental to the affective life of cyberspace, an affect of the kind of emptiness that follows a surfeit. Continual presence measures no distance or difference between times. This suggests that the loss of landscape, or space, is in its affect a digital occasion for a surfeit of desire itself.

Whatever is not *now* in cyberspace is in some sense dead matter, the inert remnants of a digital connection. Indeed, much of cyberspace is inert, a graveyard of unused or inaccessible code, space junk with no space. The hallucinatory aspect of the cyberspace images relates to the immediacy of the connection that delivers not another oppositional duality, but a radical alternative, as though time were the definitive other that is being misrecognized in visual hallucinations. One certainly has to admit, however, that the immediacy is still an ideal, given the time most commercial computers take to download data at this point. In fact, practically speaking, there is more waiting in cyberspace than there is connecting. The point is that the cyberspace imaginary is already disrupting habits of dualistic thought. It is complicating distinctions based on differences between here and there, material and digital, fact and fiction.

Present Thinking

In the early thrill of cyberspace, the connections to theater seemed obvious. Both could be understood as spaces where real acts took place in hypothetical conditions; where what counted as real was determined by consent; and where imagination and action intersected. Both raised the ever-fascinating questions about truth and illusion, pragmatism and idealism, real and unreal. Theater offered cyberspace a semantic grounding in spatial terms: an imaginary place for real events. Digital practices reciprocated by expanding the theatrical field to ever-wider dimensions, allowing audience users to see, hear, and interact with events in a space that was otherwise at a great distance.

Brenda Laurel offered theater to software programmers in her 1993 book, *Computers as Theater*.[13] Using Aristotle's *Poetics*, she described the human-to-machine "interface" as a spatial environment where objects could act as agents. The Aristotelian model limited the analogy but was apparently quite useful to programmers trying to represent digital actions to nontechnical users. Theater analogies offered a way to regard digital functions as mimetic, standing between the material and imaginary. Laurel's analogy necessarily ignored the material differences between theater and computers and further made no distinction between theater as a place for seeing and dramatic narrative as a structure of events. She reiterated a classical notion of action and agency and avoided the fact that algorithmic operations are antithetical to spatial concepts of action and unrelated to bodies and placement.

Nevertheless, theater is already taking part in the cultural and epistemological shift through its fresh emphasis on performance. Less by relation to each other than to a broader cultural *episteme,* performance and cyberspace manifest a shift from spatial to temporal modes of thinking. "The effect of technology on theater," for example, goes far beyond the technological wonders of computerized light boards, or holographic projections, or simultaneous interactive events in multiple locations. However fascinating the special effects, and however much they play with fresh images or collapse distances, theater has already had the capacity to participate in the broader cultural changes through its sense of occasion.

The tension of the shift appears in the disciplinary struggles between "drama," "theater," and "performance" as each tries to claim its centrality. Each one has a legitimate claim to both history and practice. "Performance" inhabited theater long before there were buildings to inhabit, but only recently has performance taken a significant and distinguishable place as a practice, an analytic method, and an object of study. The relatively recent highlighting of performance—from within the context of theater—represents a way of thinking that matches the shift enacted by cyberspace. Both organize perception around the moment of representation more than the content of representation. They furthermore belong with new formations of academic disciplines, cultural productions, ethnic identities, and social practices, all of which are forming ways of thinking on the run rather than in repose, in terms of processes rather than categories.

Thornton Wilder recognized some time ago that "in the theater it is always now." The "now" has simply been taken out of the spatial confines of theater into the epistemological and cultural discourses. The chronic resistance to performance as a valid object of study signals the contradictions it presents to spatial ways of knowing. Performance, being always now, is a singularity that has no substitute. Not being a thing, performance must play in real time. Gilles Deleuze writes of "repetition and difference" to distinguish two modes of thinking: *generality,* in which by means of resemblance and equivalence, one term can substitute for another; and *repetition,* which concerns singularities that can be neither exchanged nor substituted for one another. "Generality, as generality of the particular, thus stands opposed to repetition as universality of the particular. The repetition of a work of art is like a singularity without concept, and it is not by chance that a poem must be learned by heart."[14] Deleuze goes on to propose that both Kierkegaard and Nietzsche made repetition "the fundamental category of a philosophy of the future."[15]

Both cyberspace and performance, in utterly practical ways, materialize the "now." Unlike theater, however, they do not necessarily frame the now in some special aesthetic context. In disavowing a necessarily special aesthetic place, they lend themselves to a kind of discourse that sheds spatial referents and invokes transience and singularity as a model for thought. The two concepts share interests in the materialization of time as actions, occasions, or events. Even site-specific performance produces place as an intersection of past and present. Site-specific performances are not the "empty spaces" of theater, the seeing place; they are, generally, occasions for seeing place as a temporal collapse. Neither performance nor cyberspace is necessarily aligned with "liveness" or the spatiality of real bodies and things, though much of performance art might contest that statement. For both performance and cyberspace, "liveness" has much less to do with living bodies than with "live," meaning simultaneous, in real time. That kind of "live" may or may not have anything to do with mechanical reproduction or organic life. "Live" shifts the question of presence from its spatial sense of here to its temporal sense of now.

The consequence of invoking the vanishing present is that both words successfully resist the function of a category, which is so fundamental to Western thought. In classical taxonomies, categories are spatial to the degree that they "hold" particulars. They name the field (a spatial image) within which a variety of particular instances can—more or less comfortably—graze among their common features while ignoring their differences. Such discriminatory space defines the power, the wealth, and the violence of categories. But neither "cyberspace" nor "performance" works as a category because there is no defining attribute that can account for all their particulars. Separately, both cyberspace and performance institute the philosophy of repetition as a practice, not a concept. One can perform in cyberspace or use digital communications in performance, but neither action makes cyberspace and performance equivalent. Yet as demonstrations of the "philosophy of the future" (which is now), each escapes the confined disciplinary spaces of philosophy and recognizes singularity as a mode of thinking that acts and is present across a social and disciplinary spectrum of particulars. Each is an empty concept because each is spaceless. Neither can classify the particulars or discriminate among them.

When I say *cyberspace,* for example, I might be referring to anything from William Gibson's book *Neuromancer,* to virtual reality, to computer generated sensations, to interactive fantasy worlds, to the World Wide Web, to MUDS (multi-user domains) and/or GUI (graphic user interface), flight simulation, hypertext research, hypertext cross-marketing, e-mail, record keeping, institutional memory, chat or chess games, on-line therapy, virtual universities, gambling, buying, and certainly sex, story writing, music composition, telepresence for business, telepresence for art, robotics for medicine, robotics for service, robotics for fun. Any one case would fail to typify others; each would have its local particularity. It is legitimate to ask if one can even write about cyberspace since in itself it is a meaningless term, inseparable from its fictional origins and its cultural applications. Even using examples of cyberspace such as the jennicam has severe limitations. Examples not only do not represent a generality for cyberspace, they are obsolete almost as quickly as they are written.

As a concept in which a general principle or common attribute binds particulars, the category of *cyberspace* is unthinkable. Even as a medium it is unstable because its equipment is constantly changing. But I find the same difficulty—and possibilities—if I try to think of *performance* as a category. To exemplify performance, do I refer to a tribal ritual or a production of *Cats!,* the operation of my car, my breakfast ritual, or an evening with Karen Finley? How does performance equate Yoruban drama, Mardi Gras, and Jane Addams's Hull House? If I take one performer, say, Rachel Rosenthal, and try to extrapolate an idea of performance from *Rachel's Brain,* one of her solo shows, that will tell me little about Betty Buckley's performance in *Cats!* or Bill T. Jones's *Still Here.* I will derive a theory that may well belong to her work but is very likely not to be quite apt for Yoruba rituals, my breakfast, *Cats!,* or my particular iteration of gender. For every specific example or definition of cyberspace or performance there will be other examples that not only do not relate, but will raise entirely different questions. The two words are almost mathematical in the way they refer not to things but to actions. They are at most indexes for very specific, local activities. Neither has specific attributes because each is an operation, like an algorithm—not a thing, like a carrot. In other words, having the character of an index, they refer to particulars but do not represent a category for particulars. This makes both words antiphilosophical, which is actually to say anti-

Aristotelian: they lack the spatial requirements of philosophical catego-rizing that draws a line, sets out a boundary, and encompasses an idea. It is impossible to survey the landscapes of these two terms from visual or perspectival standpoints.

Marvin Carlson's book *Performance* is an excellent example of fac-ing up to the difficulties in conceptualizing performance. He traces the difficulty to W. B. Gallie's notion that certain kinds of concepts, like art and democracy, are "essentially contested" and have "disagreement about their essence built into themselves."[16] Carlson cites the position that the "continuing dialogue," articulates "a fuller understanding of the conceptual richness of performance." I would not disagree except to point out that underlying this statement is the assumption that *perfor-mance* is a concept when it is more accurately useful only insofar as it is *not* conceptual and has nothing built into its essence. Performances are not necessarily *similar* to each other. Rather, there is *sameness* in the degree to which any particular can count as performance. *Performance* functions precisely because it does not draw a line between what is and is not performance. At most performance is an act of instantiation, but it has no content apart from what it instantiates. Performance attaches itself to particulars in the sense that one speaks of a performance *of* the car, *of* the market, or *of* Ethel Merman. In each case, however, the par-ticular instances themselves donate whatever qualities the performance might have. On its own, performance is without both substance and quality, yet it is emphatically actual. Occupying no conceptual territory on its own, performance is an abstract term for a lived event. The word is fully implicated in materiality without having any matter that defines it. It shares this aspect with the word *site*, which in itself signifies a func-tional abstraction: a site of disaster, a site of memory, a site of mourning, a site of performance. "Siting," like performance studies, makes preci-sion possible without having any precision of its own.

Performance thus is not the measure of a space, even metaphori-cally. Instead, it marks out the temporal dimension of an act as it emerges from nothingness into actuality. It signals an event whose mate-rial actualization evades the problematic terms of true and false, real and imaginary. As Carlson and others suggest, there are rarely strong argu-ments for excluding any particular definition of performance in order to propose a truer one. Instead, uses and definitions of the word tend to be additive. Any one of its many uses does not erase or negate other uses. But that is not so much *conceptual* richness as an accumulation of mate-rial abundance. Performance does not open itself to analysis as much as it generates long lists of particularities: things, events, objects, uses of language, social movements, identities, that are *performative,* which is to say they are actualized in action. But particulars gather no moss.

On the Road Again

With its focus on the actualization into the now, performance eludes the durational space of narrative without erasing the possibility of narrative in a spatial register. But performance puts a show quite specifically on the road. One might think of Anna Deavere Smith's ongoing work entitled *On the Road: In Search of American Character.* Much of the critical focus has been on the virtuosity of Smith's imitations of her many interviewees. But along with the significance of her work with multiple identities is the significance of the title. The title insists that the work is constantly in process, that every segment is incomplete, and the core is about being on the road, searching, remaining open. Although undeniably "theatrical," Smith's work occasions an investigation of how a dramatic and performance form takes place between the reality of the people she interviews, the ever-changing shape of her performances, and the relationship between herself and the speakers. Above all, these relationships are fluid, and that very fluidity is the mode in which to understand the openness of the work not in terms of reality and illusion, truth and fiction, actor and character, but of motion that does not erase dichotomies but discounts them. In other words, the ontology of motion is not a solution to those dichotomies, which is why she has been criticized for seeming to refuse to take a stand on the one hand, and being too overtly political on the other. Movement does not resolve or synthesize the differences between real and imaginary, truth and illusion, nor does it allow any rest in one position or the other. Instead, it points out the conceptual nature of those differences and the actuality of time's constant departure.

Performances like Smith's that combine the "real" and the "performed" blur the sharp differences between performer, persons, and characters. The questions about whether real people count as characters, whether interviewing counts as playwriting, or whether she is an author or a recorder derive in part from a false conflation of a concept of identity with the body. That is, the questions arise from a sense of identity as a thing that, like the body, occupies a space, or, worse, "occupies the body." How, then, can two "identities" occupy the same body at the same time, as they seem to in Smith's performances? Both performance practices and cyberspace technologies counteract such a metaphysics of substance in their chronic displacement, implying perhaps that the body and identity must be considered temporal intersections more than substances.

"Exposition," the setting of the present moment and character identity in terms of a past, mentioned above by Virilio, belongs to a narrative whole that requires duration and space. The identities and situations of Smith's people need no more exposition than the change of a hat or the use of a telephone. Each one is a passing figure in the rhythm of the whole. To grasp the work means letting go of categorical differences such as *news* and *fiction,* or *imitation* and *reality*. The tension between those categories leads to calling the work *ambiguous*. But the dilemma is wholly conceptual, abstract. Ambiguity is not so much the point as is the force of specificity that keeps the actress and the character and the reality of the person interviewed fully present, without fusing them. Actress, character, and person are distinct but inseparable, attached temporarily for the duration of a performance.

How similar is that to the figure in cyberspace whom Marcus Novak identifies as a "collection of attributes given names by travelers, and thus assembled for temporary use, only to be automatically dismantled again when their usefulness is over"?[17] Cyberspace, in other words, models a way to understand the self as process rather than substance insofar as it disengages a fixed mental sense of identity and more closely replicates the fluidity and change of the body in time, not its occupation of space. The apparatus further models a way for seeing that a body, in all its neurophysiological bioelectrochemical being, *is* memory. Cyberspace, like performance, temporalizes spaces of identity. If cyberspace has any richer version of multiple identity than that of adolescent boys playing Dungeons and Dragons, it is less in terms of pretending to be something else than in terms of relinquishing a sense of a spatial, contained self for one that "is always a doing, though not a doing by a subject who might be said to preexist the deed."[18] Identity occurs not just at, but as, a site of passage.

The work of Robert Ashley discussed by Arthur Sabatini in this volume offers a paradigm for the aesthetic and the communities that arise when travel displaces subject matter and the passing of time consumes space. Ashley's work is an excellent instance of how performance actualizes transformation, even when it is recorded. That is, travel is not the subject of his work; it is the means, whose end is itself. Travel is a self-expressive mode that does not seek an object. Ashley's work is made up of the double movement of going and coming such that departure is a constant. The work—personal, political, material, imaginary—is in *transit:* restless, changing, fugitive. For travel is the mode of performance whose "life," in Peggy Phelan's familiar phrase, "is always in the present."[19] *Now,* the present moment, is necessary, real, *and* imaginary.[20] This fact does not preclude representation, by mechanical reproduction or otherwise, because it is essentially an empty fact, like the category itself. Nor does it erase the space and matter to which time is bound. *Now* is the condition but not the content of performance because it consists only of force, not substance. *Now* is a medium that subtends all media. It typifies the uncanny combination of real and imaginary belonging to the discourses of cyberspace and performance. Performance is the fugitive medium, guaranteeing that the fugitive is real even though it is not a "thing," constituting a mode of knowledge that consists of the chronic presence of change, chronic loss, loss of chronology, all within the sameness of every *now.* Truth is not a proposition about the real in this epistemology; it is rather repetition of the now, of the sameness of now that is always new.

Michel Serres writes a "philosophy of movement" in *Angels: A Modern Myth.*[21] In a virtuoso performance of images and prose, including Christian iconography, Greek myth, modern transportation, computer chips, fictional dialogue, dance, griffins, gods, airplanes, and angels, he translates the ubiquity of movement, the variability of its technologies, and the mythic dimensions of planes, trains, and automobiles into book form. His method is mimetic rather than discursive, but the mimesis is performance. Not a mirror of a world in motion, which could only be a blur, but a repetition of movement's sameness, which is continually new—"the universality of the particular." For repetition, as Lacan insisted and Deleuze elaborated, "demands the new. It is turned towards the ludic."[22] This means, among other things, that performance and cyberspace impose few formal restrictions on the truth status of content, which in any case I am claiming to be the now. When "now" is the content, however, there is no exchange value, for there is no "thing" to exchange. Digital technologies equalize content in terms of information, which means that so-called real life is itself no more than an exchange of data in cyberspace, instead of a measure of difference between true and false, reality and illusion, and their relative values. Like the notion of performance, there is something inescapably actual about the event, but there are no truth claims, no value judgments.

There is a similar phenomenon in those performances in which a solo performer blends autobiography and performance without erasing the distinction. This kind of performance (like Jenni's and Ana's) resurrects "real life" as an aesthetic appeal and a point of commonality with an audience. The autobiographical performer in particular fixes on the importance of individuality and the value of material details. She is extending the modernist tradition focused on what Georg Lukács calls "the *principle* of individuality."[23] On that principle, he suggests that in the new drama, "character becomes much more important and at the same time much less important. . . . The drama comes to be built upon mathematics, a complicated web of abstractions, and in this perspective character achieves significance merely as an intersection."[24] Taking that intersection to be both materially specific and conceptual (society, history, psychology, culture), the individual is a site who must ask not "What is truth?" but "What is real?" Cyberspace merely gives the principle of "intersection" a working apparatus.

Within the space of theater, performance is the intersection for a complicated web of temporality, reality, and the imaginary. The range of solo performers who play the real stretches from the immensely popular and commercially successful to the fringes of performance art. Spalding Gray, John Leguizamo, Danny Hoch, Josh Kornbluth, Rob Becker, Sandra Bernhardt, Guillermo Gómez-Peña, Deb Margolin, Karen Finley—this group only begins to touch the number of people who currently perform solo shows and move between stand-up comedy and the avant-garde. Solo performance of personal material is what one could call a twenty-first-century cogito (I perform therefore I am). Indeed, performance provides assurance that a life is actual, even if it (a subject, identity, story) is not exactly true. With an immediate connection between the performer and her story, she presents herself, let's say, "postpretense," not necessarily with certifiable truth but in the "principle of individuality."

True life, in this context, is both an aesthetic of disappearance and a commodity, confirmed in the proliferating real-life dramas on television. But in theatrical practices too, the solo performer makes repetition and difference an aesthetic practice. If there is a proposition in that aesthetic, it is the truth of death, announcing that through the passage of time, individual, particular lives matter and that particularity is a common denominator. If there is something of an hysterical insistence on this in mass culture, with the proliferation of real-life shows—home videos, going-along-with-the-cops shows, the one hundred most horrific car crashes caught on tape, news as person-on-the-street opinion, not to mention courtroom TV, personal video-camera websites—one can nevertheless read it as a sign of a victory over dominant, central authorities and representational government (in which somebody else speaks for me) and as compensatory expression of spaceless space. The solo performer and the person in an interactive virtual reality signal the normalizing of the transfers between real and imaginary where, as in performance, transformation occurs, simultaneously "'not itself' and 'not not itself.'"[25]

When Anna Deavere Smith performs her interview pieces, she is especially careful to keep the hesitations, the ums, ers, and uhs, in her re-presentation of people she interviewed. She very precisely chooses her physical indicators: a pair of round, black glasses, a yellow pencil, an old telephone. The precision of her choices is not only indicative of her respect for the people she plays, it is also, I believe, the cause of the huge range of responses to her work: from falling down adulation to political and personal condemnation. The precision of her performances recalled to me a section from Italo Calvino's *Six Memos for the Next Millennium*. There he uses the term *exactitude* for this quality of suggestiveness in the real. Of the exactitude that creates "situations propitious to the indefinite state of mind" Calvino says, "What he [Leopardi] requires is a highly exact and meticulous attention to the composition of each image, to the minute definition of details, to the choice of objects, to the lighting and the atmosphere, all in order to attain the desired degree of vagueness."[26] This comes full circle to the ways in which performance and cyberspace belong to a paradigm in which the particular, concrete, and material can be indexed but not categorized. Both offer the "desired degree of vagueness" of the spaceless, temporal Real that escapes both the certainties and the ambiguities of representation. Nevertheless, they must attach themselves to particularity and exactitude, for without things they are nothings. *Performance* and *cyberspace* are contested only in spatial epistemologies where they fight for territory. But as indexes for realities that have no substitutes, they both materialize the endless repetition of the death of the present and bring about encounters with a Real that is no-thing but a vanishing act.

NOTES

1. Charles Baudelaire, *The Painter of Modern Life and Other Essays*, trans. Jonathan Mayne (New York: Da Capo, 1964), 13.

2. Michel Foucault, *The Order of Things: An Archaeology of the Human Sciences* (New York: Random House, 1973).

3. William Gibson, *Neuromancer* (New York: Ace, 1984), 51. Science fiction has consistently provided models for thinking about technological advance in the science-real worlds. Gibson's cyberspace is an intersection of digital data, human consciousness, and graphic images where distance is not measured by space but by the time it takes to connect. It is a direct connection of a human

mind and digital data, free of the body's "meat." It is an infinite set of connective permutations, appearing and disappearing where orientations of the body—up, down, front, back, right, left—are meaningless because the space is mathematical. Hallucinatory and impossible, it is a mind space where Gibson's hero, part cowboy, part detective, part antihero, and part computer jockey, "jacks in" to computer systems that effectively control the planet.

4. <www.jennicam.com>.

5. <www.anacam.com/anatomy> (1999).

6. Raymond Williams, *Television: Technology and Cultural Form* (Hanover, N.H.: Wesleyan University Press, 1974), 19.

7. By writing "the Real" I mean to introduce the Lacanian distinction between the Imaginary and Symbolic projections into the world and that which persists regardless of those projections. The Real is material, not metaphysical, but is comprised of temporality, of the now that both passes and endures, and is only most evident when accidents happen. It is that which is always present and always missed in the way that the moment of death is always missed because it is the imperceptible, immeasurable difference. Jacques Lacan, *Four Fundamental Concepts of Psycho-Analysis*, ed. Jacques-Alain Miller, trans. Alan Sheridan (New York: Norton, 1981).

8. Anson Rabinbach's book *The Human Motor: Energy, Fatigue, and the Origins of Modernity* (Berkeley and Los Angeles: University of California Press, 1992) has an excellent account of the cultural consequences in the attempts to conform the human body to the rhythms and systems of machines. He looks historically at modern labor derived from the needs of time-motion efficiency to the modernist sense of "fatigue, neurasthenia, and civilization."

9. Paul Virilio, *The Aesthetics of Disappearance*, trans. Philip Beitchman (New York: Semiotext(e), 1991), 59–60.

10. <www.anacam.com/anatomy>.

11. The notion of a "missed encounter" depends on the double sense of "presence," that of space and that of time. Spatial presence does not guarantee an encounter with the other when the other is dead to the present moment, nor does temporal presence guarantee copresence in space. The screen has stolen Ana's image but she has given away her image. Like the sardine can that does not see Lacan (*Four Fundamental Concepts*, 91), Ana does not see me. Though I am within the "scopic field," her failure to see me obliterates my presence even as she exhibits herself and calls for my gaze.

12. Gertrude Stein, *Picasso* (New York: Dover, 1984), 49–50.

13. Brenda Laurel, *Computers as Theater* (Reading, Mass.: Addison-Wesley, 1993).

14. Gilles Deleuze, *Repetition and Difference*, trans. Paul Patton (New York: Columbia University Press, 1994), 4–5.

15. Deleuze, *Repetition and Difference*, 5.

16. Marvin Carlson, *Performance: A Critical Introduction* (London: Routledge, 1996), 1.

17. Marcus Novak, "Liquid Architectures in Cyberspace," in *Cyberspace: First Steps,* ed. Michael Benedikt (Cambridge: MIT Press, 1994), 235.

18. Judith Butler, *Gender Trouble: Feminism and the Subversion of Identity* (New York: Routledge, 1990), 25.

19. Peggy Phelan, "The Ontology of Performance," in *Unmarked* (New York: Routledge, 1993), 146.

20. This idea of time goes back to Augustine, who says, "I know well enough what it is, provided nobody asks me; but if I am asked what it is and try to explain, I am baffled." *The Confessions,* trans. Henry Chanwick (Oxford: Oxford University Press, 1991), book 11, xiv.

21. Michel Serres, *Angels: A Modern Myth* (Paris: Flammarion, 1995).

22. Lacan, *Four Fundamental Concepts,* 61.

23. Georg Lukács, "The Sociology of Modern Drama," trans. Lee Baxandall in *The Theory of the Modern Stage,* ed. Eric Bentley (New York: Penguin, 1976), 435.

24. Lukács, "Sociology of Modern Drama," 435–36.

25. Bert O. States, "Performance as Metaphor," *Theatre Journal* 48, no. 1 (1996): 21.

26. Italo Calvino, *Six Memos for the Next Millennium* (Cambridge: Harvard University Press, 1988), 60.

Contributors

Jane Palatini Bowers is Professor of English at Hunter College, Professor of Theatre and American Studies at the Graduate School of the City University of New York, and Associate Director of the CUNY Honors College. She is coeditor of the *Journal of American Drama and Theatre* and is the author of two books on Gertrude Stein, the first of which, *"They Watch Me as They Watch This": Gertrude Stein's Metadrama* (1991), was a *Choice* Outstanding Academic Book of 1991–92. She was a 1996–97 Fellow at the Bunting Institute of Radcliffe College.

Charlotte Canning is Associate Professor of theatre history, theory, and dramaturgy in the Department of Theatre and Dance at the University of Texas at Austin. She is the author of *Feminist Theaters in the U.S.A.: Staging Women's Experience.* Her articles have appeared in *Theater, Theatre Journal,* and *Theatre Annual,* as well as several anthologies.

Marvin Carlson is the Sidney E. Cohn Distinguished Professor of Theatre and Comparative Literature of the Graduate Center of the City University of New York. He is the author of *Performance: A Critical Introduction, Theories of the Theatre: A Historical and Critical Survey, from the Greeks to the Present, The Theatre of the French Revolution, Goethe and the Weimar Theatre,* and other books and articles on dramatic literature, history of the stage, and theatrical theory. He is the founding editor of *Western European Stages* and winner in 1994 of the George Jean Nathan Award for dramatic criticism. He is the recipient of the Association for Theatre in Higher Education Career Achievement Award for Contribution to Academic Theatre, as well as the American Society for Theatre Research Distinguished Scholarship Award.

Una Chaudhuri is Professor of English and Drama at New York University. She is the author of *No Man's Stage: A Semiotic Study of Jean Genet's Plays* and *Staging Place: The Geography of Modern Drama,* as well as numerous articles on drama and theater in such journals as *Modern Drama, Theater,* and *Theatre Journal.* She is a contributing editor to *Theater,* for which she served as guest editor of a special issue on theater and ecology. She is editor of *Rachel's Brain and Other Storms: The Performance Scripts of Rachel Rosenthal.*

Elinor Fuchs is Professor of Dramaturgy and Dramatic Criticism at the Yale School of Drama. She is the winner of the George Jean Nathan Award for Dramatic Criticism and the *Choice* Outstanding Academic Book Citation for *The Death of Character: Perspectives on Theater after Modernism.* She is the editor of *Plays of the Holocaust: An International Anthology* and coauthor of *Year One of the Empire,* which won the *Drama-Logue* Best Play award for its Los Angeles production, and she was guest editor of *The Apocalyptic Century,* a special issue of *Theater.* Her articles have appeared in numerous scholarly journals and anthologies, as well as the *Village Voice* and *American Theatre.* She has been the recipient of a Bunting and two Rockefeller fellowships.

Stanton B. Garner Jr. is Professor of English at the University of Tennessee, where he teaches courses in modern drama and dramatic theory. He is the author of *The Absent Voice: Narrative Comprehension in the Theater, Bodied Spaces: Phenomenology and Performance in Contemporary Drama,* and *Trevor Griffiths: Politics, Drama, History.* His article "Rewriting Europe: *Pentecost* and the Crossroads of Migration" won the Association for Theatre in Higher Education 1998 Essay in Criticism Award.

Daniel Gerould is the Lucille Lortel Distinguished Professor of Theatre and Comparative Literature at the Graduate School of the City University of New York. He is the translator and author of books and articles on Polish and Russian theater, including *Witkacy* and *The Witkiewicz Reader.* Also among his books are *Guillotine: Its Legend and Lore,* and *Theatre/Theory/Theatre: The Major Critical Texts.* He is editor of *Slavic and East European Performance* and of the *Polish and Eastern European Theatre Archives.*

Julie Stone Peters is Professor of English and Comparative Literature at Columbia University. She is the author, most recently, of *Theatre of the Book: Print, Text, and Performance in Europe, 1480–1880* (Oxford: Oxford University Press, 2000) and has written extensively on the history of theater and performance. She is currently working on a book on the history of text and performance in the law.

Alice Rayner is Associate Professor and Chair of Drama at Stanford University. Her books include *Comic Persuasion* and *To Act, to Do, to Perform: Drama and the Phenomenology of Action.* Her essays on dramatic literature and theater phenomenology have been published in several journals. Currently she is working on a study of theater as memorial.

Joseph Roach is Charles C. and Dorathea S. Dilley Professor of Theater at Yale University. He previously served as chair of Performance Studies at New York University, director of the interdisciplinary Ph.D. program in theater at Northwestern University, and chair of Performing Arts at Washington University in St. Louis. He is author of *The Player's Passion: Studies in the Science of Acting,* and *Cities of the Dead: Circum-Atlantic Performance.*

Marc Robinson is Director of Theater Studies at Yale College and Associate Professor Adjunct of Dramaturgy and Dramatic Criticism at the Yale School of Drama. He is the author of *The Other American Drama* and the editor of *The Theater of Maria Irene Fornes* and *Altogether Elsewhere: Writers on Exile.*

Arthur J. Sabatini is Associate Professor of Performance Studies in the Department of Interdisciplinary Arts and Performance Program at Arizona State University West. He has taught at New York University, Drexel University, and the University of the Arts in Philadelphia. He holds a Ph.D. in Performance Studies from New York University and has published extensively on performance, poetry, new music, and culture. He is currently writing a book on Robert Ashley.

Natalie Crohn Schmitt is Professor Emerita, Theatre and English, University of Illinois, Chicago. She has published *Actors and Onlookers: Theatre and Twentieth-Century Scientific Views of Nature* and forty refereed articles and book chapters including eight on Yeats's plays. She received a fellowship from the National Endowment for the Humanities and a concomitant residency at the Stanford University Humanities Center to write a book on Yeats's theater aesthetics that she is presently completing. She has also directed Yeats's plays.

Matthew Wilson Smith is a doctoral candidate in theater at Columbia University. His articles have appeared, or will shortly be appearing, in *Modern Drama, Theater, The Oxford Encyclopedia of Theatre and Performance,* and the anthology *Architect of Dreams: The Theatrical Vision of Joseph Urban.* His dissertation is entitled "From Wagner to VirtualReality: On the Mechanics of the Gesamtkunstwerk."

W. B. Worthen is Professor and Chair of the Department of Theater, Dance, and Performance Studies at the University of California, Berkeley. He is the author of *Shakespeare and the Authority of Performance, Modern Drama and the Rhetoric of Theater,* and *The Idea of the Actor,* as well as articles on performance theory, postcolonial theater, and a range of plays and playwrights. He has also edited *The Harcourt Brace Anthol-*

ogy of Drama and *Modern Drama: Plays/Criticism/Theory,* is à past editor of *Theatre Journal,* and current co-editor of *Modern Drama.*

Edward Ziter is an Assistant Professor in the Department of Drama at New York University. He has published articles in *Theatre Survey* and the *Wordsworth Circle.* His book, *Imagining the Orient on the Victorian Stage,* is forthcoming from Cambridge University Press.

Index

Abdoh, Reza, 6

Abstract expressionism. *See* Expressionism

Adorno, Theodor, interpretation of *Endgame*, 84–85, 87, 92

Aerial perspective: and Cocteau, 98; in operas of Robert Ashley, 332; and "panoramic city" according to de Certeau, 104; in performance of *You—the City*, 113; in Renaissance memory theater, 48; in theories of Stein, 47, 126, 140

Agrarianism. *See* Landscape; Rural

AIDS, 115

Akalaitis, JoAnne, 6

Albee, Edward, 99

Alberti, Leon Battista, *Della Pittura* (1435), 18

Alienation effect. *See* Brecht, Bertolt

Althusser, Louis, 296n. 9

America: creation of national identity of through Disney, 267–68; and "geomythology," 44; history of music in relation to landscape of, 153–54, 326, 328; history and consciousness of, in operas of Robert Ashley, 322, 324, 331–40; ideology of the landscape, 31; landscape and nationalism in, 24, 216–18; landscape as art in, 24; landscape of West in, 25–26, 210–14; and landscape of, in plays of Mac Wellman, 154–55; and national character of landscape of, according to Stein, 130; politics/place of, in Latino/a identity, 280–82; and postwar romanticism, 269; rural landscape and the Chautauqua circuits in, 209–25; theater and landscape in Stein-influenced dramaturgy, 145–57

American Buffalo (Mamet), 100

America Play, The (Parks), 39–43, 151

Amusement parks, 264, 265, 275, 330. *See also* Disney, Walt

Anderson, Laurie, 282

Andreyev, Leonid, staging of *Life of Man* by Stanislavsky, 317

Angel City (Shepard), 36, 99–100

Antiquarianism, 191–92

Apocalypse: in plays of Beckett, 92; in Eastern European symbolist drama, 311–14

Appadurai, Arjun, 27n. 7

Appia, Adolf, 317; and "rhythmic spaces," 162

Appleton, Jay: "The Integrity of the Landscape Movement," 3; theory of "prospect, refuge, hazard" in *The Experience of Landscape*, 12, 20–21

Arcadia. *See* Pastoral; Utopia

Aristotle, 315; poetic theory as opposed to cyberspace theory, 359, 363; and the "six elements" of tragedy, 1–2

Artaud, Antonin: and Christian narratives, 243–45; concept of "sacred theater," 228; concept of "true theater," 231, 237, 249; experience of, in the Mexican Sierra Madre, 5, 228–50; and India and Tibet, 229; influence of Balinese and Cambodian dance on, 229–31; interest of, in "primitivism," 230–31; interpretation of the Mexican Revolution, 235–36; and landscape of the maternal/feminine, 246–50; and language in theater, 231, 233; letter to André Derain, 234–35; Mexican landscape, view of, 233–34, 237–50; and "The Mountain of Signs," 238–39; and ritual, 239–50; search for origins of self, 243; and space/landscape, 233;